PHILOSOPHICAL STUDIES

MACMILLAN AND CO., Limited
LONDON · BOMBAY · CALCUTTA · MADRAS
MELBOURNE

THE MACMILLAN COMPANY
NEW YORK · BOSTON · CHICAGO
DALLAS · ATLANTA · SAN FRANCISCO

THE MACMILLAN COMPANY
OF CANADA, LIMITED
TORONTO

PHILOSOPHICAL STUDIES

BY

A. E. TAYLOR

MACMILLAN AND CO., LIMITED
ST. MARTIN'S STREET, LONDON
1934

No. 67.

COPYRIGHT

PRINTED IN GREAT BRITAIN
BY R. & R. CLARK, LIMITED, EDINBURGH

PREFACE

THE papers here collected, with the exception of the first, have all appeared in print at different dates; the order of their present arrangement is very different from that of their composition. Naturally, things are said in some of them which I should now say rather differently, if at all. But I have felt bound to leave the essays substantially as they were written, except for the deletion of a few mere errors and the insertion of an occasional qualifying foot-note. I could indeed have wished, in connection with the third and longest of them, to take account of the friendly criticisms contained in the second edition (1933) of Dr. Stenzel's *Zahl und Gestalt bei Platon und Aristoteles*, had not that work appeared too late for such a purpose. It must be understood that all comments on Dr. Stenzel's views are based on the *first* edition of his essay (1924). In connection with the fourth paper I must at once call attention to the facts that there is now, as there was not when the essay was written, an adequate critical text of the Στοιχείωσις Θεολογική of Proclus, that of Professor E. R. Dodds (Oxford, 1933), and that Professor Dodds has convinced me both that the doctrine of the "divine henads" is really due to Syrianus, not to Proclus himself, and that the attempt made in the essay to "rationalize" this doctrine is unsatisfactory, though I have not thought it right to disguise my shortcomings by alteration of the text. Three of the essays were originally delivered as public lectures, the sixth at Manchester in connection with the celebrations of the six hundredth anniversary of the canonisation of St. Thomas Aquinas in 1924, the seventh before the British Academy in 1926, in commemoration of the three hundredth anniversary of the death of Francis Bacon, the ninth before the University of Cambridge as the Leslie Stephen lecture of 1927.

I have to express my thanks for the permission to republish, in the case of the second, fourth, tenth, and eleventh essays, to the Aristotelian Society and the publishers of its *Proceedings*, Messrs. Williams & Norgate; in that of the third, fifth, and eighth, to the editor of *Mind* and the publishers, Messrs. Macmillan; in that of the sixth, to Mr. Basil Blackwell; in that of the seventh, to the President and Council of the British Academy; in that of the ninth, to the Syndics of the Cambridge University Press. My best thanks are also due to Messrs. R. & R. Clark for the pains they have taken with the printing of the volume.

A. E. TAYLOR

EDINBURGH, *March* 1934

CONTENTS

AESCHINES OF SPHETTUS

WHEN the philosopher Socrates was on his trial, he urged that his accusers, if they believed their own charges, ought to have produced evidence of his bad influence on the young from the fathers and elder brothers of his junior companions. Among other persons, actually present in court, he named in this connection Lysanias of the deme Sphettus, the father of one Aeschines (*Apol.* 33 *e*). Aeschines, we see, was at this time a young man, presumably at most not older than Plato, whose eldest brother, Adimantus, is named by Socrates in the same way. From *Phaedo* 59 *b* we learn that Aeschines was one of the group of devoted friends who were present at the philosopher's death. Plato tells us no more of him, and Xenophon never mentions his name. What was known or surmised about him in Alexandrian times we learn from later writers. Most of it is collected in the brief biographical sketch of Diogenes Laertius (ii. 60–64), and seems in the main trustworthy, if we discount one or two bits of manifest tittletattle. According to this narrative, Aeschines was always in needy circumstances, and this one fact disposes of a tale put about by Idomeneus of Lampsacus, a member of the clique of Epicurus, that it was really he who made the plan for getting Socrates out of prison ascribed to Crito by Plato; out of spite, according to this story, because Plato resented the friendship of

Aeschines with Aristippus (D. L. ii. 60, iii. 36). More than thirty years later, Aeschines, like other Socratic men, tried to profit by the temporary zeal of Dionysius II. for philosophy at the beginning of his reign. He came to Syracuse, we are told, with some of his dialogues, but was at first neglected, until he had been preferred to the young king by the good offices, of Plato according to Plutarch (*Moral.* 67 *d–e*), according to the detractors of Plato, of Aristippus (D. L. ii. 61, iii. 36). Apparently he only returned to Athens some years later, after the capture of Syracuse by Dion in 357 B.C. (D. L. ii. 63). For the rest of his life he took private pupils and composed speeches for the law-courts (D. L. ii. 62). Athenaeus (611 *e*) has preserved the proem of an interesting discourse against him, ascribed to Lysias, on behalf of a creditor who claims to have lent him the means to start in a perfumery business, on the strength of a simple faith that a disciple of Socrates could be trusted to pay his debts, but to have been rudely disillusioned. Like other creditors of Aeschines, he found he could recover neither interest nor principal. If the speech was really composed by Lysias, the law-suit must be dated long before the voyage to Syracuse. The tales of sharp practice need mean nothing worse than that Aeschines, like borrowers all the world over, wanted to "renew" when his creditors were not too willing.

The one point of capital importance in the Alexandrian stories is that Aeschines founded no school, and had no philosophy of his own to recommend. We may fairly suppose, then, that he, at least, had no motive for mystification in his picture of Socrates. His dialogues were highly esteemed for their pure and simple Attic style. According to the most careful writers, there were seven which were certainly genuine, *Alcibiades*,

Aspasia, Axiochus, Callias, Miltiades, Rhinon, Tel-auges. There was a foolish story that these were really the work of Socrates, and had been given to the nominal author after the philosopher's death by Xanthippe (D. L. ii. 60, Athenaeus 611 *d*), a story which at least implies that they were supposed to reproduce the personality and manner of Socrates with remarkable fidelity. It is this which makes him of special interest to the student of Plato as a possible "control" of the greater writer's methods of work. Unfortunately, there is no certain means of knowing which writer was first in the field, though I shall try immediately to give probable reasons for assigning the priority to Plato. However that may be, since Aeschines had no doctrine of his own to "push", representations of Socrates in which we find him in accord with Plato have a fair claim to be accepted as substantially true to fact.

One interesting consideration is at once suggested by the very titles of the seven dialogues. It is a striking feature of Plato's account of Socrates that he is depicted as closely connected from an early date with the personal circle of Pericles, a representation hardly in keeping with some modern views of the philosopher as a sort of "working-man of genius" outside the influences potent in the "upper circles" of the day. Aspasia, Alcibiades, his uncle Axiochus, Callias the "millionaire", all of them closely connected in one way or another with Pericles, figure in Plato among the habitual associates of Socrates; other personages introduced into the dialogues who illustrate the same point are Zeno, Protagoras, Damon the musical theorist, Pythodorus, Cephalus, Pyrilampes (Plato's own stepfather), and his family. All of them are in one way or another specially connected with Pericles. Now four out of the seven dialogues of Aeschines (*Alcibiades, Aspasia,*

Axiochus, Callias) are shown by their titles to be concerned with members of this group, and the titles of two of the other three confirm the suggestion thus made about the philosopher's "social standing". The Miltiades after whom a dialogue is named is not the famous son of Cimon, but is certainly a near relative, cousin or nephew. This reminds us that Archelaus, the teacher of Socrates, had belonged to the circle of Cimon, the son of the hero of Marathon. Rhinon, who gives his name to a dialogue of which nothing but the title is known, is pretty certainly the man of the name who was the leading figure of the board of Ten which took temporary control of affairs at Athens after the fall of the Thirty, and who is said by Aristotle to have shown himself a καλὸς κἀγαθός in that trying position. Socrates is thus shown by Aeschines, as well as by Plato, as standing in close relations with the most famous of ancient Athenian houses, the Alcmaeonidae (Pericles), Philaidae (Miltiades, Alcibiades), Eteobutadae (Callias). This should, I believe, go far to make us suspicious of the later story, which first appears in extant literature in a satirical allusion of Timon of Phlius, according to which Socrates was the son of a working stone-cutter or statuary. We may reasonably suspect this of being no more than an Alexandrian misunderstanding of the playful allusion of Plato's Socrates, in the *Euthyphro*, to Daedalus as his ancestor, an allusion still rightly understood by the fourth-century author of *Alcibiades I* (121 *a*), and correctly explained by the *scholium* on that passage. If this is so, though either comparison is misleading, it would be truer to speak of Socrates as belonging to a family of *ci-devants* than to call him a man of the *bas peuple*.[1]

---

[1] Grote had long ago seized on the point that Socrates belonged to "the ancient gens" of the Daedalidae. (*History*, ed. 1888, vii. 82.)

It is a curious fact about the literary methods of Aeschines that he seems specially to have affected for his dialogues the form of *narrated* drama (with Socrates, apparently, for the narrator). We can prove this for the *Alcibiades*, where, as the extant fragments show, Socrates was made to describe *ex post facto* the unbounded ambition and arrogance of Alcibiades as a lad, and his own attempts to convict him of ignorance of self. The *Aspasia* must have been of the same type, since it contained a narrative by Socrates of a conversation between Aspasia, Xenophon, and Xenophon's young wife (Cicero, *De invent.* i. 31. 51), and apparently also a report (by Socrates) of the relations of Aspasia with Lysicles, her protector after the death of Pericles. Probably, though not demonstrably, H. Dittmar is right in supposing that in both dialogues Socrates was represented as joining in a discussion of the character of a notable person recently deceased. The case is not so clear with the *Callias*, of which we know little but that it described the διαφορά between Callias and his father (Athenaeus, 220 *b*), whether διαφορά here means "quarrel" or "difference in character", and that it was Plutarch's source for an anecdote about the neglect of the just Aristides by his wealthy relative (Plut. *Aristid.* 25). For chronological reasons the Callias of this anecdote cannot be the associate of Socrates who figures in Plato's *Protagoras* and Xenophon's *Symposium*, and at a later date as a person of considerable importance in Xenophon's *Hellenica*, the butt of Aristophanes and Eupolis, and the "villain" of Andocides' speech on the *Mysteries*, but must be his grandfather, the second of the name. But whether the διαφορά of the dialogue means a "difference", in whatever sense, between this Callias and his father, or between Callias No. 3, the Callias of Plato and Xenophon, and *his* father

does not seem to me so clear, though Athenaeus appears
to me to suppose the latter to be intended. According to
him there was also in the dialogue an attack on Protagoras and Prodicus in which Prodicus was reproached
with having been the teacher of Theramenes. This shows
that Callias III was a character in the dialogue, since
it was he who had notoriously spent his money lavishly
on "sophists" and had been depicted as the patron of
Prodicus and the rest in the *Parasites* (Κόλακες) of
Eupolis. It follows, I think, that the dramatic date of
the conversation must have been at some time when
Theramenes had brought himself into general odium.
This could hardly be before 411, and is most naturally
taken to be some years later, *e.g.* in 405, when the
Athenian people were in the mood of self-condemnation
which followed the unconstitutional execution of the
Arginusae generals, and anxious to make Theramenes
the scapegoat for the proceedings. (Aristophanes, in
the same way, in this very year makes a malicious
point against Euripides by mentioning Theramenes as
the kind of man produced by his theatre.) I suggest,
then, as *probable* that in the dialogue Callias III—
the Callias of Plato—was the chief personage, as we
have seen that he was also a character in the *Aspasia*,
and that *he* was made to tell the story of a διαφορά between his grandfather Callias II and *his* father, the
anecdote about Aristides being part of the story.

All we know of the *Axiochus*—not, of course, to be
confused with the "spurious" work of that name
fathered on Plato—is what Athenaeus tells us (220 *c*),
that it contained a bitter invective against Alcibiades
as a hard drinker and seducer of women. (In another
place Athenaeus quotes from Lysias the scandal that
Alcibiades and his uncle Axiochus kept one wife between them for their common use at Abydos, and that

a daughter of this woman, whom each of the pair
fathered on the other, was afterwards the mistress of
both.) It is clear that the two men, who were both exiled
over the famous scandal about the "profanation of the
Mysteries", were alleged to have spent their years of
exile in very discreditable courses, much like Byron at
Venice. This explains how Aeschines comes, in a dialogue *Axiochus*, to be attacking Alcibiades as a lecher.
From the nature of its contents, this also must have
been a reported dialogue. The parties incriminated
must have been discussed in their absence (and presumably, after their deaths?).

From the *Miltiades* nothing remains but a eulogistic
description of the model youth and boyhood of Miltiades, son of Stesagoras. I should suppose the Stesagoras in question to be the cousin of the Miltiades of
Marathon of whom we read in the sixth book of Herodotus, but for the express statement by Herodotus (vi.
38) that this person left no son. In any case the combination of the names Miltiades and Stesagoras is
reasonable proof that the person meant belonged to the
same famous family, the great house of the Philaidae.
We are told that he "gave such attention to his body"
in early life "that he is still in better condition than any
of his contemporaries", a remark which shows that he
is supposed to be of an advanced age, and would be in
place if he is supposed to be a *nephew* of the more famous
Miltiades and a cousin of Cimon. As a pure conjecture,
I would suggest that the context of the passage may
probably have been a general encomium on the old-
fashioned education given to Attic boys before the rise
of the "sophists", much in the spirit of the "Righteous
Argument" of the *Clouds*. Presumably the speaker was
defending this type of education against that made
popular by Protagoras, and in that case it is hardly

likely that the words are spoken by Socrates. If they are, I should suppose that they are a reproduction of an alleged earlier speech of someone else on the subject, so that we are again dealing with a reported dialogue.

The *Telauges* is shown by the words "said I" (ἔφην ἐγώ) in one of its two surviving sentences to have belonged to the same type. Thus we can be fairly sure that four, if not five, of the seven dialogues had this form. For the rest we have no direct evidence, though there is perhaps a piece of indirect evidence which should count. I have mentioned the curious later tale that the real author of the dialogues was Socrates himself. This is a mere idle tale, to be sure, but it occurs to me that it could not have arisen, even as a bit of Alexandrian literary gossip, if Socrates had not spoken all through the seven dialogues as the narrator, as he does in Plato's *Republic*. If this reasoning is sound, it follows that all seven were of the same simple type of narrated conversation as Plato's *Charmides* and *Lysis*. And if this is so, I think a further consequence follows with high *probability*. Since the prose dialogue pretty clearly arose by direct imitation of the dramatic sketch, or mime, it is natural to suppose that the earliest dialogues to be written were of the "directly dramatic" type, and that the *narrated* conversation is a subsequent improvement, intended to provide fuller openings for characterisation of the speakers. Now among the Platonic dialogues, those which usually impress readers with a sense that they are first attempts, like the two called after Hippias, are of this directly dramatic type; the early *reported* conversations, such as the *Charmides*, seem to reveal a more practised hand, and this conclusion is borne out by the more special evidence of "stylometry". This is intelligible enough if Plato had to discover for himself the form most suitable to his unusual gifts of humour and dramatic characterisation. If there had already been a model in this kind before him, it is hard to think he could ever have been blind to its suitability to his genius. It seems to me therefore most probable, though not demonstrable, that Plato was first in the field as the inventor of the Socratic discourse, and that the form of the dialogues of Aeschines was imitated from that of the *Charmides* and its fellows, and not *vice versa*.

It is of more interest to consider how far the remains of Aeschines confirm the portrait of Socrates with which Plato has made us familiar. Such scanty quotations, naturally enough, contain little which throws light on the personal appearance, manners, or habits of the hero, though the extant opening words of an unnamed dialogue, perhaps the *Alcibiades*, "we were sitting on the benches in the Lyceum from which the *athlothetae* direct the competition", at least bear out one of Plato's statements about the favourite haunts of Socrates. It is also worth notice that an Aeschines who can only be the Socratic made the statement that Aristippus of Cyrene was first attracted to Athens by the reputation of Socrates (κατὰ κλέος Σωκράτους, D. L. ii. 65), exactly as Xenophon relates the same thing about Simmias, Cebes, and Phaedondas. This is in keeping with the representation of Plato that Socrates had very early attracted the attention of men like Parmenides and Protagoras, and enjoyed, as he is made to say himself in the *Apology*, the universal reputation of being an exceptional man; it is inconsistent with the view which has sometimes been mooted that no one outside his own little circle knew anything much about him, even as late as the date of the *Clouds*. Aeschines, like Plato, clearly assumed that an "intelligent foreigner" would hear of

B

Socrates as one of the notabilities of Athens, much as an inquiring Frenchman or German in the eighteenth century would hear of Samuel Johnson as one of the notabilities of London, and that such a man might quite naturally visit Athens expressly to gratify his curiosity about Socrates. One later writer at least seems to have kept this representation in mind. There still exists a Syriac version, dating from the sixth century of our era, of a Socratic dialogue in which a stranger, anxious to know the real fate of the soul after death, explains to Socrates that he has come to him for an answer to the question on the strength of his widespread reputation. The name of the stranger is given in the version as Herostrophos, which appears to be a mere miswriting of Aristippus (the second *r* being the only difference between the two words written in the Syriac character).

For evidence of the thought and manner of Socrates as represented by Aeschines we have to go to the three dialogues of which we can still make out something of the main argument, *Alcibiades, Aspasia, Telauges*. We may begin with the *Alcibiades*, from which we possess, besides briefer citations, one fairly continuous passage preserved pretty fully by Aelius Aristides in his 46th oration, and now in some respects capable of fuller reconstruction from a papyrus (No. 1608) published in vol. xiii. of the Oxyrhynchus papyri. This long fragment, in which Socrates is describing his attempts to influence the youthful Alcibiades, runs as follows (Fr. 1, Krauss, amplified from Oxyrhynchus papyrus 1608):

". . . to have treated your parents as Themistocles is said to have treated his? Why, God-a-mercy, Socrates! said he. And do you think men must necessarily be incompetent musicians (ἀμούσους) before they are competent (μουσικούς), incapable horsemen (ἀφίππους) before

they are capable (ἱππικούς)? I think they must be incapable first in both cases, said he. [Here follows a
mutilated passage in the papyrus, in which Alcibiades
apparently spoke severely about the youthful undutiful-
ness of Themistocles.] . . . "and that Apollodorus made
a good apology for the common-place man (ὑπὲρ τοῦ
φαύλου). But, said he, there is one thing I could hardly
have believed—that Themistocles was disowned by his
father. A man must be a very common fellow indeed, and
far gone in insanity to involve himself in that kind of
quarrel and enmity with his own parents; even a small
boy would know how to avoid such a thing. Why,
Alcibiades, said I, do you think it so shocking a thing
to quarrel with one's parents that anyone and everyone
must < avoid > it . . ." [Here follow a few broken lines,
and then we come to the passage previously known
from Aristides.] "So, as I could see that he was
emulous of Themistocles, I went on thus, Since you
presume to find fault with the life of Themistocles, reflect that . . . [here five lines are lost] "to know such
things as that, Socrates. Well then, has it ever struck
you that all this vast territory which is called Asia, and
stretches from one end of the sun's journey to the other,
is subject to one man? Of course, he said, to the Great
King. You know then, I said, that this monarch led a
force against ourselves and the Lacedaemonians, in the
confidence that if he could subdue our two cities, the
rest of the Greeks would be very ready to become his
subjects. He threw the Athenians into such dismay that
they deserted their country and fled to Salamis, first
electing Themistocles their commander, and authoris-
ing him to deal with the situation at his discretion. In
fact, the supreme hope of deliverance for Athens lay
upon his plans for the defence. Themistocles was not
moved to despair of the situation by the inferiority of

the Greek cities, and the superiority of the Persian in
naval and military equipment and financial resources;
nay, he understood that if his opponent should not
surpass him in *counsel*, his other advantages, great as
they were, would avail him little, and his conviction
was that success falls as a rule to the side whose affairs
are directed by the better man. As, in fact, in this very
case, the King felt his situation the weaker from the very
day that he encountered a better man than himself.
Themistocles disposed of his forces, great as they were,
with such confidence that when once he had defeated him
on the water he urged the Athenians to break up the
bridge the King had built. Failing in this, he sent a report
to the King contradicting the resolutions adopted by the
city, to the effect that he was himself doing his best to
save the King and his force by opposing the Athenian
demand for the destruction of the bridge. Hence it is
not merely ourselves and the Greek world who regard
Themistocles as the author of our deliverance; the very
King whom he defeated believed that he owed his preservation to him, and to him alone, such was his pre-
eminence in intelligence. Consequently, when he was
exiled from the city, the King rewarded him for his
supposed preservation by the gift of the whole government of Magnesia, and many other presents. Thus even
in exile he was more flourishing than many Athenians
who were at home, unmolested and in the highest repute
for merit. Who has a better claim, then, to be considered
the most powerful man of his age than Themistocles,
the generalissimo of the Greeks, and conqueror of a
king whose dominions reach from sunrise to sunset?
And yet, Alcibiades, said I, you must remember that
though he was all I have said, all his service was not
enough to save him from exile and disfranchisement at
the hands of the city, but proved too little. What then,

think you, must be the case with mere ordinary men
who bestow no tendance on themselves? Is it not a
miracle if they succeed, even in trifles? Nor must you
charge me, Alcibiades, said I, with thinking irre-
ligiously and oddly of Fortune and the supernatural,
because I credit the man with *science* of all he accomplished, and hold that none of these exploits were due
to Fortune. I should find it much easier to prove to you
that the irreligion is on the side of those who disagree
with me than they could to prove as much of me, since
they believe that Fortune comes indifferently to the
evil and the good, that Heaven does not favour the
more deserving as the more pious party."

The two remaining shorter fragments come from the
framework in which this narrative was set. They are as
follows: "Had I imagined I could benefit him by any
rule of *art* (τέχνῃ), I should certainly plead guilty to
gross folly. But in point of fact, I supposed this advantage over Alcibiades had been given me by Providence
(θείᾳ μοίρᾳ) and there is nothing in this to be surprised
at" (Fr. 3, Krauss). "My passion (ἔρως) for Alcibiades
was like the experience of the Bacchanals: when the
god takes possession of them, they can draw honey and
milk in places where others cannot even get water from
the wells. It was just so with me; I knew no doctrine
(μάθημα) which I could benefit a man by teaching him;
still I imagined I might make *him* the better by my
companionship because of my passion for him" (διὰ τὸ
ἐρᾶν. Krauss, Fr. 4).

To deal first with the two briefer fragments. We see
from them that Aeschines concurs with Plato on two
capital points connected with the personality of Socrates. He, like Plato but unlike Xenophon, ascribed to
him a very special relation to Alcibiades, going back
to the boyhood of the latter, and, in the earlier years

of the headstrong youth, at any rate, a very marked influence over him, an influence which Socrates hoped to use for the moral betterment of a youth of such brilliant promise. The strength of this influence was indicated in the dialogue, as we learn from Aristides, by the effect of Socrates' account of Themistocles on the lad. He drove him to lay his head on his knees and shed tears of despair at the contrast between his own "preparation" for public life and that of his prototype (Cf. Plut. *Moral.* 69 *f*). Also, Socrates was made to describe his own feelings for the wayward and brilliant lad in the language of exalted passion. He calls it ἔρως and compares it with the condition of a Bacchic votary in the hour of actual "possession" by the god. Aeschines thus agrees with the representation of the early relations between the two men familiar to us from Plato's *Symposium*, and moreover agrees with Plato in crediting Socrates with the temperament of the "lover", the fourth species of μανία described in the *Phaedrus*. This is entirely unlike the colourless version of the matter given, for apologetic reasons, in Xenophon's *Memorabilia*, where it is vital to the writer's purposes to minimise the connection between the two men, because, as his own language shows, the gravest of all the charges against the philosopher which he has to meet is that Alcibiades and Critias had been his "pupils". Since Xenophon has thus an obvious motive for understatement, whereas it is not conceivable what common motive Plato and Aeschines could have had for exaggeration, it should be obvious which account is likely to be the truer to fact. It is possible, no doubt, that the dialogue of Aeschines may be later than the *Symposium* and is influenced by it, but even if that should be so, it would be significant that Aeschines should evidently accept Plato's representation as in keeping with his own recollections of his old friend and teacher.

The second point seems to me still more important. Not only does Aeschines agree with Plato, and disagree profoundly with Xenophon, in making Socrates disclaim the possession of any ready-made ἐπιστήμη or τέχνη, but he also definitely connects the "fine frenzy" of the lover, as Plato does, with the personality of Socrates. This is, to my mind, one among the other reasons for holding that in the famous "erotic discourses", as elsewhere, Plato has artistically suppressed his own personality. Whether Plato had the temperament he and Aeschines agree in ascribing to Socrates, or had not, is, it seems to me, a question we have no means of answering. Like others, I may have my own personal conviction on the point, one way or the other. But naturally I cannot treat my personal conviction as evidence of its own truth. It should, however, be clear that if we trust the agreement between Aeschines and Plato as proof that the temperament ascribed to Socrates in the *Symposium* is that of the historical man, a whole large literature which has grown up around the name of Plato will have to be relegated to the limbo of unverifiable hypotheses. Not a few deserving students, particularly in Germany, continue to find in a certain form of "erotics" the key to both Plato's personality and his philosophy. If it should prove to be the fact that what has been taken for profound self-disclosure is really a masterpiece of inspired portrait-painting, the whole of this literature loses its supposed value for the biographer of Plato.

As minor points of agreement with Plato we may observe, as I have already said, Socrates' disclaimer of the possession of any ἐπιστήμη or τέχνη which could be imparted to a pupil, with the implication that, as the

Apology puts it, he had never had a real μαθητής; his young friends did not stand to him in the relation of pupils to a preceptor, though, at the same time, it is suggested that association with him might be expected to make them "better men", a phrase which really pre-supposes the doctrine of the "tendance of the soul" as the great business of life expounded by Plato in the *Apology* and elsewhere. We note, too, certain familiar tricks of speech, like the phrase θεία μοίρα.

When we come to the long continuous passage about Themistocles, we see again that its purport is a double one, and agrees with that of so many of the discourses of Plato's Socrates. The underlying thought is that the secret of success in life and in statesmanship is something which is called by two names, both familiar to us from Plato, ἐπιστήμη and ἐπιμέλεια αὐτοῦ, "care for the self". And the point to be made appears to be that even Themistocles, though he tried to "prepare" himself, and was better qualified for public life than the self-confident youth who dreamed of surpassing him, did not really possess the true ἐπιστήμη, did not "care for himself" in the right way. He rightly judged that the victory would be decided, not by numbers nor wealth, but by the person-ality of the commanders on either side; but with all his knowledge, he did not make a true success of his life. He ended in disgrace and exile,—not such an exile as a Socrates might have accepted from loyalty to high principle, but an involuntary exile which meant the ruin of his whole scheme of life. The main thought of the dialogue would thus appear to have been this. Themistocles, the model whom Alcibiades is anxious to surpass, had an immense advantage over his rivals in sagacity, invention, knowledge of affairs; yet he had not *the* knowledge a man must have to make his life a moral success, the knowledge how

to keep the law
In calmness made, and see what he foresaw.

He did not "care for himself" in the proper way.

Behind all this lies the set of ideas worked out later by some pupil of Plato in a dialogue obviously based on that of Aeschines, the *Alcibiades I*, where it is argued that "tendance of the self" is the secret of moral success, this tendance must rest on a true knowledge of the thing tended, and this thing, the "self", as distinguished from the instruments it wields, is the soul; so that the true statesman must, before all things, be a man who makes it the business of his life to see that his own soul, and those of those for whom he acts, are "as good as possible". We thus recover the familiar thesis that the virtues are all one and the same thing, *knowledge* of good, and the fragments of our dialogue are an important link in the chain of evidence by which the theory is vindicated for the "historical Socrates".

We note, also, that the appeal to the careers of Athenian public men is used in much the same way in which it is employed by the Socrates of Plato. The comments on the final collapse of the career of Themistocles reminds us at once of the thesis of the *Gorgias*, that the famous leaders, from Miltiades to Pericles, may have been good "body-servants" of the people, but cannot be pronounced true statesmen, since they regularly ended by being disgraced by the society they had "tended", and thus must have been deficient in the knowledge on which all "tendance" of a creature should be based; they did not really *know* what good is, and therefore, whatever they may have done for the subjects of their "tendance", they could not make them *good*. Here too, I believe, we can detect at least one echo of the actual phraseology of Socrates, when the words are put into his mouth that Themistocles was the superior of Xerxes τῷ φρονεῖν. As Burnet has observed, the use of φρονεῖν in the sense of "to be wise", "to be intelligent" is definitely non-Attic, being, in fact, a loan from the vocabulary of Ionian science. The word is peculiarly in point on the lips of the old disciple of Archelaus, the man against whom Aristophanes raised a laugh by calling him a φροντιστής, his "brave notions" φροντίδες, and his house a φροντιστήριον.

Possibly we should attend to a further point, though this is more conjectural. We see that the description of Themistocles' amazing career was preceded in the dialogue by some observations, now lost to us, about an ugly incident in his early life, his alleged repudiation by his father Neocles (Aeschines is likely to be the source from which this incident has passed into Plutarch's *Life* of Themistocles). We cannot, of course, be sure what use was made of this anecdote. But it looks as though Socrates were saying, in the immediate context, that just as a man begins by being a bad horseman before he is a good one, Themistocles must have begun, as we all begin, without the knowledge which enables a man to "care for himself". (His quarrel with his father will be proof of the fact.) Socrates is thus openly or covertly attacking the theory that "goodness" comes by nature. I therefore suspect that he must have been made also to dwell on another point, duly made in the *Alcibiades I*, as it is by Plato in the *Protagoras* and *Meno*, that, if "goodness" is not simply born in us, neither do we pick it up from our parents, as we do our native speech. I suspect that the story of Neocles' quarrel with his son was used to show that the son cannot be supposed to have "learned goodness" from a father who disowned him.

(The meaning of the allusion to a defence of the "vulgar man" (the φαῦλος) by Apollodorus can, I be-

lieve, no longer be explained. It should, at any rate, be
clear for chronological reasons apparent to any reader
of the *Symposium*, the apologist for the φαῦλος cannot, as
Burnet suggested to the editors of vol. xiii. of the
Oxyrhynchus papyri, be Apollodorus of Phalerum, son
of Aeantodorus, known to us from the *Symposium*,
Apology, and *Phaedo*. He would be still unborn in the
days when Socrates was conversing with the youthful
Alcibiades.)

The *Aspasia* also presents fresh and interesting points
of contact with Plato. The precise structure of the dialogue is unknown, but it looks as though Socrates,
speaking presumably after the death of Aspasia, dwelt
on her remarkable abilities. We know that this was
proved by two considerations. Someone, probably Socrates, told the story of her connection with Lysicles in
the years immediately after the death of Pericles, and
insisted on the point that Lysicles owed his temporary
success as a δημήγορος to her instructions. Apparently the
thought was that Aspasia was able to train him in the
political ideals and methods of Pericles. (Plutarch,
Pericles 24, and the valuable scholium on Plato *Menexenus*, 235 *e*.) Her practical wisdom was also illustrated
by the story referred to by Cicero (*De invent*. i. 31.
51 ff.), Quintilian (v. 11. 27 ff.) and Victorinus, of the
good advice she gave to Xenophon and his young wife
about the avoidance of conjugal disagreements. There is
a curious problem here to which I can only refer in passing. Though the name Xenophon is not uncommon, it
is difficult to think of any known Xenophon, with a
marked taste for farming and horsemanship (referred
to by Aspasia), who could well have been introduced
into the dialogue as a young married man, except
the well-known writer. And Cicero, who had the full
text before him, clearly made the identification, since

Xenophon, in his mouth, without further specification, can hardly mean anyone else. But this Xenophon left Athens in 401, and never saw Socrates alive again. He was a very young man at the time, and not yet married to the only wife he is certainly known to have had. And we cannot well suppose that Aeschines committed a gross error about the personal affairs of a contemporary whom he must have known well: this kind of "anachronism" is hardly in nature. It seems to me easier to believe that the well-known Xenophon should, in early manhood, have married and lost a wife who happens not to be mentioned elsewhere in extant literature. After all, young married women are exposed to certain perils by the very fact that they are young married women, and if Xenophon lost a wife early in life, there is no place in his writings where a reference to the fact would be particularly relevant.

The real interest of the dialogue is independent of these personal issues. From the notices preserved to us, it is clear it contained a discussion of the possibility that any woman could exhibit the capacity for affairs presupposed by the story of the help given by Aspasia to Lysicles. It must have been to meet a doubt on this point that someone (most likely Socrates) was made to appeal to two earlier precedents, that of a certain Thargelia, like Aspasia an ἑταίρα of Miletus, who was said to have used her fascinations freely to enlist prominent persons in Thessaly and elsewhere in the cause of Xerxes against Hellas, and that of a real or imaginary Persian princess Rhodogyne, who had the reputation of an "Amazon", and was honoured by a statue in which she was figured with half-braided hair, the tale being that, receiving the news of a rebellion as she was at her toilet, she hurried into the field "as she was". We are not actually told by the later writers who allude to the stories into whose mouth Aeschines put them, but since Maximus of Tyre (xxxviii. 4) relates an incident which must come from a dialogue about Aspasia, that Socrates advised Callias (III) to put his son under Aspasia's tuition, and Athenaeus (220 *b*) that Callias was spoken of, and called by someone a κοάλεμος in our dialogue (where he was therefore presumably a personage), it seems to me that the story about Thargelia, and presumably therefore also about Rhodogyne, was told by Socrates to prove that the qualities he ascribed to Aspasia were not without precedent. The two stories together are intended to support the familiar Socratic tenet on which Plato has based the developments of *Rep.* v., that "the goodness of a man and that of a woman are the same". Since the two commonly recognised chief forms of the goodness of a man are valour in the field and prudence in counsel, the two stories are meant to show that neither is confined to one sex. We have thus evidence from Aeschines that however much in the details of *Republic* v. may be "development" due to Plato, the central thought that both sexes should be expected to take their share in the work of administration and military life is strictly Socratic.

There is one further remark suggested by what we know of the *Aspasia*. H. Dittmar, in his valuable edition of the remains of Aeschines, rightly dwells on the point that it was the writers of Socratic dialogues, particularly Aeschines and Antisthenes (and to a lesser degree Plato in the *Menexenus*), who, so far as we can see, created the romantic Pericles-Aspasia *motiv*. The treatment of the subject by the contemporary comedians, Cratinus, Aristophanes, and the rest, was not romantic. In their view, Aspasia was simply a "whore" and "bawd", and Pericles a "lecher". Dittmar further contends that the Socratics so far agreed with the

comedians as to regard the devotion of Pericles to his
lady as a mere sensual weakness, and a proof that he
was no true philosophic statesman. Now though Antisthenes, the immediate source of the well-known story
that Pericles never left his house without kissing Aspasia
good-bye, is likely enough, in view of his known
opinions, to have held such a view, I confess I find it
hard to think Aeschines had set him the example. If
we take this view, we must suppose that all that was
said in the dialogue about the capacities of women, including the advice of Socrates to Callias, was meant for
irony pure and simple. But our existing fragments do
not enable us to judge whether the "irony" which is so
characteristic of Socrates in Plato was reproduced by
Aeschines or not. And we can hardly conceive the great
asserter of the "unity of virtue" treating the thesis that
the "masculine" virtues are not confined to the male
sex in a mere spirit of *persiflage*. Is it not more probable
that Aeschines meant his account of the ability of
Aspasia to be taken seriously? The conclusion is, I believe, borne out by the parallel with Plato's *Menexenus*,
where Socrates professes to have learned his patriotic
speech from Aspasia, who is also said to have inspired
the famous "funeral oration" of Pericles. The speech
in the *Menexenus* is only half ironical; it is a subtle
mixture of sound patriotism with superficial "chauvin-
ism". It could not have been put into the mouth of a
πολιτικός of the kind in whom Plato believed, a statesman inspired by genuine *knowledge* of good, but it is
exactly the sort of compound of nobility and baseness,
wisdom and prejudice, to be expected from one whose
"goodness" rests on uncriticised "opinion", and this,
according to the Platonic view, was the case with
Pericles himself.

The remaining dialogue of which it is possible to say

something, the *Telauges*, again throws light on a side
of Socrates duly represented in Plato, but often forgotten, his relations with Orphic and Pythagorean
ascetics and "salvationists", and so helps to illustrate
the *Euthyphro* and *Phaedo*. Like Plato, Aeschines
seems to have represented the philosopher's attitude
towards such persons as a curious blend of appreciation
and detached criticism. (Demetrius Περὶ ἑρμηνείας remarks that a reader might be puzzled to know whether
the account of Telauges was meant by Aeschines as
θαυμασμός or as χλευασμός.) Little is known of the structure of the dialogue (which, as we have seen, was a
reported one), except that it introduced, besides Telauges, two personages familiar to us in members of the
Socratic circle, Critobulus, the fashionable and dissipated son of Crito, who figures in Xenophon and in the
Euthydemus, and Hermogenes, the half-brother of
Callias III, known to us from the *Cratylus* as interested in Orphicism, and from Xenophon's *Apologia* as
the professed authority for Xenophon's account of the
last days of Socrates. Whether Cratylus, who appears in
Plato as a friend of Hermogenes, was also a character
in Aeschines, as Burnet has maintained, is not so clear,
though Aristotle's remark that Aeschines (presumably
our author) had used the expression τοῖν χεροῖν διασείων of
Cratylus points in that direction (Arist. *Rhet.* 1417 b 1).

Telauges is not otherwise known to us. The name
belongs to Pythagorean legend, in which it appears as
that of a son of Pythagoras, but the person meant by
Aeschines was clearly a man of the same time as Hermogenes himself, since one of the very few later notices
of the dialogue (Proclus in *Cratyl.* 21) tells us that
Hermogenes was reproached for not caring for the
necessities of his ἑταῖρος Telauges. Presumably then,
Telauges is a real person of the time of the Archidamian

War, a practitioner, as we shall see directly, of extreme asceticism and simplification of life, and probably a Pythagorist of the "strict observance". (Only a man belonging to such a circle is likely to have received such a name, just as no one in our own society is likely to be called Ignatius or Aloysius, unless he comes from a family with Roman Catholic connections.) The little we know of the argument of the dialogue comes partly from Athenaeus (220 *a*), partly from an allusion in the note-book of Marcus Aurelius (vii. 66). Athenaeus, or rather the speaker in Athenaeus, uses the dialogue to support the charge that the philosophers are even more satirical rascals than the comedians. Aeschines, he says, in his *Telauges*, satirises Critobulus for his stupidity and foulness of life, and raises immoderate laughter against Telauges on the score of his slovenly habits. He depicts him as hiring a ἱμάτιον from a fuller for half an obol a day, going about in a κώδιον—apparently a sort of leather apron—lacing his sandals with thongs of esparto-grass. (The text of the rest of the sentence seems too corrupt for certain restitution, so that we only hope Dittmar is mistaken about the very un-savoury trait with which he completes the picture.)

The reflections of the Stoic emperor really tell us little beyond the fact that he had read Aeschines. How can we be sure, he asks, that Telauges may not have been a better man than Socrates? It is no sufficient answer to tell of the splendid figure made by Socrates before his judges or in the prison. The question is not what Socrates seemed to human observers to be, but what he was in the inner man, whether his attitude was dictated by pure love for virtue for her own sake.

It seems to me foolish to see, as some critics have seen, in these remarks an attempt, in the interests of the "Cynic" ideal, to set up Telauges as a rival to Socrates.

The Emperor means only what Kant meant when he said that apparently heroic discharge of duty may be prompted by a disguised vanity which destroys its moral worth, and all we can really infer about the dialogue of Aeschines from this passage is that *in the dialogue* Socrates figured as the type of the truly virtuous man, Telauges as the caricature. Marcus is saying that you cannot be sure that Socrates really has this superiority, unless you can read to the bottom of his heart.

Putting the two notices together, it seems safe to say that the main point with Aeschines must have been to contrast Socrates at once with Critobulus, an exquisite and dandy who is "foul within", and with Telauges, who tries to make external raggedness and dirt a proof of real goodness. The point was worth making, since the association of Socrates with persons of this type, the extreme simplicity of his life, and the poverty of his later years might lead to misapprehension. We all know what play Aristophanes in the *Clouds* makes with the suggestions of rags, dirt and beggary. We remember again, that in the curious story preserved by Xenophon of the philosopher's relations with Antiphon, his lack of a shirt and of changes of raiment to meet the changes of the seasons are brought up against him. The suspicion that he was something not very different from the kind of fanatic who despises cleanliness, neatness, and decency had to be refuted by those who cherished his memory. It would be the more resented that the leading Socratic men—if we except the eccentric Antisthenes—were not of the type which finds slovenliness attractive. The "spruceness" of the young men of the Academy in particular was made by comic poets ground for an accusation of foppishness. Aeschines contrasts the decent poverty of Socrates with the deliberate filthiness of Telauges in the same spirit which prompted the recollection or invention of the rebuke to Antisthenes, who had paraded the rent in his cloak, "the tear shows your—vanity". It is presumably for the same purpose that Plato is careful to let us know that, for all his usual severe simplicity in such things, Socrates could and did "dress", and apparently dress well, for such an occasion as Agathon's party. Even in the most "unworldly" of the Platonic dialogues, when Socrates is enlarging on the theme that the cult of the body is something that must be despised by the man who means to "make his soul", we are only told that such a man will condemn "fine clothes and shoes and such adornments of the body,—so far as it is not a downright necessity to have them" (*Phaedo*, 64 *d*). The qualifying clause marks the difference between a Socrates and a Telauges. It is meant to show that the simplicity of the Socratic life is not based on superstition, and has nothing to do either with veneration of dirt or with disregard of the decencies of civilised living. Socrates, to put the thing in modern language, has no "evening" coat; it is not that he thinks the wearing of one sinful, but that he cannot afford one, and the reason why he cannot is that all through a protracted "world-war", he has been too busy with his mission to the souls of men to give a thought to his property.

We may conjecture that Socrates was made to condemn at once the elegant of the type of Critobulus, who is still neat and dressed without but filthy within, and the Pythagorist who lodges a clean soul in a "pigsty". Perhaps it was to anticipate a possible rejoinder from Telauges that his squalor was the inevitable effect of poverty that Socrates made the remark, whatever it was, which Proclus takes as censure on Hermogenes for neglect of his friend. The only actual words preserved from the dialogue are quoted by Priscian: "let us reap some benefit from the excellence of your intelligence" (or? "purpose" διανοίας); "again, Solon the legislator is dead, but to this day we owe great benefits to him". Nothing can be built on such scraps, but they read like part of an argument against "fugitive and cloistered virtue". The point seems to be that

> If our virtues
> Did not go forth of us, 'twere all alike
> As if we had them not.

Perhaps it is not fanciful to see in this a remonstrance from Socrates, the active missionary, addressed to Telauges, a "contemplative", who not only "lights his torch for himself", but by cultivating habits which make his company insupportable, actually smothers it "under a bushel". But this is, of course, avowedly pure conjecture.

[1928]

II

PARMENIDES, ZENO, AND SOCRATES [1]

THERE is a laudable unwritten custom of well-bred society by which metaphysical discussions are carefully excluded from polite conversation. The reason of the rule is probably, as Mr. Jourdain has lately explained, that such discussions commonly involve the perception of jokes of the fourth order, and jokes of a higher degree than the second, or at best the third, are imperceptible by all but an insignificant minority of mankind. Hence the prohibition of their perpetration in general conversation is an easy and obvious deduction from the principle of the Categorical Imperative. History, however, presents us with two brilliant exceptions to the general rule: the conversation held at a memorable tea-party between Alice, the Mad Hatter, and the March Hare, and that which, if we may believe Plato, took place at Athens at a certain celebration of the Panathenaic festival, some time about 451 or 450 B.C., in the house of the well-known admiral and politician, Pythodorus, the son of Isolochus, between Parmenides, Zeno, and the youthful but already distinguished Socrates. Mr. Jourdain has already published an entertaining and illuminating commentary on one of these singular conversations: I propose this evening to invite your attention to some points of interest connected with the other.

---

[1] Allusions to Professor Burnet's views, unless otherwise stated, are to the analysis of the *Parmenides* in his volume, *Greek Philosophy: Thales to Plato*.

I cannot, of course, undertake to deal here with so wide a subject as the purpose and argument of the *Parmenides* considered as a whole. All that I intend is to offer a slight contribution to the history of early Greek logical theory by attempting to throw some light on one or two lines of reasoning which are made prominent in the dialogue, and I shall select for special consideration two topics, the use made by Parmenides of the appeal to an infinite regress, and his attempted Refutation of Idealism. Before I can deal with either point in detail it will be necessary to say something in general about the dramatic setting which Plato has provided for the discussion, a subject on which the commentators, so far as I am acquainted with them, have been unduly silent.

If we examine the *Parmenides*, as we have the right to examine any dialogue of Plato, simply as a work of dramatic art, we shall see at once that it has certain peculiarities which give it a unique place among the Platonic "discourses of Socrates". Its form, to begin with, is unusually complicated; it is a narration by an otherwise unknown speaker of a narration of a narration of a conversation. Hence its "formula", as Professor Burnet calls it, is "Antiphon said that Pythodorus said that Parmenides, Zeno, or Socrates said such and such a thing". The scheme is, of course, far too cumbrous to be kept up at all rigidly, and Plato repeatedly allows himself to drop for convenience into direct reproduction of the conversation. So far as this scheme goes, however, the *Parmenides* does not stand alone; we have an almost exact counterpart in the *Symposium*, with the exception that there the speaker who relates what he had heard about the famous dinner in honour of Agathon's victory is himself a known person, and that his story has come to him at only one remove, so that the formula reduces to "Aristodemus told me that Socrates, or Aristophanes, spoke as follows". The full singularity of the scheme adopted for the *Parmenides* only becomes manifest from a rather fuller examination of the imaginary circumstances of the recitation. The speaker who relates Antiphon's account of Pythodorus' account of the interview between the three famous philosophers is indeed named, but beyond his mere name we learn no more of him than that he belongs to a group of citizens of Clazomenae who take a keen interest in philosophy (μάλα φιλόσοφοι, 126 *b*). Where, or to whom, he is speaking we are not told. The scene is certainly not in or near Athens, and to judge from the way in which the word οἴκοθεν, in his opening sentence, is explained by the addition ἐκ Κλαζομενῶν, it is not in Clazomenae. We are really entitled to say no more than that the story of the meeting of Socrates with the Eleatic philosophers is related somewhere by a person interested in philosophy to a like-minded audience. This complete silence about the place and the personnel is a thing unparalleled in the rest of Plato's dialogues. In the case of directly dramatic dialogues, the mere presence of Socrates himself provides sufficient indication of place. Even in a work which avoids all more specific references, like the *Philebus*, we are at least sure that we are to imagine ourselves in Athens or its immediate neighbourhood. The *Theaetetus* is supposed to be read aloud at Megara long after the conversation which it records, but the opening discourse between Euclides and Terpsion is intended to make it quite clear when and where and in what circumstances the reading takes place. So in the *Phaedo* Plato is quite careful to direct our attention to the point that Phaedo's narrative of the master's last day on earth is delivered some little while after the

event before the Pythagorean community of Phlius.
With reported dialogues the case is much the same.
Apollodorus in the *Symposium*, for example, expressly
explains that his recollection of Aristodemus' narrative
is just and vigorous because he had rehearsed the whole
only a day or two before (πρῴην) in conversation with a
friend as he walked from his home in Phalerum to the
city. In the *Republic*, Socrates repeats a conversation
in which he had been the central figure only the day
before, and we are told just where it had been held, in
the house of Polemarchus in the Peiraeus; in the
Protagoras he has only just left the circle in the house of
Callias when he meets the friend to whom he relates the
events of the day. Even in the *Laws* what we may call
the stage directions are perfectly clear and distinct. The
Sophistes and *Politicus*, indeed, so far as their contents
go, have nothing to indicate time and place, but both
are carefully attached to the *Theaetetus* in such a way
as to date them immediately after the filing of the
accusation against Socrates in the year 400–399. That
the immediate speaker in the *Parmenides* should be, as
he is, quite uncharacterised, and should be speaking no
one knows where and to no one knows whom, is quite
against Plato's usual practice, and the departure from
custom has, therefore, presumably a reason.

Still, if we learn little about Cephalus, the one
definite thing that we do learn is significant enough. We
are expressly told that he and his friends made the
journey from Clazomenae to Athens for no other purpose than to learn from Plato's younger half-brother,
Antiphon, the details of the conversation between
Socrates and the Eleatics (πάρειμί γ' ἐπ' αὐτὸ τοῦτο,
δεησόμενος ὑμῶν, 126 *a*, and the more express statement
of 126 *b* just below). This conversation, we must remember, is supposed to have been held when Socrates, who

was born in or shortly before 470 B.C., was still "exceedingly young" (σφόδρα νέον, 127 c), *i.e.* not later than about 450. It is assumed that, at the time when Cephalus is speaking, all the persons who had actually been present on this memorable occasion were already dead, and a correct account of what happened could only be obtained from Antiphon, who, we are told, had heard the tale from Pythodorus, in whose house the meeting took place, so often that he had got it by heart (εὖ μάλα διεμελέτησεν, 126 c). That Proclus is right in pointing out that the death of Socrates is presumed in this narrative is obvious. So long as one of the parties to the original conversation was alive, it would have been ridiculous to make Cephalus go to a second-hand source for his information. How long after 399 Cephalus is supposed to be speaking cannot perhaps be decided. Antiphon is now no longer a μειράκιον but a young man, but, in the absence of any positive knowledge about the date of his birth, we can draw no inferences from this. The important point is simply that the journey of Cephalus to Athens must be supposed to happen not less than half a century after the meeting of the three philosophers, and quite possibly a number of years later. What may we reasonably infer from Plato's assumption of this story as the basis for his dialogue? First of all, I think it is clear that Professor Burnet is right (*Phaedo*, p. xxiii) in calling attention to Plato's habit of calling attention to the fact that he could not have been personally present at some of the scenes which he describes. Thus the device of making Apollodorus repeat at second-hand from Aristodemus the incidents of the *Symposium* serves to remind us that Plato, who was a mere boy at the time of Agathon's tragic victory, could not have been present at its celebration, and is not proposing to speak as an eye-witness.

Similarly, the insistence in the *Parmenides* on the point
that there is now only one person living who can satisfy
the curiosity of Cephalus, and that he himself had got
his knowledge, when a mere lad, from a much older
man who is now dead, is an effective device for warning
us that the scene to be described belongs to a very
remote past, of which Plato could himself have no direct
knowledge. And we may suspect that one reason for the
pains which he has taken to explain how the narrative
was passed on by Pythodorus to Antiphon and by Antiphon to Cephalus is to make it clear that it has been
derived from sources entirely independent of himself.

To the reader this means, of course, that Plato de-
clines to pledge his personal credit for the historical
accuracy of all the details. If we find the Eleatic philosophers apparently conducting their dialectic with a
special view to fourth-century controversies between
Plato and his contemporaries—well, Plato has as good
as told us that he is not responsible for the accuracy of
the narrative. He was not there to hear what Parmenides and Zeno actually said, and the version he
puts before us makes no profession to come in any way
from Socrates. It is what Antiphon professed to have
learned from Pythodorus; we might be interested to
know whether Socrates would have confirmed it on all
points, but . . . Socrates is unfortunately no more, and,
even for what Pythodorus said, we have only the recollection of one much younger man whose testimony cannot be subjected to any process of control, and must be
taken for what it is worth. In no other dialogue has
Plato been at such elaborate pains to make it quite clear
that he has left himself free to colour his account of a
conversation in the distant past with an eye to the philosophical situation in the present.

But there is another and even more important

inference suggested by the opening narrative of the dialogue which, so far as I know, has never yet been pointed out with sufficient plainness. The initial assumption of the story about Cephalus and his visit to Athens is that the meeting of Socrates with the famous Eleatics was not merely an historical fact—that it was so seems to be now the current view of most writers on the history of early Greek philosophy—but that it was an event of absolutely first-rate importance. It is taken for granted that the conversation of the three philosophers was so notable that half a century or more afterwards it was remembered as something of remarkable interest by the friends of Cephalus at Clazomenae, who, indeed, sent to Athens for the express purpose of getting the true account of what had passed from the one person on earth who could supply it.

Of course, I do not suggest here that it is necessary to suppose that the mission of Cephalus to Athens is an historical fact. It is most likely to be no more than an artistic fiction on the part of Plato. The really important point is that Plato should have thought the story, true or false, sufficiently plausible to make use of it as he does. It implies at the very least that the philosophers of Clazomenae took the same sort of interest in Socrates and his doings which the *Phaedo* attests for the Pythagoreans of Thebes and Phlius and the *Theaetetus* for the philosophers of Megara. Nor would it be hard to account for the existence of this interest. When all the available evidence for the dates in the life of Anaxagoras are carefully compared, it seems almost certain that the prosecution which terminated that philosopher's thirty years of residence in Athens must have occurred somewhere about 450 B.C.,[1] in spite of the general agreement of modern historians in favour of placing the

---

[1] See my article on the subject in *Classical Review* (xi. 81 ff.).

event nearly twenty years later. This explains among other things why in the *Phaedo* the influence of Anaxagoras on Socrates is represented as exerted partly at second-hand, partly through his book, and nothing is said of any personal intercourse between the two men, why again in the *Greater Hippias* Socrates is made to contrast Anaxagoras as one of the "ancients" with the men of his own time, why the doxographic tradition, which goes back to Theophrastus, always mentions not Anaxagoras himself but his successor, Archelaus, as the teacher of Socrates, and finally how Anaxagoras was able, between his disappearance from Athens and his death in the opening years of the Peloponnesian War, to organise a philosophical school in Ionia, which appears to have been still in existence in the time of Epicurus. It also explains the interest of the philosophers at Clazomenae in Socrates. For Clazomenae was the native city of Anaxagoras himself, and though all the accounts agree in naming Lampsacus as the actual centre from which he propagated his philosophy after his enforced retirement from Athens, we may be sure, even if the history of Epicureanism did not prove the point, that science continued to be studied in Ionia generally, and that the fame of a brilliant pupil of Anaxagoras' successor, Archelaus, would be sure to spread to the birthplace of Anaxagoras himself. A meeting of Socrates with the great Eleatics would be memorable as marking the beginning of the process by which the science of the Ionian East and the Italian West were for the first time brought together at the only place which, for historical reasons, was adapted to serve as a general clearing-house for Greek speculations— the Athens which was already becoming the great political and commercial centre of the civilisation of the Mediterranean basin. Hence the naturalness of the fiction that even after more than half a century the event should have been so vividly recollected that the scientific men of Clazomenae sent a special deputation to recover a detailed account of it from the only living man who was in a position to supply one.

It should also be borne in mind that there are special reasons why it is humanly certain that a young man of philosophical genius living in the middle of the fifth century, and already feeling dissatisfied, as we are told in the *Phaedo* Socrates was dissatisfied, with the current Ionian views about science, would make a point of being introduced to the most famous representatives of Western ideas. In the *Parmenides* itself all that we are told by way of explanation of the presence of Parmenides and Zeno in Athens is that they had come to visit the Panathenaic festival. To understand the full meaning of this we need to recur to information supplied partly by the poem of Parmenides himself, partly by statements made in the Platonic *Corpus* and elsewhere about Zeno. Our thanks for the preservation of the eschatological proem to the poem of Parmenides are due to Sextus Empiricus, who inserted the whole of it in the first of his treatises "against the dogmatists" (Sext. *Adv. mathematicos*, vii. 111). The recent re-examination of the manuscripts by Mutschmann for his still incompleted edition of Sextus, shows that according to the best text Parmenides began his verses with an invocation to the divinity ἢ κατὰ πάντ' ἄστη φέρει εἰδότα φῶτα, "who guides the man who *knows* through all cities". This means, of course, that Parmenides himself was in the habit of travelling from city to city and giving epideictic displays of his philosophy. Like the evidence, which goes back to Isocrates, for the actual education of Pericles by Anaxagoras, the allusion shows how far it is from being true that there was in the middle of the fifth century any hard-and-fast line of distinction between the man of science and the so-called "sophist" who undertook the "education of men" as a profession. We *need* not, of course, suppose that Parmenides made nothing by his *epideixeis* any more than that Anaxagoras derived no personal advantages from his position as instructor to Pericles. If Protagoras came to be popularly regarded as the inventor of the sophistic profession, we must remember both that according to the account of Plato he must have been in the field at least twenty years at the date of the visit of Parmenides and Zeno to Athens, and that the special novelty of his programme was not that he was paid for his services but that he substituted the art of political success for science as the subject of his instructions.

About Zeno the case is even clearer. It is quite beyond reasonable doubt that Zeno not only taught for pay but that he must have settled in Athens and practised his calling there for some considerable time. This is explicitly stated in a dialogue, the *First Alcibiades*,[1] which though probably not Platonic, is at any rate shown by its style and contents to be a fourth-century Academic work little if anything later in composition than the latter years of Plato's life. We are there expressly told that two well-known public men of the fifth century, Pythodorus son of Isolochus—and it is manifestly he, as Proclus saw, who is the Pythodorus of our dialogue—and Callias the son of Calliades, the commander who fell honourably before the walls of Potidaea, paid him 100 minae each for his instructions. Zeno's permanent residence in Athens is equally implied by Plutarch's story that Pericles had been one of his hearers, and by the well-known allusions of

[1] 119 *a*.

Aristotle to dialogues in which Zeno and Protagoras figured as discussing problems connected with the notion of the infinitesimal. In fact, it is precisely this professional activity from which Zeno derived the name of "the sophist". Writers who wish to distinguish Zeno of Elea from Zeno of Cittium and other persons of the same not unusual name call him ὁ σοφιστής, not, as Earl Russell has imagined, by way of disparagement of his mathematical paradoxes, but simply because he did, as a matter of fact, follow the calling of a paid instructor of young men, just as we might speak to-day of "So-and-so the Army coach" or "Such-a-one the journalist". And if we will believe Plato, as there is no reason why we should not, acquaintance with Zeno's works had already had a great influence on the mind of Socrates himself in early youth. According to the famous autobiographical passage of the *Phaedo*, prominent among the difficulties which had led Socrates to the formulation of his doctrine of Forms were not only the problem raised by Anaxagoras about growth and nutrition (*Phaedo* 96 c), but Zeno's puzzle about unity and plurality (96 e), and the method of "hypothesis" finally adopted by Socrates as the only proper instrument of philosophical inquiry is just that method of Zeno in which the *Parmenides* represents him as receiving a lesson from the two earlier philosophers.

The situation, in fact, as imagined by Plato, and as likely to have occurred in fact, is that Socrates has just thought out *for himself* as a theory which will solve both sets of difficulties, the doctrine of Forms. (That this solution is genuinely his own is stated with the utmost distinctness. Parmenides' very first question, on hearing it (130 a), is αὐτὸς σὺ οὕτω διῄρησαι ὡς λέγεις, "Have you made this distinction of which you speak by yourself and for yourself?"; αὐτός here means just what it does in such a phrase as αὐτοί ἐσμεν, "we are by ourselves", and it is implied in the whole passage that the answer is affirmative. The theory of Socrates is plainly something of which Parmenides is hearing for the first time, though it is so far constructed on lines familiar to him that he only requires to hear it stated once before showing himself an acute and formidable critic of it.) Plato's assumption then is that the meeting between the Eleatics and Socrates was a memorable event in the history of Greek philosophy for very obvious reasons. Socrates had already been interested in the work of Zeno, but, according to Plato's account, had hitherto not been under the personal influence of Zeno. Zeno is, it appears, in Athens for the first time, since it is implied that all the copies of his book which have got abroad there are reproductions of a surreptitious copy: the true text has now been brought to Athens for the first time by the author (127 c). Such a first meeting between the greatest thinkers of an earlier generation and Socrates in the very flush of his first eager speculation must necessarily be of moment, and hence Plato can readily ask us to believe that men might take much pains to secure an authentic account of the interview even fifty or sixty years later. In fact it would be just the death of the last survivors of the party that would make persons with an interest in the history of ideas feel the necessity to obtain a narrative of the kind without further delay.

I have dwelt so long on the character of Plato's piece of introductory narrative because, as it seems to me, if I have divined its purpose correctly, an inference of some importance may be made about the reasoning to which it preludes. We shall naturally expect, if the whole work is to be of a piece, that the proper historical illusion will be kept up throughout it. However many covert shafts Plato may be aiming at contemporaries of his own living towards the middle of the fourth century, we shall expect that his drama will respect the unities sufficiently to be in its main lines true to the spirit of the fifth century. The chief lines of reasoning, however they may be worked out into detail, should be such as might naturally have been followed in a discussion of the age of Zeno. And we can see that Plato really felt this too. The whole form of the dialogue with its ingenious antinomies has, as Professor Burnet has said, been adapted to the pretence that it is just one of those exhibitions of the Zenonian dialectic to which Aristotle refers. It pretends to be just such a dialogue as that quoted by Aristotle in which Zeno was represented as posing Protagoras with the notion of *petites perceptions* which are "beneath the threshold". It may, in my own opinion, be fairly said that, so far as the main lines of discussion are concerned, there is little if anything in Plato's *Parmenides* which might not have been said at an actual joyous passage of arms between dialecticians in the middle of the fifth century. To prove this statement completely it would be necessary to subjoin an elaborate critical commentary on the whole dialogue, taken clause by clause. But I propose to do something towards establishing the point in the present paper by singling out for consideration two arguments put forward in the early part of the dialogue which have always attracted a great deal of attention,—that which turns upon the logical objection to an "infinite regress", and that in which Plato's Parmenides anticipates Kant's attempt to make a formal refutation of "Idealism".

To appreciate these pieces of dialectic it is necessary to begin by understanding exactly what is the point in the doctrine of Forms, as propounded by the youthful Socrates, against which the Eleatics are directing their attack. Unfortunately modern writers on Plato have often approached the *Parmenides* with a complete misunderstanding of its main purpose. They have supposed Socrates to be asserting, Parmenides and Zeno to be disputing, the existence of "Forms which are only to be apprehended by thought". This is a misconception which is fatal to any real insight into the dialogue. Parmenides and Zeno nowhere raise any difficulty about the existence of such Forms as the proper objects of knowledge; in fact, since the very "One" of which their own philosophy speaks is just such a Form, and is, in fact, called by the equivalent name μορφή in the poem of Parmenides himself, they could not well make a difficulty on the point. From their neglect to ask for any explanation of the matter, we must assume that they are supposed already to know quite well what sort of thing a Form is, and to have met before persons who believe in the reality of such Forms. Indeed, if Proclus is right in taking it as familiarly known that the extreme "friends of Forms" criticised in the *Sophistes* are Italian Pythagoreans, the Eleatics must have known all about the matter. What does strike them as unfamiliar in the theory expounded by Socrates is that he believes in Forms "of the things we perceive", and it is about this very assertion of a precise correspondence between Forms and "things we perceive" that they ask the question whether he had really hit upon the doctrine for himself. The whole object of the dialectical difficulties which they go on to raise is to suggest to Socrates that it is impossible to give a coherent account of the relation asserted in his theory to subsist between a Form and the sensible things of which it is the Form, and Parmenides ends his dialectical examination of the doctrine by the express declaration that though, as can now be seen, Socrates

D

has formidable difficulties to face before he can claim
to have justified the assumption of Forms of things,
philosophical thought is impossible unless there are
Forms (135 *a–c*).

We have, therefore, to bear in mind that the object
of the argumentation is not to throw a doubt on the
existence of Forms, but to urge the need for a plain
and explicit account of the *relation* which Socrates
commonly called that of *participation*, by which a thing
is connected with what he calls the Form of that thing.
As Professor Burnet says, expressing the point with
perfect exactness in the terminology of a later generation, it is not the existence of the intelligible but the
existence of the sensible which is, according to Parmenides and Zeno, the *crux* in Socrates' theory. And,
in fact, it was precisely the crux. In the account given
in the *Phaedo* sensible things figure as mere temporary
vehicles of a number of Forms; they are, apparently,
what they have sometimes been called by later thinkers,
meeting-places of universals, terms which sustain complexes of relations, but what more than this a thing is
does not appear. It would seem that Socrates himself
felt that this could not be the last word on the matter;
at any rate, he is careful in the *Phaedo* to suggest a
plurality of names for the relation between thing and
Form, and appears not to be wholly satisfied with his
account of it. That Plato himself felt the necessity of
giving a different doctrine on the point is manifest not
only from the *Timaeus* and *Philebus* but from the hints
furnished by Aristotle's criticisms of him. The impression left by the *Parmenides* is that Plato at least
wishes us to think that Socrates had quite early in life
struck into the right line of thought, but to the day of
his death had never been able to follow it up with
complete success. Indeed our dialogue even *professes*

to give the reason for his partial failure; he had never in his early life had a thoroughly adequate training in hard and dry dialectic. He was trying to define "beautiful" and "right" and "good" and the other Forms before going through a sufficient "discipline" in hard logic, or, in other words, his interests were too exclusively ethical and not logical enough. To myself this passage (*Parm.* 135 *c–d*) has all the appearance of being intended to suggest a serious criticism of what Plato felt to be a weak spot in the Socratic philosophy. I find it quite incredible that such a direct criticism should be levelled either at a purely imaginary person, who had no existence outside his creator's imagination, or at some unnamed person, Plato himself in an earlier stage of his development, or some disciple of Plato, or some Socratic man, under the disguise of the Master. With so much in the way of preliminary orientation we may turn to the treatment of the two specific arguments I have selected for consideration. And I will begin with the argument from the illegitimacy of the infinite regress, which occurs twice over, at *Parm.* 132 *a–b*, and *Parm.* 132 *d–e*. I will begin by a fairly literal rendering of the relevant passages:

"I suppose your reason for thinking that there is in each case such a one Form is this. When you judge that several things are big, perhaps when you consider them all you hold that there is one and the same Form, and hence you think that 'the big' is one." "You are right."

"But if you consider together in the same way *the* big and the other big things, will there not again appear one big something in virtue of which they all appear big?" "So it would seem."

"Then there will appear a second Form of bigness, over and above *the* big and the things that partake of *the* big, and there will be a third on the top of all these in virtue of which they will all be big. Thus each of your Forms will no longer be one but indefinitely numerous."

[Socrates hereupon makes the suggestion that the difficulty might be evaded by supposing that a Form is only a "thought in a mind", and this leads to what I have called the *Refutation of Idealism*. He then tries the alternative explanation that the relation of a thing to a Form is simply that the Form is a type, and the thing is *like* the type. This is met by recurrence to the argument from the regress as follows.]

"Then if anything is *like* the Form can the Form be other than like that which has been stamped with its likeness, in so far as it was modelled on it? Can the like by any artifice be prevented from being like what is like it?" "Certainly not" [*i.e.* the relation of *likeness* is symmetrical]. "And must not the like and its like both partake of one identical something?" "They must." "And that by partaking of which likes are like—will not it be just the Form?" "To be sure it will." "Then it follows that nothing else is like the Form, nor the Form like anything else. Otherwise besides the Form there will always appear another Form, and if *it* is like anything, still another, and there will be an unending series of fresh Forms, if the Form proves *like* that which partakes of it."

The argument from the "infinite regress" is thus employed first against the general theory of the "participation" of things in forms and then, in a specialised form, against the suggested identification of the relation of "participation" with the relation between a copy of an original and the original.

The questions which naturally occur to us on reading the two passages are two, whether the reasoning ascribed to Parmenides in the dialogue is sound, and what, so far as we can still discover, was the history of this type of argument in antiquity before Plato composed the *Parmenides*? Has Plato invented the difficulty which Zeno is made to raise for himself? Or was it invented by some contemporary and unfriendly thinker as a criticism on the type of doctrine expounded in the *Phaedo*? Or is it possible to hold that it is at least historically possible that the real Zeno may have argued in this fashion against theories which were actually current in his own times? The answer usually given to these questions is, I think, that the reasoning is valid, or at least that Plato has not given any reason to think it invalid, and further that, as it is said we know from Alexander of Aphrodisias, the argument was invented by the Megarian logician Polyxenus and is identical with that often alluded to by Aristotle as the τρίτος ἄνθρωπος or "third man". What I propose to show is that the appeal to the regress, though valid against certain ways in which the doctrine of Forms might be understood, is not valid against anything which Plato has advanced anywhere in his writings, that there is no ground for supposing it to be identical with the argument of Polyxenus and that it is not what Aristotle usually has in mind when he speaks of a certain type of argument as the "third man". I will consider first the more general form of the objection.

The argument as formulated by Parmenides at 132 amounts to this. The reason, and the *only* reason, why we should believe in *Forms* is that when many particulars have a common predicate—*e.g.* when it is true to say of several men that each of them is *tall*—this must mean that they have a common character, a common objective determination to which the common predicate of speech answers, and this common character is *one* and the same definite determination. That is *why* we say that though the particulars are *many* there is *one* Form in which they all "partake". But, Parmenides contends, we may once more ascribe this common predicate not only to each of the several "particulars", but also to their "common nature" itself. We can say not only that A_1 is great or good or beautiful, A_2 great or good or beautiful, A_3 great or good or beautiful, but that *greatness* is great, *goodness* good, *beauty* beautiful, and so on. Thus if the resemblance between A_1, A_2, A_3 requires to be accounted for by saying that each of them is an "instance" of A, by parity of reasoning we must say that since A itself has a predicate in common with A_1, A_2, A_3, there is a second Form—call it $A^{(1)}$ of which A, A_1, A_2, A_3 all "partake", and the same considerations will avail to establish in the place of every Form A postulated by the theory of Socrates, a simply infinite series of Forms A, $A^{(1)}$, $A^{(2)}$, ..., $A^{(n)}$ ..., $A^{(\omega)}$. And this, it is assumed, is an absurdity.

Now, in the first place, I should like to observe that this argument, whatever it is worth, is not directed against the reality of Forms or universals, but against the possibility of appealing to that reality as a ground for believing in the revelations of sense-perception and an explanation of what we mean when we make a perceptual judgement. It is not the doctrine that there are νοητὰ εἴδη and that we can be acquainted with them, but the doctrine that what we perceive by our senses —"sense-data"—"partake in" them and thus acquire a secondary reality which furnishes the starting-point of the argument, and, as I shall try to show immediately, the conclusion that there is not *one* form of "good", "beautiful", etc., but a whole hierarchy of orders of good, beauty, etc., is not *per se* absurd. The real difficulty is that if this is so the theory of Forms becomes useless as a device for "saving the appearances" of the world as perceived by sense. The argument is exactly in the right place when put into the mouth of an Eleatic who wishes not to "save" these appearances, but to "give them a fall" ($\kappa\alpha\tau\alpha\beta\acute{\alpha}\lambda\lambda\epsilon\iota\nu$ $\tau\grave{\alpha}\varsigma$ $\alpha\grave{\iota}\sigma\theta\acute{\eta}\sigma\epsilon\iota\varsigma$), and if valid against Socrates it is only valid because Socrates is the champion of perception against ultra-Rationalism.

First, then, as to the validity of the general argument from the "regress", which has always been much affected by metaphysicians as an instrument for the discomfiture of their rivals. It is still often assumed that a theory which leads to an "indefinite regress" in any form is thereby logically discredited. I cannot myself agree with this view. It seems to be no better than a prejudice based on that confusion between infinity and indeterminateness which has been finally exploded by the researches of modern mathematicians into the character of infinite collections. The doctrine that only the finite has determinate structure or order is one which a few hours' study of any elementary work on the Theory of Assemblages is sufficient to explode. Hence I think Russell is plainly right in distinguishing between a harmless and a logically vicious type of the "regress". There can be no logical objection to the "regress" so long as it is constituted merely by implications between propositions. It is no objection either to the significancy or the truth of a proposition p_0 to say that p_0 implies p_1, which again implies p_2, and so on interminably. For there is no reason why each of an endless series of propositions $\{p\}$ should not be true. In fact, on the hypothesis of "Idealists" of the kind who usually make the most frequent employment of the "regress" against their opponents, every *true* proposition p *must* imply an infinite series of true propositions. For they commonly hold that a proposition cannot be true without being actually known by some mind and that this is part of what we *mean* by calling p true. Hence the true proposition p implies, on their theory, the true proposition, "x knows p", and this, being itself a true proposition, again implies "y—who may of course be identical with x—knows that x knows p", and so on *in indefinitum*.[1]

Professor Royce has correctly drawn this conclusion, and since it is a fundamental article of his philosophical belief that to be known by someone is part of what we mean by being true, he rightly accepts the view that this particular "regress" must be accepted. But he seems also to make the further assumption, which is not warranted by his premises, that it is *never* an objection to a philosophical doctrine that it leads to the "regress". Here, again, I think Russell clearly right in holding that there is one kind of "regress" which is always fatal to any hypothesis which implies it. No intelligible proposition can be such that an infinite "regress" arises in the very attempt to state its meaning. An apparent proposition p_0 which turns out to be such that we cannot state its meaning without first stating as parts of that meaning the infinite series of propositions p_1, p_2, ..., p_n, ..., p_ω, must be no proposition at all but a mere unmeaning noise. For, as we can never exhaust an infinite series by enumeration of its terms, we could never know definitely what such a p_0 means, and every proposition must have a fully determinate meaning. Hence for us, at any rate, p_0 is no proposition at all. The importance of this distinction will be seen when it is remembered that all the attempts made by philosophers,

---

[1] This doctrine must be carefully distinguished from the statement given in all works on symbolic logic that "true propositions are implied by all propositions". The reference here is to "material implication"; what the philosophers referred to in the text mean is apparently "formal implication",—a very different thing.

and notably by Kant, to discover contradictions in our notions of space and time involve only a "regress" of the harmless kind; they only show that certain propositions, if true, involve the truth of an infinity of other propositions, as there is no reason why they should not. So, again, if Zeno's well-known argument from indefinite divisibility were alleged as a reason for denying that a line can be divided at all, there would be an open fallacy. It was only valid *ad homines* because part of the case of his opponents was that a point is a minimum length. As an argument for Spinoza's thesis of the indivisibility of real extension it is no more cogent than it would be to argue that there can be no such number as 1 because there is an infinity of rational fractions less than 1. We cannot, however, meet the argument of Parmenides against Socrates by urging that the "regress" of which he speaks is of the harmless kind. If he is right in finding that "regress" in the theory of μέθεξις, the "regress" is vicious and shows that the theory of Socrates is indefensible. For the reasoning is as follows: Two things A_1 and A_2 are both A (*e.g.* Socrates and Zeno are both men), because they have a common "nature" (humanity), and it is *only* because they possess this common nature that we can truly predicate the same term of them. But we can predicate A of A itself in *precisely the same sense* in which we predicate A of A_1 and of A_2 (*i.e.* we can say that Humanity is human, or Man is a man, exactly as one can say Zeno is human or Socrates is a man). Hence A, A_1, A_2 must, on our own theory, have a still more ultimate common nature, and so on indefinitely. Hence you will never be able to say exactly what it is that Zeno and Socrates have in common; you do not know what the predicate you assert about both of them *is*.

Thus the solution of the puzzle, if there is one, cannot lie in admitting the "regress" but pronouncing it harmless; if the theory of Socrates is to be defended at all, it must be shown that the alleged "regress" does not really arise. That is, we must deny the tacit premise of Parmenides that a universal can be predicated of itself as it is predicated of its "instances". A_1 and A_2, we must say, have the common nature A, or are "instances of" A, but A and A_1 are not two "instances of" A; A has not to itself the relation it has to A_1 or to A_2. We may say of two white things that each of them is white, but we must not say in the same way that whiteness, or white, is white. Or, to use Plato's language, which makes the point clearer, though we may say that a white surface *has* whiteness, or white colour, we must not say that white colour, or whiteness, *has* white colour or whiteness. We must say that a concept, or meaning, or intension can be predicated of each constituent of the corresponding extension, but can never be *predicated* of itself,—in fact that the subject-predicate relation is an alio-relative. This seems to me an obvious truth which is only concealed from us by the linguistic fact that we commonly use the same word "is" to symbolise both predication and identity. "White is white", "goodness is goodness", and the like, if they are significant expressions at all, are not predications but assertions of identity. They mean that "white is the same thing as white", etc., but "Socrates is a man" does not mean that Socrates is identical with Man. To say that snow is white means that snow *has* the colour white. What that means I must not discuss here, but, whatever it means, it would be nonsense to say that whiteness, or white colour, has a white colour, as snow has. White *has* not itself any colour at all; it *is* a colour.

The solution of Parmenides' puzzle, then, is that

identity and the relation of predicate to subject are
different and disparate, and this is why every system of
logical symbolism has always found it necessary to avoid
the trap laid for thought by the inexactitude of ordinary
speech in this matter. Hence the alleged "regress" does
not really arise from the original statement about the
"participation" of things in Forms or universals. It
arises not from the doctrine of Socrates himself but
from Parmenides' skilful combination of what Socrates
had said with the further premise that the Form "participates in" itself. (τί δ' αὐτὸ τὸ μέγα καὶ τἆλλα τὰ
μεγάλα; οὐχὶ ἕν τι αὖ μέγα φανεῖται ᾧ ταῦτα πάντα
μεγάλα φαίνεσθαι; 132 a.) So, to recur once more to my
example, the "common nature" of all white things is
just their white colour, but the "common nature" of a
thing and a colour cannot itself be a colour, and *you do
not need to know what it is* in order to know what the
white colour which is the "common nature" of all white
things is. You can know what "white" is without re-
quiring to have any view on the question what colours
and things other than colours have in common. Hence
no "regress" is involved in the *meaning* of the assertion
that such and such a particular "partakes" in such and
such a Form. It is perhaps important to note that the
source of the apparent fallacy, the ambiguity of "is",
is also, as Plato was to show in the *Sophistes*, the source
of all the old "eristic" difficulties about negative propositions. Since, as everyone admits, Plato saw and
explained the ambiguity so far as it affects the possibility
of significant denial, it is only reasonable to suppose he
was aware of the presence of the same ambiguity in the
argument we have just analysed. But it would have
been bad art, and probably also bad history, to allow
the youthful Socrates of the dialogue to see through and
expose the fallacy. Consequently Plato does not let him

discuss it at all. He is made to turn without discussion to a fresh point. Historically, I take it, this means that the appeal to the "regress" had been used against the doctrine of μέθεξις, but presumably after the death of Socrates himself. The persons who used it must have meant primarily not so much to discredit the doctrine that the proper objects of knowledge are intelligible Forms as to deny that these Forms are in any way connected with the things and events of the perceived world. That is, they must have been logicians with an ultra-intellectualistic bias like the "friends of Forms" mentioned in the *Sophistes* whom Proclus identifies with Italian Pythagoreans.

The detailed examination of the history of the argument has to begin with the consideration of certain passages in the *Metaphysics* of Aristotle and the explanation given of these passages by Alexander of Aphrodisias. Aristotle more than once makes the statement that the "most finished" versions of the theory of Forms lead to a difficulty which he speaks of as the "third man". Thus at *Met. A*, 990 b 15, where he is arguing that the reasons currently given in the Platonic school for believing in the Forms and their relation to the world of sense-data are not above criticism, he says ἔτι δὲ οἱ ἀκριβέστεροι τῶν λόγων οἱ μὲν τῶν πρός τι ποιοῦσιν ἰδέας . . . οἱ δὲ τὸν τρίτον ἄνθρωπον λέγουσι, "of the more accurate (but the meaning is rather 'more finished', 'more subtle') arguments, some lead to Ideas of relations . . . others involve the difficulty of the 'third man'" (tr. Ross). The same remark occurs, and, so far as the words I have cited go, in identical language, except that ἀκριβέστατοι is substituted for ἀκριβέστεροι at *Met.* 1079 a 11. From the facts that Alexander in his commentary refers to the argument with which we have just dealt as an example of a "third man" argument,

and also mentions the Megarian "sophist"—*i.e.* formal
logician—Polyxenus as the inventor of a form of the
"third man", it has become customary to say that τρίτος
ἄνθρωπος is a name for what we call the appeal to the
"indefinite regress", that the controversial use of this
appeal was invented by Polyxenus, and that it is to this
that both the *Parmenides* and the Aristotelian references
allude. According to this now generally accepted view,
Plato is here recalling and dramatically ascribing to Parmenides a criticism directed—so it is assumed—against
Plato himself by Polyxenus. The dramatic justification
of this is that Polyxenus belonged to a school whose
founder Euclides was originally a disciple of Parmenides. If, however, we read the passage of Alexander
with proper care, we shall see that we must not assume
without discussion either that Polyxenus invented the
particular argument rehearsed in the *Parmenides*, or
that it is the *Parmenides* argument to which Aristotle is
alluding in the *Metaphysics*. We must therefore consider
the whole question for ourselves in a little detail.

It may be as well to begin with a brief statement of
what is known about the personality of Polyxenus. Our
one contemporary reference to him comes from the
correspondence between Plato and Dionysius II. In the
last letter of the correspondence as arranged in our
texts, which is also the earliest in order of time and
belongs to the year 366–5, Plato mentions that he is
sending to Dionysius a person whose society will, he
hopes, be agreeable to him and to Archytas. This person is Helicon of Cyzicus, a member of the astronomical
school of Eudoxus, and, Plato adds, one who has
enjoyed the society of a certain unnamed pupil of
Isocrates and Polyxenus, one of the disciples of Bryson
(τῶν Βρύσωνός τινι ἑταίρων, 360 *c*). Thus Helicon was
apparently selected by Plato on the ground that he

would be able to represent at once the mathematics and astronomy of Eudoxus, the political ideals of Isocrates, and the formal logic of the Megarians; from the context it is clear that, though Plato thought well of his man, his feelings towards persons of Megarian antecedents were not at this date over-cordial. The important point for my purposes is, however, that the reference gives us, in a rough way, the date of Polyxenus. He is a disciple of Bryson, whose interesting contributions to the problem of the quadrature of the circle are discussed by Aristotle in the *Posterior Analytics* and *Sophistical Refutations* in an unappreciative and pedantic way, which suggests that the *maestro di color che sanno* did not really understand the nature of the problem. Now, Bryson was one of the original members of the Megarian school, and had been a personal associate of Socrates, as we see from the fact that Theopompus, the historian, a pupil of Isocrates, in an attempt (fr. 247) to depreciate Plato, charged him with borrowing his ideas from Aristippus, Antisthenes, and *Bryson*. Polyxenus thus belongs to the second generation of the school of Euclides, and must be, roughly speaking, contemporary with Plato, so that it is quite credible in itself that he may be the author of criticisms referred to by Aristotle and by Plato himself in a work as late as the *Parmenides*.

I can hardly carry the discussion further without actually quoting almost in full what Alexander said about the "third man" in his comment on *Met. A*, 990 b 15, as there are several points in his statement to which I would direct attention. This, then, is what he says:

"The argument which brings in the 'third man' is as follows: They [*i.e.* the believers in Forms] say that the substances which are predicated generally are the true and proper substances [κυρίως εἶναι τοιαῦτα. *I.e.* the Academy, unlike Aristotle, who regards individual things like 'this horse', 'this man', as the primary substances, regard universals or kinds, 'man', 'horse', etc., as the 'true and proper' substances, whereas Aristotle will only allow them to be called substances in a secondary and derivative sense], and that these are the Forms. Further, things which are *like* one another are so in virtue of participation [μετουσία, a word never used by Plato in this connection, as Professor Burnet has noted] in one and the same something which properly is that [*i.e.* is 'horse' or 'man', or whatever each of two like things is said to be], and this is the Form. But if this is so, and if that which is predicated in like manner of several things, when not identical with any one of those things, is another thing over and above them—and it is just because the Form of Man, though predicated of particular men, is not identical with any of them that it is a *kind*—there must be a *third* man besides man particular—as, *e.g.* Socrates or Plato—and the Form, which last is also itself numerically one.

"Now, there was an argument used by the sophists and introducing the 'third man' to this effect. If we say 'there is a man walking' we do not mean that Man, in the sense of the Form, is walking—for the Form is unmoving—nor yet a determinate particular man—and how can we mean this if we do not recognise the man? We are aware that *a* man is walking, but not *who* the particular man is of whom we assert this; we are saying that another *third* man different from these [*i.e.* different from both Man and from this or that man whom we know] is walking. Ergo, there is a *third* man of whom we have predicated that he is walking. To be sure, this argument is sophistical, but an opening is made for it by those who postulate the Forms. And Phanias says, in his reply to Diodorus, that the sophist Polyxenus introduces the 'third man' in these words: 'If man is man in virtue of partaking and participation [κατὰ μετοχήν τε καὶ μετουσίαν, both words non-Platonic in this sense] in the Form, or αὐτοάνθρωπος, there must be a man who will have his being correlatively to the Form. This cannot be the αὐτοάνθρωπος, who *is* the Form, nor yet the particular man who *is* by *participation* (μετοχή) in the Form. The only alternative is that there is yet a third man who *is relatively* to the Form.

"The 'third man' is also demonstrated thus: If what is truly predicated of a plurality of subjects *is* a reality alongside those of which it is predicated and distinct from them—and those who postulate the Forms believe they can prove this . . ., if so, I say there will be a 'third man'. For if *Man* as predicate is other than the *men* of whom the term is predicated, and has a substantial being of its own, and if *Man* is predicated in like manner, both of particular men and of the Form, then there must be a third man distinct both from the particular men and from the Form. And in the same way a fourth, predicable in like manner of this third man, of the Form and of the particular man, and again a fifth, and so on *in indefinitum*. This argument is identical with the first, since it was assumed that like things are like in virtue of their participation (μετουσία) in one and the same thing."

Now, it is to be observed that we are here offered three distinct arguments, each of which brings in a "third man"; one is ascribed to the "sophists", that is, according to the Aristotelian use of that word, the Megarian logicians generally, the second by name to the Megarian Polyxenus, and the third is identical with the argument put by Plato into the mouth of Par-

menides. It is only in this last version, which Alexander
gives in two forms, that any question of a "regress"
arises, and *this* argument is not that attributed to Polyxenus. The other two will easily be seen on analysis
to be of a quite different type. The first, that of the
"sophists" generally, is based on the ambiguity of the
indefinite article, or, in Greek, of the common noun
without any article. If I say, as I quite well may, "a
man is walking down the street" without knowing *what*
man it is whom I see at the far end of the street, though
I am saying what is true and significant, I plainly do
not mean that "humanity" is going down the road.
Particular men may be met in the Strand, but you
would hardly expect to encounter Man, "the substance
of men which is Man", there. And I do not mean that
this or that known man, Lord Kitchener or Russell,
is going along the Strand, since by hypothesis I do not
know who the man in question is. Hence besides "Man"
with the capital and Lord Kitchener or Russell, the
words "a man" or "man" must have some third sense.
This is, of course, simply true. When I say "Man is
fallible", I mean by Man what Socrates would have
called "just man", the *Form* of man. When I say "a
man wrote *Hamlet*", if I have any knowledge of English literature I mean that *Hamlet* was written by a
particular man whose name, birthplace, and so forth I
could mention if I chose. But when I say "a man wrote
Junius", I—who am not convinced by any hypothesis
yet put forward on the identity of *Junius*—mean neither
that the Form of man, Man with the capital, wrote
Junius nor that, *e.g.*, Philip Francis or Edmund Burke
wrote *Junius*. I really mean to assert the disjunctive
proposition "either *a* wrote *Junius*, or *b* wrote *Junius*.
or *c* wrote *Junius* or . . ." and so forth, where *a*, *b*, *c* . . .
stand for the different individuals of English speech

E

who were alive and adult during the whole period in which the *Letters of Junius* were appearing. I mean that some one of this set, though I do not know which, was the author. That this observation was well worth making is shown by the fact that Russell has had to make it again at some length in his *Principles of Mathematics*. But it is not in any way inconsistent with the theory of Forms. It is no objection to a doctrine of *universalia in rebus* or even of *universalia ante res* to say that it cannot tell me which of the many beings who "partake of" humanity wrote the *Letters of Junius*. If, as would seem, the argument is Megarian, it shows no trace of being directed against Socrates or Plato; it is merely a correct reflection on the ambiguity of the article such as would naturally occur to anyone interested in the formal development of logic.

The argument of Polyxenus is rather different and distinctly more subtle. Our view of its exact purport must depend on a point of textual criticism. In my rendering I have followed, with just a shade of doubt, a transposition of the words of one clause suggested by Clemens Bäumker. Professor Burnet, in his recent work on *Greek Philosophy from Thales to Plato*, does the same thing, but oddly enough subjoins an interpretation which seems only possible if the transposition is *not* made. As I understand the passage, the argument is this: According to the theory of Forms, *man* means (1) the Form of Man, (2) each of the particular men who, on this theory, have an inferior kind of reality due to their "participation" in the Form. Thus *man* in sense (1) is identical with the Form, in sense (2) depends on and derives his being from the Form. Polyxenus maintains that there must be a third sense intermediate between the two. There should be a "man" who is not identical with the Form and yet is "on the same footing" with it, not derivative like the "particular" man.

The point of this can, I think, be illustrated by what we know to have been Plato's doctrine about the objects studied in geometry. As we know from Aristotle, he held that these "mathematicals" are "intermediate" between Forms and sensibles. Thus the Form of circularity is one and only one; the circle as a type of plane curve is one determinate type, and all circles belong to this same type. The round figures we draw with ink or chalk are not really true to the type; they are only approximations, or, in the language used by Socrates in the *Phaedo*, "they are not circles, but would like to be circles if they could". But the circles of which Euclid reasons stand in an intermediate position. There are *many* of them. We talk, *e.g.*, of *two* circles which cut or touch, or of a nest of concentric circles, or of the three circles each of which touches one side of a triangle and the two other sides "produced". Yet each of the geometer's many circles is an *exact*, and not, like the visible round figure, a merely approximate realisation of the one type. Now, as I understand Polyxenus, he was arguing that on the theory of Forms there ought always to be something which mediates between the Form of Man and the imperfect embodiments of it which figure in actual life as the geometer's circles mediate between "*the* circle" of Analysis and the things we draw on paper or on the blackboard. But *there seems to be no such thing in the case of Man*. This reasoning is most naturally understood as a criticism directed against that very extension of the doctrine of Forms from mathematics to cover the realm of organisms about which Socrates himself is made to express a doubt in our dialogue at p. 130 *d*. If this was really the point Polyxenus intended to make, his criticism appears to me to speak very highly for his philosophical acumen. Plato himself indicates in the passage to which I have just referred that the recognition of Forms of organisms is one of the most ticklish points in the whole theory. How he himself in the end escaped from the difficulty cannot be considered here, as any serious discussion of the matter would require an elaborate investigation of what Aristotle has told us about the Platonic reduction of philosophy to arithmetic. But it may at least be said that the Platonic doctrine, as known to Aristotle, only preserves the conceptions ascribed in the *Phaedo* to Socrates by a transformation which makes them at first sight almost unrecognisable. For my present purpose it is enough to note that if I have rightly discerned the real point of Polyxenus, his criticism must have been specially directed against Plato himself and no other, and this would explain why it is, as a matter of fact, never answered in the *Parmenides*, where it would be an anachronism to put Platonism, as distinct from the cruder doctrine expounded in the *Phaedo*, into the mouth of the youthful Socrates. For the conception of this gradation from Forms or numbers through mathematicals down to sensibles is always connected by Aristotle with what he represents as the personal theories of Plato. He ascribes it to Plato as peculiar to himself, as an ἴδιον Πλάτωνος, in a way in which he never ascribes the general theory of Forms to him. Professor Burnet, who takes a different view, remarks, indeed, that the words used in the account given by Alexander on the authority of Phanias of Eresus, an original member of the Lyceum, of what Polyxenus had said, to represent the relation between a Form and a sensible, μετουσία, μετοχή, are not technical terms of Plato's vocabulary, and infers that the argument of Polyxenus was not specially directed against Plato. I

do not myself think the inference of much weight. If
it proves anything, it should surely prove that the
criticism of Polyxenus was not directed even against
Socrates, for it is Socrates who, in Plato's writings,
habitually talks of μέθεξις as the relation between
sensibles and Forms. The only other person in the
dialogues who ever says much about the matter is the
Pythagorean Timaeus, and he avoids the use of the
words μετέχειν and μέθεξις in a very remarkable
manner, for which I shall directly give the true reason.
But if the argument is meant neither to tell against
Socrates nor against Plato, against whom is it directed?
Do we know of any other "friends of Forms" who held
the view that sensible things are what they are by "participating" in Forms at all, except just Socrates and
his associates? Professor Burnet who, like myself, regards this account of sensible things as the distinctive
contribution of Socrates to the theory of Forms is, I
think, under a special obligation to face this question.

With regard to his one definite argument, that from
the un-Platonic character of the *words* μετουσία and
μετοχή, I might remark (*a*) that even if it were absolutely certain that the actual words of Polyxenus have
undergone no modification in reaching us at two removes, I see no reason why his preference for μετοχή
as the verbal noun to μετέχειν should be regarded as
proof that he is not thinking of Plato. μετοχή is, at any
rate, as old as the fourth century as a verbal noun to
μετέχειν. Thus in *Met. Z,* 1030 a 11 ff., we are told
that "nothing which is not a species of a genus will have
an *essence* (τὸ τί ἦν εἶναι), only species will have one,
for in these the subject is not held to *participate* in the
attribute" (ταῦτα γὰρ δοκεῖ οὐ κατὰ μετοχὴν λέγεσθαι),
where the so-called "Alexander" sees a direct
allusion to the Socratic-Platonic doctrine. δύναται τὸ οὐ

κατὰ μετοχὴν νοεῖσθαι ἀντὶ τοῦ οὐ κεχωρισμένα ἐστὶ τὰ εἴδη
καὶ οὐ καθάπερ φησὶ Πλάτων κατὰ μετοχὴν αὐτῶν τὰ καθ'
ἕκαστά ἐστιν "the words *is not held to participate* may be
understood to mean that the species are not separable,
and individuals do not exist in virtue of *participation* in
them, as Plato asserts" ("Alexander" *in loc.*). Aristotle
again uses μετοχή as the noun of μετέχειν at *Ethica
Eudemia*, 1217 a 29, though without reference to the
theory of Forms. The *word* indeed is used by Plato
himself in one of his latest writings, *Ep.* vii. 344 *e*,
though not in a technical sense, ὡς παιδείας δὴ μέτοχος
ὤν, ἧς οὐκ ἄξιος ἦν ἀγαπῶν δόξαν τὴν περὶ τῆς μετοχῆς
γενομένην. Μετουσία, again, though not a Platonic or
Aristotelian word, is no coinage of a later age but
belongs to the Greek of Aristophanes and Demosthenes,
and I have observed the use of it in later Platonists as
an equivalent for the Platonic μέθεξις. (*b*) And, as an
illustration to show that inferences from verbal expressions must not be pushed too far, I would remind
Professor Burnet that he himself expresses a doubt
whether the name "indeterminate duality" given by
Aristotle to the continuum called by Plato the "great-
and-small" is Platonic, though he has, of course, no
doubt that the concept is characteristically Platonic.
Similarly, it is notorious that Aristotle expresses the
Platonic theory of matter by the statement that "Plato
says in the *Timaeus* that space (χώρα) and matter (ὕλη)
are the same", though Aristotle must have known that
as a matter of language the *Timaeus* does not use the
word ὕλη in the sense of "matter" at all. I am, therefore,
not convinced by the linguistic argument that the reasoning of Polyxenus is aimed at someone other than Plato.

Now let us see how the argument will be affected if
we refuse to make the transposition of words introduced
by Bäumker into the passage about Polyxenus. In the

MSS. of Alexander the text runs thus: "If man is man by partaking or participation in the Form or αὐτοάνθρω-πος, there must be a man who has his being relatively to the Form. But neither the αὐτοάνθρωπος who *is* the Form, nor the particular man, is in virtue of participation in the Form. The remaining possibility is that there should be a third man who has his being relative to the Form." If this is what Polyxenus said, he must mean one and the same thing by "having one's being relative to" the Form and "partaking in" the Form. The sense then is: What do you mean by the man who is said to "partake in" the Form of man? You cannot mean Man, because Man does not "participate in" but *is* the Form. And you do not mean this or that actual man; therefore you must mean "man" in some unintelligible third sense. Thus understood, Polyxenus simply assumes it as conceded by those against whom he is reasoning that this and that man do not "participate in" the Form, that is, as Professor Burnet says, the actual men stand in *no* relation to the Form. He is not attempting to prove this but making it one of the premises of his syllogism. But once more we have to ask ourselves against whom such a polemic can be directed. Can we point to any "friends of Forms" who admitted that things of some kinds "partake of" Forms but held that none of these things are sensibles? Such a theory is, no doubt, an abstract possibility. We can imagine a philosopher holding that all the "things" which "partake in" Forms are what Plato called "mathematicals",—the many circles, triangles, etc., of the geometer, not "sensibles". And something like this may—nay, almost must—have been the doctrine of the "friends of Forms" criticised in the *Sophistes*. But Aristotle is explicit and emphatic on the point that the phrase about "participation" was never Pythagorean.

The Pythagoreans, he says at *Met. A*, 987 b 11, "said that things are by *imitation* of the numbers, whereas Plato said it was by *participation*". (This, I may observe in passing, is the simple explanation of the fact that the Pythagorean speaker in the *Timaeus* talks throughout of μίμησις, not of μέθεξις.) And he is equally clear in the same context that it was *sensibles* which were said to "have their being by participation". Thus, whether we follow Bäumker in his transposition or not, it still seems to me plain that the argument of Polyxenus is aimed against either Plato or Socrates as he is represented in Plato, and more probably than not against Plato himself.

As I understand Alexander's account of the matter, he means that this argument is a special application of the more general one to which he refers simply as an "argument of the sophists", and of which he says that it was provoked by those who "separate the common (nature) from the particulars". This seems to mean that even the more general form of the argument was devised for the purposes of the polemic against Plato. I agree with Professor Burnet that Alexander does not say that Polyxenus invented the "third man", but only that he "brought it on the stage" (for this seems to be the metaphor underlying the expression εἰσάγειν λόγον), but I think he means that the special form of it which he quotes from Phanias was due to Polyxenus. However this may be, the really important point is that the argument ascribed to Polyxenus, like that put down more vaguely to "the sophists", does not turn on an indefinite "regress". You could not use either of these "sophisms" to show that there must be a "fourth" or "fifth" man, and Alexander shows himself to be quite aware of this. Hence I think that we must at least come to the conclusions that—

(*a*) The argument from the "regress" is only one special form of a type of reasoning popularly known as the "third man".

(*b*) This type of reasoning was clearly quite well known in the time of Aristotle, since he would not otherwise have referred to it by a nickname. Even the special form which brings in the "regress" was no novelty when Plato wrote the *Parmenides*, since he makes Socrates allude to it in passing as something that requires no detailed explanation in a much earlier dialogue (*Republic*, 597 *c*).

(*c*) The version of the "third man" specially due to Polyxenus does not bring in the "regress", and therefore cannot be what Plato has in view in the *Parmenides*.

If I am asked from whom then did the argument about the "regress" come, I have to answer that I do not know. But one thing at least is significant. In the *Parmenides* this argument is used twice, once, as we have seen, against the notion of sensibles as "participating in" Forms, and a second time against the notion of sensibles as copies of Forms. That is, it is used against the Pythagorean as well as against the Platonic formula. This suggests that the argument is very possibly originally anti-Pythagorean, and that the employment of it against the μίμησις formula may go well back to the fifth century. In fact, it belongs to the same class of reasonings as those of Zeno against infinite divisibility and has all the appearance of coming from the same source. I see no anachronism therefore in supposing that it comes from Zeno himself, and is just the sort of objection that would probably have been made by him and Parmenides to the youthful Socrates if he expounded to them the doctrine which the *Phaedo* represents him as formulating in his early manhood.

Indeed I shall be surprised if Zeno had not already used the "sophism" against the Italian "friends of Forms".

In the face of these results, it is not unreasonable to raise the question whether, in spite of his modern interpreters, Aristotle is really thinking of the "regress" at all when he urges that the most "finished" discourses of the Academy lead to the difficulty about the "third man". He *might* be referring to one of the "third man" arguments which do not bring in the "regress". It is true that Alexander seems to have taken the same view as the modern interpreters, since his explanation of this remark identifies the objection meant by Aristotle with that which he raises at *Met. A*, 991 a 1, which is a simple reproduction of the *Parmenides* passage (see Alexander in *Metaphysica*, 991 a 1). But against this I would set the consideration that none of the other passages in which Aristotle speaks of the "third man" seems to have any connection with the "regress".

At *Met. Z*, 1039 a 2, there is a passing reference in connection with an argument to prove that no "universal" is an οὐσία, an individual *substance*, and that consequently all "universals" are attributes, not things (οὐδὲν σημαίνει τῶν κοινῇ κατηγορουμένων τόδε τι ἀλλὰ τοιόνδε). If you deny this, Aristotle says, "the third man and other difficulties will arise". There is nothing here to show that he is thinking of the "regress", and it is more natural to suppose that he is not. The sense seems to be simply this. Suppose that a "universal predicate" really is the name of a *this* or individual thing. Then when I say "Socrates is a man" what *this* is denoted by the word "man"? Not the Form, for the Platonists themselves, at whom the argument is aimed, say that Socrates *is* not the Form, but only "partakes of" it. And not a determinate individual, Socrates or another, since "Socrates is Plato" would obviously be false, whereas "Socrates is a man" is true, and "Socrates is Socrates" manifestly, though true, does not mean the same thing as "Socrates is a man". Thus if the word "man" in the supposed proposition denotes an individual *this* at all, it must denote a *third* man, who is neither Socrates nor Man with a big M, and this, it is assumed, is absurd. It is quite clear, I think, that this is all that Aristotle means here.

A second passage occurs in the very doubtfully authentic book *Met. K*, 1059 b 8. Here again there is no question of a "regress", and the argument is exactly that which I have supposed to be intended by Poly·xenus, that if there are Forms answering to all universals, there ought also to be men and horses and the like intermediate between the Forms and the sensible things, just as the "mathematicals" are intermediate between Forms and visible diagrams. The writer's words are: "Even if one postulates the Forms there is a difficulty about the question why it is not with other things of which there are Forms as it is with mathematicals. I mean that they place the mathematicals between the Forms and sensibles as a third class over and above the forms and the things in our world (οἷον τρίττα τινὰ παρὰ τὰ εἴδη τε καὶ τὰ δεῦρο, b 7), but there is no third man or third horse besides the Form and the particulars (τρίτος δ᾿ ἄνθρωπος οὐκ ἔστιν οὐδ᾿ ἵππος παρ᾿ αὐτόν τε καὶ τοὺς καθ᾿ ἕκαστον)."

The one other reference to the "third man" in the Aristotelian corpus is in the work *On Sophistical Refutations*, which is in effect an unfriendly examination of the formal logical paradoxes of the Megarian school.

At 178 b 36, in an account of the fallacies of figure of speech—*i.e.* fallacies which arise from confusing one "figure of predication" or "category" with another—

Aristotle includes among them the argument that "there is a third man over and above the Form and particular men" (ὅτι ἔστι τις τρίτος ἄνθρωπος παρ᾽ αὐτὸν καὶ τοὺς καθ᾽ ἕκαστον). This argument, he says, is one of the fallacies of "figure of speech" because it turns on treating a general term such as "man" as if it stood for τόδε τι, a *this*, whereas it really stands for a τοιόνδε, a *tale* or *such*. That is, in Aristotelian language, it mistakes an attribute or predicate for a substance—a substance being by definition just that which can only be subject, never predicate, in a proposition. The reference again is manifestly not to fallacious appeals to the "regress"—it would be quite impossible to regard these as *"in dictione"*—but to the simplest form of "third man" argument. Alexander rightly says in explaining the passage that the argument meant is that according to which when we say "a man is walking" we are speaking neither of Man nor of a determinate and known man. *I.e.* the fallacy lies in treating the words "a man", when they really mean "one and only one of the members of the class man, but I do not know which member", as if they meant "this particular man whose name I could give if I chose". Aristotle's own remark on the logical error is that "it is not the *isolating* (or *exponing*, τὸ ἐκτίθεσθαι) of the universal which leads to the 'third man', but the assumption that the 'exponed' universal is a *this*"—i.e. a particular existent (*S.E.* 179 a 3). The paradox, that is, is not due simply to the legitimate insistence on the distinction between "some man or other" and "this particular man", but to the further illegitimate assumption that "some man or other" is an object of the same type as Zeno, Socrates, or Plato, though different from them.

We are justified then in saying that though, as Alexander tells us, Aristotle had made some use of the argument from the alleged impossibility of the "regress" in his lost work περὶ ἰδεῶν, there is no passage in his extant works in which the τρίτος ἄνθρωπος need be understood as referring to the "regress". It *need* not be understood so in his remark that certain Platonic arguments about the Forms lead up to the "third man"; it *cannot* be understood so in any of the other passages. I conclude then that Aristotle's allusions to the "third man" as a paradox implied by Plato's theories about Forms has nothing to do with the problem of the "regress". He only means that on the interpretation he always gives to Plato's language, viz. that the Form is a kind of particular existent, it *would* be a valid objection that the subject of such a proposition as "some man or other is walking" must also be *another* particular thing.

Before I proceed to deal more briefly with the second argument from the "regress", I will, to keep to the actual order of development in the *Parmenides*, examine the section which immediately follows that we have just dismissed, and which I called the *Refutation of Idealism* (*Parmenides* 132 *b–c*).

Socrates now makes the suggestion that all the difficulties about the unity or multiplicity of the Form may be avoided if we look on Forms merely as "subjective", as "ideas in our own heads", or, in his own words, as "thoughts" (νοήματα) which are not "in" things at all, but only "in souls" (ἐν ψυχαῖς), *i.e.* in the minds that think the thoughts. If a Form is just a "thought" and is not really "in" anything but the mind which has the thought, it seems obvious that my thought of "man" is the same thought whether I think that Socrates is a man or that Zeno is a man. So we seem here to have an account of Forms which allows of the "presence" of one Form to many particulars without leaving an opening for an opponent to urge that the Form cannot be really one if the particulars are really many. For now all that will be meant by saying that the one Form is present to many things will be that we can think the same predicate of each of them—and this seems to be a fact of everyday experience. Such a doctrine clearly amounts to what in modern days is called "Idealism" in the strict and proper sense of a much-abused word— the view that the "unity" or "common nature" of a class, and similarly the relations which connect existents ("double of", "cause of", "husband of", and the like) are the "work of the mind" or are "put by the mind" into a "raw material" supplied by sense.

I shall therefore use the name "Idealism" for the view which is thrown out in this section of the *Parmenides*, merely adding that in some degree or other this view has deeply coloured most European philosophy from Locke's time to our own. By calling the section a *Refutation of Idealism* I mean, that is, a refutation—and to my mind the neatest and most unanswerable I know of—of the theory that unity and relational order are the "work of our minds" or "put by our minds" into experience. The Platonist point is that we no more "put" the universal into things than we create "things" by perceiving them or thinking about them. We *discover* a pre-existing order just because it is there to discover. (It is true that Plato also held that order is the "work of the mind" in the sense that it has been "put into" things by God, but he did not hold that God's knowledge that things are relationally ordered is the logical *prius* of their being so ordered.)

In view of the confidence with which it is often asserted on the strength of a glaring fallacy of ambiguity that Plato was an "Idealist" in some modern sense of the word, it should be noted that the present passage is the only one in all his works where it is ever suggested that a Form is an "idea in the mind" or a "mental state", and that the suggestion is only made to meet with a refutation which is unanswerable and is accepted as such by Socrates (132 *c*, ἀλλ' οὐδὲ τοῦτο, φάναι, ἔχει λόγον). This, of itself, should show that the interpretation of Plato which goes back to Philo the Jew, and still has its defenders, according to which a Form is a "thought in the mind of God", is untenable. It is true that in his Refutation of Idealism Plato is thinking, primarily at least, of thoughts in the minds of men, but the principle of his argument would be valid against the attempt to identify the universals which pervade the world, and give it its structure with processes in any mind whatsoever. Plato would have agreed in principle with the observations of Bolzano (*Wissenschaftslehre*, i. 113, 115): "It follows no doubt, from the omniscience of God, that every truth, even if it is neither known nor thought of by any other being, is known to Him as the Omniscient, and perpetually present in His understanding. Hence there is not in fact a single truth which is known to no one. But this does not prevent us from speaking of truths-in-themselves as truths in the notion whereof it is in nowise presupposed that they must be thought by someone. For, though to be thought is not included in the notion of such truths, it may still follow from a different ground, *i.e.* from the omniscience of God, that they must at least be known by God, if by no one else. . . . A thing is not true because God knows it to be true; on the contrary God knows it to be true because it is so. Thus, *e.g.*, God does not exist because God thinks that He exists; it is because there is a God that this God thinks of Himself as existing. Similarly God is not almighty, wise, holy, etc., because He conceives Himself as such ; *e converso*

He thinks Himself almighty, etc., because He really is so."

With Plato, then, an εἶδος or ἰδέα or Form is always the *object* of a thought, that of which someone thinks, not the process of thinking nor any psychological characteristic of that process, not knowledge, but something which is known. Thus the number 2, as we learn from the *Phaedo*, is a Form, but my ψυχή is not a Form, and still less is that which takes place in my ψυχή when I think about the number 2 a Form; 2 and my thinking about 2 are as distinct as my (dead) grandfather and my present thinking about him. The view which is here suggested only to be dismissed differs in holding that 2 *is* the same thing as my thinking about 2, or at least is so connected with my thinking about 2 that a proposition about 2 is only true when I, or some other thinker, happen to be thinking about 2, and *because* someone is thinking about 2.

This "Idealist" view, which identifies a Form with the νόημα or thought of the Form, can perhaps be fairly expressed in modern phraseology as follows. (I do not know if any writer puts the point exactly in this way, but readers of modern works on the "theory of knowledge" will, I believe, admit that my statement of it is an impartial expression of a widely disseminated doctrine.)

The universe is throughout made up of a multitude of process-contents (the doctrine called Mentalism by Sidgwick). Each specific mental process has *its* own specific "content", or more precisely each cognitive process has its specific "content", that which is thought in it, and these contents are, of course, propositions. No two processes have precisely the same "content", or, at any rate, the "content" is never the same if the "processes" differ in any way beyond occurring at different points of absolute time or in different minds. On the other side the specific content only exists—the special proposition is only true—as an "aspect" of the corresponding process, and this seems to be the reason why those who hold views of this type always call the propositions which we think "contents". They mean that, *e.g.*, a true proposition about the number 2, such *as* that $2 \times 2 = 4$, is related to my thinking about the number 2 in the same way in which the pleasantness is related to the consciousness of endeavour in an unthwarted conation, and they also usually mean something further. The suggestion is really a double one: (*a*) that identity, difference, causal relation and all the other types of relation recognised by science only *are*, and the propositions which assert them only are *true*, while someone is actually thinking that they are; and (*b*)—and this is an even more important point—that by saying that they *are*, or that the propositions which assert them are *true*, we actually *mean* that someone is thinking that they are. Few really competent thinkers indeed go the whole length of maintaining the position explicitly and consistently, but it ought, I think, to be held by anyone who accepts the principles of Kant's critical philosophy or believes with Green that relations are the "work of the mind", and it is hard not to suspect that it is latent in Mr. Bradley's view of the relation of the "that" and the "what" in experience. I know, of course, that the distinction of the "that" and the "what" may be insisted on by a philosopher, as, for instance, by Aristotle, who regards it not as a distinction of "aspects", but as falling entirely within the object of cognition or experience. And it is therefore possible that Mr. Bradley does not really mean what his language seems to me to imply. But his insistence that there *is* nothing at all in the Universe except "finite centres of experience" tells the other way, as there seems to be no reason for accepting this doctrine except the allegation that to be *means* "to fall within the experience of a finite centre", apart from the assertion that the objects of thought are "aspects" of the process of thinking. (And compare the use made at p. 15 of *Appearance and Reality* of the argument that "primary qualities" depend for their *perception* on an "organ" to show that they are not "real", and the unqualified assertions on p. 144 of that work that "to be real, or even barely to exist, must be to fall within sentience", and that "there is no being or fact outside of that which is commonly called psychical existence".)

As I have said already, I do not see that the general character of the theory is altered by the substitution of God's mind for our minds as the ψυχή in which the process is supposed to go on. For the view in question is not simply that what *is* is always present to God's thought, that God actually thinks all true propositions, but that when you say "this is so"—*e.g.* when you say that the greater angle in a triangle is subtended by the greater side, or sin x is a periodic function, or that prussic acid is a poison—you *mean* that God knows that these things are so. The word "true" then ceases to have any meaning as applied to God's thinking, since the proposition "what God thinks is true" is reduced to the empty tautology that "what God thinks is what God thinks". The peculiarity of the theory is thus that it treats the philosophical question about the function of universals and relations in the real world as if it were a psychological question about the details of mental processes. The refutation put into the mouth of Parmenides shows the impossibility of Idealism if we mean by Idealism the doctrine that the knowing mind *makes* its objects in the act of knowing them, or that *what* I think is an "aspect" of the process of thinking.

The reasoning proceeds thus. The view that Forms are "thoughts" itself implies, of course, that each thought is a thought *of* something, or *about* something. No thought is a thought of, or about, nothing at all. We sometimes say, to be sure, that we are "thinking of nothing", but that is only another way of saying that we are not thinking at all. You can no more be thinking and yet thinking of nothing than Alice could really meet "Nobody". Of course, you can think about the number o, but o is not nothing but something ; it is, *e.g.*, the cardinal number of all the combatants at the battle of Salamis who are now living in London. On the process-content theory itself, then, there can be no process to which there is not a corresponding content. And this content is something determinate, or as Parmenides says, a τὶ or *somewhat*, different from the other *somewhats* which are the contents of other and different processes. What you think of at all you think of as having a determinate character of its own, not as a featureless blank. (This is the element of truth which is distorted into an absurdity in the Hamiltonian dictum that "to think is to condition".) Thus the "content" of your thought, being a *somewhat*, is something that *is* or has being, a νόημα is always a νόημα of an ὄν τι (132 *c*). This was, of course, as a matter of historical fact the main tenet of Parmenides himself, who declared *what is* to be *one* on the ground that you can only think of τὸ ἐόν; you cannot think of anything else, because anything other than τὸ ἐόν must be μὴ ἐόν (what has *no* being), and μὴ ἐόν is merely an empty name to which no real thought corresponds. "It is possible for It to be, but it is not possible for nothing to be." As Plato was to show in the *Sophistes* the only way to meet the paradoxes of Eleatic Monism is to deny the premise that "what is not is just nothing at all", and to insist that "what is not" in one sense "is" in another sense. The proposition that what is thought of is and its contrapositive that what is just nothing at all cannot even be thought of are unassailable. Fully expressed, the proposition that every thought is a thought of something that is means that, whatever you think of, you think of as *being already* so-and-so, already occupying a definite place and standing in definite relations to other constituents of a world which your thinking of it does not create. You never think of anything as having *no* other further reality, no other determination, beyond the mere fact that you are now thinking about it. There is no such thing as an *ens rationis* or as the mere "being for thought" of which some philosophers talk.

(To indicate more exactly what this means and what it does not mean, let me show how it bears on the familiar question of the "subjectivity of secondary qualities". It does not necessarily follow, from the principle that whatever is perceived or thought has a being which is not merely a "being for thought" or "for perception", that things have colours when no eye is looking at them. The sort of realism implied by what Parmenides has just said would be quite consistent with the view that colours depend for their existence on our eyes, and that the colours of the things in this room no longer exist when it is left empty. What the doctrine denies is that the existence of the colours is dependent on our *minds*. It may or may not be that our eyes help to create the colours; it is false that our minds make them by attending to them. The mere fact that we may attend to details in a scene which we had at first overlooked proves that whether or not, *e.g.*, colours depend for their existence on a physical relation to a retina,

they do not depend on a psychical relation to a mind.
Whether they exist where there is no eye to see them or
not, when seen they are qualities of the objects we see,
not qualities of our minds. However we answer the
question what becomes of them when there is no eye
to see them, it is at least certain that colours are not
"subjective", they do not exist "in" the mind, but, in
the only sense such a phrase can have, "without the
mind".)

It follows then that the "content" of the process in
which you think of a Form is always *one* something.
It is "some *one* specific somewhat which *that* thought
thinks as present in all the instances" (ὃ ἐπὶ πᾶσιν
ἐκεῖνο τὸ νόημα ἐπὸν νοεῖ, μίαν τινὰ οὖσαν ἰδέαν, where
ἐπόν must of course be taken with ὅ and not with
νόημα). Parmenides means, to put the point in more
modern language, that even on the "Subjectivist" or
"psychologising" or "Idealistic" view, there are determinate universal *meanings*, though on this view these
meanings are held to be the "other aspect" of the
occurrence of specific mental processes. He next adds
that, since each of these meanings is a universal, each
of them must be what Socrates calls a Form, a point of
identity *in* the particulars of existence, a "common
nature". Next we combine with the result thus deduced
the Socratic premise that a particular derives its existence entirely from its "participation" in a Form or
Forms, in other words that it is just a bundle of universal predicates and relations, and what follows? *I.e.* what
follows if we assert (1) that a thing is just a complex of
universals and (2) that universals are "the work of the
mind"? Well, it follows that if things are made of universals and relations (which is what Socrates is maintaining) and if further these universals and relations only
are as "aspects" or characters of mental states, then

either everything is made of mental states and all things think (πάντα νοεῖν), *or else* that there are "unthinking thoughts" (ἢ νοήματα ὄντα ἀνόητα εἶναι. Some good scholars have rendered the phrase "unthought thoughts", but I submit that this is impossible Greek at least for Plato. The only place in good Attic Greek where ἀνόητος means anything like "not thought" is *Phaedo* 80 *b*, where the soul is said to be νοητόν, "apprehended by thought", but the body ἀνόητον— *i.e.* apprehended not by thought but by sense-perception, and there, as Professor Burnet remarks in his edition of the dialogue, Plato is making a pun; ἀνόητον gets an otherwise impossible meaning from the antithesis with νοητόν. The regular meaning of the word in ordinary classical Attic is "silly", and this is enough to show that its literal sense was felt to be "unthinking".)

The alternatives then are these: either all things whatever—including steam-engines as Mr. Bradley once observed apropos of Mill's version of Idealism— *are* mental processes, *or* there are thoughts which are *not* mental processes. The first alternative is transparently absurd; the second contradicts the very doctrine from which it has been deduced, which was that for every "content" there is a process which is inseparable from it. An umbrella, for example, is not a complex of mental processes, though Mr. Spencer does somewhere talk of performing the feat of making the set of visual states which he calls his umbrella move past the set of visual states he calls the sea and sky. On the other hand "unthinking thoughts", thoughts which are all "content" without any process, are impossible according to Subjectivism itself. The plain conclusion is that the whole attempt to treat the objects of thinking as "aspects" of the process of thinking leads to impossible results (οὐδὲ τοῦτο ἔχει λόγον).

It may be worth while at this point to leave the text of the *Parmenides* and ask whether after all we cannot escape this admission by a way of which Plato has not thought. Certainly the existence of "unthinking thoughts" seems quite impossible even on the premises of the Mentalist himself. But what of the other alternative that "all things think"? Common sense regards it as absurd, and so do Parmenides and Socrates in our dialogue. Yet many things which common sense is prone to call absurd seem to be true, *e.g.* in mathematics, and a fair-minded controversialist would probably allow that it is no disproof of a doctrine in theology to say that it looks absurd to untutored common sense. No one who knew his business would go to the "man in the street" to learn whether there are in God three *personae* in one *substantia* or whether the rational soul is derived by generation from one's parents. So there seems to be no intrinsic reason why a metaphysical proposition which sounds paradoxical to the "man in the street" should not be true. And, to say nothing of our professed Pampyschists, Dr. McTaggart has vigorously maintained that the Universe consists exclusively of souls. So it may be as well to ask whether, in spite of Parmenides, either "mental states" or "souls" may be the only things there are. I do not myself think we can make either assertion. To begin with, on any theory, it could only be of the particular existents in the Universe that we could say that they were all states of mind, or all souls, and the Universe contains much besides its particular existents. Suppose that all particular existents are souls. Then the Universe includes not only these souls but their various attitudes to one another, and no one will say that if *A* and *B* are souls, *A*'s love for *B* is a third soul, and *B*'s recognition of *A*'s love a fourth. We get rid of this particular difficulty if we say not that all particular existents are souls, but that they are mental states. But this view, too, has to face equal difficulties. It involves, of course, the denial that there are such things as minds or selves which have or own the states. This denial, however, though I myself think it philosophically bad, is made by men of eminence, and I will not dispute it here. But what about, *e.g.*, "the hopelessness of A's love of B" or "the absurdity of C's opinions about D's philosophy". These, at any rate, can hardly be mental states, but they are as much constituents of the Universe as A's love of B or C's opinions about D themselves.

Even so, we have only touched the fringes of the real difficulty. Assuming problematically the more moderate position that souls (or, if you prefer it, mental states) are the only particular existents in the Universe, we have to ask, in this society of souls (or mental states), what do the souls (or states) think of and know? Do they only know, can they only think of, the propositions of Psychology? In our own case, we certainly suppose ourselves to know propositions about many particular existents which are not propositions of Psychology, and unless all these propositions without exception are false, there must be particular existents which are not souls nor yet mental states. Thus I may believe that there is at this moment a round pebble lying on my garden path, or that the pen with which I write these words was made by Messrs. Macniven & Cameron, and these propositions, which assert the existence of the stone and the pen, certainly do not convey psychological information about souls or mental states. Even if stones and pens *have* souls or mental states, it is pretty clear that they *are* not souls or mental states, and that a statement about the weight of the stone or the hardness of the pen is not an assertion about a mental state. Again, we believe the gravitation-formula to be a statement which is true, or nearly so, of a certain relation between certain particular existents, but the relation which it expresses is not a relation between minds or states of mind.

Thus if Pampsychism only means that everybody *has* a soul or a mental life, it implies, rather than denies, that there are non-mental particular existents. But if it means that all existents *are* minds or mental states, and all the relations between them relations falling within the purview of Psychology, it seems to be proved false by the existence of the other sciences.

If we finally try to maintain the other alternative offered to us by Parmenides in a modified sense, by holding that things may be thoughts without being *my* thoughts in particular, because it is always possible that what I am not actually thinking of is always being actually thought of by other men, or by God, we are really no better off. That things which I have no ground for supposing to be actually thought of by any being but God may yet be real existents seems to be clear from the simple fact that an unknown body may cause perturbations in the behaviour of a known one. Neptune existed, not merely before Adams or Leverrier discovered Neptune, but before anyone had observed the perturbations in the periodic motion of Uranus which led to the discovery. It would be gratuitous to assert that because the perturbations existed before we discovered them there must have been non-human astronomers who did know about them. And though it may be reasonable on other grounds to believe in an omniscient God who, being omniscient, did know about the perturbations and their cause before we suspected either, it seems nonsense to say that God's knowledge of the existence of Neptune is what we *mean* by the existence of Neptune. For we should then have to say that what Adams and Leverrier discovered was not Neptune but the fact that God knew about Neptune. So, as Bolzano says, "There is a God" does not *mean* that "God thinks that there is a God". We might make this point even clearer by asking what an atheist means when he says "There is no God". He cannot mean (*a*) "I, *A. B.*, think there is no God", for if he meant that he could prove his proposition by merely proving his sincerity in making it. But no sane man thinks you can prove a proposition to be true by merely proving that you honestly believe it. Nor can he mean (*b*) "Men in general think there is no God". It is just because he knows they think there is a God that he gives himself the trouble of trying to reason them out of their mistake. And he assuredly does not mean (*c*) that "God thinks there is no God", for if he means that, what has become of his atheism? Again, even if every proposition which is true is thought by someone, it is certainly not true that whatever is thought by anyone is true, and this of itself shows that to be true is not the same thing as to be thought true by someone. And though both the propositions "whatever God thinks is true", and "whatever is true is thought by God" may be true, yet "to be true" cannot *mean* "to be thought true by God", for this would lead at once to a vicious regress. "God is", *e.g.*, would have to *mean* "God thinks He is", and this again would not merely imply but *mean* "God thinks that He thinks that He is", and so on. Hence the real meaning of the statement "God is" would be unknown and unknowable, at least to a human intelligence.

Thus it seems clear that neither to *be* nor to *exist* can mean the same thing as to be thought of, and, as we have no empirical reason for believing that whatever is or exists is also thought of, we cannot deny that there may be any number of existents the existence of which is not known to any mind, unless we can, on independent grounds, assert the existence of at least one omniscient mind. In that case it would be true that whatever is or exists is actually known, not because it is any part of the meaning of being or existence to be known, but as Bolzano says, because there is an omniscient mind. I need hardly add that in this case it would not in the least follow from the existence of an omniscient mind that all the other existents known by that mind are themselves mental. There is no more reason to think that a mind can only know minds than to suppose that an eye can only see eyes or a nose only smell noses.

It is an interesting question from what quarter the suggestion that Forms may be νοήματα, "thoughts", originally came. It is certainly very unlikely that Plato should have invented this gratuitous false interpretation merely for the sake of refuting it, but it is not at all easy to say with whom the idea originated. Proclus, if he knew, keeps his information to himself, and most modern expositors seem to think they have done their duty when they have made a reference to Berkeley. Grote, however, with his usual scholarship and conscientiousness, really tries to solve the problem. He observes (*Plato and the other Companions of Socrates*, vol. iii. p. 64, *n.* 2, ed. 1885) that Aristotle expressly alludes to the same view at *Topics*, 113 a 25, where he says that εἰ τὰς ἰδέας ἐν ἡμῖν ἔφησεν εἶναι, if your opponent in a dialectical encounter has maintained that the Forms are "in us", *i.e.* are states of our minds, you might meet him by arguing that his thesis leads to the simultaneous affirmation of contradictories (*e.g.* as a believer in Forms he must admit *ex hypothesi* that Forms are changeless, but if they are "in us" they change their position as we move about). A few pages further on (*op. cit.* p. 74, *n.* 2) Grote connects the thesis that Forms are "thoughts" in "souls" with the doctrine that *qualities* (the *word* is, of course, a piece of Aristotelian *Categorienlehre*) are ψιλαὶ ἔννοιαι, "mere notions". Simplicius says in a scholium on Aristotle's *Categories*, 8 b 25, that this subjectivist view was specially held by the Eretrian school of Mene-demus, of whom we really know nothing except that they, like the Megarians, were famous for formal dia-lectic and that they must have been influenced by Eleaticism, since it is recorded of Menedemus (Dio-genes Laertius, ii. 135) that he refused to recognise negative propositions. On the scanty evidence we possess, Grote's conjecture that Plato's *Refutation of Idealism* is meant to refer to this view seems to me the best that can be made.[1] Antisthenes, as usual, has been suggested as the object of the criticism on the strength of the saying ascribed to him, "I can see a horse, but I never saw horse-ity". This is less likely. Antisthenes was perhaps dead when the *Parmenides* was written, even if the *mot* in question is authentic, not to add that the point of the alleged saying is not that "horse-ity" is a thought, but that is an empty *name*.

Socrates now offers another suggestion which leads to a second appeal to the impossibility of the "regress". He suggests that the difficulty about the Unity or Plurality of the Form may be escaped by thinking of Forms as παραδείγματα, fixed "models" or "types" of which sensible particular existents are "imitations" or "representations" (ὁμοιώματα). The precise meaning of the statement that the particular existent "partakes" in the Form will then be that it is a "likeness" or "copy"

---

[1] Only if so, the doctrine must have been older than Menedemus, who belongs to the early third century.

of the "type", and it is easy to argue that there is no reason why any number of "likenesses" may not be "copies" of one "type", just as any number of impressions may be struck from one die or any number of engravings reproduced after the same original. It must be carefully borne in mind that in this new formulation of the theory the relation between the particular existent and the Form is not merely similarity or resemblance, but the relation of copy to original. The particular does not merely resemble the Form, but further is derivative from and dependent on it. It is this further relation of derivation which gives Parmenides an opening for a fresh application of the objection to an infinite regress.

There are many interesting questions about the relation between the new formulation of Socrates' theory and that which had been given earlier in the dialogue, which I am obliged to pass over as irrelevant to the purpose of this paper. I will merely note that the "imitation" version of the relation of particular to Form was, as we have learned from Aristotle, the Pythagorean one, and apparently older in date than the "participation" formula. Parmenides does not admit that the change in phraseology leads to any improvement in sense. He sets himself to argue (1) that the new version of Socrates' theory is still open to the objection that it leads to the "regress", and (2) that it has the still graver fault of leading by rigid logical consequence to a pure agnosticism. It is only with the first of these criticisms that I am to deal here. The argument of Parmenides is briefly as follows. If a particular existent is a "likeness" of a Form, then not only must it be like that Form, but the Form must be like it, since "being like" is, as we should now say, a symmetrical relation, a relation which is its own converse.

But, according to the theory itself, whenever two things are like one another, they are so *because* they "partake of" one and the same Form. Hence, since we have just admitted that particular and Form are like one another (*e.g.* that the Form of "man" is like Zeno or Socrates), our own theory requires us to hold that the particular and its Form both "partake of" a second Form. That is, employing the explanation just given of what is now supposed to be meant by "participation", the particular and the Form of which it is a copy, must both be copies of a second Form. And in the same way we shall argue that the second Form, the first Form, and the particular existent, are all like one another, and are therefore, on our own premises, copies of a third Form, and so on without end. The only way to avoid this "regress" is to deny the proposition "if A is like B, B is always also like A", and so to make it possible to hold that a particular existent is like a Form and yet the Form not like the particular. As this seems hopelessly paradoxical, it appears that we must say "it cannot be a virtue of likeness that things participate in Forms" (133 *a*).

Now, as to this argument, the alleged "regress" is plainly a vicious one, since the point of the reasoning is that we cannot even state what we really mean when we say, *e.g.*, "Socrates is like the Form of Man", without going through in succession all the terms of an endless series. Also, on his own premises, the reasoning of Parmenides seems wholly sound, and we are thus driven, as he says, to admit that the puzzle can only be solved if it is possible to hold that a particular existent and a Form are not, on the theory under examination, like one another in the same sense in which two particular existents which are members of the same class are like one another. More precisely, what we need to be able to say is that the relation between Form and

particular existent symbolised by calling the second a
"likeness" of the first is asymmetrical. Fortunately this
position, which Parmenides calls paradoxical, is quite
easily defensible. Proclus says truly that the solution of
the difficulty is this. The relation of likeness which
holds between two copies of the same original *in virtue
of the fact that* they are copies of the same original does
not hold between copy and original. Thus, though the
resemblance between two engravings may justify the
belief that they are copies of the same painting, it does
not follow that this painting and the engravings are
alike in any sense which would justify us in believing
that all three are copies of a still older painting. As
Proclus puts it, the copy is a copy of its original, but
the original is not a copy of the copy. The relation
really meant by Socrates when he spoke of particulars
as "likenesses" of Forms was not *mere* likeness in some
point or other, a symmetrical relation, but the kind of
likeness which there is between an original and a copy,
likeness *plus* derivation, and this relation is asymmetrical. Parmenides only proves his point because
Socrates is so "young" and unpractised in formal logic
that he allows the proposition "sensibles are likenesses
(ὁμοιώματα) of Forms" to be reworded in the shape
"sensibles are like Forms". The fallacy becomes manifest in a simple case. My *carte-de-visite* photograph and
my living face may be like one another, but the likeness
is not such that it could be argued "This photograph is
a likeness of you, *ergo*, by conversion, you are a likeness
of it". You can argue that since my reflection in a
looking-glass is like me, therefore I am like it, but you
cannot argue that since it is the reflection of me, I am
the reflection of it. This is how Socrates permits Parmenides to argue when he allows him to substitute for
the statement that a sensible thing is a likeness of a

Form the very different and much less specific statement that a sensible thing is like a Form.

When it is argued that since two sensibles which are like one another are, *ex hypothesi*, both "copies" of the same Form, therefore a Form and its "copies", being like one another, must all be "copies" of another Form, everything turns on the question whether "like" bears the same meaning throughout the premises. In point of fact it does not, and this is where the fallacy comes in. No particular existent is like a universal in the same way in which two instances of the same universal are like each other. Thus two green leaves are like one another in the sense that they both have the same colour, but a green leaf and the colour green are not like one another in this sense, since green *has* no colour but *is* a colour, the leaf *is* not a colour but *has* the colour green. Two men are alike in exhibiting the same type of bodily or mental structure, but John Smith and the human organism, or John Smith and "the human mind", are not alike in this sense, since the bodily or mental organisation characteristic of men is not itself a body or a mind. To take a case which touches the doctrine of Forms as expounded by the Platonic Socrates even more closely, two pairs of things, say a pair of gloves and a Parliamentary "pair", are alike in having the same cardinal number; there are two gloves, there are two members of Parliament. But a pair of gloves and the number 2 are not thus alike, for 2 is not a pair. There are two gloves, but not "two units" in 2, since 2 is not two numbers but one number, though Aristotle could not see this and is very wroth with Plato for having said that numbers are not generated by addition.

Let it be carefully noted what these examples show. They do not show that a Form, or universal, and a set of particular existents are not in some way "like" one another. They do not, for instance, show that the Form of man and Socrates may not both be "copies of" or "partake in" some Form. But they do prove that the Form of man and Socrates cannot both be "copies" of the Form of *man*, and it is *this* absurdity which Parmenides was trying to extract from the statements of Socrates. He wanted to show that what Socrates calls *the* Form of man is really not one Form at all, but an endless hierarchy of Forms of man of ascending orders, and in fact, a "well-ordered series of type *ω*". Unless he can show this he has not proved that there is a *vicious* "regress" implied in saying that two men are alike because they both "imitate" or embody the same Form. If it is true that the particular man and the Form of man both "imitate" a further Form, which is not the Form of *man*, that is a harmless truth. The regress to which it gives rise is only an endless chain of implications. But if it were true that there is not *one* Form of man but an endless series of them, you would never be able to say *what* it is of which two particular men are "copies" or embodiments, and *this* is the pretended objection to the theory of Forms. Just so it creates no difficulty in arithmetic that if there is a finite integer, say 2, there must be another integer which comes next after 2, and another which comes next after that, and so on without end. But all arithmetic would come to an end if instead of one number 2 there was an infinity of 2's, so that 2 came an infinite number of times after itself.

I hope then that I have made it clear that the vicious regress which follows logically enough from the premises used by Parmenides does not follow from the assertions of Socrates of which the premises of Parmenides are an ingenious perversion. So far, the principle of the theory of Forms, that the making of intelligible propositions, and consequently all science, depends on the pervasion of the Universe by universal types of structure and schemes of relation which are neither particular existents nor inventions of the knowing mind remains unshaken by the criticisms we have passed in review. But it is clear from the way in which Socrates receives these criticisms without attempting to answer them, as well as from the express declaration of Parmenides at 135 c that the failure of Socrates to repel his assaults is due to his lack of practice in dialectic, that Plato means us to understand that though the theory is at bottom sound and rests on a right perception of the character of scientific knowledge, its originators were not possessed of the logical equipment required to formulate it in a way which would ensure it against grave objections. For this purpose the theory required to be reshaped by a master of logic and pure mathematics, and the reshaping was the task of Plato's maturest thought. The form in which the theory finally emerges from his hands was never embodied in his dialogues. In them he remained true to the words he twice wrote to Dionysius II. that there would never be a σύγγραμμα Πλάτωνος, an exposition of the philosophy of Plato. But its general outlines can be still recovered by careful study of the unsympathetic and often not very intelligent polemic of Aristotle as well as from the indications preserved in the remaining fragments of later Platonists.

[1916]

III

FORMS AND NUMBERS: A STUDY IN PLATONIC
METAPHYSICS [1]

I

WE all know the famous chapter in Aristotle's *Meta-physics* (*A*, 6) where Aristotle sums up the Platonic doctrine about the ἀρχαί and calls attention to its points of disagreement with Pythagoreanism. As all my readers will, doubtless, recollect, Aristotle holds that the differences between the otherwise very similar doctrines are two: (1) the Pythagoreans say that the constituents of number are the unlimited (ἄπειρον) and limit (πέρας), Plato that they are "the one" and the "great-and-small", or, as it is alternatively called, the "indeterminate duality" (ἀόριστος δυάς). (There are really two points of difference here; the One, which, as we know from other passages, was regarded by the Pythagoreans as derivative, being the simplest "blend" of their ἀρχαί, πέρας and the ἄπειρον, appears in the Platonic version as itself one of the underived "constituents" of number, the "formal" constituent, as Aristotle calls it; the other,

---

[1] With the whole of what follows I must ask my reader to compare Milhaud, *Les Philosophes-Géomètres de la Grèce*, bk. i. c. 2, bk. ii. cc. 4, 5 ; Burnet, *Greek Philosophy, Part I.* 320-324; Stenzel, *Zahl und Gestalt bei Platon und Aristoteles.* I have to apologise for repeating much which is common property, but it is necessary to do so if I am to make it quite clear exactly where these writers seem to me to have stopped short of what seems the precise truth. [I reprint these pages as they were originally written. The modifications to the second edition of Dr. Stenzel's book (1933), which confessedly bring his views rather nearer to those I am urging, would require a separate essay for their discussion.]

or "material" constituent, is a duality of some kind.) Aristotle's language (*Met.* A, 987 b 25) shows that this is the peculiarity which strikes him as specially remarkable. (2) Though both parties agree that things are somehow made of numbers, the Pythagoreans simply identify these numbers with the things we perceive by our senses: Plato distinguishes the two, and further interposes an intermediate class of "mathematical objects" (μαθηματικά) between them.

It is obvious, as most recent scholars have seen, that Aristotle is not talking here about anything of the nature of a "senile aberration". He identifies this doctrine unreservedly with the teaching of Plato, and this must mean that no other "Platonic theory" was known in the Academy all through the twenty years between Aristotle's entrance there and Plato's death. If he has not explained what the formula means more fully, the reason must be that he believed himself and the contemporaries for whom he was discoursing to understand its sense without any explanation on his part.

Naturally enough, the meaning is not so obvious to us, who have to rely for our knowledge of Plato's teaching in the Academy on chance observations of Aristotle himself eked out by a very few statements of contemporary Academics preserved by his later commentators. It does not follow that the true interpretation cannot be recovered with pains and industry. In fact, my object in this paper is to show that three recent scholars, M. Milhaud in his *Philosophes-Géomètres de la Grèce* (1900), Prof. Burnet in *Early Greek Philosophy, Part I.* (1914), and Dr. Julius Stenzel in his important recent work, *Zahl und Gestalt bei Platon und Aristoteles* (1924), have been, as the children say, very "warm" in their search for the key to the puzzle. But I believe none of them has ever quite tracked down the quarry, probably because none of them has adequately interpreted the one passage in Plato which is more nearly than any other the explanation, *Epinomis*, 990 *c* 5–991 *b* 4. M. Milhaud ignores this important page altogether, except for the passing citation of a single phrase, presumably on the ground that it comes from a "spurious" dialogue. Prof. Burnet makes some use of the first half of it (*op. cit.* p. 322); Dr. Stenzel, with a sound perception of its importance, quotes and comments on nearly the whole of it (*op. cit.* 91 ff.) and would, I believe, have given the full interpretation, but for the want of mathematical knowledge which he candidly confesses in his *Preface*. Yet the mathematics required for complete understanding of the whole are really very elementary; if they were not, I should not venture to attempt the solution which I now propose to students of Plato for their judgement and censure.

I must make a beginning with the familiar passage of Aristotle. The thing which strikes him as singular is not simply that Plato, like the Pythagoreans, should have attempted a derivation of numbers from two components, but that he should have made one of these components, the one which Aristotle calls in his own terminology the "matter" of numbers, a duality, and that this duality should have been a "great and small". And quite clearly this is the point from which investigation should start. Why was Plato dissatisfied with the simpler statement that the "matter" of number is an ἄπειρον? And again why, if it is to be a couple of some kind, is it a couple of the *great* and *small*? If we could only identify the particular problems which have suggested the general formula, we might be able to answer these questions. In the light of the passage from the *Epinomis* it is possible, I believe, to identify the problem or problems almost beyond a doubt, and thus to penetrate to Plato's meaning by reconstructing a piece of mathematical history.

Before I proceed further, however, I must mention two explanations which I feel bound to dismiss as insufficient, though on the right lines, so far as they go. It is quite insufficient to say, in the well-known words of Plato's disciple, Hermodorus (Simplicius *in Physica*, 247, Diels; *Greek Philosophy, Part I*. 330) that "those things which are spoken of as having the relation of great to small all have the 'more and less', so that they can go on to infinity in the direction of the 'still greater' and the 'still less'." This may explain why an ἄπειρον *may* be called a duality; it does not explain why it *must* be called so. The point is made in so many words in the *Philebus* (24 *a* ff.) where Plato is careful to make Socrates work with the old Pythagorean antithesis of the ἄπειρον and πέρας; if it were all that is meant, there seems no reason why Plato should have made any modification in the formula, or why, if he had done so, Aristotle should not dismiss the change, as he does the substitution of the word μέθεξις for μίμησις, as a mere change of language. Also, the remark throws no light on a point on which Milhaud, Burnet, and Stenzel are all, rightly as we shall see, agreed, that the Platonic formula is somehow connected with the doctrine of "irrational" numbers. If there were no numbers but the rationals, it would still be true, as Hermodorus says, that there can be an infinity of, *e.g.*, lengths greater and again smaller than a given length, of notes "sharper" or "flatter" than a given tone. Hermodorus may, no doubt, have known that his words do not give the full explanation of the Platonic doctrine. It is quite possible that he went on to explain further, but if he did, Simplicius must have cut his excerpt short before reaching the principal point, and that is hardly likely in a man of his intelligence. Or Hermodorus may not have thought fit to say all he could have said. He has certainly not told us all we want to know before we can see why Plato should have been dissatisfied with the Pythagorean formula.

Again, when Milhaud, Burnet, Stenzel, all look for the explanation of the formula in the conception of the value of an "irrational" by successive approximations to a "limit", they are plainly on the right track, as the passage of the *Epinomis* we have to deal with shortly demonstrates. Their explanation comes much nearer being the whole truth than the remarks quoted from Hermodorus by Simplicius. Yet it is not the whole of the truth. The thought of "convergence to a limit", important as it is, does not really explain why it should be necessary to replace the ἄπειρον by a "duality" and why the "duality" should be a "great and small". An example or two will make this clear. Consider the series $1, 1/2, 1/4, 1/8 \ldots 1/2^n \ldots$. We see at once that the series "converges to the limit" 0, since, by taking n large enough we can make the difference $1/2^n - 0$ less than any assigned rational fraction σ, however small. But though the endless sequence of the terms is a good example of an ἄπειρον, it is not clear how it can be an example of a "great-and-small". Since each term is one-half the preceding term, the series proceeds in a single direction, that of "the small" or "defect". Now consider the series formed by taking the sums of $1, 2, 3 \ldots n \ldots$ terms of our first series, $1, 1 + 1/2, 1 + 1/2 + 1/4, \ldots$ $1 + 1/2 + 1/4 + \ldots 1/2^n \ldots$. This again "converges to the limit" 2, as we all know. But again, the series proceeds in a single sense. Each term, $3/2, 7/4 \ldots$ is greater than the preceding. Thus our series is emphatically not a "great *and* small". The inevitable inference is that when Plato replaced the Pythagorean ἄπειρον by the "duality" of the "great and small", he was thinking of a specific way of constructing infinite convergent series which his interpreters seem not to have identified. I propose to show what the method was, by indicating the precise problem from which Plato was starting.

What the problem was we are all but told in so many words in the *Epinomis*, to which we must now turn. (It is irrelevant for the immediate purpose to enter into a discussion of the authenticity of the dialogue, though I may confess here my own conviction that it is genuine. Those who have adopted the ascription to Philippus of Opus usually recognise that the author is an immediate scholar of Plato, specially competent in mathematical matters, and that the work was issued from the first along with the *Laws*. Even so much is sufficient ground for holding that we may accept the matter of a mathematical passage from the dialogue as genuinely Platonic with reasonable confidence. If our exegesis should make it appear that the passage actually gives the clue to Plato's language about the "great and small", then, I submit, reasonable confidence passes into complete assurance. Incidentally also, such a result would, I take it, put the authenticity of the dialogue beyond question. That a "stylometrist" already determined to bring out a different result, examining the few pages of the dialogue under the microscope, should succeed in detecting some small peculiarities of the diction, as compared with that of *Laws* i.-xii., would prove nothing on the other side. If any slight departure from a stylometric average is proof of spuriousness, what single page of any author is safe from the first critic who has his reasons for wishing to get rid of it?)

I come then to the critical passage of the *Epinomis*. We must begin by recalling the context in which it is set. The ostensible purpose of the whole dialogue is to answer the question what scientific studies are indispensable in a member of the "nocturnal council", the standing Committee of Public Safety, as we might call it, which watches over the general well-being of the community of the *Laws*. We are first told that the maintenance of a high standard of public piety will be the first concern of this council. That piety may be wholesome and rational, the Olympians are to be replaced as the primary objects of the public cultus by the heavenly bodies, the "great works" which, by the strict conformity of their apparently mazy dance to mathematical law, most specially declare the wisdom of the Creator. The fundamental business of the authorities who enforce this cult of the host of heaven is to impress it on men's minds that the heavenly bodies are not capricious creatures, like the fabled Olympians, but move in accord with law. And to satisfy men of this, it is necessary to ascertain the rhythmic periods of the movements of each "planet" and express them in terms of the period of any other. Consequently, the members of the council must not only be astronomers, they must also be thoroughly versed in all the preliminary knowledge which the astronomer will need for the execution of the task just mentioned. (Thus, exactly as in the *Republic*, before we come to astronomy itself we are conducted through the stages of a preliminary mathematical training. But there is this difference between the *Republic* and the *Epinomis*—it is just the difference between the mathematical science of the age of Socrates and that which Plato, with the work of Eudoxus and Theaetetus before him, was hoping to inaugurate—that, whereas the *Republic* specifies three preliminary sciences, arithmetic, plane geometry, solid geometry, the *Epinomis* introduces a new and extended conception of number which has the effect of bringing the whole of the prolegomena to kinematics under the single head of arithmetic. Arithmetic, as now conceived, is the whole of what is strictly science in the "pure" mathematics.)

The speaker now proceeds to develop his views in a page which defies all formal grammar, probably not so much because it is badly "corrupted", though there are one or two points at which we are tempted to emend— as because the syntax is that of thought, and the words have never been subjected to revision with a view to circulation. If they are notes of Plato, "transcribed from the wax" with scrupulous piety after his death, this is intelligible; it is harder to understand, if they were deliberately set down by any one who meant them to be read as they stand. To avoid unnecessary prolixity, I will therefore merely give such a résumé of the general sense as remains unaffected, whatever view we take of the text and grammar of the various clauses. We shall need, he says, various μαθήματα, first one which deals with numbers simply as numbers (αὐτοὶ ἀριθμοί), not as embodied in anything, and studies the "generation of the odd and even" and the character (δύναμις) they impart to nature (990 c 5-8). Next we must study what has been very ludicrously called "mensuration" (γεωμετρία), but is really an art which assimilates to one another *numbers* which are not similar in their own nature, by reference to surfaces (or areas). This art is a more than human miracle in the eyes of those who can appreciate it (990 d 1-6). Then comes another art which deals with *numbers* "raised to the third power and similar to volumes" (τοὺς τρὶς ηὐξημένους καὶ τῇ στερεᾷ φύσει ὁμοίους), and once more makes similar a second class of numbers not naturally similar. This is what the inventors who first hit on it called "gauging" (στερεομετρία). This again is a miracle in the eyes of those who understand how "all nature" (ὅλη ἡ φύσις) is moulded in form and kind (εἶδος καὶ γένος ἀποτυποῦται) as the function (δύναμις) and its converse (ἡ ἐξ ἐναντίας ταύτῃ) move about "the double" in each progression (*i.e.* geometrical, arithmetical, harmonic, 990 *d* 6–991 *a* 1). The simplest form of "the double" is the ratio 2/1, from this we get, in geometrical progression, the second power 4/1, and the third 8/1. With this third term 8/1, "the double" has advanced to "volume and the tangible". If we treat 1 and 2 as the end terms of an arithmetical or harmonic progression and insert the arithmetical mean 3/2 and the harmonic mean 4/3 (or, if, to get whole numbers for all the terms, we consider the A.P. 6, 9, 12 and the H.P. 6, 8, 12) we have the secret of music (991 *a* 1–*b* 4).

The general drift of the argument may be considered before we come to detail. The connection in thought is this. To compare the various astronomical periods with one another, we need arithmetic. We begin the study with the arithmetic of the integers or natural numbers, and we must remember that it is explicitly announced that (1) the integers are to be studied as "pure", not as "embodied", and (2) that the study is to involve an account of their γένεσις or derivation. The point of the first statement is to guard against the confusion, into which it is so easy to fall, between an integer and a collection of which it is the cardinal number. What is meant is that, though every pair consists of two things, every triplet of three, and so on, the number 2 is not a pair of numbers, nor the number 3 a triplet. This is important for two reasons. It makes it clear that though there may be many pairs of things, there are not many 2's but only one 2, the number characteristic of each and every pair, and again, that though a pair, *e.g.*, of gloves is made up of two gloves, 2 is not made up of two 1's. 2 is not two 1's, but one 2, and it does not "contain" any 1's. We see therefore that the standing Aristotelian criticisms, which regularly assume that there are as many 2's as there are pairs, as many 3's as triplets, and again that integers are generated by the summation of 1's, are irrelevant as criticisms of Plato; they are no more than dogmatic affirmations of a non-Platonic, and manifestly false, theory of the nature of the integers. We see also that in the account of the "generation" of integers of which the *Epinomis* speaks, they are meant to be generated in some other way than by summation of 1's, that the integer $(n + 1)$ will not be defined as the sum of the integer n and the integer 1. The point could not be stated by Plato in just this way, because the numerical notation at his disposal did not enable him to use a general symbol, like our $(n + 1)$ or Peano's improved symbol $(n +)$, to stand for "the integer immediately after a given integer". His way of stating it is to say, as we know from Aristotle he did say, that "numbers" cannot be "added" (are not συμβλητοί).

The transition from the remarks about arithmetic to the comments on "geometry" and "stereometry" has an obvious motive which is not expressed in words. Arithmetic, we are told, must be cultivated because it will be required for the determination of the periods of the heavenly bodies. But it is not the fact, and the *Epinomis* anticipates the knowledge that it is not the fact, that all the ratios we shall have to consider in our astronomy, the ratio, *e.g.*, of the lunar month to the year, or day, or of one planet's period to that of another, can be accurately stated as "ratios of one integer to another". The number of days in the lunar month, or of lunar months in the year is not a whole number, and we must be prepared to face the possibility that it is not a rational fraction. Hence the astronomer will need in his calculations to manipulate "surds". He will require

to estimate such ratios as that of the side to the diagonal
of a square, that of the diameter of a circle to its circumference, of the diameter of a sphere to the edge of each
of the regular solids inscribed in it, and of each of these
edges to the rest. We may note in this connection that
the two last-mentioned problems are actually discussed,
in connection with the constructions for the inscriptions
of the regular solids, "the figures of Plato", in the 13th
Book of Euclid's *Elements*, and we may be quite sure
that the author of the *Timaeus* was deeply interested in
them. We may fairly assume that when Theaetetus
completed the Pythagorean geometry by discovering
the constructions for the icosahedron and octahedron,
he did not neglect to make this determination of the
magnitude of edges part of his investigation. It is clear,
then, that our astronomer will need to be able to determine the values of irrational quadratic and cubic roots,
and to determine them with as close an approximation as
his problems demand. Since such values were actually
found by geometrical constructions, the common view
was that the determination of them belongs not to
arithmetic but to geometry, and so long as arithmetic
is conceived of simply as the study of the integers, geometry must, of course, be regarded as a wholly distinct
science, since it is full of "incommensurable magnitudes", but there are no "incommensurable integers",
the position pertinaciously defended by Aristotle. The
Epinomis insists, on the other hand, that the real
scientific problem has nothing in itself to do with the
"measuring of land" or the "gauging of solids", but is
numerical. In other words, when we have learned how
to evaluate the square and cube roots of the integers,
we have, in principle, solved the problem of determining
the length of the side of a regular polygon of given area,
or the edge of a regular solid of given volume. The rest

is no more than a special application of our arithmetical discovery. (The insight shown by this view may well be illustrated by a very similar remark which occurs some- where in Couturat's work *De l'Infini mathématique*. Most of us commonly think of π as "the ratio of the circumference of a circle to its diameter", and again of *e* as the basis of the system of natural logarithms, *i.e.* of a series devised for the practical purpose of facilitat- ing calculations. But the numbers π and *e* have a much more general significance than this. As Couturat says, even if we never had to survey a circular area or to make elaborate calculations, we should come upon *e* in the prosecution of analysis by the discovery that e^x is the function of *x* which is its own derivative, and we should discover π from such purely numerical considera- tions as that $\pi/4$ is the limiting value to which the sum $1 - \frac{1}{3} + \frac{1}{5} - \frac{1}{7} \ldots$ converges as the number of the terms summed increases indefinitely.) Thus we may say that the passage of the *Epinomis* under our consideration is historically important as the literary record of the first discovery of the "real numbers", if we are careful to bear in mind that the writer confines his attention only to those real numbers which are necessitated by the geometrical problems familiar to him, the quadratic and cubic irrationals. He does not envisage a series which would contain the whole of the algebraic num- bers, still less has he any conception of the "tran- scendental numbers". (The problem of the quadrature of the circle had, as we know, already been raised in the fifth century, but naturally enough, no one in Plato's time was in a position to say that π might not turn out to be a quadratic surd. That it is not an alge- braic number of some kind was only finally proved by Lindemann in our own days.)

So far, then, we have reached the result that astronomical problems force on us the extension of arithmetic by the discovery of a method of evaluating quadratic and cubic "surds", and a corresponding enlargement of our conception of number which will enable us to include these "surds" among numbers. What the required method of evaluation is to be is at least hinted in the words which follow. We are now told that if we take the simplest of all numerical ratios, that of the "double" 2/1, and its reciprocal, the "half", 1/2, and study them in the light of the doctrine of progressions, they will disclose the whole secret of science. The latter part of this explanation, which deals with music, calls for no comment. It points out simply that 1, 3/2, 2 is an arithmetical progression, 1, 4/3, 2 an harmonic, and that the ratios 3/2 : 1, 4/3 : 1 correspond to the fundamental melodic intervals of the scale, the fifth and the fourth, so that we can get as many octaves as we wish by merely repeating them thus, 1, 3/2, 2, 3, 4 . . ., 1, 4/3, 2, 8/3, 4. . . . Here we are not going beyond familiar Pythagorean ground. The immediate meaning of what precedes is, of course, that 1, 2, 4, 8 . . . is a geometrical series composed of the powers of 2, and is the simplest example of the proposition that the areas of similar polygons are in the ratios of the second powers of their sides, those of the volumes of similar solids in those of the third powers of their edges. But there is clearly more intended than this, and we must discover what that more is before we shall see the connection between what had been said about the generalisation of number and these remarks about geometrical progression. The "double" had been in the fifth century the subject of one disturbing problem, that of the "common measure of the side and diagonal", where the problem is to know what must be the length of the side of a square if its area is to be double that of a given square. In Plato's

own time it gave rise to another problem, with which
Plato is traditionally said to have been concerned, the
"Delian problem" of finding the length of the edge of
a cube whose volume is double that of a given cube. In
other words, the fifth century had been concerned with
the question what is the "square root" of 2, the fourth
was trying to find the "cube root" of 2, and I suggest
that the language of our passage is meant as a definite
allusion to this. The underlying thought would thus be
that the theory of arithmetic will only be complete when
we have learned how to give a numerical expression for
$\sqrt{2}$ and $\sqrt[3]{2}$—and thus, by the way, solved the "Delian
problem"—and have then proceeded to generalise a
method for the evaluation of the rest of the quadratic
and cubic "irrationals".

If these were the special origins of Plato's conception, it ought not to be difficult to determine what kind
of method he has in view, and then to answer our former
question about the reason for the name "great-and-
small". There was already in existence in the latter part
of the fifth century a rule for making approximations to
the value of $\sqrt{2}$, the rule to which Plato apparently
alludes in *Rep.* 546 *c*, where he makes Socrates speak
of 7 as the "rational diameter of 5". The meaning is that
since $7^2 = 49$ and $5^2 = \frac{50}{2}$, $\frac{7}{5}$ is an approximate value of
$\sqrt{2}$. The "diagonal" (διάμετρος) of 5, that is the length
of the diagonal of a square whose side is 5, is, by the
Pythagorean theorem, $5\sqrt{2}$, and this is an "irrational",
but 7/5 approximates fairly closely to it, since $7^2 =
2 \times 5^2 - 1$. Of course it would be possible to suppose
that such approximations were originally discovered
empirically. One might, for example, write out a list of
the "squares" of the integers from 1 to 100, and then
pick out, by inspection, every pair of values which
would satisfy the equation $y^2 = 2x^2 \pm 1$. This would

yield us the pairs of integral values $x = 1$, $y = 1$; $x = 2$, $y = 3$; $x = 5$, $y = 7$; $x = 12$, $y = 17$; $x = 29$, $y = 41$; $x = 70$, $y = 99$. But there is a general rule, given by Theon of Smyrna (Hiller, p. 43 f.) for finding all the integral solutions of the equation, or, as the Greek expression was, for finding an unending succession of "rational diameters", that is, of increasingly accurate rational approximations to $\sqrt{2}$, the "ratio of the diagonal to the side". The rule, as given by Theon, is this. We form two columns of integers called respectively "sides" and "diagonals". In either column we start with 1 as the first term; to get the rest of the "sides", we add together the nth "side" and the nth "diagonal" to form the $n + 1$th "side"; in the column of "diagonals", the $(n + 1)$th "diagonal" is made by adding the nth "diagonal" to twice the nth side. Fortunately also Proclus (*In Remp.* Kroll ii. 24-25, 27-29; *ibid.*, *Excursus*, ii. p. 393 ff.) has preserved the recognised demonstration of this rule; it is a simple piece of geometry depending only on the identity $(a + b)^2 + b^2 = 2(a/2)^2 + 2(a/2 + b)^2$, which forms Euclid's proposition II.10. Since the students of the history of Greek geometry seem agreed that the contents of Euclid II. are all early Pythagorean, there is no reason why the rule given by Theon should not have been familiar not only to Plato, but to Socrates and his friends in the fifth century. The probability is that they were acquainted with it, and thus knew how to form an endless series of increasingly close approximations to one "irrational", $\sqrt{2}$.[1]

[1] It may be noted in passing that the interest in finding the value of $\sqrt{2}$ is not prompted by purely "geometrical" considerations. Since one approximate value is $17/12$, for $17^2 = 289 = 2 \times 144 + 1 = 2 \times 12^2 + 1$, 17 is *very nearly* $= 12\sqrt{2}$. If it were strictly true that $\sqrt{2} = 17/12$, it would follow that $17^2 = 288$, and therefore $= 16 \times 18$. Thus, 16, 17, 18, would be a geometrical progression and we should have $18/16$ or $9/8 = (17/16)^2$. This would enable us to divide the musical interval of the tone into two equal semi-tones. The irrationality of the "diagonal" is thus connected with a corresponding irrationality in music.

We note at once that the ratios obtained by forming the "sides" and "diagonals" are identical with what we call in modern language the successive "convergents" to $\sqrt{2}$, formed by expressing the "irrational" as an unending continued fraction. I hope the reader acquainted with a little elementary algebra will pardon me if I explain this point briefly for the benefit of students of Plato whose school mathematics have been neglected through no fault of their own.

To express a quadratic surd as an unending fraction, we start from the identity $(\sqrt{a}+b)(\sqrt{a}-b)=a-b^2$. Thus in the case where $\sqrt{a}$ is to be $\sqrt{2}$, we can put $b=1$, and the identity becomes

$$(\sqrt{2}+1)(\sqrt{2}-1)=2-1, \text{ i.e. } \sqrt{2}-1=\frac{1}{\sqrt{2}+1}.$$

We then proceed as follows:

$$\sqrt{2}=1+(\sqrt{2}-1)=1+\cfrac{1}{\sqrt{2}+1}=1+\cfrac{1}{2+(\sqrt{2}-1)}$$

$$=1+\cfrac{1}{2+\cfrac{1}{(\sqrt{2}+1)}}=1+\cfrac{1}{2+\cfrac{1}{2+(\sqrt{2}-1)}}=1+\cfrac{1}{2+\cfrac{1}{2+\cfrac{1}{(\sqrt{2}+1)}}}.$$

Where we see that by substituting $\dfrac{1}{(\sqrt{2}+1)}$ for $(\sqrt{2}-1)$, whenever the second expression recurs, we shall ultimately get the unending fraction

$$\sqrt{2}=1+\cfrac{1}{2+\cfrac{1}{2+\cfrac{1}{2+\cfrac{1}{2+\dots}}}}$$

The successive "convergents" to the value of this fraction are formed by "stopping it off" at the first, second,

. . . nth step in the formation. Thus they are the rational numbers

$$1, \; 1 + \frac{1}{2}, \; 1 + \frac{1}{2 + \frac{1}{2}}$$

and so forth. The reader will readily see that they correspond precisely to the series of "diagonals" and "sides" given by Theon, the numerator and denominator of each being one of the pairs of integral solutions of the equation $y^2 = 2x^2 \pm 1$.

On examining the way in which the unending "continued fraction" and its "convergents" are formed, we at once note the following points:

(*a*) Each "convergent" is a nearer approximation to the required value than the one before it. Thus $17/12$ is a nearer approximation to $\sqrt{2}$ than $7/5$, since if we take 2×5^2 as $= 7^2$, we are wrong by 1 in 50, but, if we take 2×12^2 as $= 17^2$, we are only wrong by 1 in 288.

(*b*) The convergents are alternately rather less and rather greater than the value to which they are approximations. Thus $7/5$ is less than $\sqrt{2}$, since $7^2 = 2 \times 5^2 - 1$; $17/12$ is $> \sqrt{2}$, since $17^2 = 2 \times 12^2 + 1$. 7 and 5 are, in fact, solutions in y and x of the equation $y^2 = 2x^2 - 1$; 17 and 12 are solutions of $y^2 = 2x^2 + 1$.

(*c*) The interval, or absolute distance, between two successive "convergents" steadily decreases, and by taking n sufficiently large, we can make the interval between the nth and $(n + 1)$th convergent less than any assigned rational fraction σ, however small, and can therefore make the interval between the nth convergent and the required "irrational" smaller still than σ.

(*d*) The method is manifestly applicable to any "quadratic" surd, since it rests on the general formula

$$(\sqrt{a} - b) = \frac{a - b^2}{(\sqrt{a} + b)}.$$

It is most readily applicable when a, whose "square root" is required, is an integer of the form $m^2 + 1$, since in that case, by taking $b = m$, we reduce our fundamental formula to the simple form $(\sqrt{a} - 1) = \dfrac{1}{(\sqrt{a} + 1)}$.

Thus we get at once such results as that

$$\sqrt{5} = 2 + \cfrac{1}{4 + \cfrac{1}{4 + \dots}} \qquad \sqrt{17} = 4 + \cfrac{1}{8 + \cfrac{1}{8 + \dots}}$$

But we can also use it with a little more trouble to yield, e.g.,

$$\sqrt{3} = 1 + \cfrac{1}{1 + \cfrac{1}{2 + \cfrac{1}{1 + \cfrac{1}{2 + \dots}}}}$$

and similar results.

The general character of the procedure is thus that in the expression of $\sqrt{a}$ as an "unending continued fraction," by forming the series of "convergents" we pin down $\sqrt{a}$ between two values, one of which is a little too small and the other a little too large, but the difference between the too small and the too large is decreasing at every step and can be made less than any fraction we like to assign, though we never quite get rid of it, because we cannot actually arrive at a last convergent. To put it another way, in approximating to $\sqrt{2}$ by this method, we are not merely approximating to a "limit", we are approximating to it from *both* sides at once; $\sqrt{2}$ is at once the upper limit to which the series of the values which are too small, 1, 7/5, . . . are tending, and the lower limit to which the values which are too large, 3/2, 17/12, . . . are tending. *This*, as it seems to me, is manifestly the original reason why Plato requires us to substitute for the ἄπειρον as *one* thing, a "duality" of the great and small. $\sqrt{2}$ is an ἄπειρον, because you may go on endlessly making closer and closer approximations to it without ever reaching it; it never quite turns into a rational number, though it seems to be on the way to do so. But also, it is a "great-and-small" because it is the limit to which one series of values, all too large, tends to decrease, and also the limit to which another series, all too small, tends to increase.

The meaning of what is said in our passage of the *Epinomis* about plane geometry will thus be that the real problem of the study is to evaluate all quadratic surds ($\sqrt{3}$, $\sqrt{5}$, etc.), by the same method which has proved successful in the case of the "double"; they are all, in modern phraseology, to be expressed as unending "continued fractions", and our conception of number is to be enlarged to include these "irrationals", which by the proposed method can be made rational to within whatever "standard" we like to adopt. It is the indispensability of providing a means of checking the interval within which the "error" of an approximation falls which is the real reason for replacing the single ἄπειρον by a "duality".

Thus, for example, when we know that $\sqrt{2}$ lies somewhere between 1 and 3/2, our work is not really done. We are not to say that it simply is one of the "infinitely numerous" values between 1 and 3/2. By taking the next pair of "convergents", 7/5 and 17/12 we can exclude it from that part of the interval (3/2 – 1) which lies between 1 and 7/5 and again from that part of it which lies between 18/12 and 17/12. The alternation of the too small which is steadily increasing and the too great which is steadily decreasing is demanded if we are to estimate the amount of error incurred by taking a given approximation as the true value of our "irrational".

It may be worth while to note here that this absolute necessity for the revision of the Pythagorean formula would not have existed if the Greek arithmeticians had possessed our method of developing irrational "square roots" as unending decimal fractions. When we employ this method to evaluate $\sqrt{2}$ and get the result that $\sqrt{2} = 1 \cdot 41421, \ldots$ we are approaching our "irrational" only from one side, that of the "too small". Any approximation got by taking n significant figures to the right of the decimal point will be too small, because there are always still more significant figures that can be added. Yet we are able to assign a limit to the amount of the error. Thus I can say at once that the value $1 \cdot 4$ is too small by an amount which lies some-where between $\cdot 01$ and $\cdot 02$. And yet, even so, we have not quite got away from the "duality". If I merely said that $1 \cdot 4$ is "too small", this would leave much too wide a margin of error, since the possible error might be anything between $\cdot 00000 \ldots 1$, when I may suppose as many o's as I please, provided only that the number is finite, and $\cdot 009999 \ldots$ where again, the 9's may be as numerous as you please, so long as their number is finite. If we are to make any accurate estimate of the error, still more, if we are to be able to diminish it *ad libitum*, we must be able to confine our approximation between a μέγα and a μικρόν. We do this habitually in our elementary calculation, when we follow the rule that if we wish to get an approximation right to n "significant places", we must first work it out to $(n + 1)$ places, and then, if the $(n + 1)$th figure is greater than 5, increase the nth by 1; for example, if we wish to give the value of π "to four places", we must not write $3 \cdot 1415$, though 5 is really the fourth figure in the "decimal"; we must write 3·1416, since the full calculation would give 3·14159. . . .

The task which the *Epinomis* would impose on the "geometer" would, in the absence of a numerical notation resting on the principle of position, be a formidable one. We can conceive two possible ways of executing it. One would be the purely empirical one of forming a table of the successive "squares" of integers by actual multiplication and then picking out on inspection suitable pairs. Thus, to find $\sqrt{3}$, we might try to pick out from such a table the pairs which satisfy one of the equations $y^2 = 3x^2 - 2$, $y^2 = 3x^2 + 1$. The solution of the first equation would give the first, third, fifth, . . . those of the second the second, fourth, . . . "convergents" to the continued fraction

$$1 + \cfrac{1}{1 + \cfrac{1}{2 + \ldots}}$$

. But this procedure would not only be exceedingly tedious, in view of the great number of multiplications involved; it would have the further difficulty that the requisite equations are hard to detect except in the most favourable cases. We may, therefore, feel fairly sure that a fourth-century student of the problem would attempt to establish the equation by finding a geometrical construction on the basis of Euclid, *Elements* II., as we know from Proclus was actually done for $\sqrt{2}$. But these constructions themselves would often be difficult to discover, and I have not been able as yet to learn whether any such constructions can be shown to have been actually known in the fourth century. Is there any proof that there was a known construction of this kind for $\sqrt{3}$? Perhaps some special student of the history of mathematics may be able to answer the question. If there was not, we must understand the *Epinomis* as simply indicating a programme for Academic mathematicians of the future.[1] In any case, it should be noted that the principle of the method, the pinning down of an irrational between a "too large" and a "too small" which are made to approach one another indefinitely, is the same which was employed for the finding of the areas of curvilinear figures and the volumes of solids with curved surfaces, as when, *e.g.*, the area of the circle was treated as intermediate between that of a circumscribed and a similar inscribed polygon and these two areas then made to tend to equality by supposing the number of the sides of the polygon increased.

The "stereometer's" problem is next said to be in principle the same. His business is to express surd "cube roots" as limits of series of approximation which are alternately too large and too small. Here, again, we have the materials for a question which I should like to propose to special students of the history of mathematics. Had the mathematicians of the fourth or third century a method of extracting such "roots", and if they had, what was it? The restriction of the treatment of irrationals in Euclid X. to quadratic surds may possibly be evidence that no such method was in the possession of Euclid or his Academic precursors, since one cannot believe that they would not have utilised it,

---

[1] See on the whole subject Zeuthen, *Histoire des mathématiques dans l'antiquité et dans le moyen âge*, 43-52, for the difficulties to be faced. The one such approximation to an irrational square root preserved in the literature before the time of Hero of Alexandria seems to be the value of $\sqrt{3}$ given by Archimedes in *Dimensio Circuli*, iii. He assumes that the value is intermediate between 265/153 and 1351/780 (*op. cit.* 49). Both fractions occur among the convergents to $1 + \cfrac{1}{1 + \cfrac{1}{2 + \cfrac{1}{1 + \cfrac{1}{2 + \dots}}}}$, the expression of $\sqrt{3}$ as a "continued fraction", the former being the ninth and the latter the twelfth term of the series. It is not clear to me why the more accurate 989/571 was not taken as the value which errs by defect.

if they possessed it, for the solution of the "Delian" and similar problems. (The solutions known to us are all geometrical, not arithmetical.) In any case, if the Academy anticipated, as the language of the *Epinomis* would naturally suggest, that the problem could be solved by a method analogous to the construction of endless continued fractions, their anticipations were premature. The problem resists this treatment for the simple reason that the product $(\sqrt[3]{a} - \sqrt[3]{b})(\sqrt[3]{a} + \sqrt[3]{b})$ is irrational. Yet we can exhibit cube roots in a form which displays the regular alternation of the "great" and the "small", though by a method unknown to the ancients. For we can in general write $\sqrt[3]{x+y} = \sqrt[3]{x} \times \sqrt[3]{(1 + y/x)}$ and then proceed to expand $(1 = y/x)^{\frac{1}{3}}$ by the Binomial Theorem, since it is easy to show that $(1 + y/x)^{\frac{1}{3}}$ is convergent if y/x is < 1. Hence, when once we have found $\sqrt[3]{2}$, we can find in succession $\sqrt[3]{3}$, $\sqrt[3]{4}$ and the rest. For $\sqrt[3]{2}$ itself, things stand rather differently, as we cannot throw $(1 + 1)^{\frac{1}{3}}$ into the form demanded. We can, however, show that the series arising from the expansion of $(1 + 1)^{\frac{1}{3}}$ is convergent by considering that the terms, apart from the first, form a series in which each term is numerically less than the preceding, and that they are alternately positive and negative. This proves that the sum of them converges to a limiting value, and consequently the sum of them with the addition of the first term, 1, is also convergent. In practice the method is not employed, for the reason that a considerable number of terms have to be calculated in order to secure any accuracy of approximation. We are not entitled to assume that the Academy actually possessed any method by which $\sqrt[3]{2}$ could be calculated, and the Delian problem solved arithmetically, rapidly, and accurately. We should rather take the *Epinomis* to express the natural hope that the method which had disposed of the fifth-century problem of "side and diagonal" would prove directly applicable to all the "irrationals" as yet recognised, quadratic and cubic alike.

I submit, then, that the character of the series of what we call the "convergents" to an endless continued fraction supplies the reason for the denomination of the irrational as μέγα καὶ μικρόν; in the power the method affords of restricting the value of the irrational within limits which can be made to approach one another as nearly as we wish, we have the motive for the correction of the earlier formula; in the anxiety to clear up the mystery of the "side and diagonal" we can see the starting-point of the conception. If this is so, we understand the origin of the formula guaranteed by Aristotle, that the part played by the "formal" element in a "number", the one, is to *equalise* (ἰσάζειν) the "great" and the "small".[1] Since the series of convergents, alternately too small and too large, never actually comes to an end, there is always an "inequality"or tension between the "great" and the "small", and thus always a still unrationalised "matter" in the "number". But since we can make the interval between two consecutive convergents less than any assigned rational interval, the tension is steadily growing fainter as you pass along the series. It would come to rest in a complete "equality" if, *per impossibile*, two successive convergents could have an identical value. They would then not be two values, but one; the "interval" would be reduced to zero. This never actually happens, but it "all but happens"; you cannot come literally "as near as nothing" to a rational fraction which, when multiplied by itself, gives the product 2 or 3 or 5, but you *can* come *nearer*

---

[1] *Met.* M, 1081 a 24, where ὁ πρῶτος εἰπών definitely ascribes the expression to Plato.

than anything which is not literally o to such a fraction. Thus we might say of the "irrational" in the phraseology of the *Phaedo*, that though it never quite succeeds in being a rational, "it tries its very hardest to be one", and misses by immeasurably less than the traditional hair's breadth. This means that if we are to equate Forms with "numbers", as Aristotle assumes that Plato did, and also to say, with the *Epinomis*, that "irrational roots" are numbers, and therefore Forms, the relation the *Phaedo* assumes for "sensible things to Forms, must also exist among the Forms themselves". The "irrational" is a Form, but it is always trying, and never quite succeeding in the attempt, to exhibit the Form of a "rational". (The unending "decimal" tries its hardest to "recur".) This is, in principle, why the στοιχεῖα of the Forms are the στοιχεῖα of all things.

We may illustrate this point in a little more detail from the *Timaeus*. It is true that the speaker there is a fifth-century Pythagorean and that his repeated insistence on the provisional and tentative character of all his mathematical physics shows us that Plato does not wish to take the responsibility for precise details. But the existence of the dialogue itself is sufficient proof that the general type of view which pervades the dialogue is meant to be regarded as sound. There all the sensible characters of bodies animate and inanimate are made to be functionally dependent on the geometrical structure of their corpuscles. The structure of the corpuscles again is determined by that of their faces, and that of the faces by the structure of the two types of triangle from which they are built up. Now the triangles are determined in everything but their "absolute magnitude", which is asserted by Timaeus (57 *d*) to be variable within limits, by the triplet of "numbers" which gives the ratios of their sides to one another, and this triplet in each case introduces irrationals. For the isosceles right-angled triangle, it is the triplet (1, 1,√2) and for the "right-angled scalene" adopted as the foundation of three of the five regular solids, the triplet (1, √3, 2). If you know how to "approximate" within as near an interval as you please to √2 and √3, you know how to form these triangles, and thus you are possessed of the secret on which all the physical characters of the realm of becoming depend. The στοιχεῖα of the "numbers", √2, √3, are, in the end, the στοιχεῖα of γιγνόμενα. It is worth noting that the two triangles might equally have been specified by giving the ratios between their *angles*. This would give the triplets (1, 1, 2), (1, 2, 3), where no irrational appears. In Speusippus, Fr. 4, where these triangles and their significance for solid geometry are described, *these* ratios are mentioned, but nothing is said about the others. This is significant, since the passage is given in the *Theologumena Arithmetica* as an extract from a work by Speusippus, the *Pythagorean Numbers*, based on the teaching of Philolaus. We may infer that the originators of the doctrine of the "elementary triangles" reached it by a consideration of the angles of the two figures, and if they knew, as they pretty certainly must have known, that the ratios of the sides, in both cases, introduced the "scandal" of the "incommensurable", they kept a decent silence on the point. Plato, on the other hand, calls express attention to the ratios of the sides, and is silent about those of the angles, but for the single remark that there is a certain "beauty" about these triangles, which presumably means that the ratios involved between their angles are the simplest λόγοι of integer to integer, 1 : 1, 1 : 2, 1 : 3. Thus he makes Timaeus bold enough to insist on the very point which is embarrassing to the Pythagorean conception of number, but, in the interests of historical verisimilitude, will not let him say that his geometrical ἀρχαί have still more ultimate arithmetical ἀρχαί, "surd" numbers. He allows the speaker to escape with the ambiguous remark that "God knows" what ἀρχαί there can be more ultimate than the triangles (*Timaeus*, 53 *d*).

In the *Theaetetus* (147 *d*) we are told that the Pythagorean mathematician Theodorus has just been explaining to the lad Theaetetus and his friends that 3, 5 . . . 17 have no rational square roots. This plainly does not mean that Theodorus merely explained that these numbers have no integral square roots; this is obvious and could have been said in a sentence. Nor can it mean that Theodorus actually possessed and explained the method of approximating to $\sqrt{3}$ and the rest. If a Pythagorean in the year 400 could have given such a method, there would have been no novelty about the Platonic view of number. We must suppose that Theodorus is supposed to be able to demonstrate the irrationality of the various numbers, $\sqrt{3}$, $\sqrt{5}$ . . ., without knowing how to construct them, and to show that the construction involves an endless series. The simplest way in which this might be done would be to employ the kind of reasoning by which it is proved in a theorem appearing in some MSS. at the end of Book X. of Euclid's *Elements*[1] that $\sqrt{2}$ is irrational. The method is to prove that if there is a rational root, the absurd consequence follows that a certain fraction both is and is not stated "in its lowest terms". Thus, if we suppose that $\sqrt{3} = (1 + m/n)$ where m and n are integers and have no common factor, it is easy to prove that our equation demands that both m and n shall be even numbers, and therefore have the common factor 2, contrary to the hypothesis. The method could be used for any of the numbers stated to

[1] Heiberg, *Euclides*, iii. App. pr. 27.

have been investigated by Theodorus. Also, in some cases, as Zeuthen has pointed out,[1] it would be possible to apply the method given in Euclid X. 2 for the finding of a G.C.M., and to show that a given rational magnitude and a second magnitude under consideration have no G.C.M., and therefore the second must be incommensurable with the first. (Thus it is easy to see from the construction of Euclid II. 11 that the two segments into which a straight line is divided in the proposition have the ratio $\sqrt{5} - 1 : 2$, and then, by using Euclid X. 2, that the two segments have no G.C.M.) Zeuthen reasonably infers that the irrationality of the expression $\sqrt{5} - 1$, and consequently of $\sqrt{5}$, must have been known to Theaetetus in this way. (It does not follow, though it is possible, that Theodorus had actually demonstrated the fact. We might suppose that Plato is taking certain propositions, due to his own associate Theaetetus, and dramatically feigning him to have learned them from his old teacher, though in view of the admittedly Pythagorean character of the "geometrical algebra" of Euclid II, I think it probable that we may go a step beyond Zeuthen and ascribe the propositions in question to Theodorus.)

In the *Meno* again (83 *a-e*) the immediate object of the cross-questioning of Meno's page is to establish the point that $\sqrt{2}$ lies somewhere between 1 and 1·5. The *Republic* (546 *c*) shows that Socrates is familiar with the closer approximation 1·4 (7/5), and we may suppose that if it had been necessary for his purpose, he could have continued his elenchus until this had been made plain, *i.e.* that he knew the construction given by Proclus for approximation to $\sqrt{2}$.

To sum up, then, the special points I want to make are these:

[1] *Op. cit.* p. 45.

(*a*) The fundamental novelty about the Platonic theory is that it represents the first discovery, in an incomplete form, of the real *numbers*, as the ultimate determinants of geometrical structure, and so mediately of the physical characters of things.

(*b*) That the real numbers are conceived of as the common limit to which two "infinite" series "converge". The terms of the one series (that of the odd "convergents" of the complete double series) are always "too small", but the defect is steadily diminishing; the terms of the other (the series of the even "convergents") are all "too great", but the excess steadily diminishes. This is why the "material" constituent of number must be called the μέγα καὶ μικρόν.

(*c*) The origin of the whole theory is to be found in the discovery of the "side-and-diagonal" numbers which form an endless series of increasingly close approximations to $\sqrt{2}$. Plato holds that the business of "geometry" is to discover similar series for all the quadratic surds.

(*d*) The rise of solid geometry in the Academy, leading as it did to problems involving "cube roots", creates a demand for the formulation of a similar method of approaching the cubic surds alternately from the side of the too great and from that of the too small. Here again, the simplest case of the general problem is that of finding a series for $\sqrt[3]{2}$ (the "Delian problem"). Theoretically the construction of such series of approximations to cube roots from the two sides alternately is readily performed, though it involves algebraical methods not possessed by the Greek mathematicians. Practically the method has little value, since the number of terms which must be taken into account to secure a moderately accurate approximation is inconveniently large.

There is one further observation, more important than any of the foregoing, which can only be made here with the utmost brevity. The Platonic theory is inspired by the same demand for pure rationality which has led in modern times to the "arithmetisation of mathematics". The object aimed at, in both cases, is to get rid of the dualism between so-called "continuous" and "discrete" magnitude. The apparent mystery which hangs about the "irrationals" is to be dispelled by showing how they can be derived, by a logical process which is transparently rational at every step, from the integers and the "rational fractions", or λόγοι of integers to integers. It is precisely the same process, carried further, which we see in modern times in the arithmetical theory of the continuum, or in Cantor's further elaboration of an arithmetic of the "transfinite". In all these cases, the motive for the construction is to get rid of an apparent mystery by the discovery in the seemingly unintelligible of the principle of order of which the integer-series is the perfect and ideal embodiment. "Forms are numbers" because "order is Heaven's first law", and number is the type and pattern of order. The task which still awaits us is to consider the nature of the further and final step by which the conception of number as the determination of a "material" (the great-and-small), by "form" or "order" was extended to cover the case of the integers themselves. So far as we have gone, the integers and their order have figured as given data, but the harder problem remains to detect the elements of matter and form within the integer-series itself. We must not be surprised if we find that the Platonic theory, so far as we can discern its character, was less successful in dealing with this than with the easier problem of the rationalising of the irrational.

II

The present essay will not attempt to deal with the whole intricate problem of the Platonic theory of the integers and Aristotle's criticisms upon it. It would be absurd to dispose in a few pages of a subject which has cost M. Robin several hundred large pages for the mere full display of the materials for a conclusion. I can, at best, offer a *vindemiatio prima* effected by the *intellectus sibi permissus*. It will be enough to discover, if we can, what the theory must have been in its broad outlines to give rise to the kind of strictures it provokes from Aristotle. We shall gain something if we can see that these strictures are not mere explosions of wilful petulance, and yet that the doctrines which provoked them represent a real advance in mathematical thought, in spite of features which rightly rouse grave misgiving. I believe it will appear from our discussion that the number-theory of the Academy is in much the same position as the Calculus before the purification of it from bad logic in the days of our fathers. The main ideas are sound and fertile, but the formulation given to them involves illogicalities. The remedy for such a situation is neither, with Aristotle, to dismiss the theory on the ground of these illogicalities, nor, like rash admirers of Plato, to pretend that the illogicalities are not there. It is to reconstruct the theory with a more exact and subtle logic, and so to show that its apparent paradoxes are incidental excrescences; the only way to get bad logic out of a philosophical theory is to have more logic, not less.

I start from the assumption, justified by the whole tenour of the Aristotelian criticism, that the doctrine of the One and the "great-and-small", apparently derived from the study of irrationals, was at once extended to

I

the integers themselves. It is always in this form, as a theory about integers, that Aristotle deals with it. We can readily see that the thought of the "real numbers" as limits of series of rationals, once introduced, would not be confined to irrational real numbers. For the limit to which an infinite series of rationals converges need not be an irrational. Thus, for example, the sum of n terms of the series $1 + \frac{1}{2} + \frac{1}{4} + \frac{1}{8} \ldots$ converges to the value 2, that of n terms of the series $1 + \frac{1}{3} + \frac{1}{9} + \frac{1}{27} \ldots$ to the value $\frac{3}{2}$, and in general, obviously the "sum to infinity" of a decreasing geometrical progression with rational terms is rational. This would be apparent at once from consideration of the process of unending bisection to which Zeno had directed attention. We see at once from a diagram that as the process continues, the successive points of bisection, C, D, E, F . . . , approach nearer and nearer to the terminal B, and that, since

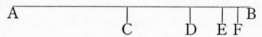

bisection never becomes impossible, we can make the interval between a point of bisection and B less than any assigned interval σ, however small σ may be, by merely continuing the bisection long enough. In other words the sum $1 - \frac{1}{2} - \frac{1}{4} - \frac{1}{8} \ldots$ converges to the value 0 as the number of terms summed increases "indefinitely". It is on this consideration that Eudoxus based the principle of his method of "exhaustions", that if from the greater of two unequal magnitudes there be taken more than its half, from the remainder more than its half, and the same process be continued, a finite number of subtractions will leave us with a remainder less than the smaller of the two given magnitudes (Eucl. X. 1). The rule implies the knowledge that such sums as $1 - \frac{1}{3} - \frac{1}{9} - \frac{1}{27} \ldots$, $1 - \frac{1}{4} - \frac{1}{16} - \frac{1}{64} \ldots$, converge to limiting values which are rational and not $= 0$ (in the first case to $\frac{1}{2}$, in the second to $\frac{2}{3}$).

In these particular cases, indeed, we do not see the μέγα καὶ μικρόν, since the sum of $r + 1$ terms of such a series is always less than the sum of r terms. But it is easy to give an example which is a μέγα καὶ μικρόν. Thus, take the sum $1 - \frac{1}{2} + \frac{1}{4} - \frac{1}{8} \ldots$ We see at once that it can be written as $(1 + \frac{1}{4} + \frac{1}{16} \ldots) - \frac{1}{2}(1 + \frac{1}{4} + \frac{1}{16} \ldots)$, and that it is therefore $\frac{1}{2}(1 + \frac{1}{4} + \frac{1}{16} \ldots)$, and so converges to the value $\frac{4}{3} \times \frac{1}{2} = \frac{2}{3}$. These considerations prove, as I have said, that if a μέγα καὶ μικρόν is a "real number", the "real numbers" cannot all be "irrationals", and that the duty of a sound arithmetical theory is to provide for the derivation of the whole series, including its rational members, on a single principle.

This involves a consequence of the first importance, which has only been definitely realised in very modern times. The "real number" 2 cannot be the same entity as the integer 2, for the reason that the integers are pre-supposed as a series from which the "real numbers", including the "real number" 2, have to be derived. Hence no "real number" is an integer and no integer a "real number", though the distinction is concealed by our convenient and economical habit of making our numerical *symbols* do double duty. The reality of the distinction is seen as soon as we attempt to use the method we have been describing to furnish the necessary *definitions* of "real numbers". If I am going to introduce the sign $\sqrt{2}$, for example, I must define it, and if I define it by saying that it stands by *definition* for the value to which the "side-and-diagonal" series $1, \frac{3}{2}, \frac{7}{5}, \frac{17}{12} \ldots$ converges, the very statement presupposes the integers, 1, 2, 3, 5, 7, 12, 17, as already given and known. Since the process of forming "convergents" thus presupposes the integers as the "matter" out of which the convergents are formed by a proper selection, it manifestly cannot be employed to "derive" the series of the integers themselves. Yet, as the history of arithmetic proves, it was inevitable that there should be an initial confusion between the integers and the corresponding "real numbers", and that the necessity of making a rigid distinction should only be discovered by later reflection on the consequences of the confusion. This makes it intelligible why the theory of the derivation of number from the determination of the "great-and-small" should have been extended to the integers themselves. At the same time, it prepares us for the discovery that the simple transference of the notions of the "One" and the "great-and-small", in the form in which they are serviceable in the theory of the irrationals, to the logical derivation of the integers themselves will prove logically unsatisfactory. We are thus in a position to do what many students have found impossible, to be just at once to the Platonic theory as containing the germs of a true theory of whole number, and to the objections of Aristotle. We are neither called on to regard the Platonic theory as a "senile aberration" (the real meaning of the German euphemisms about *Zahlenmystik*), nor, in our admiration for Plato, to treat Aristotle as a mere carper or a pure fool, as I fear even C. Ritter, who has done more than any living German writer for the understanding of Plato, tends to do. It should really be equally incredible that Plato meant anything but a piece of rational mathematics by his theory, and that Aristotle was a mere envier of his master's reputation or a common ass. We shall not look in Aristotle for a mathematician's appreciation of mathematical new conceptions, but we shall look for, and we shall find, intelligible protests against something which, on the face of it, appears to conflict with the logic of common sense. We shall be prepared to admit that the criticisms may so far hit the mark as to show that the Platonic new idea can only be "saved" by a re-casting which removes some very fundamental Aristotelian objections. Aristotle, no doubt, was one of those numerous persons who cannot follow a piece of mathematical reasoning until it is turned into the language of "common sense", but we shall do well to remember the saying of W. K. Clifford that "algebra which cannot be translated into good English and sound common sense is bad algebra".[1]

The particular application I would make of this observation is this. It is quite clear that if the proposed conception of a number as a determination of the ἄπειρον of the "great-and-small" originated, as we have tried to argue, from consideration of the quadratic and cubic "irrationals", it was extended to cover the case of the integers themselves. It is on the application to the integers that Aristotle's criticisms directly bear. If the "numbers" in question had all been "irrationals", which Aristotle himself followed the older tradition in regarding as μεγέθη, or ποσὰ συνεχῆ, in contradistinction to ἀριθμοί or ποσὰ διωρισμένα, he would have been obliged to make the criticism, which he never does make, that the so-called ἀριθμοί of which the Academic analysis holds good are not ἀριθμοί at all, but μεγέθη, and that the definition thus confuses the two εἴδη of τὸ ποσόν, which are in fact ἀντιδιῃρημένα. Again, his apparent standing confusion of the ἀόριστος δυάς of the great and the small with the αὐτὸ ὅ ἐστι δυάς, the integer 2, would be so gross as to be wholly incomprehensible unless the integer 2 actually played the part of a factor in the derivation of "number", as it can only do if the integers are thought of themselves as having a δυάς as one of their factors. If

[1] *Common Sense of the Exact Sciences*, p. 21.

there is a logical confusion of two wholly distinct concepts in Aristotle's strictures, the only reasonable explanation is, though I fear it is one to the neglect of
which in the past I must myself plead guilty, that the
confusion had been made before him by the Academic
champions of the theory themselves, and that his
acquiescence in it therefore does not affect the value of
his criticism as an *argumentum ad homines*. Thus when
he tells us (*Met.* M, 1082 a 12) that "the indeterminate
dyad, as they say, lays hold of the determinate dyad
and so makes two dyads", this ascription to the ἀόριστος
δυάς of "doubling" — whether by multiplication or
division—what it "lays hold of", where the confusion
of it with the integer 2 is manifest, must be an actual
piece of the Academic theory, as the words ὥς φασί
imply. (And, in the absence of any evidence, we are not
entitled to maintain that the confusion is not Plato's
own but merely that of inferior disciples.) So the type
of criticism which is exemplified by the argument of
Met. M, 1084 a 23, that if 4 is the form of horse and 2
that of man, "man will be a part of horse", bad as it is,
at least implies that according to the Platonic theory
the integers 2 and 4 are among the "numbers" of which
the "One" and the μέγα καὶ μικρόν are the factors, just
as the complaint of the next lines (1084 a 25-27) implies
that *the* Form-numbers *par excellence* are the integers
from 1 to 10. It is still more important to realise the
implication of the passage *Met.* M, 1081 b 12-22, where
Aristotle's point is that in a sound theory the integers
must be logically derived in their "natural" order, 1, 2,
3, . . . but "if this is so numbers cannot be derived, as
they derive them, from the dyad and the one. For 2
(the dyad) is a part of 3 and 3 of 4, and so on throughout the series. But what was derived from the 'first
dyad' (the integer 2) and the indeterminate dyad was

the integer 4". The whole point of the criticism is that in the Academic theory, 4 can be defined without defining 3, *i.e.* the Academic deduction of the integers does not give them in their "natural" order. Aristotle's own theory that each number of the series is made from the preceding by adding 1 to it is a piece of very bad logic, but this does not affect the perfect soundness of his contention that a correct theory ought to define the integer $(n + 1)$ in terms of n, and so yield the "natural" order, a point which is fully recognised by Russell when he calls the finite integers those which can be obtained by mathematical induction, and by Frege when he defines the whole series as "the successors of o". The criticism would be meaningless if the Academy had not defined the numbers up to 10 in an order other than the "natural". This consideration of itself would be fatal to the diagram of the derivation given on p. 31 of Dr. Stenzel's penetrating study of the Platonic doctrine,[1] which does succeed in getting the successive integers from 1 to 10 in the familiar order, and is thus shown to be un-Academic. Dr. Stenzel's method is, in fact, to start with 1, and to derive from it the two next integers 2 and 3. He then derives two more integers from each of the two thus obtained and regards the process as one to be continued indefinitely. We thus get the diagram

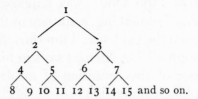

8 9 10 11 12 13 14 15 and so on.

The obvious criticisms on this procedure are (*a*) that it disregards the plain indications of Aristotle that the numbers from 1 to 10, the numbers of the "decad", held

---

[1] *Zahl und Gestalt bei Platon und Aristoteles* (ed. 1.), p. 31.

a privileged position in the Academic theory, and (*b*) that it is not clear by what sort of derivation the author supposes himself to be getting his new integers from an old one at each step. He apparently thinks that, *e.g.*, the application of the "indeterminate dyad" to 1 produces 2 and 3, its application to 2, 4 and 5, and so on. But this is barely consistent with the express statement (*Met.* M, 1081 a 14) that the function of the ἀόριστος δυάς is to be δυοποιός of whatever it "gets hold of". You cannot make 3 from 1 or 5 from 2 by any process of doubling or halving.[1] Presumably Dr. Stenzel's thought is that, since his method somehow always derives from any integer *n* the *two* integers 2*n*, 2*n* + 1, the transition from *n* to 2*n* is always the work of the dyad which is δυοποιός. Exactly how the transition from *n* to 2*n* + 1 is to be described is not clear. I suppose it illustrates the function of the other constituent of number, the "One". But if the Platonic method of generating the odd numbers had been Dr. Stenzel's, it would have been a criticism Aristotle could hardly have missed that half the integers, on the theory itself, *are* got by the "addition" of a "unit". I find this irreconcileable with Aristotle's insistence on the "addition of 1 to 1" as a point which, it is implied, was not recognised in the Platonic theory, and also with his statement that the function of "the One" was supposed to be that of "equalising" something, a statement for which we have already seen the evidence. I am thus driven to conclude that, though all Dr. Stenzel says in his book about the importance of the definition of an ἄτομον εἶδος by the process of logical division is of the highest value, he has gone astray in supposing that we can directly discover

[1] One might add that Aristotle's language seems to make it plain that 2 was not supposed to be derived from 1 by "doubling," but was, like 1 itself, assumed as a datum. He clearly means to say that the first and simplest example of the "doubling" power of the "dyad" was supposed to be given by 2 × 2 = 4. See *infra*.

the Platonic theory of the logical structure of the integer-series from the teaching of the *Sophistes* and *Philebus* about διαίρεσις κατ' εἴδη. (Perhaps he has forgotten also that the *Philebus* is clear on the point that διαίρεσις does not proceed necessarily by dichotomy. We divide a "kind" into the fewest sub-kinds necessary at each step, but not necessarily, as the *Sophistes* had done, always into two and no more, *Philebus* 16 *d*.)

What is meant by "equalising" I think we can see best from the use of the same word in connection with the doctrine of "directive justice" in the fifth book of the *Nicomachean Ethics*. It will be remembered that the main thought there is that the commission of a wrong creates an inequality between two parties who were before, and ought to be, equal. *A* has now an advantage and *B* a disadvantage, and the business of a dicastery, in assessing its award, is to transfer to *B*'s side of the account with *A* just so much as will cancel the inequality and leave the parties in the state of "equality" which existed before *A*'s unlawful act. This is done by striking a kind of "arithmetical mean".[1] So much is clear, whatever view we take on the special points about which interpreters have diverged from one another. There is another equality besides absolute or arithmetical equality, that which Aristotle calls "equality of proportion", and Plato in the *Gorgias*, "geometrical equality", but when "equality" is spoken of without qualification it means absolute equality, and when "equalising" is spoken of in the same unqualified way, what is meant is the taking of an arithmetical mean. The arithmetical mean between b and a, $(a + b)/2$ (where I assume $b > a$), is said to "equalise" this because the difference $b - (a + b)/2$ is identical with the difference $(a + b)/2 - a$.

---

[1] *E.N.* 1132 b 10 ff.

If we apply this to the case of numbers, we see at once that it implies that an odd number $2n + 1$ is to be looked on not as the result of adding 1 to $2n$, but as the result of taking the arithmetical mean between the two even numbers $2n$ and $2n + 2$. These two numbers, being both even, are themselves the product of the activity of the "indeterminate dyad" which "doubles" something. The "equalisation" of a great and small is effected by the arithmetical mean, $2n + 1$, because the mean "falls short" of the greater, $2n + 2$ by the same interval by which it "exceeds" the less, $2n$. It follows, I submit, that we are to think of the integers from 1 to 10 as "generated" in the following manner:

(1) The ἀόριστος δυάς, by doubling whatever it "lays hold of", originates the "power-series" 1, 2, 4, 8, as is clearly taught by what is said of the "double" in *Epinomis*, 990 *e* and *Met. M*, 1081 a 21, b 20.[1]

(2) Next we "equalise" the "great and small" by taking the arithmetical mean between the two adjacent even numbers 2 and 4, viz. 3.

(3) The double of 3 is next produced by the action of the "dyad", and we get 6.

(4) We now get the "mean" between 4 and 6 and 6 and 8; this gives us 5, 7.

(5) The "dyad" lays hold of 5, and this gives us 10.

(6) Finally we obtain the "mean" between 8 and 10, 9.

The resulting order is thus 1, 2, 4, 8, 3, 6, 5, 7, 10, 9, and we note that the odd integers, apart from 1, are all got by what is really division by 2, $2n + 1$ being

---

[1] 1 is supposed to be given already as a datum needing no derivation. I have spoken, for brevity's sake, as though 2 is to be taken as the result of an application of the ἀόριστος δυάς to 1. This is the view which ought in consistency to be taken of 2, if the underived constituents of the integers are the "One" and the "indeterminate dyad". I shall give reasons later on for thinking that in fact the "dyad" was only used to obtain even numbers greater than 2, and that 2 itself was treated, though it should not have been, as a primitive datum of the theory.

regarded as $\frac{1}{2}(4n + 2)$; the even integers are got, apart
from 2 itself, which will be considered later, by multiplication by 2. Thus the series once more illustrates
the phrase of *Epinomis* 990 e ἀεὶ περὶ τὸ διπλάσιον στρεφο-
μένης τῆς δυνάμεως καὶ τῆς ἐξ ἐναντίας ταύτῃ. We must add
to what we have already said about this phrase that the
whole integer-series is produced by doublings and their
inverses, halvings.

There is just a little uncertainty about the precise
arrangement of the five last terms of the series. We
might get 5 before 6, if we supposed that step (2) covers
the insertion of a "mean" between 2 and 8, as well as
a "mean" between 2 and 4. And 6 itself might again be
got, not as 3 × 2 but as the "mean" between 4 and 8.
Or again, we might try to get the odd numbers 3, 5, 9
immediately after the series 1, 2, 4, 8 by "limiting" the
advance of the "doubling dyad". The third step would
then be the doubling of 3 and 5, and the fourth and last
the "limiting" of the "advance" of the dyad from 6.
Thus we should get an order given by Robin (*Théorie
Platonicienne*, p. 282), 1, 2, 4, 8, 3, 5, 9, 6, 10, 7. But
the evidence seems to me to indicate that *only* odd numbers are derived by the process called τὸ ἰσάζειν, and
against the last suggestion we have the double consideration that it destroys the *symmetry* of a regular
alternation of multiplication and "equalisation", and
also that it obtains the odd numbers by a method which
Aristotle would have described as the addition of 1 to 1.
If half the integer-series had actually been derived by
the Platonists in this way, it seems to me that Aristotle
could not have failed to make the telling objection that
it is illogical to scruple at getting all the integers by
the method you yourself employ for getting half of them.
Yet he never makes any such point, but assumes rather
that it is characteristic of the Academy to make no use

whatever of "addition of 1 to 1". And, in fact, on the view adopted here, this is the case. Unless we make an exception for 2, no term of the series has been simply derived from that which immediately precedes it in the "natural" order. Hence I believe that the order we have given is the one really intended. It is the same as one given by Robin (*op. cit.* 447-9), and I think the method of obtaining it described there is identical with that given above, though M. Robin does not notice the use of ἰσάζειν in the *E.N.*, and does not explicitly explain that one of the two operations involved is the taking of the "mean". Hence I did not myself see the superiority of this arrangement over that proposed *op. cit.* 282, until I happened to reflect on the use of ἰσάζειν in the *Ethics*.

If the reconstruction thus attempted is sound in principle, it should show us that there is real point in Aristotle's criticism. Several of his contentions must in fairness be allowed to be valid. (1) Thus though he is manifestly in error in supposing that the higher integers contain the lower as "parts" of themselves, and more generally in thinking that an integer n which is > 1 is a collection of n "units", he is wholly right in objecting to any number-theory which generates the integers in any but their "natural" order. To say nothing of the practical inconvenience of having to prove separately the endless "inequalities" which we should require to establish if we started with such a series as Plato's method would give us, it is a *logical* fault in the theory that it requires two distinct principles of method for the generation of the integers, the operation × 2 for the even, and the operation ÷ 2 for the odd. Both, no doubt, may be said to be operations with the "double", but they are different operations, one the inverse of the other, and operations, like *entia*, are not to be multiplied *praeter necessitatem*.

And there really is a single formative principle which governs the logical structure of the whole series of finite integers; they have a definite type of order, different from any other, which it is important to recognise. It is only when they are arranged in the "natural" order that we see at once what this type is, that of a "well-ordered" infinite series, *i.e.* one in which there **is a** first term and in which every term has one and only one next succeeding term. That you could not discover this in an integer-series constructed by what seems to have been Plato's method is obvious. The order of the first five integers would, indeed, be unequivocally fixed as 1, 2, 4, 8, 3. But we might doubt whether the immediate successor of 3 should be got by "equalising" 2 and 8, so as to yield 5, or by applying the "dyad" to 3 so as to yield 6. It is not clear what the "integer next after 3" on this scheme is. Mathematicians recognise the soundness of Aristotle's point when they define the finite integers as those which can be reached by "mathematical induction", or "induction from n to $n + 1$". Aristotle's error in supposing that because a collection of $n + 1$ things contains n things and 1 thing over, the integer $n + 1$ contains the integer n and a 1 over does not affect the real force of his criticism. He is in precisely the same position as Berkeley and others who condemned the Calculus for employing the notion of "vanishing" magnitudes. They were quite right in saying that the theory of the Calculus, as formulated by its exponents, introduced vanishing magnitudes which are treated as somethings which are turning into nothings, and that to talk of such nothing-somethings is to talk nonsense. But the criticism really hit not the Calculus itself but only the inaccurate analysis its exponents had given of their own method. So Aristotle's criticism affects not the thought the Academics were trying to express, but the faulty expression they gave to it. His appeal to the process of counting as indicating the lines on which a correct logical theory of whole numbers should proceed (*Met.* M, 1080 a 30) is perfectly sound; unfortunately, it destroys his own doctrine of the generation of the integer-series by successive additions of 1, since we do not count, "one, one, one, one . . . ," but "one, two, three . . . ," as he has to admit in so many words.

(2) Again, it seems to me probable that Aristotle is not himself to be made responsible for the curious confusion of the number 2 with the ἀόριστος δυάς which runs through so much of his argumentation. When we compare the statements that 4 is produced "as they say", from the "first dyad and the indeterminate dyad" (M, 1081 b 21), that the indeterminate dyad, "as they say", laying hold of the determinate dyad makes two dyads, for its character by definition is to double what it lays hold of (τοῦ γὰρ ληφθέντος ἦν δυοποιός, M, 1082 a 12-14), that ἡ ἀόριστος δυὰς δυοποιός ἦν (M, 1083 b 35), it seems impossible to doubt that the Platonists, and presumably Plato himself, definitely regarded multiplication by 2 as the work of the ἀόριστος δυάς. And here there clearly is a bad mistake in logic. There is nothing "indeterminate" either about the process or about the result of "doubling". It is true, indeed, that multiplication in arithmetic is strictly, like addition, an operation on collections, not on the cardinal numbers of the collections. But the operation is one which has a perfectly determinate rule, and when both the collections involved are finite, as in the case of the "multiplication of 2 by 2", there is no ἀπειρία anywhere in data, process, or results. The data are collections of classes of two members each, the process is that of forming the "logical product" by combining each member of each of the two classes with

each of the other, and the logical product is a class with the determinate number 4. The combinations of couples which can be constructed out of the members of the couples (a, b) and (c, d) are (ac), (ad), (bc), (bd), and no others. Thus it should be the "first" or "determinate" dyad which is both multiplier and multiplied, and Aristotle is justified in making difficulties about the appearance of an "indeterminate dyad" in the character of multiplier. 2 is not an "indeterminate coefficient".

(3) And this leads to a further problem. What about the "first dyad", the integer 2, itself? If 4 results from the operation of the "indeterminate dyad" on 2, does 2 result from its operation on 1? Or must we regard 2, the "prime dyad", as an original datum for the theory, by the side of 1 and the ἀόριστος δυάς? From the very passages of *Met.* M which have just been cited above, when we remember that there are no similar allusions to a "laying hold of" 1 by the "dyad", it seems to me clear that the "doubling" of 2 was supposed to be the first example in the integer series of the working of the ἀόριστος δυάς. And the same thing, as I still think, is the only possible explanation of the perplexing remark of A, 987 b 33, that Plato made one of the constituents of his numbers a "dyad" because numbers are so easily generated from it, as from a matrix—ἔξω τῶν πρώτων. The πρῶτοι, which form the exception to the statement, are, I think, certainly 1, the "unit", and 2, the "first dyad". We have seen already that all the others are very easily "generated" by combining the two operations of multiplying by 2 and finding an arithmetical mean. *If* the first operation of "doubling" you will admit is the multiplication of 2 by 2, of course 2 itself, like 1, will not be one of those so generated. And since, as Aristotle implies, the Platonic theory forbids you to generate 2 by "adding 1 to 1", obviously you *cannot* "generate it" by a

multiplication of 1 by 2, thus presupposing 2 as one of the factors which generate itself. You must assume that 2 is there as something "given", no less than 1. And this leaves you with three underived data instead of two, 1, the "indeterminate dyad", 2. These difficulties are really inseparable from the attempt to make "doubling" the function of the "indeterminate dyad", and are therefore justly chargeable not on Aristotle, to whose memory I would hereby make an *amende honorable* for former utterances, but on the πρῶτος εἰπών, Plato himself.

The real source of the trouble is a curious one. It is that 1 is a term of the series of "powers" of every number whatever, that, as we express it, $x^0 = 1$, whatever number x may be, or, differently expressed, that $\log_x 1 = 0$, for all values of x. The mere statement of the point makes it clear that the first step to a theory which would avoid both the illogicality of confusing 2 with a couple of 1's, and the necessity of assuming 2 as well as 1 as a datum for the construction of the integer series, could not be taken until the notion of an arithmetical zero was clearly formed, that is, until it was understood that there is an "integer 0", and that 0 is the first of the whole numbers. But, though the Academic conception of the line as the "fluxion" of a point, like the Platonic name for the "point", ἀρχὴ γραμμῆς, shows that Plato and his followers had definitely conceived of a zero magnitude which is the geometrical analogue of the "number 0", the very fact that "the One" was treated as an underived constituent of number, this "One" being, as Aristotle's criticisms plainly show, regarded as identical with the number 1, proves that they had not thought of replacing 1 as the first term of the integer-series by 0. Hence the integer 2 creates a great difficulty for their number-theory. Once you have got 2, as we have seen, you can easily go on to "derive" all the other even integers. But how are you to get your original 2? There seems nothing for it but to presuppose that it is given as a datum needing no derivation. And yet, even if one winks at the ascription of "doubling" to the wrong "dyad", the "indeterminate", one's logical sense must be shocked by having to hold that one is not to regard $1 \times 2 = 2$ on the same footing with $2 \times 2 = 4$. If one does assimilate the two propositions, one would be led straight to the identification of the 2 by which 1 is multiplied in the first equation with the "indeterminate" dyad which ἦν δυοποιός. The ambiguity about this "dyad", which seems at once to be and not to be the integer 2, is thus not due to a blunder on Aristotle's part; it is inherent in the Platonic account of number itself.

Yet the thought at the bottom of the theory is far too valuable to be surrendered. We cannot fall back, like Aristotle, on the view that an integer n is a "sum" of n 1's, since that is manifestly nonsense. No integer contains the integer 1 or any other; it is strictly true that integers are not συμβλητά, and that our language about adding them to one another is a convenient and inaccurate abbreviation. When we say that $7 + 5 = 12$, what we really mean is that if we have a collection a with 7 members and another collection b with 5 members, and proceed to form the "additive class", "things which are either a or b", the cardinal number of this new class is 12. If there are 4 greater prophets and 12 minor prophets, there will be 16 persons in the collection of persons who are prophets, major or minor. But there is no number 12 or number 4 in the number 16. It is the two sets of prophets, not their cardinal numbers, which are "addible".

The importance of the Platonic theory, in spite of the easily recognised logical difficulty about the two "dyads", is perhaps best brought out by stating it in a way which throws its apparent paradoxicality into the strongest relief. It refuses to employ addition as a means of generating numbers, but employs multiplication and its inverse operation, division. This shocks common sense, which regularly looks on multiplication as an equivalent to repeated addition, regarding $x \times y$ as an abbreviation for $x + x + x \ldots$ to y terms. Yet the view implied in the Platonic theory is a sound one and that of common sense unsound, though we should never discover the fact in our practical operations with numbers. So long as we are concerned only with finite integers, it is true that multiplication may be treated as no more than a compendious substitute for repeated additions. But when we look into the logical character of the two operations, we shall see that it is not the same; logically multiplication is an independent operation with a principle of its own. In addition, as has been already explained, what we really do is to form a new collection which has for its members those and those only which were members of one or the other of two original collections. The fundamental logical process is that of forming the notion of the collection "*a* or *b*" from the notions of the collections *a* and *b*. In multiplication, on the other hand, when we multiply the collection *a* by the collection *b*, the underlying notion is that of the "multiplicative class", and this is generated on a totally different principle. We combine each member of *a* with each member of *b* to form a couple; the number of couples thus obtained is the number of the "product" of *a* by *b*, each couple being one of the members of the "multiplicative class".[1] Thus $5 \times 3 = 15$ means that if

---

[1] Here and elsewhere in this essay, I am, of course, wholly unoriginal, merely repeating, in a rough and approximate way, what the reader will find put with full scientific precision in works like Whitehead's and Russell's *Principia Mathematica*, Russell's *Principles of Mathematics*, Frege's *Grundgesetze der Arith-*

we have five things, *a*, *b*, *c*, *d*, *e*, and three things *a*, *β*, *γ*, 15 is the number of distinct couples in which one member is taken from the group *a*, *b*, *c*, *d*, *e*, and the other from the group *a*, *β*, *γ*. The logical process underlying addition is disjunctive, that which underlies multiplication is combinative. The extraordinary method by which the Platonists appear to have constructed the δεκάς arises from an over-hasty application of a truth which is, in itself, of the first importance.

To return to the construction of the integer-series itself. It is manifest that the curious process by which the successive integers are reached in an order which is not the "natural" one cannot stand against the criticism of common sense. The fatal objection to any such construction is that the "natural" series of the integers is a particularly important type of order and that no other arrangement of them exhibits the type in the same transparent way. Thus, suppose we have already completed the δεκάς and wish to continue the series. We shall first have to apply the "dyad" to 6, the lowest integer to which it has not already been applied, and this will give us 12. Then by "equalising" 10 and 12 we get 11. But the procedure obviously implies that we already know that there is one and just one empty space to be filled between 10 and 12, that there is a "number next after 10" and that it is also the number "next before 12". And this, in turn, implies that the integers in their "natural" order are already known before the process of derivation by means of the "dyad" begins. We cannot condemn "common sense", speaking through Aristotle, for finding such a construction incoherent. Indeed, if the contention of our former essay was

metik, and the like. To readers who know these works I apologise for dragging in what is so much more competently given there, on the ground that many persons who are interested in Plato seem too much frightened by the titles of such works as I have named to consult them for themselves.

correct, and the method really originated from an attempt
to determine the value of "irrational real numbers" in
terms of the integers, the transference of it to the derivation of the integer-series itself was morally bound to
lead to incoherence. If a "one" and a "dyad" are to be
discovered as the constituents of the integers themselves,
they cannot be identical with the "one" and the "dyad"
which figure in the derivation of the algebraic "surds";
at best, we can only expect the analysis of the formation
of integers to reveal constituents which function in an
analogous manner. The confusion of the analogous
with the identical has already met us as characteristic
of Greek number-theories in the form of the identification of the real numbers 2, 3, . . . with the corresponding
integers. It is only what we should expect that the same
logical confusion should encounter us again in the
ascription of the function of "doubling" to the "indeterminate dyad" instead of the "first dyad", which
has led to so much of the Aristotelian criticism. On the
other hand, we cannot regard Aristotle's justified objections to the theory as any justification of his own view
that integers are generated by "addition of 1 to 1". If
we neglect the confusion between integers and the collections of which they are the numbers already spoken
of, there is still a simple difficulty which is enough to
annihilate this "common-sense" explanation. If I say
"how many are 1 and 1 and 1 and 1?" I am asking a
question which I cannot answer unless I am already
acquainted with the series 1, 2, 3, 4. To count, I have
to know that when, *e.g.* in this illustration, a stop is
made in the repetition of the words "and 1", the *fourth*
"1" has been reached, and no other. Once more, the
integer-series is tacitly assumed as already known in
the very theory offered to describe its generation. One
might have seen this from the simple reflection that we

do not learn to count as children by saying "one, one, one . . .", but by saying "one, two, three. . . ." I can only learn by counting on my fingers that "1 and 1 and 1 are 3", if I have already learned to count the fingers as "one, two, three . . ." Hence the first task of an arithmetical kind for a young child is to get the names "one, two, three . . ." *in their right order* stamped on its memory, and it is very amusing to listen to children as they acquire certainty about this order by repetition, and to observe how hard they find it not to miss out some of the terms or to invert their order.

If we analyse the actual method by which we can successively define each of the integers in terms of the preceding, we shall see that, in fact, it may be said to be dependent throughout on the notions of *a* "one" and *an* "indeterminate" dyad, or great-and-small. What functions as the "one" is the notion expressed in language by the indefinite article "a" or "an", and what functions as the "dyad" is the notion expressed by "any". These are not, of course, the same things as integers of any kind; in particular "a" does not mean "one"; it is a notion already possessed by the youngest child who can point to a thing and say "ball" or "dog", long before it has even begun to learn to count. Given these elementary notions we can proceed to derive the integers in order in the way regularly followed by modern philosophical writers. Roughly the procedure is as follows.

We begin by defining the first member of the series, o. To do this we need, besides the notion of "any", the general logical notions of true and false and of a propositional function and its "arguments".[1] By a

---

[1] Here again I am, of course, simply borrowing as much as is necessary for my purpose of the terminology of Frege, Whitehead, and Russell, and am aiming at no more precision than is strictly necessary for my immediate purposes. I may give a general reference to the first chapter of the *Introduction* to *Principia Mathematica*, vol. i., and to Frege's essay *Funktion und Begriff*.

propositional function, for our purposes, we mean whatever can be significantly asserted about anything; we
denote it by such symbols as ϕ, ψ, χ, written before a
pair of brackets. By an argument to a function we
mean anything of which the assertion in question can
be made so as to yield a significant statement. Such
arguments may be denoted by the symbols, a, b, c . . .,
and when we wish to consider the function alone, leaving it an open question whether any argument can be
supplied which converts it into a true statement, we
may indicate this by using the symbols, x, y, w . . . Thus,
e.g., $\phi(x)$ may mean "is bald", $\psi(y)$, "is infallible", etc.
Then if a denotes Julius Caesar and b the Pope, $\phi(a)$
will be the proposition "Julius Caesar is bald", $\psi(b)$ the
proposition "the Pope is infallible". So much premised,
we might define o by saying that if every proposition
$\phi(a)$, $\phi(b)$ . . . is false, the number of the "values of x
which satisfy $\phi(x)$" is o, by definition.

We may then go on immediately to define 1, in terms
of the conceptions used in our definition of o, thus: 1 is
the number of "values" which satisfy $\phi(x)$ if (1) some
proposition of the form $\phi(a)$ is true, and (2) "$\phi(b)$ is
true" implies that b is identical with a. If this is the
definition of 1, we can proceed at once to define 2 thus:
2 is the number of values of x which satisfy $\phi(x)$, provided that (1) some proposition of the form $\phi(a)$ is true,
(2) some proposition of the form $\phi(b)$, where b is not
identical with a, is true, (3) if $\phi(c)$ is true, either c is
identical with a or c is identical with b.

More generally, when once the integer n has been
defined, we proceed to define its immediate successor
$n + 1$ by the conditions that $n + 1$ is the number of
values which satisfy $\phi(x)$ if (1) there are n distinct arguments a, b . . . n, such that $\phi(a)$ is true, $\phi(b)$ is true . . .
$\phi(n)$ is true; (2) $\phi(p)$ is true and p is not identical with a,

not identical with b, . . . not identical with n; (3) if $\phi(q)$ is true, either q is identical with a or is identical with b, . . . or is identical with n, or is identical with p. Thus, what I mean by saying that there were three triumvirs is that the two propositions, "Octavian was a triumvir", "Antony was a triumvir" are true (Octavian not being the same person as Antony); that the proposition "Lepidus was a triumvir" is true, and that Lepidus was not Octavian nor yet Antony; that if there is any person of whom it is true that he was a triumvir, that person is identical with Octavian, or identical with Antony, or identical with Lepidus. *E.g.* it is true that Augustus was a triumvir, but that is because Augustus was the same person as Octavian; it is true that M. Aemilius was a triumvir, because M. Aemilius was Lepidus; or, to put the matter in a different way, $n + 1$ is the number of members of a collection if it includes a collection with n members, if it has also a member which is not a member of this collection of n members, and if whatever is a member of it is identical either with some member of the collection of n or with the member, not included in the collection of n, mentioned in the last clause.

All this is wholly trite and familiar and I only repeat it here for the sake of making the following points clear. (1) the notion "a" or "an" is not the same as the notion "1", as is shown by the fact that we have to use it as part of the definition of 1. To put it quite popularly, "There is one reigning King of England" means "there is a reigning King of England—George V—*and there is no other*". (2) The notion of "any" is not the same as the notion of "all". It means "any you may please to take", "any which turns up", not "each and all". Hence we can employ it in cases where it might be doubtful whether we could speak of "all", a definite totality. In speaking, *e.g.*, of "any integer" we do not commit ourselves to the view that there are propositions which can be significantly made about "all integers" or "every integer". We can speak significantly of "any region of space" without by implication denying Prof. Alexander's view that space is not a "whole". This is why there is no logical fallacy involved in the use of the notion "an" as a datum presupposed in the definition of the integer 1; it is also why the notion of "an" by itself, without that of undefined plurality, would not be sufficient for the definition of 1, and why, for example, the belief that "there is a God" is not the same as the belief that God is one.

If the Platonic line of thought was really that which has been indicated, we can see that though, in a sense, it is true that the "material" of the integers is a "great-and-small" or "indefinite duality", in fact, the concept of indefinite multitude, the actual working-out of the thought has committed the double confusion of this duality or dyad with the integer 2, and of the antithetic notion of "an" with the integer 1. Were there no numbers but the integers to take into account, the older Pythagorean analysis which made the constituents of number limit and the unlimited and treated the "unit" or integer 1 as itself the simplest combination of these constituents might fairly be held to be more satisfactory than the amended version of it which presupposes 1, and apparently 2, as initial data calling for no derivation, and so enables Aristotle's criticism to get home. This seems to me good ground for supposing that the necessity of the modification was due to the fact that Plato and his friends started from the consideration of something other than the integers, and that their theory of the derivation of the integers was a further development motived by the desire to transfer to number as a whole a theory originally adapted to the special case of the irrationals. So long as the "real and rational" numbers are not distinguished from the integers, it is inevitable that, *e.g.*, the integers 2, 3 and the irrational real numbers $\sqrt{2}$, $\sqrt{3}$ should be regarded as terms of one and the same series subject to one and the same law of derivation. The confusion which seems to play havoc with the theory is one which could not have arisen if it were the case that all the values to which infinite series converge were irrational. The integers and the "real numbers" would then have stood out as two distinct series and there would have been no temptation to bring both under a single formula. And here, again, we may do a tardy justice to the stalwarts of the older tradition who, like Aristotle, insisted that though there may be irrational geometrical magnitudes ($\mu\epsilon\gamma\acute{\epsilon}\theta\eta$), there are no irrational $\dot{\alpha}\rho\iota\theta\mu o\acute{\iota}$. If their distinction on this point between geometry and arithmetic had been obstinately sustained by the mathematicians, the development of modern mathematics would have been impossible. The one-to-one correspondence of points in a plane with couples of real numbers which is the very foundation of Descartes' analytical geometry would have been ruled out. Yet, at bottom, there is a real justification for their protest against the "new" arithmetic of the Academy, though they do not express the justification in the right way. What they are trying to say is something which is quite true, that the integers and the real numbers are two distinct series and that no term of the one is a term of the other. The important principle embodied in the insistence on this radical distinction between $\dot{\alpha}\rho\iota\theta\mu o\acute{\iota}$ and $\mu\epsilon\gamma\acute{\epsilon}\theta\eta$ is that the real numbers cannot be obtained from a set of logical data by the method which yields us the series of integers, the "inference from n to $n + 1$", "mathematical induction".

This is both important and obvious. "Inference from
n to $n+1$" presupposes that $n+1$ has a determinate
meaning, *i.e.* that in a series derived by this method
every member has one determinate "immediately next"
member, as is the case with the integers. The integer-
series is the standing type of a "well-ordered" infinite
series, satisfying the conditions that there is a first term
of the whole series and that every term has one and
only one term which is next after it. It might appear, at
first sight, that the series of rational fractions does not
conform to the type, since there is, *e.g.*, no rational fraction which, in what we call the order of magnitude,
comes next to a given fraction, But, as is well known,
we may rearrange the rational fractions in such a way
that the condition is satisfied. Thus if I begin the series
thus, $\frac{0}{1}, \frac{1}{1}, \frac{0}{2}, \frac{1}{2}, \frac{2}{1}, \frac{2}{2}, \frac{0}{3}, \frac{1}{3}, \frac{2}{3}, \frac{3}{3}, \frac{3}{2}, \frac{3}{1}, \dots$, it is manifest
that I can continue the series endlessly and that by the
law of its formation, every term has a definite next following term, and that no rational fraction will appear
more than once, and none will be omitted. (The same
thing would be true, if for brevity's sake one suppressed all the fractions with o for their numerator after
$\frac{0}{1}$ and reduced all others to their "lowest terms".) Thus
the series of rational fractions can be made to correspond one-to-one to that of the integers, and so has the
same "ordinal number". But the case is altered when
we come to the real numbers. It is true that the "algebraical" real numbers, those which are the roots of
equations with integral indices and rational coefficients,
can be arranged as a well-ordered series, and that the
real numbers known to the Academy, the quadratic
and cubic surds, are only an infinitesimally small selection out of this multitude (Couturat, *De l'Infini mathématique*, 622 ff.). But when we take into account the
whole "real number" series, including the "transcend-

ent" as well as the "algebraical" real numbers, the correspondence with the integer-series breaks down. The continuum of real numbers appears definitely not to be a well-ordered series. Attempts have been made, including one by the late Philip Jourdain in *Mind*, to show that it must be possible to arrange it as one, but to the layman, like myself, these proofs have a suspicious appearance of assuming the conclusion, under a thin disguise, as a premise for its own demonstration, and they do not seem to have convinced the mathematicians. And it is suggestive that their authors never seem to have ventured to put their view to the test by producing a sample segment of the continuum of real numbers rearranged by their own methods. We may probably take it as certain that the continuum of all the real numbers is a series of a type different from that of the integers or any series whose terms can be made to correspond one-to-one with the integers. It is, at any rate, certain that we cannot logically derive the series from that of the integers by the methods by which we can develop the integer-series itself or derive from it the series of rationals or that of *algebraical* real numbers, which have the same type as the integer-series itself. Neither Aristotle nor the Platonists he criticises could have known this, but it is the real justification of his stubbornness in opposition to them, though it is amusing to recollect that, as we saw in our former study, the only "irrationals" with which Aristotle was acquainted, the quadratic and cubic surds, *can* be derived from the integers by the methods to which he objects and that the whole series of algebraical real numbers has the same type of order as the integers. The strength of his position on this point only appears when we take into consideration the "transcendent" numbers of which he could have had no conception. (Of course I am not forgetting the simple fact that a transcendent number can be expressed as the limit to which a series of rationals converges, as when we write $\dfrac{\pi}{4} = 1 - \frac{1}{3} + \frac{1}{5} - \frac{1}{7}$ ... *ad infin.* We could not calculate them, if this were not so. What I mean is that, on the one hand, such a series itself is not yielded by the method Plato appears to have contemplated, but presupposes acquaintance with the exponential and logarithmic functions, and, on the other, that the difference of order-type between the integers and the continuum of the real numbers is the vital difference embodied, though Aristotle could not know the fact, in his own contrast between ἀριθμοί and μεγέθη.)

To sum up, then, the main points I offer for consideration are these:

(1) The peculiar Platonic theory of the constitution of number probably originated in the conviction that the quadratic and cubic surds which figure in geometry, especially in the solid geometry created by Theaetetus, compel us to recognise "irrational numbers". As an historical point, we might conjecture that the prominence given to the topic of irrational μήκη in the *Theaetetus* may very possibly indicate that Theaetetus himself, in the Academy, influenced the development of Plato's convictions in this direction.

(2) Probably the character of the theory was determined by the fact that it started from knowledge of a rule for finding the successive "convergents" to $\sqrt{2}$, regarded as a "continued fraction". The anticipation was that all quadratic and cubic "surds" could be treated by this method, and it is from the alternation of convergents which are alternately too small and too large that the notion of the "indeterminate duality" has arisen.

(3) Owing to the fact that the values to which such infinite series converge need not be irrational, it was inevitable that the "rational" real numbers should be confused with the integers, and that the attempt should be made to extend the theory to the whole field of known numbers, the integers and the quadratic and cubic surds, regarded as a single series.

(4) But the extension to the integers involves a deformation of the theory which leads to confusion of "the One" and the "indeterminate dyad" with the integers 1 and 2, and the unfortunate assigning to this "dyad" of the function of "doubling", which should really have been connected with the "auto-dyad" or integer 2. It also involves deriving the integers in an arrangement other than their "natural" order, for two reasons. The powers of 2 have to precede the other integers of the decad, and further no odd number $2n + 1$ can appear until $2n$ and $2n + 2$ have already been obtained. A number $2n + 1$ will always follow *after* $2n + 2$.

(5) Hence Aristotle's criticisms, so far as they concern these features of the doctrine, are justified. There is also a certain justification, unknowable to Aristotle himself, for his insistence on the distinction between ἀριθμοί and μεγέθη.

(6) At the same time, the Platonic formulae, as applied to the integers themselves, correctly anticipate two important points of a true number theory, the necessity of a strict derivation of the integer-series from more fundamental logical notions and the logical independence of multiplication on addition.

(7) The identification of the forms (εἴδη) with numbers means that the "manifold" of nature is only accessible to scientific knowledge in so far as we can correlate its variety with definite numerical functions of "arguments". The "arguments" have then themselves

to be correlated with numerical functions of "arguments" of a higher degree. If this process could be carried through without remainder, the sensible world would be finally resolved into combinations of numbers, and so into the transparently intelligible. This would be the complete "rationalisation" of nature. The process cannot in fact be completed, because nature is always a "becoming", always unfinished; in other words, because there is real contingency. But our business in science is always to carry the process one step further. We can never completely arithmetise nature, but it is our duty to continue steadily arithmetising her. "And still beyond the sea there is more sea"; but the mariner is never to arrest his vessel. The "surd" never quite "comes out", but we can carry the evaluation a "place" further, and we must. If we will not, we become "ageometretes".

[1926]

IV

THE PHILOSOPHY OF PROCLUS

We have seen in recent years a remarkable awakening of intelligent interest in the Neo-Platonist philosophy which our grandfathers and their fathers were content to deride without understanding. We have learned that the Neo-Platonists were neither magicians nor emotionalist *schöne Seelen*, but systematic philosophers addressing themselves to the philosopher's task of understanding the world in which he lives as seriously as Aristotle or Descartes or Kant. No one writing to-day on the history of Greek thought about God, man, and nature would be likely to mistake so great a metaphysician as Plotinus for an apologist for polytheism or a New England *littérateur* born out of due time. Still the rehabilitation of the Neo-Platonists has hardly so far led to an adequate appreciation of Proclus, by far the most important member of the school after its great founder, though an honourable step has been taken in this direction by Mr. Whittaker.

This neglect of Proclus is unfortunate in more ways than one. For the historian of thought his importance is hardly second to that of Plotinus himself. It is in the main from him that Christianity received the Neo-Platonic impress still distinguishable in orthodox theology under all the disguise of a formal Aristotelianism. It is true that before the date of Proclus Christianity had been deeply influenced by Neo-Platonic ideas derived from Plotinus through such intermediaries as St. Augustine. But the main sources of the unmistakable Neo-Platonism in the great scholastic philosophers are two, the writings of the so-called Dionysius, themselves the work of some Christianised follower of Proclus, and the work *De causis*, commonly supposed in the Middle Ages, though St. Thomas was better informed, to be Aristotelian, though it is really a Latin rendering of an Arabic work based on the very treatise of Proclus to which I shall directly invite your attention. It was from these sources that the schoolmen of the golden thirteenth century derived the peculiar theory of causality upon which their conception of the Universe rests, and it is most instructive, as an illustration of the impossibility of drawing any real dividing line between ancient and modern thought, to find Descartes, in the very act of professing to construct a new way in philosophy, assuming as his fundamental principle and treating as evident "by the natural light" of the understanding just this same theory. Proclus again is the author of the only work that has come down to us in which the attempt is made to exhibit the main principles of the Neo-Platonic doctrine, in the strict order of their logical connection as a well-articulated whole. In many ways a student of Neo-Platonism would be well advised to begin his reading with the brief but pregnant Στοιχείωσις θεολογική or *Elements of Neo-Platonism* of which I am to speak this evening. He will find there, brought together in a compact form and expressed with a special view to logical precision, just the leading positions he requires to understand in order to find his way in the multitude of occasional essays we call the *Enneads* of Plotinus. He will also find that the style of the author presents far fewer difficulties. Proclus has, indeed, none of the splendid bursts of spiritual eloquence which at times carry the reader of Plotinus off his feet. His is emphatically the *sermo pedester*. But, by way of compensation, he makes no such demands on his reader as Plotinus in his uninspired moments. He neither defies the rules of grammar nor perplexes his sentences by Plotinus' trick of incessantly interweaving with his own words imperfectly quoted phrases from Plato. If you approach him with a decent working knowledge of Greek, you will find his style on the whole less difficult and less encumbered with technicalities than Aristotle's, and not more arid than, say, that of John Stuart Mill in English. If he is dry to the taste of many readers, it is only for the same reason that Mill's *Logic* is dry to readers of the same class; the nature of his subject requires him to pursue a train of close argumentation to its logical issue, and affords no scope for the eloquence which appeals to the imagination.

The one real difficulty which besets the student of the Στοιχείωσις is the wretched condition of the text.[1] As regards this, in some ways his most important book, Proclus has been most unfortunate in his editors. To the schoolmen only part of the work was known in the Latin version of William of Morbeke. Since the invention of printing, so far as I am aware, only two texts have been published. The Greek was first printed in 1618 by Aemilius Portus at the end of his folio edition of the much longer but infinitely less valuable *Six Books on the Theology of Plato*. Of Portus it is hard to speak worse than he deserved. His Greek text was made from bad manuscripts and swarms with errors equally fatal to grammar and to sense. The Latin version which accompanies it proves that he was quite incapable of translating even an uncorrupt and simple Greek original

---

[1] [Now remedied by the edition and translation of Professor E. R. Dodds. *Proclus, The Elements of Theology*, Clarendon Press, 1933.]

with any fidelity. The worst stumbling-block is created, however, by his wholly senseless method of punctuation. On the whole, Portus seems to have a preference for placing a full stop or even beginning a new paragraph in the middle of a sentence. The first translation into English was made from this execrable text in 1816 by that curious eccentric, Thomas Taylor, "the Platonist", and, so far as I know, there has never been a second until the praiseworthy but insufficient enterprise of Mr. Ionides. Taylor deserves great respect for his real devotion to Platonic studies, but as a translator he was badly handicapped by the hopeless badness of his text, and in an only less degree by his own want of Greek. His book is now very rare, and probably most of you may never have seen it.

In 1832 the *Elements* obtained a second editor, the notorious Frederic Creuzer, better known as responsible for the unsatisfactory but typographically beautiful Plotinus of the Oxford University Press. Creuzer was one of the mystagogues of Schelling's coterie, who professed to find the key to all philosophies in Orphic, Eleusinian, and Samothracian *orgia* of which they knew nothing and no one else much. He also stood in relations with Hegel, whose adulatory letters to him suggest some unpleasant doubt of that philosopher's competence to act as an expositor of things Hellenic. The whole brood of quacks to which Creuzer belonged, as I may remind you, was finally blown into the air by the scathing exposure of Lobeck's immortal *Aglaophamus*. Creuzer, had he been less incompetent, might perhaps have produced a decent text of the *Elements*, as he received from Schweighäuser the readings of a manuscript then at Strassburg which corrects many of the worst faults and fills up many of the lacunae of the inferior MSS. on which Portus had relied. Unfortunately, Creuzer knew very little Greek, and thought he knew a good deal. Hence, though he inevitably made a great advance on Portus by adopting many of the readings furnished by Schweighäuser, he rejected to his notes scores of others which should have been adopted. A conscientious editor would, of course, have made or caused to be made a complete collation of Schweighäuser's MS., but it is not clear from Creuzer's prefatory account of his own proceedings whether he did more than record such readings as he thought fit. What is worse, he retained the sense-destroying paragraphing and punctuation of his predecessor, and, though he professed to have revised the Latin version of the Greek, very little examination shows that, while removing some bad errors, he introduced a goodly number on his own account, so that his rendering is often a mere trap for the confiding and unwary.[1] The text has not been edited since Creuzer, and the Strassburg MS. was lost in the siege of 1870. At the present moment, any reader who is to understand his author requires to construct a working text for himself by the aid of such light as Creuzer's records of the readings of the Strassburg MS. afford.[2] Fortunately, the *usus et norma loquendi* of the author enable this to be done with a reasonable approach to certainty in all matters of moment.

I propose in the following pages to give some general account of the method and contents of Proclus' work, leaving the task of criticism to others. It should, of course, be remembered that the doctrine expounded is not, except on one or two points, peculiar to the author.

---

[1] Creuzer re-edited the text, many years later, and no more satisfactorily, for the firm of Didot. We have had to wait until 1933 for Professor Dodds to produce a text founded on real knowledge of the MSS.

[2] Happily, since the appearance of Professor Dodds's text, this statement is no longer true.

His object is to give a compendious summary of the
principles of the whole Neo-Platonic school, and in the
main the doctrines expounded are those which were
held in common by all the thinkers who looked back to
Plotinus as the restorer of what they took to be the
philosophy of Plato. There are perhaps only two points
on which Proclus diverges from Plotinus, both duly
recorded by Mr. Whittaker. Like most of the later
members of the school, Proclus rejects the possibility,
admitted by Plotinus, that the soul may lead a double
life, lapsing, as the phrase was, from eternity into time
and mutability only in her least worthy elements, while
her higher and nobler activities remain in the purely
spiritual world "unfallen". Proclus, like nearly all the
Neo-Platonists from the time of Iamblichus, maintains
in the last proposition of his book that the soul, when
she "falls", falls wholly and in every part. This modification of the doctrine of Plotinus, as Mr. Whittaker
has said, seems to have been due, at any rate in part, to
reaction against what was felt as an over-strained
idealism. Even to his devotees Plotinus seemed to be
preaching an other-worldliness which was not quite
wholesome. It is the same feeling which comes out in
the commentary on the *Republic*, where Proclus makes
a vigorous defence of the Homeric stories and the
tragic drama against the censures of Plato's Socrates.
But there was also a sound logical reason for the revision of the older view; the theory of Plotinus was felt
to be inconsistent with the unity of human personality.
It involved something like what our Anglo-Hegelians
call a "faculty psychology", and it is on this ground
that Proclus rejects it in the *Elements*. You cannot reconcile the unity of our mental life with the distinction
between a "fallen" and an "unfallen" part in the soul.

More important, and much more difficult to inter-

pret, is a doctrine which appears in the very middle of
the book, and affects the whole subsequent exposition,
the doctrine of the divine Henads or Unities which
Proclus identifies with the "gods many" of Hellenic
religion. On the probable meaning of this doctrine—
which appears to be peculiar to Proclus[1]—and the
reasons for insisting upon it, I hope to offer a suggestion
in the right place. For the moment I must be content
to introduce my digest of Proclus' metaphysics by some
general remarks on the method and arrangement of his
manual.

Perhaps I need hardly say that Proclus will wholly
disappoint a reader who comes to him eager to hear
about ecstasies and other abnormal psychological
wonders. These things belong to the personal religious
life, not to philosophy. Even in Plotinus, for all his
personal saintliness, the passages where the mystical
"rapt" is dwelt on are few and far between, and there
is no suggestion that it is attended with any of the
abnormal psychological excitements on which the
adepts and *illuminati* lay stress, and in a logical exposition of the metaphysical doctrine of the school there is
no occasion to mention ecstasy at all. In philosophy, as
Mr. Whittaker has rightly said, the Neo-Platonists are
from first to last rationalists. Like Descartes, they believe themselves to have found a strictly logical and
coherent theory of God, Man, and Nature, and they
are as ready as any other philosophers who have ever
lived to expound their reasons for their convictions.
The manner and method of Proclus are, in fact, much
those of the great rationalists of the seventeenth century
from Descartes to Leibniz and Locke. In method, in

---

[1] (Prof. Dodds has, however, made out a strong case for the view that the
actual author of this doctrine was Syrianus, the immediate teacher of Proclus.
See *Elements of Theology*, p. xxiv. 257 ff.)

particular, he recalls at once two famous names in modern philosophy, Spinoza and Hegel. Of Spinoza, he reminds us by the care with which his method is based on that of Euclid and the geometers, of Hegel by his insistence upon the grouping of notions in triads. These resemblances, however, must not blind us to equally important differences. As far as regards the use of the "geometric method" goes, its employment is, of course, not peculiar to Spinoza; nor is there really anything specifically geometrical about it. It is merely the method known to the ancient mathematicians as synthesis, the systematic exhibition of a body of truths in the order of increasing logical complexity, the simplest being placed first, and the more complex exhibited as a series of successive deductions from them. It is thus the natural method of any thinker who has to expound a system of true propositions, and is concerned not with the historical problem of showing how they were originally discovered, but with the purely logical problem of indicating the implications which hold between them. It used at one time to be thought that there was some special connection between the matter of Spinoza's *Ethics*, and the method adopted for exhibiting it. This is, of course, a mere misapprehension. Any body of demonstrable propositions can be thrown into the form of the "geometrical method". Spinoza had been preceded in its use by Descartes, who gave, in the *Answers* to the objections against his *Meditations*, a formal "geometrical" proof of the real distinction between body and mind, and Spinoza's own first use of the method was to employ it on an exposition of Cartesian doctrine with which, as he candidly avowed, he did not himself wholly agree. Proclus uses it precisely because it is the method now called the "hypothetical-deductive", originated by Zeno and explained at length by

Socrates in the *Phaedo* of Plato. It consists simply in putting forward a theory or hypothesis, or set of postulates, as the explanation of a group of "appearances".

The consequences of the "hypothesis" are deduced at length, for the purpose of seeing whether they accord with the "appearances". If they do, the appearances are said to be "saved"; if they do not, some other hypothesis must be discovered which will save them. In the case of Proclus the appearances to be "saved" are just the whole body of all that we know, or think we know, about the things in the Universe, and the justification of his philosophical postulates is that these known truths about minds, souls, and bodies are "saved" in their entirety by the postulates of Neo-Platonism. (There is, of course, no question of dismissing the "appearances" as illusions or transmuting and transforming them into something other than what they are. We are throughout kept faithful to the principle enunciated by Butler in what is perhaps the most weighty single sentence ever uttered by any philosopher: "Everything is what it is and not another thing".) Proclus believes that his postulates do in fact "save" all the appearances and are therefore true, but there is no miraculous virtue about the mere use of the method. If you start with false premises, it will not prevent you from drawing conclusions which are also false. Spinoza, too, understood this quite well, as is shown by his use of the method in an exposition of Descartes where it brings out results which are false in Spinoza's opinion precisely because it has relied on false premises. As a point of history, it was the geometers of the Alexandrian age who took over the synthetic method with much else from the philosophy of Plato, not the philosophers who borrowed it from the mathematicians.

As to the parallel with Hegel, again, it is instructive

to observe precisely how far it holds. Proclus, like Hegel, believes that the triadic arrangement reproduces in thought the order of the links by which the richest of realities, the *ens realissimum*, is connected with the poorest and meanest. Only, in spite of appearances, he really begins at the end of the ladder where Hegel left off. Hegel, you will remember, opens his *Logic* with the notion of *Being*, on the ground that it is the most empty, abstract, and insignificant of all concepts, and works up gradually through increasingly fully determined concepts to the Absolute Spirit, the most significant of all. Proclus, on the other hand, begins with an even simpler concept than Being, Unity, or the One —precisely because he believes it to be, like God in the philosophy of the Christian schools, the richest and fullest of all concepts—and works downwards from it through the successive series of Minds, Souls, and Bodies to what he regards as the poorest. Again the method by which successive triads are found is widely different from Hegel's,—to my own thinking, not for the worse. Hegel's method, as we know, was first to take a concept, next to discover a contradictory opposite for it, and then to look for a third which could be plausibly represented as contradicting the contradiction. The procedure of Proclus is less heroic, but more readily intelligible. He usually arrives at a triad by first calling attention to two members A and B, which are doubly disjunct. A, that is, has the characters x and y, B those of not-x and not-y. He then argues that if A and B are both found as terms of a serial order of connected concepts, they cannot be in immediate juxtaposition. There must be an intermediary which resembles A, let us say, in having the character y and B in having the character not-x. The full reason for insisting on this necessity of an intermediate link between two doubly disjunct terms will only appear as we come to speak of the logically most important thing in the system, the Neo-Platonic doctrine of Causality. The importance of this theory can hardly be exaggerated, though it is one of the pleasant ironies of history that Proclus' exposition of it should have provided the Christian religion, which he so heartily disliked, with just the instrument it needed for the elaboration of its doctrine of God, and should a second time have given Descartes the basis of the argument for the existence of God without which he could not take the first step beyond the mere affirmation of his own existence.

It has been truly said by Mr. Whittaker that the general theory of the world which Proclus elicits from his initial postulates forms something like a *via media* between Leibniz and Spinoza. We have a Monism with an Absolute as the logical and causal *prius* of every-thing but itself, but just because Proclus goes farther back than Spinoza in his quest for a simple first prin-ciple, the Absolute is a theistic Absolute, a trans-cendent Deity who is the source of existents, their char-acters and the relations between them.

We meet with *causa sui* and *substantia* (if we may take the latter as a rendering of the Greek οὐσία), but they are not the Absolute; their place is a secondary one. There are also monads of various orders, but, since the Neo-Platonist theory of causality makes all causality transitive—even in the case of the *causa sui*—the monads are not "windowless" and we escape all the paradoxes connected with the Pre-Established Har-mony and its ambiguous relation to God's "choice of the best". For the same reasons we are left free to accept at their full value all the familiar facts which tell so powerfully in favour of an Interactionist theory of the relation of Mind and Body. Moreover, the very

insistence on the transcendent character of the Deity
and the transitiveness of Causality make it possible,
against Spinoza, to assert the permanent reality of individual souls, and against Leibniz the genuine reality
of brute inanimate matter. The Neo-Platonist philosophy thus aims at uniting coherently the strongest
points in what are commonly thought the incompatible
doctrines of Monism and Monadism. As the choice
seems to lie between Monism and Monadism for all of
us who can find no refuge either in Kantian Agnosticism or in some pure Materialism, the type of view
represented by the epitome of Proclus may perhaps
fairly claim to have more than a merely antiquarian
interest.

I shall probably succeed best in the attempt to give
an account of the Neo-Platonist metaphysics at once
concise and reasonably intelligible to students of philosophy who have no previous acquaintance with Neo-
Platonist literature by allowing myself to sit rather
loose to the actual terminology and order of the propositions of Proclus, and to deal only with the central
conceptions of the system. It will be found that the
notions of chief importance in the development of the
system are those of the transcendent character of the
One, the ultimate source of the Universe, and its
identity with the Good which, as Plato had taught, is
at once the motive power throughout the life-history of
the Universe and the goal or aim of all processes, the
causal relation which connects the One with the various
stages of its evolution, and every stage with every other,
the principal stages of this evolution, or, as the Neo-
Platonists call it, "progression", and the process of
"inversion" or "reflection" which is always found
associated with progression and serves to make the
system formed by the One and its manifestations into a

complete and harmonious whole. If we take our main topics in this order, the One, Causality, Progression, Inversion, we shall not indeed be following the order of Proclus quite exactly, but we shall not depart very far from the main structural outlines of his work.

He begins then, as was natural to a Platonist who had the *Philebus* well-nigh by heart and had commented at enormous length on the *Parmenides*, with the earliest and most stubbornly persistent of all philosophical antitheses, that of the One and the Many, which had, in fact, dominated all Greek thought from the time that it was first insisted upon by Parmenides and Zeno. The two conceptions of unity and plurality are not, strictly speaking, co-ordinate. Logically, and therefore ontologically also, the One is antecedent to the Many because it is involved in the very conception of a Many or Aggregate or Assemblage ($\pi\lambda\hat{\eta}\theta os$), that it is, to use the old Pythagorean and Euclidean definition $\pi\lambda\hat{\eta}\theta os\ \mu o\nu\acute{a}\delta\omega\nu$, an Assemblage of units. It is the same thought which leads Leibniz to begin his *Monadology* with the proposition that the complex presupposes the simple. A modern mathematical logician would hardly be satisfied with the form of Proclus' proof, which, as is common with him, is a *reductio ad absurdum* based on the alleged impossibility of an infinite regress. The real point is, however, independent of this assumption, and amounts to the contention that a well-ordered series must at least have a first term, though it need have no other, or again that all complexes, even if their degree of complexity be infinite, must, as Leibniz said, be complexes of individuals. To take other illustrations of the same principle, if logical classes are to "exist", there must be at least one thing which is not a class but an individual, if "classes of classes" are to "exist" there must be at least one class which is a class not of classes but of individuals; if truths of what Russell calls the "first order" are to be possible, there must be at least one thing which is not a true proposition but an individual about which a proposition can be made; if there are to be truths of the second order, there must be at least one truth of the first order, and so on *in indefinitum*.

The propositions which follow furnish the basis for a Philosophy of Transcendence as opposed to all "immanence doctrines" of the ἓν καὶ πᾶν type. Whatever "partakes of the one", *i.e.* whatever can have oneness predicated about it, is in a sense "one thing", but in a sense also not-one or many. As our Anglo-Hegelians say, it is one in virtue of being a *whole* of parts, not-one or many in virtue of being a whole of *parts*. It is a unity but it is not Unity. The oneness we ascribe to such wholes must be something other than any of them. This is why Plato and the Platonists say that they *are* not "one" but "partake of" the One. What follows prepares the way for the enunciation of the theory of Causality. Whatever produces anything other than itself (*i.e.* is the source of its existence) is superior in kind to that which is produced. This is the principle implied in the characteristic Neo-Platonic conception of evolution as "progression" or "emanation" (a word, by the way, which is not with Plotinus and Proclus a technicality but an illustrative metaphor). It is also the principle denied by every philosophy which treats *epigenesis* as the final word in evolutionary theory. The proof of this proposition is interesting, and depends on the implied assumption that causality is a transitive relation and that its terms are substantival entities, not events. Either the entity produced by a causal agent is itself capable of producing something further, or it is not. If it is not, this very fact establishes its inferiority to its own cause. If it is, its effects are either superior to, equal to, or inferior to itself. The second possibility may be excluded as it leads to the conclusion that there is no hierarchy of better and worse, no difference in levels of value, among things, and this is assumed to be plainly at variance with the "appearances". The third possibility is that evolution is a steady process of epigenesis by which the inferior gives rise to the superior. But this, too, is unthinkable. For if an agent could produce certain perfections in that on which he acts, he could equally have produced at least as much perfection in himself, since, *ex hypothesi*, he had sufficient power, and his failure cannot be due to lack of will, since by a universal law all things tend to attain the Good as far as their powers reach. (This, it will be recollected, is the reason given by Descartes for holding that he is not himself the perfect being.) Universally, then, the cause from which anything derives at once its being and its specific character is higher in the scale of goodness than its own effects.

Further, from the Platonic principle that all Beings seek for the Good, and their whole life is determined by the pursuit of it along the lines possible to them in virtue of their various specific constitutions, it follows that the Supreme Good, the first term in an ordered hierarchy of goods, cannot itself be one of these Beings or the totality of them. Just because it is what all beings strive to obtain, it must be beyond them all. It must be, as Plato had put it in the famous passage of the *Republic*, ἐπέκεινα οὐσίας, "on the other side of Being". It cannot be a "good something" but must be just "the Good", that whose whole character is goodness and nothing else. Good is not a predicate of it; Good *is* it. It needs only the further step of identification of the Good, thus conceived, with the One, that is the identification of the

Universal End with the Universal Source, to convert
the logic of Proclus into a theistic theology agreeing
with that of the Christian Church, in looking on God
as a transcendent Being distinct from the Universe or
whole of creatures and internally simple, not like an
Herbartian "real" or the "bare monad" from the
poverty of His nature, but just because all the perfections which are found in diffusion among His creatures
are wholly concentrated and interpenetrant in their
source. This is, in fact, what the schoolmen mean when
they tell us that *Deus est suum esse*, and again that each
"attribute" of God is God Himself. We are specially
warned against confusing the Good with the "self-
sufficing". A self-sufficing being can, indeed, meet all
its needs out of the plenitude of its internal resources;
it can live, so to say, by the consumption of its own fat.
But the very statement implies that such a being *has*
needs, though it can always meet them. *The* Good,
being "good" *simpliciter*, has no needs to meet. We
must not mistake it for a magnified Stoic Cato. We may
not even say of it, that it is "filled with good". It *is*
Good, and therefore must be called, as Proclus more
than once calls it, "more than full", ὑπερπλῆρες. The
epithet seems meant to indicate the Neo-Platonist
answer to the obvious question why there should be a
Universe at all. Why should the Good not be alone to
all eternity in a state of single and perfect blessedness?
How comes there to be a world of creatures who aspire
to it? The Neo-Platonist explanation is that which Plato
had long before put into the mouth of Timaeus. Goodness is, of its very nature, a self-imparting or self-
communicating activity. It cannot keep itself to itself,
but *must* overflow, much as Christians have said the
same thing of love. Unlike Christian theologians,
Plotinus and Proclus do not represent the creative

activity in which Goodness finds its outlet as one of "free choice". To them this would have implied that Goodness might conceivably not have imparted itself to anything, and therefore might not have been wholly good. Finally, they agree with Spinoza that God acts *ex legibus suae naturae*, though, unlike him, they are stout assertors of Providence and Final or Intentional Causality, and are careful to treat Free Will (τὸ αὐτεξ-ούσιον) as a reality. The difference between them and Spinoza is really much greater than their divergence from the thought of Christian scholastics. Indeed, this latter divergence is much reduced when we recollect that, according to the schools, neither free choice nor anything else can be *universally* asserted of God and of any creature. The difference from Spinoza goes deeper. For Proclus would understand by the "laws of God's nature", the law of *Goodness*, whereas in Spinoza it is no part of the nature of *Deus-substantia* to be good, and even the distinction between good and bad in human character and conduct comes perilously near being dismissed as an illusion in the famous appendix to the first Part of the *Ethics*.

The formal identification of the One with the Good —derived, of course, from Plato himself—which turns Proclus' "First Cause" into God is effected by the help of the famous definition of Eudoxus, "the good is that at which all things aim". Such a good or end of appetition is manifestly a principle of unification and co-operation. Health, for instance, is the body's good, and health is just the harmonious organisation of all the constituents and members of the body. *Salus populi* is the good of a society of men, and it is realised in virtue of the *conatus* or *nisus*, conscious or otherwise, of each member of the body politic after it. Wherever you find good you find it as a common object of appetition to the members of a πλῆθος, and it is this *nisus* after one and the same end which makes the πλῆθος a unity-in-multitude. So, if the creatures really form a Universe—and it is the presumption involved alike in thought and action that they do—it is because all of them are striving up to "the measure of the light vouchsafed" towards a common principle of Good which is beyond and above them all. It sounds a paradox, but it is thus the fact, that the One is the unifying principle in the Universe just because it is itself not "in" the Universe but "beyond" it. The general line of thought is thus very similar to that which is followed by Professor Varisco in the last chapter of his *Massimi Problemi*, where he sets himself to argue that the question whether the Universe as a whole, has value (is good) or not depends upon the prior question whether, as he phrases it, "Being has other determinations than the concretes, in which case the traditional conception of Being is transformed into the Christian conception of God". Proclus answers this question affirmatively; it is a matter of terminology that what Professor Varisco speaks of as "determinations of Being other than the concretes", are called by Proclus ὑπερούσια, the things "above" being.

At this point, it will be convenient for a moment to desert the actual order of our author's exposition, which is designed with a view to preparing for the distinctions to be drawn between Minds, Souls, and Bodies, and anticipate a little by explaining the doctrine of Causality upon which his further account of the Universe depends. Causality, as I said before, is always, to the Neo-Platonists, a transitive relation. It implies two related terms, the producer (τὸ παράγον) and the produced (τὸ παραγόμενον), and these are never events.

The cause or producer is always an agent or the

activity of an agent; the effect produced may be the
existence of an individual or a quality of an individual,
or both. As the relation is not one between events, it is
not necessary that it should involve temporal sequence,
and the Neo-Platonists were thus free to maintain with
Aristotle that the historical sequence of events has no
beginning. That the Good is the Great First Cause,
means with them simply that everything depends, both
for its existence and its special character, on the Good;
but for the Good there would be nothing. It does not
mean that there was a time when the Good was not
"overflowing", and there was no world of creatures.
Further, the way in which the agent or cause works is
by imparting its own characteristics to that of which it
is the cause. This is, of course, because *operari sequitur
esse*, and it is in virtue of being what it is, that a cause
causes just such effects as it does and no others. The
effect is thus "like" its cause, or an "image" of it, but
since, as we have already seen, it is a cardinal point in
the system that what is produced is always an inferior
and imperfect image of what produces it, the causal
relation is asymmetrical, and Proclus thus agrees with
Russell on the fundamental importance of asymmetrical relations. As Proclus and Plotinus are fond of
putting it, the cause is imperfectly "mirrored" in its
effects. It irradiates them, but they are at best broken
lights of it. The Neo-Platonists would have been only
in imperfect sympathy with the numerous modern
philosophers who have maintained that the relation of
cause and effect is really identical with the logical relation of antecedent and consequent. They would have
agreed that the cause is always the "reason why", since,
in their view, the causal relation is always a case of
"participation"; the effect is what it is because the cause
is what *it* is. But they would never have admitted either

M

that temporal sequence is an illusion or that to complete insight it would be possible to reason from effect to cause with the same certainty as to effect from cause, precisely because they hold that the effect *is* not the cause but only "participates" in it, and therefore only mirrors it partially. On their view there is always more in the cause than is ever reflected in the effect. It is notable that Proclus is careful to warn us that the transitivity of the relation is not done away with, even in the case of things which may be said to be "self-caused" (αὐθυπόστατα), because they contain in themselves the source of their own motions. As we know from Plato, this is the case with all souls, and it is the defining *proprium* of a soul, in contradistinction from all other existents, that it has "its principle of movement within itself", or is "that which can move *itself*". Even here, the Neo-Platonists, following the lead of Aristotle, say that though the terms of the causal relation are identical, it is still a dyadic relation and transitive. For this reason *causa sui* cannot, as with Spinoza, be identified with the "great first cause". The One, because its Oneness *is* itself, is not *causa sui*. It is simply uncaused.

Strictly speaking, the phrases self-moving or self-caused (αὐτοκίνητος) must not even be used of Intelligence or Mind, for Intelligence or Mind is (as Aristotle had held) something which remains itself unmoved or unchanged, but gives rise to the internally initiated changes in the soul. Hence, by putting the *causa sui* at the head of his hierarchy Spinoza is, from the point of view of Proclus, opening his account of things in the middle. He can only take into his reckoning Souls and the Bodies which are moved by those Souls. He has left out of consideration all that is really of highest moment in the universal order.

A last point of fundamental importance in this doctrine of Causality is that, as Proclus is careful to state, the higher up in the hierarchy a cause is, the lower down the scale are its effects felt. The reason is that what comes nearer to the Absolute One in the scale is, being a truer reflection of the One, a unifying principle of higher order than what is more remote. Hence the unifying power of the One or Good extends to the whole Universe. Everything in the Universe, down to the mere unformed matter which is the ideal lower limit of dispersion and lack of organisation, derives its being from the One or Good. As Socrates said, everything is, and is what it is, because it is best that it should be so. The activity of Mind does not reach so far down, precisely because Mind is not itself the supreme or divine principle, but merely its most immediate reflection. We can, indeed, satisfy ourselves of this by the simple consideration that Mind does not make matter. It is true that order and structure are everywhere put into matter, even into inanimate matter, by Mind. For Divine Providence extends to the inorganic as well as to the organic world, and again human intelligence, which within its own limits mirrors Providence, shows itself constantly at work shaping inorganic matter by the introduction of form. But Matter is not existentially dependent on Mind; it is something which from the point of view of Mind is *vorgefunden* as an instrument of expression, not created by Mind itself. There is no ultimate dualism in the system, since Minds and all the things which are existents are alike existentially dependent on the transcendent One or Good: but if you forget the One, and start with Mind as your *ens realissimum*, you will be led to such a dualism, just because Mind is found everywhere correlated with an object, not Mind, to which it is related alike as knower and as organising principle. It is just by not accepting

Idealism in the modern sense, by not equating the *ens realissimum* with Mind, that the Neo-Platonists avoid dualism.

Again, the Soul is a less adequate mirroring of the One than its Mind or Intelligence. In fact, the Soul directly mirrors Mind or Intelligence, and reflects the One only at second-hand. And again we see that the causal activity of the Soul ceases to show itself before that of Mind. The activity of the Soul consists, in fact, precisely in communicating to another its own *proprium*, life. It is just the principle of life, and what it does to things is to bestow life on them, to endow them with the special kind of unity and organisation characteristic of organisms. Now not all bodies are capable of receiving this kind of unity and structure, but only some. There is organic matter, but there is also inorganic matter, and on dead or "inorganic" matter the Soul can exercise no influence. It can mould to its own ends the protoplasm of which our bodies are formed; it cannot dwell in or "inform" stocks and stones. But Mind, as we have seen, can give form to inorganic matter. A cabinet-maker or a statuary can not merely beget sons and daughters, but he can also, because he is not only an animal but an intelligent one, fashion cabinets or statues out of boards and stones. So universally, the higher the rank of a causal agent the more far-reaching are its effects, and, in particular, we may say of the Good which stands outside the whole series of existents and is above "being" that there is a sense in which *its* effects extend beyond the realm of existents and affect what is "below" being. For, as we have seen, inorganic bodies fill the lowest place in the system of existents. The "bare matter" which we are constrained to think of as that which is common to them all is never found actually existing.

It is like the limit of an infinite absolutely convergent series, to which each successive term makes a closer approximation, though it never appears itself as a term of the series, or, to be more precise, it is like the limit of an infinite series whose terms, though all positive, tend to zero. Thus, as Aristotle had held, such mere matter may be called μὴ ὄν, "the non-existent", and can only be conceived by way of negation. Just as God is implicitly thought of by Neo-Platonists and Christian schoolmen as a simple being, who is at the same time the subject of all positive predicates, "bare matter" is a simple being which is the subject of no positive predicates. Yet the One stands in causal relation even with this mere negation. It is because of the presence of the One that what exists is not this bare potentiality of being something, in other words, that there really is something and not nothing. The idealist of the modern type is naturally tempted to call this shadowy universal "substrate" or "first matter", which is nothing in particular, a "creation" or "fiction" of our minds, but the Aristotelian and Neo-Platonic thought seems to me the truer. Of course we only arrive at the notion by a process of comparison and abstraction, but comparison, if we consider it rightly, only discovers, it never creates. That there is something common to the most elementary existents, which is never found itself actually existing, is a discovery. If the "something common" were not really there, no process of comparison would ever conduct us to it; comparison would be, as the Anglo-Hegelians say abstraction is, always falsification.

It is a corollary of this conception of causality that a predicate may be said to be contained in its subject in any one of three ways. Since a cause is mirrored in its effect, i.e. its activity consists in imparting its own character, so far as that is possible, to the effect, whatever is characteristic of the effect may already be said to be contained in the cause. It is not there exactly as it is in the effect, since the effect is an imperfect image of the cause. In the cause the character of the effect is present "in a more perfect manner", in intimate conjunction with other characters which do not appear in that particular effect, but only in other effects of the same cause. To borrow Leibniz' metaphor the effects of a cause are perspectives, each reproducing the cause from one special point of view. In the effect itself the character in question is said to exist καθ' ὕπαρξιν—*i.e.* it is strictly only of the effect that we can *predicate* the character in question. (The expression καθ' ὕπαρξιν is obviously coined by analogy with the use of the verb ὑπάρχειν in Aristotelian logic, where A ὑπάρχει τῷ B is the standing way of saying *B* is an *A*, or *A* is predicable of *B*.) In the effects of the effect, the same character again will be found imperfectly mirrored or represented, or, as Proclus says, "by participation". In scholastic Latin these distinctions are carefully kept up. The characters of an effect are said to be "formally" in itself, but "eminently" in its cause; Descartes' familiar assertion that what is thus "formally" in the object of an idea is "objectively" in the idea itself is a simple special case of the presence of a character "by participation" in the effects of the cause which has the character "formally", since the idea is held by Descartes to be caused by its object. The special Cartesian proof of the existence of God from my possession of the idea of God thus is proved by its very terminology to be a simple reproduction of Neo-Platonism as put into technical form by Proclus. Presumably all this Neo-Platonism reached Descartes through the medium of scholastic philosophy in his early days at Rennes, and this is why he supposed what he had been taught as a school-

boy to be so evident by the natural light of the understanding.

We can now formulate very briefly the general Neo-
Platonic conception of the world of existents and its
relation to its single internally simple, transcendent
cause, or source, the Good. It is of the nature of the
Good to overflow its own banks, to bestow itself on
something else, and this is the real answer to the questions, why there are existents at all, and why they form
an ordered and connected universe. The overflow is by
way of representation; the Good gives rise to a system
of existents which imperfectly mirror or image its own
goodness, and they in turn to "appearances" which imperfectly mirror them. It is to be noted that the imperfection of the mirroring, as Proclus tells us, is due to the
inevitable defects of the mirror. If the actual world is
not perfect, this is not due to any withholding of perfection from it by the Good. The Good is present to all
things in its super-plenitude, but they cannot receive
all that it has to give. They receive "according to their
own constitution". It is with perfection as the Scottish
divine admired by Johnson and Boswell said that it is
with happiness: the quart pot and the pint pot are both
full, but they do not contain the same measure; each is
as full as it can hold. This is, of course, an inevitable
inference from the general conception of causation as a
process of imaging, or, what is the same thing, the
principle that there is always greater excellence in the
cause than its effect. (Fully thought out the principle
would have led Christian theologians who accepted
Neo-Platonism as their philosophic basis to an Arian
doctrine of the Trinity: The Son, being the "image of
the Father", would have been "inferior to the Father"
not only "as touching His manhood" but also "as
touching His godhead".) The doctrine of Plotinus had

been that the immediate "image" of the Good is Mind
(νοῦς), and the immediate image of Mind is Soul (ψυχή),
and that Mind is thus the highest member of the chain
of actual existents. *I.e.* Mind is the highest kind of
individuality which we find as an actual existent. Mere
Soul, as we know it, *e.g.* in ourselves when we are at the
mercy of irrational passion or impulse, or again in the
immature who have not yet "found themselves", or still
more as we discern it in the lower animals, is still less
of a real complete and stable unity. The triad thus
formed by the One, Mind and Soul is the only example
of a triad in the *Enneads*. One must note carefully also
that Mind and the objects of its thought (the world as
apprehended by science) together make up the whole
of what can be properly called real existents (ὄντα),
and that Mind and its objects are inseparable. "The
objects of Mind (τὰ νοητά) do not subsist outside Mind"
was the doctrine thought by Porphyry to be peculiarly
characteristic of Plotinus, and it was precisely his stubborn doubts about this tenet which delayed his entrance
into the school of Plotinus until he had written a
criticism which was in turn refuted to his own satisfac-
tion by an earlier disciple. By this doctrine it is not
meant that the objects known by Mind are themselves
mental in the sense that they are made of "mental
states" or "processes". What is meant is that the distinction between the epistemological subject and the
epistemological object is not regarded as characteristic
of the interior life—if we may call it so—of the Absolute
One. It emerges first in the first image of that life,
which is the life of Mind. The life of Mind is always a
knower's attitude towards a known—the concept and
the thinker of the concept are inseparable, not—to borrow a distinction familiar to readers of Professor Ward
—in a psychological, but in an epistemological sense.

Actual existence then consists of Mind and what Mind knows. When we come to the life of the mere soul, not as yet rationalised, we are at a lower level. It is, compared with the waking vision of science, a sort of confused dream. Like the dreamer, the Soul, as mere soul, is itself perplexed and confused, and there is the same confusion in the object of its cognition and striving. It is a thing itself not realised moving about in a world unrealised. It belongs and its world belongs to "becoming"—the region where everything is perpetually baffling us by proving not to be what it seemed to be— not to "being".

Proclus refines something on the original statement of the doctrine. Within the primary triad itself we have to distinguish a subordinate triad. On inspection, Being, which Plotinus had treated as equivalent to Mind, breaks up into the triad of Being, Life, and Mind. For many things are, which are lifeless, and again many living things are not minds. But of this, as of the other triadic constructions which figure in rather confusing multitude in the elaborate *Six Books on the Theology of Plato*, it is not necessary to say much in a mere brief sketch like the present. Roughly, the successive more and more imperfect reflections or images of the Good may be said to be, in order of increasing imperfection, Mind, and Soul (the former being eternal both in its nature and its activity, the latter eternal in nature but temporal in its activity, and both together making up "what is"), and finally Body—temporal at once in nature and in its activities, which is what "seems", though we must remember that what "seems" really does "seem". Body as such has its place in the system: it has not to be "transmuted" or "absorbed" into something else as a condition of recognition.

Further, we must add that as Proclus conceives the

world, each member of this series gives rise to something other than itself in two different ways, or along two different lines. The source of this conception is manifest. There are many individual minds, souls and bodies in the Universe, and it does not occur to the Neo-Platonists to explain away this plurality of individuals of different types as an illusion. It is a fact which must take its place as a fact in an adequate philosophy. Hence Proclus conceives of Mind and Soul, not merely as units each of which can be "imaged" by a unit of a lower type, Mind by Soul and Soul by Body, but as first terms of series. His doctrine is that in each such series the first member generates a series of beings of the same type as itself, though each, according to its distance in serial order from the first term, is a less adequate representative of the type. There are thus, at the level of Mind, a whole series of more or less exalted Minds, and similarly, at the lower levels, a whole series of Souls and a whole series of Bodies of greater or less worth and dignity. The first member of each such series is called ἀμέθεκτος, imparticipable,[1] that is unpredicable, because it is in the strictest sense only capable of appearing in a proposition as subject and can never be predicate. (Even Descartes at the stage of reflection reached by examination of the *cogito* can only say I am *a* mind, not I am Mind.) The rest of the series are the "participated" minds or "souls". Thus, in the case of minds, the first member of the series is Mind with the capital M, the other are *the* minds of the various beings who are said each to "have" a mind.

This theory is obviously applicable to the Good or One, no less than to Mind or Soul. If Mind gives rise not only to Soul, but to a plurality of Minds, the

---

[1] (This doctrine of ἀμέθεκτα, however, is not original with Proclus, but comes to him from Iamblichus.)

Supreme One or Absolute Good must be thought of likewise as giving rise to a series of Ones which Proclus calls the "divine" Henads or Unities and also simply "the Gods". As the Good is God, so in his system the Henads are "Gods" in the plural, related to God as the minds of you and me are related to the entity we call Mind. This doctrine is, as I have said, the peculiar property of Proclus and its interpretation has caused some trouble. It has sometimes been spoken of as a mere device for saving the face of dying Hellenic polytheism. This, however, is not to my thinking its real *raison d'être*, though Proclus has filled many weary pages of his *Theology of Plato* and commentary on the *Parmenides* with ingenious attempts to identify and classify the Henads and to show that with some forcing they may be read into the traditional theology. I think the origin of the theory more likely to be what I have indicated already. Some explanation had to be found for the existence of individual Minds and Souls, some reason why this plurality should be real and why there is not just one Mind, one Soul and one Body. The doctrine of the series of Minds and Souls is already suggested by Plotinus, who always treats individual human Souls as existing, so to say, with the same right and on the same level as the *Anima Mundi*. It originates in the justified refusal of the Neo-Platonists to treat personal individuality as a kind of illusion and reduce human persons to the status of "modes" of a single *Deus-substantia*. When the theory had been thus thought out for the case of Mind and Soul, it was a mere exigence of logic to extend it to the first member of the supreme triad. It is thus, as it seems to me, the logical completion of a line of thought inherited by the whole school from Plotinus. It is a rather more difficult thing to feel sure of the interpretation to be placed on

the doctrine. Mr. Whittaker suggests the highly ingenious comparison with the modern conception of the
stars as centres of planetary systems, but avoids committing himself to an opinion about Proclus' own intention. I think one may venture at any rate on a tentative
suggestion. Just as the Imparticipable One is identified
with the Good, Proclus tells us that the various divine
Henads or Gods are ἀγαθότητες—"goodnesses", and
that each of these "goodnesses", which are all com-
prised *eminenter*—or, as his own phrase is, κατ' αἰτίαν—
in the One, forms one of the Henads or Gods. He also
connects the doctrine with the well-known passage in
the *Phaedrus* where Socrates speaks of different classes
of men, statesmen, warriors, poets, as under the protection of a particular deity. The real meaning of this,
according to Proclus, is that each different type of individual mind is linked to the One in a two-fold way; it is
a member of the series of Minds, and the first term of
this series, Mind, is derived from the One; also this
special mind is a mirroring or image of a special Henad
in the series of "divine numbers", and this Henad belongs to the series headed by the One.

On the strength of such passages one might suggest
that what Proclus has in his mind is a doctrine of the
attributes of God like that of Philo, or, again, of the
great scholastics. The scholastics speak of a plurality of
these attributes, goodness, wisdom, power, and say of
each that God's wisdom is God, God's power is God,
and the like, as may be read at length in the first book
of St. Thomas' *Summa contra Gentiles*. This may be
how we ought to understand what Proclus says about
the gods or Henads and their relation to the One God.[1]

---

[1] But for some deserved strictures on the undue assimilation of the doctrine
to that of the scholastics made here, cf. E. R. Dodds, *Proclus, the Elements of
Theology*, 270-71.

They are, I take it, the "perfections" or "excellences" which in God exist, according to scholastic philosophy, in a way compatible with God's absolute simplicity, but in His works are found displayed to a great extent separately, some of the works revealing more particularly the wisdom, others the power, and yet others the goodness of their author. The notion must, of course, be carefully distinguished from Spinoza's theory in which just what is characteristic of each attribute is that you cannot say "God's extension is God" or "God's thought is God", and cannot conceive God as really simple at all.

Thus finally, including the Henads which are "above being" and bodies which are properly speaking "below" it, we may say that the One or Good appears as the source of four orders, Gods, minds, souls, bodies, and that as the four orders form a hierarchy of "images" or "reflections" of the *ens realissimum*, so each order itself is a hierarchy of "reflections" of its own initial members. The whole system is, in modern language, a well-ordered series of well-ordered series.

There remains, however, yet another fundamental doctrine on which I have not yet touched—the theory of ἐπιστροφή or reflection backwards. "Reflection" has commonly been used in English to translate the word, but with us the expression is ambiguous and I have already been obliged to employ it to illustrate what Proclus means by the progression of Henads, Minds, and the rest from the One. "Inversion", especially for some of its mathematical associations, would really be a better word. We have already seen that the One is thought of as being at once the source of all existence and the end or good which all existents tend towards by the law of their being.

Once more, we may remind ourselves that the

thought is derived directly from the definition given by
Eudoxus, the astronomer, and adopted by Aristotle,
that the good is that οὗ πάντα ἐφίεται, that which all
things "go for". And the "all things" do not mean
simply the "sentient creation". The thought is that in
everything, sentient or insentient, animate or inanimate, there is a real *nisus* towards systematic organisation or unity. You see this *nisus*, a Neo-Platonist would
have said, at different levels in the cohesion of the
particles of a homogeneous body, in chemical affinities,
in the attraction of the plant for the insect, in the sexual
life of the animal kingdom, the family and social aspira-
tions of man, the life-long struggle of the thinker after
an organised and coherent body of knowledge, or of
the saint after the disciplined life of holiness. In all
these instances, what we discern is marked by two characteristics. The *nisus* is not, as Spinoza, being a mere
naturalist, supposed, towards self-*preservation*, but, to
use Dr. Ward's expression, towards *betterment* of some
kind, attainment of a good which is the specific good of
the creature exhibiting the *nisus*. Dr. Ward's remark
that a creature which, as we commonly say, eats to fill
its skin gets as a consequence a better skin to fill, exactly
hits off this aspect of the Neo-Platonist view of the
fundamental conatus or "will to be" in things. Again—
and Proclus would say that this is an immediate consequence of the identity of the transcendent One with
the Good—the *nisus*, because it is always a turning
back or inversion of the process by which a thing is
derived from its cause, is always a movement towards
simplification. It is always a tendency towards the
assertion of unity and individuality. A vertebrate is
more truly *one* creature than a sponge, the inner state
of cognition in a man of science or feeling and will in a
saint is one of simplicity, as compared with the state of

a man whose mind is a medley of confused and un-
systematised beliefs, or the battle-ground for perplexed
and divided counsels or passions. This is the ultimate
source of the mediaeval conception of growth in grace
as a steady "reduction of the soul to its *ground*". Unless
we have the theory of ἐπιστροφή or *inversion* well in
mind we are bound to go astray when we try to understand what a writer like Dante or à Kempis really
means by extolling *sancta simplicitas* as the highest and
best state for a Christian. I suppose we can all feel the
beauty of such a line as that famous one about the
anima semplicetta che sà nulla, or the tenderness of a
nameless English mystic's adjuration never to try to
melt the "cloud of unknowing that is between thee and
thy God", or of Ruysbroek's description of the "nought-
ing" of the soul, but, apart from Neo-Platonism, we
cannot really understand what all this *meant*.

Two points are specially important in connection
with this conception of ἐπιστροφή: (1) The fundamental
conatus of everything is the *nisus* to reverse the process
of its production—to return to its immediate source.
Macaulay quotes, as typical of the nonsense of "Satan"
Montgomery, a badly expressed line, to the effect that
"the soul aspiring seeks its source to mount". To
Macaulay this seemed unmeaning, but it is only what
Donne or Vaughan would have said better about the
soul and about everything else. But there is a vital distinction between two classes of things, those which in
being reflected back upon their source are also reflected
upon themselves, and those which are incapable of reflection or inversion into themselves. This distinction is
as fundamental for Neo-Platonic philosophy as the distinction (on which the difference between infinite and
finite assemblages depends) between series which can
be "mirrored" within themselves and series which can-

not is for modern mathematics. The point is that some
things contain the principle from which they proceed
within themselves in a way in which others do not.
"Soul", for example, is thus related to its principle,
Mind or Intelligence. As Plato had said in the *Sophistes*
and *Timaeus* νοῦς always exists in ψυχή. Of course it
might be said that, on the other hand, there are many
ψυχαί, those of animals, for example, which do not think.
I suppose the rejoinder would be that even animal instinct, as Professor Stout has argued at great length,
not only produces results which are justified at the bar
of reason, but is found everywhere working under intelligent guidance, as we see from the regular adapta-
tion of instinctive trains of action to the special requirements of the individual situation and the modifiability
of instinct by experience. There is intelligence involved
in a cat's pursuit of a mouse, though we might hesitate
to say that the intelligence belongs to the cat in the
same way in which my intelligence belongs to me. But
when you come to deal with bodies the case is altered.
Bodies, it is held, are the "images" of souls, and, as
Plato had argued, all bodily movement is produced
directly or indirectly by the prior "motions" of a soul.
And bodies share in the universal tendency to reflection back into their proximate cause. Body is only seen
at its fullest and completest when it is an *animate* body.
From the standpoint of ancient physics it would seem
natural and right to look upon inanimate bodies as
having the function of feeding and sustaining plant life,
and plants that of providing sustenance for animals,
who in their turn minister to the needs of man. And the
Platonist view was that the prime elements of all bodies,
animate or inanimate, are the same. A living body does
not differ from a lifeless one by being made of ultimately
different stuff, but simply by being organic to a soul—

by being the body *of* that soul. So that the general facts about the so-called "three kingdoms" of the popular natural histories would be just an example of the process of ἐπιστροφή on a grand scale.

But bodies, in being reflected back into their cause, are not reflected back into *themselves*. Self-reflection, inversion into self, is characteristic only of what is bodiless. Proclus offers a curious formal proof of this. The argument is that reflection or inversion into self is a relation of a whole to itself as a whole. Whatever is thus inverted, he says, must be in contact as a whole with itself as a whole, that is, it must be directly existentially present as a whole to itself. But this relation cannot hold between wholes which are aggregates of distinct parts. In them, each part is present to itself in a direct way in which no two non-identical parts are present to each other. It is this relation, only possible to wholes which are simple units, in the sense that they are not made of separable parts, which constitutes knowledge. Hence in being "inverted" into Mind, a soul not only knows Mind, but knows itself. And Mind similarly, when in contemplation it is turned back upon the One or Good, is in the very same act reflected into itself and knows itself. Bodies, because they cannot be thus directly present to themselves, know neither themselves nor their causes. The analogy between this doctrine and Leibniz' distinction between "bare" monads and souls strongly suggests that the one has been modelled on the other. From the same source, I venture to think, comes Locke's well-known language about "ideas of reflection". According to Locke these are ideas of the mind's own activities got by the mind in taking note of our own "operations about our ideas". That the mind has this power of inversion, by which its own activities become objects for its contemplation, Locke assumes as some-

N

thing which no one will deny. I suggest that both the assumption and the name "ideas *of reflection*" are due to the same cause which produced the polemic of the First Book of the *Essay* against innate principles, the general and widespread influence of Neo-Platonism on the English philosophical writers contemporary with Cudworth and Henry More. The eighteenth century saw the gradual decrease of this influence; in its latter third, writers like Gibbon had lost all sense of the meaning of Neo-Platonic language, and we thus find the *Decline and Fall of the Roman Empire* treating as gibberish doctrines which are referred to, for example, by Bacon as perfectly familiar and intelligible.

One should note that, easy as it would have been to treat the doctrine of ἐπιστροφή as the basis of an anti-rational mysticism—and this, I would suggest, is very much what M. Bergson does in his doctrine of the *élan vital*—it does not occur to the Neo-Platonist to do so. In spite of the familiarity of the school with the psychological facts about "rapts" and "ecstasies", no Neo-Platonist ever regarded these states as revealing philosophical truths. Plotinus expressly compares the state of the ecstatic with the position of a priest who has passed the veil that screens the holy of holies and left all the images of the temple behind him, and dwells on the point that it leaves behind it no memory of what it was. And when Proclus speaks of Mind as reverting in self-contemplation to its principle the One, he is not referring to "rapts" at all. There is an agnostic side to his doctrine which reappears in the orthodox schoolmen. Nothing, he says, is ἄπειρον, indeterminate, in itself, but everything is ἄπειρον, not fully determinable or fathomable, by anything that stands lower in the universal hierarchy than itself. The higher, though more rational in its own constitution, is something of a mystery to the lower, much, we might say, as a man must be a mystery to his dog. Thus in a sense the One is Unknowable, but this only means that since it is something more than Mind, Mind can only know it by the reflection of itself it has stamped on Mind. The One is, he says, in itself ἑνιαίως "after the fashion of unity", but in Mind only νοερῶς, "after the fashion of Mind". That is, I take it, Mind is not the highest and most perfect type of individuality.

The utter individuality of God, the source alike of Mind and everything else, is proper to God; but Mind, since we have minds, is the most truly individual thing *we* can understand. We can see that God is something even more individual—a more perfectly articulated and yet absolutely individual being—than Mind itself, but *what* it is like to be something more than Mind, we, not having the experience of it in ourselves, cannot say. In general, the higher is only known to the lower by its effects on the lower itself, because it is in self-knowledge that we have to come to the knowledge of what is higher than self. The "negative theology" or "way of negation"—so salutary a protection against the extravagances of ignorant imagination to those who understand its real meaning, so utter a puzzle to moderns like William James and the Pragmatists, who have criticised it without knowledge of its history—is all contained in this doctrine of the necessary limitations of our knowledge. It is the real defence of sober thought against that "wild licence of affirmation about God" with which Matthew Arnold, in reckless defiance of facts, charged mediaeval theologians, and we may more reasonably charge a good many of our popular scientific writers who would refuse to call their ultimate reality by so old-fashioned a name as "God".

(2) The other point on which there may be room for a

word or two is also an example of Neo-Platonic sobriety. The doctrine of ἐπιστροφή must not be interpreted in the light of modern theories of the *Deus-substantia* type about the unreality of finite selves and finite things in general. The existence of a plurality of finite individuals of different types is to the Neo-Platonists, as to Plato himself, an ultimate premise. Each individual has his good or end and "reverts" to it, but the process is conditioned throughout by the specific nature of the individual. He "reverts", or unites himself with his Good, in the way *his* nature permits. The bonds of individuality are not burst in the process. Bodies, in the process of inversion, do not cease to be bodies or souls to be souls. So with Mind; Mind in attaining full knowledge of itself also discerns its immediate source, God, the One,—but it does not become God or a god. "Every thing is what it is and not another thing", and in the process of ἐπιστροφή it does not cease to be what it is, though no doubt it may discover that it is much more than it had at first supposed. The reversion or inversion of Mind into the One does not mean that Mind *becomes* God, but that in self-contemplation it learns to *know* God, so far as God is comprehensible to any of His creatures. There is no question of an Absolute in which finite individuality of any kind is transmuted and transformed into the irrecognisable. Proclus, in fact—though limits of time will not permit me to follow him—professes to be able to prove the everlastingness, both *a parte ante* and *a parte post*, of every individual capable of self-inversion, that is, of every individual which is not a body. The demonstration follows the usual lines of the old rational psychology, attacked by Kant, and need not delay us. What interests me more personally is a reflection suggested by the Neo-Platonic insistence on transitive causality.

It is frequently said nowadays that the fault of the old orthodox theology lay in its devotion to a "transcendent" deity. To be in earnest with transcendence, we are commonly told, means to exclude all possibility of any real relation between God—or whatever else a man likes to call the Supreme Being—and other beings. Religion, as a personal matter, because it means intimate personal relation with the Supreme, requires a doctrine of "immanence". Against this fashionable view I wish to suggest that it is, in point of fact, just the "immanence" philosophies which have always found it impossible to have any theory of the relation of their ἐν καὶ πᾶν with the individuals we know. Either the *Deus-substantia* has to become an empty name for a mere aggregate, without any individuality of its own, or the individuals have, by elaborate logical sophisms, to be made into mere illusions.

It is palpable, as it seems to me, that this inability to recognise the reality of individuals other than the *Ens summum* is certain to be fatal to the philosophies of Mr. Bradley and Professor Bosanquet as they stand. I do not, of course, mean that these philosophies ought to be rejected, or will be rejected, because we do not like their reduction of our own individuality to an illusion. I mean rather that on careful scrutiny the arguments of these distinguished philosophers reveal themselves as variations of one single contention which turns out, on close examination, to be a *petitio principii*. My own growing feeling is—and I believe it is by no means peculiar to myself—that if Mr. Bradley and Professor Bosanquet discover their own individuality to be unreal, the reason is that they set out from the start with a *parti pris*. Naturally they do not find what they are unconsciously determined not to see. To myself it seems obvious that if there is a real supreme *principium individuationis*, it must be, as the Neo-Platonists held, an end as well as a source, and must, therefore, *of course*, stand "outside the Universe", and that it is just because it is "outside" that direct and intimate personal relations with it are possible to all of us, if indeed they are possible. This means, of course, that I feel bound to hold as a point of general theory that transitive causality and transitive asymmetrical relations are ultimate in logic. I can see no vestige of ground in logic for the assumption, tacitly or expressly made in so much of the thinking of the generation before my own, that there are no relations of one-sided dependence. Herbart's protest against Kant's assumptions about the ubiquity in the Universe of "reciprocal action" seems to me as unanswerable as it has remained unanswered. To be more precise, the particular doctrine about which I feel the greatest difficulty in Professor Bosanquet's system of thought is his theory of Causality.

What gravels me is not so much his assertion that the relation of Cause and Effect is at bottom identical with that of Antecedent and Consequent. The ancients, who called both Cause and Reason Why αἴτιον, in a sense accepted this, and I could make shift myself, perhaps, to regard Causality as a special case of the more general relation. My difficulty is with the further assertion that in a really true hypothetical proposition Antecedent and Consequent are simply convertible. This, of course, means that there are no ultimate and unanalysable relations of one-sided dependence. But why should there not be?

So, again, the assertion that *time* is not real is, I suppose, a consequence of the same view, since, if time is real (unless it can be shown that events recur in cycles), the relation before-after is transitive and asymmetrical, as all relations which generate series appear to be. This is why I feel myself that if we are not to declare ourselves frank Irrationalists, we must hold that a philosophy of the general type of Neo-Platonism is at least nearer the truth than Spinozism or those versions of Hegelianism which have had the widest currency in our Universities for the last generation.

[1918]

THE ANALYSIS OF 'ΕΠΙΣΤΗΜΗ IN PLATO'S SEVENTH EPISTLE

THE question as to the genuineness of the seventh of the thirteen letters contained in our Plato manuscripts is one of considerable importance for the History of Philosophy. If the letter is really the work of Plato, it throws a flood of light on the philosopher's early life, particularly on the nature of his relations with Socrates and the causes by which Plato was led to abandon the career of public life as an Athenian statesman, which would have been normal in a man of his birth and endowments, for the vocation of a φιλόσοφος. It is further, on the hypothesis of genuineness, of great value as giving us an authoritative version of the reasons by which Plato was led in later life to attempt an active intervention in the affairs of Sicily, and his grounds for holding that the death of Dion was no fatal defeat for his "cause". It is not, however, my object at present to examine the whole literary problem created by the *Epistles* in general, or by our letter in particular. In view of the present state of the controversy, I feel justified in assuming that the evidence, both from style and from historical allusions, is overwhelmingly in favour of the view that the seventh *Epistle* is, as it purports to be, a document belonging to the year immediately after the assassination of Dion by Callippus, and presumably, therefore, a genuine letter of Plato. There remains, however, a difficulty which is neither historical nor literary but philosophical, and it is this difficulty which I propose to discuss, and, if possible, to remove. The most remarkable passage in the letter (342 *a*–344 *d*), a digression which professes to give the justification for the well-known Platonic view that "philosophy" cannot profitably be communicated by books, but only by the direct and long-continued personal intercourse of mind with mind in the common pursuit of truth, has given great offence to students who have professed themselves unable to perceive its drift, or to feel sure that what meaning it has is genuinely Platonic. I therefore propose, to the best of my ability, to argue that the whole section has a definite purpose, that its leading contentions are in principle sound, and that good Platonic authority can be adduced for them. An examination of the passage is the more indispensable that Constantin Ritter, who strongly defends the genuineness of the letter as a whole, regards this passage as a later interpolation,[1] and that Mr. H. Richards, in his recent *Platonica*, not only speaks of its presence as possibly an "insuperable difficulty" for those who ascribe the letter to Plato, but loads the digression itself with terms of disparagement, such as "rigmarole", "skimble-skamble stuff", and the like.

I will divide my treatment of the subject into two main parts. First I shall urge briefly, against the theory of later interpolation, that the digression is strictly relevant, and indeed necessary, in the connection in which it stands, and next, in answer to the charge of unintelligibility, I will translate and interpret the passage in question as carefully as I can, adducing such parallels from the Platonic dialogues as suggest themselves to me.

---

[1] See his *Neue Untersuchungen über Platon*, Essay 7; *Platon*, i. p. 8.

I. *Relevancy.*—That a statement showing why it is futile to convey the deepest truths by means of written hand-books (τέχναι) is relevant to the matter in hand is clear from what has been said immediately before. The object is to prove that the reprehensible proceedings of Dionysius are no legitimate fruit of the Academic philosophy. For Dionysius had by no means heard the whole Platonic doctrine from its author in the days of their friendly intercourse. Indeed, he had not even asked for a full exposition, for "he professed that he already knew for himself and was sufficiently master of many things in it, and those the most important".[1] Since then Plato has heard that Dionysius has actually written a hand-book (τέχνη) on the subjects of their conversation, in which he has gravely misrepresented its purport (γεγραφέναι αὐτὸν περὶ ὧν τότε ἤκουσε, συνθέντα ὡς αὐτοῦ τέχνην, οὐδὲν τῶν αὐτῶν ὧν ἀκούοι. That is, he wrote the hand-book on his own initiative, took the credit for its contents to himself, and totally misrepresented Plato's views on the matters which had been discussed). The writer of the letter does not know whether this report is true, though he knows of others who have done the same thing, οἵτινες δὲ οὐδ' αὐτοὶ αὐτούς —apparently a colloquial way of saying that these writers were "nobodies". He will only remark that all past and future writers of books "who profess knowledge of the matters to which I devote myself (περὶ ὧν σπουδάζω), cannot possibly, in my opinion, understand one whit of the business. There is not, and God forbid there should ever be, any work of my own on the subject,[2] for it cannot be expounded (ῥητὸν γὰρ οὐδαμῶς ἐστιν,

---

[1] 341 *b*, πολλὰ γὰρ αὐτὸς καὶ τὰ μέγιστα εἰδέναι τε καὶ ἱκανῶς ἔχειν προσεποιεῖτο διὰ τὰς ὑπὸ τῶν ἄλλων παρακοάς, *sc.* from the imperfect accounts he had received before Plato's own arrival.

[2] Cf. *Ep.* ii. 314 *c*, οὐδ' ἔστιν σύγγραμμα Πλάτωνος οὐδὲν οὐδ' ἔσται. If these are not, as I believe them to be, the actual words of Plato, they must be regarded as

—a play on the mathematical meaning of ῥητόν, 'exponible') like other branches of learning (μαθήματα). It is only from long-continued personal association in the business and in a common life[1] (ἐκ πολλῆς συνουσίας γιγνομένης περὶ τὸ πρᾶγμα αὐτὸ καὶ τὸ συζῆν), that suddenly, as it were, the fire bursts forth from one soul and enkindles (*sc.* in the other) a spiritual flame which thenceforth feeds itself" (341 *c*). Consequently, the letter goes on, if it were really possible to put the "essence of Platonism" into a written book, the proper person to write the book would be Plato himself, the very man who would feel most distress if the work were ill done. Hence "if I had thought these matters could be adequately written about for the general public, and were exponible[2] to it, what nobler task could I have had in life than to write things of so much service to mankind and bring Nature to light for all to look upon?" (341 *c*). But the author's opinion is that there are very few men who can be benefited by being urged to study such subjects, and they are just those who can be trusted to discover truth for themselves with a little preliminary guidance (διὰ σμικρᾶς ἐνδείξεως). In most men the reading of philo- sophical works either leads to an undeserved contempt for what they find above their intelligence or to idle vanity about their attainments. Thus far the introduc- tory page on which the much-decried bit of analysis follows. The writer then goes on to make a special application of his general thesis to the case of Dionysius. He remarks that the most appropriate test of capacity for philosophy in a "prince" is to give him some initia-

copied from the present passage, which, in that case, must have been regarded as genuine by the writer of *Ep.* ii.

[1] That is, from the effort to lead the βίος φιλόσοφος is common.

[2] For the repeated play on the word ῥητόν cf. *Rep.* 546 *b*; here the word has primarily its literal sense, but there is a pretty clear allusion to the specially mathematical sense to which magnitudes commensurable with a "proposed" standard are said to be ῥητά (Euclid, *Elements*, x. def. 3).

tion into the subject and then observe the effect, and discover into which of the three classes just enumerated he falls. Such a πεῖρα he says he applied to Dionysius. He had one philosophic conversation with him, and found that the young king asked for no more, but claimed to be henceforth qualified to "philosophise" on his own account, and is even reported to have composed a written work on φύσις.[1] This gives the opportunity for a long restatement of the familiar Platonic view that written works are an inadequate vehicle of philosophical education. The central part of this restatement is taken up by an attempt to show that the doctrine in question necessarily follows from the nature of the problems of ἐπιστήμη on the one side, and the character of written and spoken language on the other. It is this passage (342 a –344 d) to which Mr. Richards takes special exception (though all the time regarding it apparently as an integral part of the letter). The writer then returns to the subject of Dionysius and his book (344 d), and tells us, in effect, the final verdict to which the application of his πεῖρα to Dionysius has led him. This is, as we should expect, highly unfavourable (344 c–345 c). Now it seems to me that the whole passage from the end of 341 a, where we first hear of the application of the πεῖρα to Dionysius, down to 345 c is so closely coherent that it would be impossible to excise any minor part of it and yet retain the rest. We cannot, for instance, hold that the letter as a whole is genuine, and only the particular digression about ἐπιστήμη and

---

[1] It would probably be wrong to take the reiterated allusions to φύσις as the topic of the conversation with Dionysius and of the alleged τέχνη as concerned specially with φύσις in the Aristotelian sense. φύσις throughout the passage apparently represents the subject matter of φιλοσοφία or ἐπιστήμη in general; that is, it means τὸ ὄν or τὰ ὄντα. So when we read in *Theaetetus* 173 c, of the mind as πᾶσαν πάντῃ φύσιν ἐρευνωμένη τῶν ὄντων ἑκάστου ὅλου, the context shows that this includes ethical reflexion as well as the astronomy and geometry which have just been mentioned.

language, to which Mr. Richards so strongly objects,
spurious. For where, in that case, are we to look for the
close of the interpolation? It cannot be placed *before*
the return to the case of Dionysius and his book at
344 *d*, because the allusions in 344 *b* to the ὀνόματα,
λόγοι, and ὄψεις which serve as intermediaries of communication of knowledge are hardly intelligible apart
from the full account of what is meant which was given
on pages 342, 343, and further because the metaphor
of the kindling of the flame of φρόνησις and νοῦς by the
personal intercourse of questioner and answerer in that
section is a conscious reversion to the exactly similar
metaphor of 341 *c*. Nor can we reasonably regard the
interpolation as ending at 344 *d* 2, where the letter reverts to the subject of Dionysius, because, when the
long digression has been removed, the words with which
the next paragraph opens, τούτῳ δὴ τῷ μύθῳ τε καὶ πλάνῳ
ὁ συνεπισπόμενος εὖ εἴσεται κτλ. have nothing left to
which they can refer. It is the digression itself (342 *c*–
344 *d* 2) which is the μῦθος and πλάνος in question. Consequently Mr. Richards' view that the digression on
ἐπιστήμη is senseless cannot be held by anyone who
regards the seventh letter in the main as genuine, unless
he is prepared to excise not only the piece of analysis
contained in 342–343 but the whole of the pages which
deal with the interview in which Plato applied the πεῖρα
to Dionysius and the results which he obtained.

Thus I think we may fairly say that if there is an
interpolation at all it must extend to the whole of the
pages which Ritter wishes to excise; every allusion to
the supposed "book" of Dionysius must go out. Let us
see then what the result of so considerable an excision
would be. The genuine Platonic letter will run as follows, if we epitomise its argument from the beginning
of 340, where Plato is explaining that in coming to

Syracuse for the third time he was sacrificing his own
judgement to that of Dion and Archytas, who thought
well of the "philosophical" qualifications of Dionysius
(339 c): "I undertook the journey with grave secret mis-
givings. When I reached Syracuse I thought it my first
duty to find out whether Dionysius had really been 'set
on fire' by philosophy, as was reported, or not.[1] The
most becoming way of ascertaining this in the case of a
prince (ὄντως τυράννοις πρέπων, 340 b) is to make it quite
clear to him that philosophy is a big thing and only to
be acquired by great labour of the mind (ὅτι ἔστι πᾶν τὸ
πρᾶγμα οἷόν τε καὶ δι' ὅσων πραγμάτων καὶ ὅσον πόνον ἔχει,
ibid.). Such discourse, in fact, acts as a spur to the noble
mind and incites it to learn how to walk alone without a
guide. The true votary is led on to mould his *life* in
accord with philosophy in all the affairs of business, and
to order his daily conduct in a way which will make him
quick to learn, slow to forget, able to reason soberly for
himself (340 d). But those who are not true 'lovers of
wisdom' at heart, but cherish a mere skin-deep interest
in 'points of view' (δόξαι, 340 d), will soon grow weary
of the prolonged course of study and the daily discipline
of the 'affections and lusts', and give up the quest.
Some of them will try to persuade themselves that they
are already masters and need pursue no further (ὡς
ἱκανῶς ἀκηκοότες εἰσὶν τὸ ὅλον, καὶ οὐδὲν ἔτι δέονταί τινων
πραγμάτων, 341 a). The proposed test, applied to those who
have not the diligence to follow the path to its goal,
brings out the difference between the man who blames
his teacher for his failure to make progress and him who
rightly lays the blame on his own inability to *live* as a
philosopher must (πάντα τὰ πρόσφορα ἐπιτηδεύειν τῷ

---

[1] *I.e.* whether what he had learned from Plato on his former visit had kindled
a genuine desire to know more. Cf. 338 d ff. φιλοσοφία throughout the letter
means virtually the theory and practice of the Academy.

πράγματι, *ibid.*). It was in this spirit that I spoke as I did
then to Dionysius." Hereupon, according to Ritter,
follows immediately (345 *c* ff.) the account of the growing
unfriendliness of Dionysius to Dion, on which Plato remarks that it enabled him "to see accurately how much
Dionysius cared about philosophy, and gave him the
right to feel indignant", and the narrative then runs
straight on with an account of Plato's desire to be
allowed to go home and the reluctance of Dionysius to
part with him.

Now is it not clear that, as thus restored (?), the continuity of the letter is violated? The elaborate account
of the kind of "test" (πεῖρα) appropriate to the case of
a prince has led nowhither. We are neither told whether
it was actually applied, nor, if it was, how it resulted.
We have been led to expect information as to whether
Dionysius confessed his inability to live up to the
standard demanded of the philosopher, or tried to lay
the blame for his failure on Plato, or finally posed as
having already learned all that Plato had to teach, and
being therefore free from the obligation to live any
longer *sub disciplina*. This information we get in the
letter as it stands, but not in the mutilated form which
Ritter regards as original. Indeed, in Ritter's version,
Plato is made to ascribe his discovery of the uselessness
of further attempts to make a "philosopher" out of
Dionysius not to the application of the carefully
described πεῖρα, but solely to the prince's unworthy
treatment of Dion.

This incoherence is so glaring that I venture to say
that if the letter had come down to us without the whole
passage which Ritter excises, critics would have declared with some reason that there must be a considerable lacuna in the text at the very point where Ritter
begins his excision. Some account of the application of

the πεῖρα to Dionysius would have been rightly felt to be indispensable. But when once so much as this is granted, we have to allow that the coherency of the whole "interpolation" with itself, and particularly the intimate connection of its beginning and end with what immediately precedes and follows, forbid our resorting to any theory of a minor "interpolation" covering only the two pages 342–343. There is no reasonable way of dealing with the text by excision short of cutting out the whole of what Ritter regards as "interpolated", and the whole, as we have just seen, cannot be removed without making the letter hopelessly incoherent. Either then the whole letter is spurious, a view which Ritter himself in my opinion properly rejects, or the whole is genuine, and Plato must take the blame for any unintelligibility there may be in the pages which deal with ἐπιστήμη and the reasons which make written books unsatisfactory as instruments for imparting it. This brings me to my second point, the careful consideration of the incriminated passage, and the exposition of its real meaning. I proceed then to offer a translation of the whole passage 341 b–345 c, with such interspersed comments, marked in the text by square brackets, as seem requisite. I will only premise that the reader remembers that the studies which, according to Plato, are particularly effective in producing the intellectual and moral elevation requisite for philosophy are mathematics and dialectic, the former, as commonly taught, being a propaedeutic for the latter, and that it was precisely by a course of geometry that, according to ancient tradition, the training of Dionysius for the work of kingship was begun. Consequently we shall not be surprised to find that the account of the difficulties attending the attainment and communication of ἐπιστήμη is specially concerned with the philosophy of the mathe-

matical sciences, though allusion is also made to ethical
inquiries. If we bear this in mind, we shall discover
that many of the alleged obscurities of the passage
vanish of themselves.

II. *Interpretation*.—"To be sure, I did not give a
complete exposition, nor did Dionysius ask for one. He
professed, in fact, to know and be adequately possessed
of many, and those the most important, matters for
himself by reason of what he had imperfectly heard
from others. I hear that since then he has even written
a work about what he heard at the time, in the form of
a Hand-book to Philosophy (τέχνη) by himself, which
differs utterly from what he then heard. About this I
have no certain knowledge, but I know for certain that
others have composed writings on the same topics,
though who they are is more than they know themselves.[1] Yet I can state this much of all writers in the
past or future who profess knowledge of the matters
to which I devote myself, whether on the ground of
having learned them from me or others, or as a discovery of their own. It is, in my opinion, impossible
that they should understand one whit of the business.
At least, there is not, and God forbid there should ever
be, any written work of my own about it. [Plato in the
main kept his word. We learn a little about the topics
described here as περὶ ὧν σπουδάζω from the *Timaeus*,
Philebus, and *Laws*, but for the most part we are
dependent on the reports of Aristotle.] For the matter
is not 'exponible' in speech, like other branches of study.
It is only after long fellowship in the business itself·
[*sc*. the pursuit of the philosophic life; the reiterated
τὸ πρᾶγμα seems to mean something like 'the grand

---

[1] We cannot expect to know who the persons thus referred to are, except that
they seem to be pupils with whose performances Plato was not wholly satisfied.
Readers with a sense of humour would naturally like to think of Aristotle, but to
identify the culprits at all is to be wise above what is written.

O

concern'] and in life together that, so to say, a light is
kindled in one soul by the fire bursting forth from the
other,[1] and, once kindled, thereafter sustains itself. [The
meaning is that there are μαθήματα—the rules of composition as taught by Isocrates would be a case in
point, and so would 'geometry and the kindred τέχναι',
as taught in our school-books with avoidance of all
reference to the philosophical problems they suggest—
which can be learned from a manual or τέχνη. Philosophy, being a 'way of life', or 'habit of mind', cannot
be compressed into any such spoken or written summary of rules and results. It is only by living daily
the life the Master lives, and by lying long open to
the influence of his personality, that, sooner or later, the
soul of the pupil 'takes fire'. After that moment the
sacred fire, which required at first to be fed by the example and precept of another, 'feeds' itself. The
philosopher is thus not a 'crammer' but a trainer of
men. Cf. the well-known views on the relation between
teacher and taught, and the necessity for intimate first-
hand intercourse between the riper and less ripe in mind
in *Rep.* 518*b*; *Phaedrus*, 274-276; *Theaetetus*, 149-151.]

"And yet I am sure of one thing, that if these matters
were to be expressed in spoken or written discourse, it
had been best done by myself, and further that I should
feel more distress than another if the written exposition
were a bad one. Had I thought them 'exponible' and
adequately communicable in writing for the public, to
what nobler work could I have given my life than that
of writing what would be so serviceable to mankind,
and of throwing the light of day on Reality for all men?
[This sounds arrogant, but the arrogance is only in
the sound. It is Plato's apology for giving the public

---

[1] 341 *c*, ἐξαίφνης, οἷον ἀπὸ πυρὸς πηδήσαντος ἐξαφθὲν φῶς, ἐν τῇ ψυχῇ γενόμενον
αὐτὸ ἑαυτὸ ἤδη τρέφει. The context shows that the ψυχή is that of the disciple
which catches fire from the soul of the Master.

hitherto only 'discourses of Socrates', not a set exposition
of his own philosophy. If the Platonic philosophy could
have been imparted to the world at large in a book,
Plato was obviously neglecting his duty in not writing
that book.] But I do not regard the so-called dialectical
exposition of these matters[1] as good for any but the
few who are capable of discovering them for themselves
with the help of a little guidance. As for the rest of
mankind, it would fill some of them out of all measure
with a mistaken contempt and others with a vain and
empty conceit of the sublimity of what they had
learned." [*I.e.* some would not understand a written
work on φύσις and would despise it as jargon; others,
who mistakenly thought they understood it all, would
plume themselves on their fancied intellectual penetra-
tion and forget that as yet they were only beginners
and not proficients. Readers of Herbert Spencer among
ourselves illustrate the point. Some of them are led to
despise all philosophy as high-sounding jargon; others
give themselves airs of superiority on the strength of
the supposed intellectual power shown in professing to
understand what "the general" are baffled by.]

[The upshot so far, then, is that the result of the πεῖρα
was unsatisfactory. Dionysius, by his boasts of his
knowledge, had shown himself to belong to the class of
men whose philosophy is only skin-deep, inasmuch as
he insisted that he had already reached a point at which
he had nothing more to learn from Plato, and had even,
if reports could be trusted, attempted to expound a
philosophy of his own in a book.]

"It has occurred to me to say something more at
length about these matters [αὐτῶν I take to be neuter as in

---

[1] For the meaning here given to τὴν ἐπιχείρησιν περὶ αὐτῶν λεγομένην compare
Sophistes, 239 *c*; *Laws*, 631 *a*, 722 *d*; Aristotle, *Topics*, 111 b 16, 139 b 10, and
the regular technical sense of ἐπιχείρημα in the *Topics*. The full expression is
ἐπιχείρησις τοῦ λόγου, as, *e.g.*, in *Ep*. viii. 352 *e*.

the preceding τὴν ἐπιχείρησιν περὶ αὐτῶν λεγομένην and the following λεχθέντων αὐτῶν, though it might conceivably be masculine, referring to the persons just spoken of, for whom the study of philosophy is not desirable]. There is a truth adverse to the pretensions of those who would commit any such matter to writing, a truth which I have often uttered before, but must, as it seems, repeat again now."

[Now follows Mr. Richards' 'rigmarole', about which I would make one preliminary remark. In the author of the *Laws* and *Philebus*, who, as he says himself in the *Theaetetus*, 172 d, regarded it as a mark of the 'liberal' character of philosophical discourses that the speaker is not controlled by a brief, or hampered by a time-limit, but can digress at any moment and to any length he regards as desirable, the passage must not be condemned simply because it is a digression, and to our taste a lengthy one, but only if its contents can be proved unworthy of their alleged author.]

"For everything that is [ἐκάστῳ τῶν ὄντων, *i.e.* for every concept which is an object of scientific contemplation] there are three intermediaries by which the knowledge of it must be imparted [the notion of 'imparting' is suggested by the παρα in παραγίγνεσθαι], and we may reckon the knowledge itself as a fourth thing, the object of it, which is the Knowable or Real Being, being counted as fifth; thus, (1) a name; (2) a discourse [λόγος, the example below will show that he is thinking more particularly of the λόγος τῆς οὐσίας or definition, the 'discourse' which tells you what the thing called by the name is]; (3) an image (εἴδωλον); (4) a knowledge. If you wish to understand what I am saying, you may take one example and conceive all the rest analogously. There is something which we call a circle. Its *name* is the very word we have just uttered. Next comes its

'discourse' [or definition, λόγος], a complex of names and
verbal forms [ῥήματα].¹ *E.g.* the 'discourse' of the thing
which has the names 'round', 'circle' is 'that which has
its boundary in every direction equidistant from its
middle point'. Third is what we draw and rub out,
fashion on the lathe and destroy again. These affections
do not belong to the 'circle itself' with reference to
which all these operations are performed, clearly because it is something different from what is thus con-
structed.² Fourth, there are knowledge and understanding (νοῦς) and true judgement (δόξα ἀληθής) about
all this. These must again all be reckoned as one condition which inheres neither in sounds, nor in the
shapes or colours of bodies, but in minds [ψυχαῖς ἐνόν.
I.e. knowledge and belief inhere neither in the visible
diagrams and models, nor in the spoken words of discourse; they are states of *mind*]. Hence it is manifest
that this condition is something different both from the
real circle [αὐτοῦ τοῦ κύκλου τῆς φύσεως, where I may be
pardoned for remarking that κύκλου depends on φύσεως,
not *vice versa*, αὐτὸς ὁ κύκλος, ὁ ἐν τῇ φύσει κύκλος, ἡ τοῦ
κύκλου φύσις are all synonymous in Platonic language],
and from the afore-mentioned three things. [That is,
the 'circle itself', which is the object of the geometer's
knowledge, is neither a name, nor corporeal thing, nor
a psychical thing or 'state of mind'; it is strictly what
the scholastics call a *universale ante rem*, like all the
Platonic εἴδη.]

"But of all the rest understanding (νοῦς) approximates most closely to the fifth [real being, the object of

---

¹ I have rendered ῥήματα here 'verbal forms' on the authority of *Sophistes*
262 *b*, where βαδίζει, τρέχει, καθεύδει, and τἆλλα ὅσα πράξεις σημαίνει are said
to be ῥήματα, but it is, of course, possible that the sense is more general, and that
we should translate 'predicative phrases', so as to include adjectives used
predicatively.

² Cf. *Rep.* 510 *d-e*, for the point of the distinction between a mathematical
diagram or model, and the concept which it is meant to illustrate.

scientific thought], in affinity and likeness; the others stand at a further remove. We must hold the same view of straight and curved figure, of colour, of the good, beautiful, and right, of every body artificially made or naturally generated, of fire and water and their likes [*sc.* not only of bodies but of the popularly recognised στοιχεῖα of bodies, which are, of course, *not* στοιχεῖα at all for Plato], of all organisms and all tempers of the soul, as well as with reference to all action and passion; in all these cases, unless one in some sort acquires the first four, he will never partake fully of the knowledge of the fifth."

[The application of all this to the problem of the communication of knowledge is obvious. To communicate knowledge about an object of thought, you have (1) to use a name for it, (2) to explain what the name means by stating its equivalence to a certain 'discourse' or 'definition', (3) to illustrate your 'discourse' by actual appeal to diagrams or models,—or, we may add, to the memory-images of them, which like the diagrams and models themselves fall under the general head of εἴδωλα. It is only by these intermediaries that you succeed at last in producing in another a genuine knowledge about the purely conceptual objects of genuine scientific knowledge, and we are to see directly that every stage of the process is attended by grave sources of error.]

"Furthermore, all these processes, thanks to the imperfection of language (διὰ τὸ τῶν λόγων ἀσθενές), are used no less in showing what the object is *like* than in showing what it *is* (τὸ ποῖόν τι περὶ ἕκαστον—τὸ ὂν ἑκάστου). Hence no man of understanding will ever venture to put his concepts into language (εἰς αὐτό = εἰς τὸ τῶν λόγων ἀσθενές), least of all into language which cannot be altered, as is the case with writings."

[So far the sense is quite free from difficulty, and wholly Platonic. The point is that it is a hard and barely possible thing to communicate profound mathematical and 'dialectical' truth by a written text-book illustrated with diagrams. That Plato distrusted these last we know independently from *Phaedo* 92 *d*; *Cratylus* 436 *d*; *Rep.* 510. And for this very reason he requires in the passage of the *Republic* that 'dialectic' shall be devoid of the help of diagrams (511 *b*, αἰσθητῷ παντάπασιν οὐδενὶ προσχρώμενος), much as the philosophical mathematicians of our own day demand a "geometry without diagrams".¹ This throws light upon the one apparent

¹ It may be thought that I am here forgetting that it is not 'geometry and the kindred τέχναι', but dialectic which the *Republic* forbids to employ diagrams. But the fact is that the "philosophy of mathematics", and the treatment of mathematical problems in the light of such a philosophy, form a most important part of what Plato calls 'dialectic'. It is not in its subject-matter, but in its method and its success in reaching certain first principles, as contrasted with positions merely assumed for the purpose of argument, that dialectic is discriminated from the other μαθήματα, and it is the business of dialectic to justify by deduction from ἀνυπόθετοι ἀρχαί the unproved assumptions which the ordinary mathematician uses simply as—to employ a technical term which the evidence of Proclus proves to be as old as the first generation of the Academy—αἰτήματα, assumptions which are not self-evident, but merely demanded for the sake of argument. Cf. Proclus, *Comment. in Euclid.* 188. 8, τὸ γὰρ αἴτημα κατ' ἐκεῖνον (*sc.* Aristotle) δεῖται ἀποδείξεως τινός; *ibid.* 76, οὔκ ἐστι ταὐτὸ ἀξίωμα καὶ αἴτημα . . . ὥς πού φησιν ὁ δαιμόνιος 'Αριστοτέλης, ἀλλ' ὅταν μὲν καὶ τῷ μανθάνοντι γνώριμον ᾖ καὶ καθ' αὐτὸ πιστὸν τὸ παραλαμβανόμενον εἰς ἀρχῆς τάξιν . . . ἀξίωμα τὸ τοιοῦτόν ἐστιν . . . ὅταν δὲ αὖ καὶ ἄγνωστον ᾖ τὸ λεγόμενον καὶ μὴ συγχωροῦντος τοῦ μανθάνοντος ὅμως λαμβάνηται, τηνικαῦτα φησίν, αἴτημα τοῦτο καλοῦμεν. The reference is to *Analytica Posteriora*, i. 76 b 23–34.

To avoid misconception about the character of 'dialectic' it is worth while to note that the biological researches of Speusippus known as the Ὅμοια or *Homologies* appear, as has well been brought out by P. Lang (*De Speusippi Academici scriptis*, 1911), to have been intended in the first instance as a contribution to 'dialectic' (because they subserve the process of classification), and again that the theory of surd magnitudes in Euclid X., in the same way, aims at making a *classification* of types of surds (see *op. cit.* Prop. 111, Corollary, which was very probably, as Heiberg suggests, the original conclusion of the book). The work is therefore primarily a piece of dialectic as described in the *Philebus*, as is only natural when we remember that it completes and embodies the researches of the Academicians Theaetetus, Socrates, and Eudoxus (see Plato, *Theaetetus* 147 *d*, [Aristotle], *De lineis insecabilibus*, 968 b 16 ff., Proclus, *op. cit.* 66–68 on these mathematical pioneers. The passage of the *Theaetetus* itself represents the study of surds as from the first a problem in classification.

obscurity of the present passage. What, it may be said, has the alleged ultimate source of all difficulties, the inadequacy of language, τὸ τῶν λόγων ἀσθενές, to do with the danger of reliance on diagrams? That there is such a danger we know very well. A diagram is always imperfect, and often suggestive of error, and moreover a diagram can never exhibit a problem or construction in its generality. Thus, to take the simplest examples, Euclid never proves a point which is vital in his very first proposition, viz. that the two circles described from the end-points of his given straight line *have* a point of intersection not lying on the given line. He is apparently contented to take this for granted on the strength of the diagram, though it can be, and ought to be, proved. In i. 2 his figure only illustrates one of several possible "cases" of the general problem, and so again in i. 47 the proposition would be equally true of squares constructed on the inner sides of the straight lines which compose the triangle, but the diagram does not represent this case. But what connection have these considerations with the "inadequacy of discourses"? Simply, as I suppose this, it is the inadequacy of ψιλοὶ λόγοι to render mathematical reasoning generally intelligible which drives the mathematician to eke out his "discourse" by appeals to always imperfect and often misleading diagrams and models. The ordinary man will not take in what is meant by the statement, nor be able to fix his attention on the steps of the reasoning, without some such helps for his imagination. So, again, the propositions of Euclid V. hold good of all ratios between magnitudes of any kind, those of Euclid X. for any surd magnitudes of the types discussed, but as aids to the imagination the writer regularly employs two special kinds of magnitudes, lengths and areas. And in X. we see that this habit has reacted on his thought and language; he constantly speaks of surd "lines" and "rectangles" as though the propositions he is enunciating held exclusively of lines and areas.[1] The same considerations account for the allusion to the distinction between the ὄν and the ποῖόν τι and the stress which our passage goes on to lay on the confusion between them as a source of fallacy. The way in which the distinction appears in geometry is well illustrated by some remarks made by Proclus in connection with the classification of Euclid's propositions as "theorems" and "problems". The distinction between the two, he tells us, had not originally been universally admitted in the Academy. Speusippus had regarded all geometry as composed exclusively of "theorems", Menaechmus had held that all propositions of geometry are "problems" (*Comment. in Euclid.* 77–78).

Thus the dispute, since Speusippus had taken sides in it, may not unreasonably be held to go back to the life-time of Plato himself, as Speusippus only survived his uncle by a few years, and was already an elderly man when he became head of the Academy.

Proclus goes on to trace the effect of it upon the views of later thinkers, and tells us that "Posidonius and his school defined the one as a proposition in respect of

[1] This may be illustrated by the distinction kept up throughout the book between the surd expressions called respectively μέση and μέσον. The μέση (the full expression is μέση εὐθεῖα) is defined at X. 21 as the straight line whose square is equal to the rectangle under two straight lines which are only δυνάμει σύμμετροι. Thus, *e.g.*, $\sqrt{a\sqrt{b}}$ would be a μέση since (if a and b are integers, and b not a square number) a and $\sqrt{b}$ are δυνάμει μόνον σύμμετροι. The μέσον (full expression μέσον χωρίον) is the rectangle under two μέσαι which are σύμμετροι whether μήκει or only δυνάμει (X. 24). Hence $\sqrt{ab\sqrt{cd}}$ satisfies the definition of a μέση if you regard it as the square root of $ab\sqrt{cd}$; it satisfies that of a μέσον if you regard it as the product of $\sqrt{a\sqrt{c}}$ and $\sqrt{b\sqrt{d}}$ (premising, as before, that c and d are not square numbers). The apparently hard and fast distinction between the type μέση and the type μέσον really depends only on the arbitrary selection of a straight line or a rectangle to symbolise a surd magnitude. The irrelevancy of the εἴδωλον is here the source of a confusion of thought.

which it is asked whether something exists or not, the
other as a proposition in which it is asked 'what is it?'
or 'of what sort is it?' '' (*op. cit.* p. 80), a view which
exactly corresponds to the modern doctrine that "problems" are existence-theorems.[1] It is in accord with this
view that when Proclus comes to comment on Euclid's
first "theorem", Prop. I. 4, he justifies the arrangement
by which the proposition is preceded by the familiar
"problems", I. 1–3, in the following way. "How was
Euclid to instruct us about the συμβεβηκότα καθ' αὑτό of
the triangles, and the equality of their angles and sides,
without first constructing the triangles and providing
for their genesis? Or how could he have assumed sides
equal to sides and straight lines equal to other straight
lines if he had not already considered this by way of
problems and achieved the finding of the equal straight
lines? For suppose him to say, before constructing them
(*i.e.* before showing how a triangle or a straight line
equal to a given straight line can be constructed), 'If
two triangles have the following property (σύμπτωμα),
they will also in all cases have such-and-such a second
property'; would it not be easy for anyone to retort
on him, 'But do we know whether a triangle can be
constructed at all?' Or suppose him to go on, 'If the
two triangles have two sides of the one equal to two
sides of the other'—might not one raise the question,
'But is it possible that there should be two equal straight
lines?' . . . It is to anticipate such objections that the
author of the *Elements* has furnished the construction

---

[1] Friedlein's text makes Proclus say that it was the *problem* which Posidonius
regarded as investigating "what the thing is" (*op. cit.* p. 80, l. 22, τὸ δὲ πρόβλημα
πρότασιν ἐν ᾗ ζητεῖται τί ἐστιν ἢ ποῖόν τι). As this contradicts not only Proclus'
previous statement that the doctrine of Posidonius was derived from "Zenodotus
who belonged to the succession of Oenopides" and taught that "a *theorem* asks
what is the σύμπτωμα predicated of the matter under consideration", but also his
further account of the views of Posidonius himself, I can only suppose the word
πρόβλημα to be a mistaken gloss on τὸ δέ.

of triangles (*sc.* in I. 1)—for his procedure is equally
applicable to all three kinds of triangle—and the genesis
of equal straight lines. This last he has achieved in a
double form. He both constructs such a line in general
(I. 2), and constructs it by cutting off a segment from
an unequal line (I. 3). Thus he reasonably makes the
theorem follow on these constructions" (*op. cit.* 234–
235). In the light of Proclus' account of the antiquity
of the question about the distinction between theorems
and problems, it seems natural to me to suppose that
it is to this that the language of our passage alludes.
The sense then will be simply that the effects of the inadequacy of language are felt in problems and theorems
alike.]

"I must, however, repeat the lesson I am now giving.
Every one of the circles which are drawn or fashioned
on the lathe by actual manual operation (ἐν ταῖς πράξεσι)
is full of the opposite of the Fifth, I mean, it is everywhere in touch with the Straight. But 'the circle itself',
so we say, has neither more nor less in it of the nature
of its opposite. [*I.e.* no actually described physical disc
is ever absolutely circular. At any point you please you
can make it coincide throughout a finite distance with
a physical 'straight' line. So, one might also say, in the
diagrams of our Euclids, the so-called circle and tangent can always be seen by anyone to coincide throughout a perceptible distance. But 'the circle itself', the
'mathematical' circle of which Euclid is speaking, only
coincides with the tangent at a 'mathematical' point.]
So we say that none of them [viz. the 'physical' figures
referred to] has a fixed name. There is no reason why
those we actually call round should not have been called
straight; yes, and the straight ones round. The names
would be just as fixed if we interchanged them. [*E.g.*,
to revert to the example I have just given, we may

imagine a diagram in which the so-called tangent co-incides throughout a visible interval with the so-called circle. Then, the so-called tangent is not *really* straight, nor the so-called circular arc *really* circular. So if you were to cut out this bit of the diagram and consider it by itself, it would not matter which of the visible lines you called the arc, and which the tangent.][1]

"Further the same must be said of the 'discourse', since it is made up of names and verbal forms (ῥήματα). There is no sufficiently fixed fixity in it. [μηδὲν ἱκανῶς βεβαίως εἶναι βέβαιον. This is an obvious consequence. If a mathematical term gives rise to ambiguity owing to the possibility of its being taken as standing for something we can see and draw, *a fortiori* the same must be said of a definition or other proposition containing many terms.] And there is no end to be said (μυρίος δὲ λόγος) in the same way (αὖ) of the ambiguity (ἀσαφές) of each of the four [*sc.* ὀνόματα, λόγοι, εἴδωλα, δόξαι]. But the principal point is that we mentioned just now. The ὄν and the ποῖόν τι are two different things. But when the soul is trying to know the *What* (τί), not the ποῖόν τι, each of the four presents it, in word or in fact [λόγῳ τε καὶ κατ᾽ ἔργα, where κατ᾽ ἔργα refers to the construction of the sensible diagram or model], with that after which it is not seeking,[2] and thus renders what is being stated

---

[1] Or is it simply meant that we might—since names are a matter of "convention"—have used the word "straight" to mean what we actually call "curved"? This is true, but I do not see how it can be regarded as giving rise to any difficulty.

[2] These are perhaps the most difficult words in the whole of the passage. What are we to understand by this substitution of the irrelevant question for the relevant? I think we may explain the matter as follows. The mind is said to be inquiring into the "what" of something, and the reference to a diagram or model as the source of the confusion shows that the something is a mathematical line or figure of some kind. Its τί or "what" will therefore be its defining characteristic, and to "inquire into" this τί will presumably mean to "construct" the curve or figure or what not, to establish its "existence". You will be committing the inconsequence spoken of if you attempt to demonstrate the συμπτώματα of the line, curve, figure, before showing how to construct it, *i.e.* before

and demonstrated open to refutation by the senses, and so fills everyone, speaking roughly, with confusion and perplexity. Accordingly in matters as to which, from our evil upbringing, we have not so much as learned the habit of seeking for truth, but are satisfied by any image of it which presents itself, we do not make one another ridiculous in the process of question and answer, by our ability to tear in pieces and refute the four; but in cases in which we are obliged to answer about the fifth and point it out, anyone who has the will and the ability is equal to overthrowing < his antagonist > and can make the exponent < of a truth > in speech or writing or answers to questions [*i.e.* dialectical inquiry] appear to most of his hearers to know nothing about the matter on which he is undertaking to write or speak, since the audience often forget that it is not the mind (ψυχή) of the writer or speaker which is being refuted, but only one or other of the four, thanks to its ill constitution.[1] It is the process through

proving that it is one of the objects contained in the geometer's universe of discourse. Thus Proclus' already-quoted observations about the reason for placing Euclid I. 4 after I. 1-3 amount to urging that Euclid would have committed the fault in question if he had investigated certain συμπτώματα of triangles in which two sides and the included angle of the one are equal to two sides and the included angle of the other, without having proved by implication (as Proclus assumes he has done) that a pair of such triangles can exist.

A more modern illustration would be attempting to establish some theorem about the tangent to a given curve at any point before you have ascertained that the curve has a tangent at any point.

[1] *I.e.* the man who is attempting to express a true proposition may employ ill-selected terms, or a badly expressed or otherwise imperfect definition, or may attempt to illustrate his meaning by a diagram which does not represent the relations with which he is dealing adequately. You may then make it appear that he is uttering a paradox or that what he says is at variance with what can be seen in the diagram. But you have not in this way proved that what he meant to assert is false. Thus, for example, Aristotle's "refutations" of the Platonic views about the εἰδητικοὶ ἀριθμοί turn in effect on denying that a surd expression such as $\sqrt{2}$ is a *number*. ("All number is composed of ones", etc.) This, however, is no criticism of Plato's meaning, but only of his terminology. So, again, it is no disproof of the existence of "transfinite" numbers to say that the arithmetic of "transfinites" contradicts the axiom that "the whole is greater than the part". The contradiction merely shows that the axiom only holds good of collections

them all, the transition forwards and backwards in the case of each, that last hardly gives birth to knowledge of the well-constituted in a well-constituted < mind >. But if < the mind's > constitution be ill (and this is most men's case both with respect to acquiring knowledge and with respect to acquiring what is called character), and in part also corrupted, Lynceus himself could not make such men see."

[We may, I think, illustrate the whole passage in the following way: Let us suppose a mathematician to be dealing with a branch of his study which owes its fundamental principles to the researches of the Academy, the Geometry of the Conic Sections. Let us further suppose that he is aiming at proving the existence-theorem that there are three such curves and no more; a task which, of course, involves the establishment of a correct definition of each of the three by reference to some exclusive property—an answer to the question τί ἐστι; It is at once obvious that any ambiguity of language may introduce great difficulties into the communication of his investigations on such points to others. But the same thing is equally true of the diagrams by which he attempts to remedy the imperfections of language, and make his meaning definite for his hearers. Thus, for example, if we formed our notions of the ellipse from the diagrams of the text-books, we should probably be struck by the inequality of the two axes of the curve, which the diagrams usually make prominent, and we might be led to think this inequality a universal characteristic of ellipses. This would lead to entire misconception of the relation of the ellipse to the

with a finite number of terms, and is, therefore, as it stands, badly expressed. Or, finally, you do not refute a proof that a given curve has no tangent at a given point (say the "origin") by drawing a diagram in which it looks as if there were a tangent at that point. You only show that the diagram does not represent what it stands for correctly.

circle, since we should fail to see that the circle is only one special case of an ellipse, in which the eccentricity of the curve is = o, a mistake which was actually committed by Herbert Spencer when he contrasted circular orbits as "homogeneous" with elliptic orbits as "heterogeneous". Or, again, the teacher might wish to prefix to his treatment of the separate 'conics' a general account of the properties of the 'general conic'. For the benefit of his readers or hearers, he would probably illustrate his propositions by diagrams. But in any one diagram the figure will not be a 'general conic', but definitely either parabolic, elliptical, or hyperbolic, and this may lead the beginner to confuse the properties of conics as such with those of the special conic figured in the diagram. Or, yet again, and this illustrates the remarks about the ease with which a smart ἀντιλογικός can make the mathematician look ridiculous, the lines which in a figure represent the asymptotes to an hyperbola can be seen to be such as would soon meet the line which stands for the curve, if both were produced, and the side and diagonal of the "square", measured by our rough appliances, will seem to have a common measure. Hence an ἀντιλογικός who insists on regarding the figure as the actual object of which a proposition is enunciated can readily make it seem that the geometer is uttering paradoxes which an appeal to the senses will explode. It is apropos to remember that the subtle arguments of Zeno were for centuries supposed to be idle though ingenious sophisms which might be set aside by such an appeal, though in fact they go down to the roots of mathematical philosophy. Thus we can understand what the writer means when he says that the whole series of intermediaries by which knowledge is imparted, name, definition, diagram or model, belief as to the teacher's meaning, is attended at every stage by possibility of misapprehension, and that it is only by a repeated dwelling on each of the four and comparison of it with the rest (*e.g.* repeated transition from written text to diagram, and back again from diagram to text) that the truth which the teacher is struggling to express at last dawns on his pupil's mind. For this reason alone, it would follow that, as has been already maintained, long personal association in the pursuit of truth is necessary if one philosopher-mathematician is to train up another. The same difficulty would meet us, as the writer says, in the attempt to impart knowledge of any kind but for the fact that in our daily life we are commonly content with something far short of the ideal. We think it enough that those to whom we communicate our ideas should form a mere rough-and-ready approximation to our meaning. This is, *e.g.*, all that is commonly arrived at when a man makes a speech on a social or political topic. He does not expect his audience to take in all that he means, or to frame very precise notions of the "liberty", "order", "progress", and so forth of which he speaks. He is satisfied if they catch his meaning "there or thereabouts". But it is the great merit of the μαθήματα as a mental discipline that a "there or thereabouts" standard of comprehension is not tolerated in "geometry and the kindred arts".

So much for the sense of the passage. A word on the reference to Lynceus the sharp-sighted with which it ends. Mr. Richards finds this nonsensical, and asks whether Lynceus was supposed to be able to infect others with his gift of vision. I think this a serious misunderstanding of a phrase which in itself is simple enough. Everyone knows that if, *e.g.*, you take a country walk with a keen-sighted friend, he is likely to call your attention to all sorts of minute or distant objects which you can see well enough for yourself after your atten-

tion has been directed to them, but would otherwise
have passed by unnoticed. It is in this sense that
Lynceus is spoken of as able to make other men see
things. And it is in this same ability to call a pupil's
attention to what he would otherwise have overlooked
that a good teacher may properly enough be compared
with a keen-sighted companion whose range of vision
is longer than one's own.]

"In a word, if there is no affinity[1] between a man's
mind and our study (τὸ πρᾶγμα) mere quick receptivity
or good memory will never create such an affinity [with
οὐκ ἂν ποιήσειεν we have clearly to understand συγγενῆ,
so that the construction is τὸν μὴ συγγενῆ οὔτε εὐμάθεια
οὔτε μνήμη ποιήσειεν ἂν συγγενῆ]. For it absolutely refuses
to make its appearance except in a kindred soul. Hence
neither those who have no natural attachment and

---

[1] For the thought that Philosophy demands kinship between the Reality
known and the mind that knows it, see *Republic* 490 *b*, οὐδ' ἀπολήγοι τοῦ ἔρωτος,
πρὶν αὐτοῦ ὃ ἔστιν ἑκάστου τῆς φύσεως ἅψασθαι ᾧ προσήκει ψυχῆς ἐφάπτεσθαι
τοῦ τοιούτου—προσήκει δὲ συγγενεῖ κτλ. As the *Republic* passage shows that
the thought is closely coloured by the imagery of the ἱερὸς γάμος, the allusion
in συγγενής may not impossibly be to the Attic Law of the heiress, by which the
hand of the orphan ἐπίκληρος fell of right to the next-of-kin. In any case, the
meaning is that mere quickness in learning and good memory will never make
a philosopher. A special elevation of soul and a peculiar gift of insight is indispensable. Historically we can trace back the thought that the highest intelligence is *akin* in a special way to the worthiest objects of knowledge to the
Orphic belief that while the body to which a soul is temporarily assigned consists of materials drawn from its physical surroundings, the soul itself, being a
divinity, comes from "heaven". Cf. Xenophon, *Cyropaedia*, viii. 7. 20 (in the
course of an argument for immortality manifestly drawn for the most part from
the *Phaedo*), διαλυομένου δὲ ἀνθρώπου δῆλά ἐστιν ἕκαστα ἀπιόντα πρὸς τὸ ὁμόφυλον
πλὴν τῆς ψυχῆς (earth to earth, etc.), αὕτη δὲ μόνη οὔτε παροῦσα οὔτε ἀπιοῦσα
ὁρᾶται, where the suggestion plainly is that the soul also departs at death, πρὸς τὸ
ὁμόφυλον, to its cognate gods ; Aristophanes, *Clouds*, 229, εἰ μὴ κρεμάσας τὸ νόημα
καὶ τὴν φροντίδα λεπτὴν καταμείξας ἐς τὸν ὅμοιον ἀέρα (where the allusion is to
the theory of Diogenes of Apollonia—also mentioned in the *Phaedo* as one
which had interested Socrates,—that air is, as we should now say, the vehicle
of intelligence); cf. also the lines of the Orphic plate from Petelia, εἰπεῖ· "Γῆς παῖς
εἰμι καὶ Οὐρανοῦ ἀστερόεντος, αὐτὰρ ἐμοὶ γένος οὐράνιον" κτλ., and those found
at Thurii, καὶ γὰρ ἐγὼν ὑμῶν γένος ὄλβιον εὔχομαι εἶναι κτλ. The humorous
parallel of Plato's *Timaeus* between the shape of the human head and the shape
of the οὐρανός is a fanciful expression of the same central idea.

P

affinity to righteousness and whatsoever else is fair,
though perhaps quick to learn and steadfast to retain
other knowledge of various kinds, nor yet those who
have this natural affinity but are slow to learn and for-
getful,—none of these, I say, will ever fully master the
truth about virtue and vice.[1] (< I say 'virtue *and* vice',>
because both must be learned together, and similarly
truth and falsehood about Real Being as a whole have
to be learned together, and this, as I said at first,
demands much time and practice ($\tau\rho\iota\beta\dot{\eta}$)). It is only in
consequence of a reciprocal friction of them all, names,
discourses, visual and other perceptions, with one
another and the testing of them by kindly examination,
and question and answer practised in no spirit of vain-
glory ($\check{a}\nu\epsilon\upsilon\ \phi\theta\acute{o}\nu\omega\nu$), that the light of sound judgement
($\phi\rho\acute{o}\nu\eta\sigma\iota\varsigma$) and understanding ($\nu o\hat{\upsilon}\varsigma$) flashes out on the
various problems with all the intensity permitted to
human nature.[2]

"Wherefore every worthy man ($\pi\hat{a}\varsigma\ \dot{a}\nu\dot{\eta}\rho\ \sigma\pi o\upsilon\delta a\hat{\iota}o\varsigma$) will
beware with all caution of bringing worthy matters into

---

[1] $\epsilon\dot{\upsilon}\mu a\theta\acute{\iota}a$ and $\mu\nu\dot{\eta}\mu\eta$ are similarly demanded as qualifications of the philosopher
at *Republic* 486 *c–d*, but there, as here, they form only a very small part of
Plato's requirements. He also demands a *passion* for 'truth' or 'reality', indifference to the satisfactions of appetite, "highmindedness" and freedom from all
pettiness of soul ($\dot{a}\nu\epsilon\lambda\epsilon\upsilon\theta\epsilon\rho\acute{\iota}a$) and from all unworthy fear, and various other
qualities which are here aptly summed up in the requirement of a "natural
affinity" to the object of philosophical study.

[2] The metaphor of the sudden breaking out of the flame forms, of course, a
link with 341 *c–d*, but it is ingeniously prepared for by an almost untranslatable
play on words. It has just been said that much $\tau\rho\iota\beta\dot{\eta}$ 'practice' will be required
for the acquisition of philosophy. The writer then echoes the word $\tau\rho\iota\beta\dot{\eta}$ in the
$\tau\rho\iota\beta\acute{o}\mu\epsilon\nu a$ of the next sentence, where he speaks of the process of repeated alter-
nations of attention between the words and $\lambda\acute{o}\gamma o\iota$ of a demonstration and the
diagrams which illustrate it, as one of "friction". This leads naturally to the
image of the insight which results from the process as a light kindled by "friction".
This gradual preparation through an apparently scarcely conscious figurative
use of a common word for a full-blown metaphor has always seemed to me characteristically Platonic. The point of the remark that the philosopher has to learn
at once $\tau\grave{o}\ \dot{a}\lambda\eta\theta\acute{\epsilon}\varsigma$ and $\tau\grave{o}\ \psi\epsilon\upsilon\delta\acute{\epsilon}\varsigma$ is, of course, that in the use of dialectic it is
precisely by seeing where unsatisfactory hypotheses are false that we are led
on to a truer one.

the range of human rivalry and perplexity by writing
of them. In one word, one must learn from what has
been said that when one sees written compositions by
an author, whether laws written by a legislator, or
writings of any other kind soever, these were not the
matters the writer deemed worthiest, if indeed he is himself a man of worth; such things [sc. the things the
writer deemed σπουδαιότατα] are laid up in the fairest
place the man possesses.[1] If he indeed committed them
to writing as things of greatest worth and moment,
'why then, thereafter', not gods but men 'bereft him
of his wits'.

"Well then, he who has followed this discursive tale
will know full well that whether Dionysius, or any other
man, greater or less, wrote down any of the highest and
primary truths of Nature, he must have had no sound
instruction nor understanding of anything of which he
wrote, at least not according to my conviction. Else he
would have had the same awe of these themes as I
have, and not have exposed them to the eyes of discord
and uncomeliness.[2] He could not have been impelled
to write them as memoranda for his private use (there
is no danger that one whose mind has once compassed
the truth should forget it, for it is contained in the
briefest words). It must have been done, if it were done
at all, from an unseemly vanity, whether the purpose
was to claim the knowledge as his own, or to prove his
participation in an education of which he was unworthy

---

[1] κεῖται δέ που ἐν χώρᾳ τῇ καλλίστῃ τῶν τούτου, that is, ἐν τῇ ψυχῇ, or more
precisely ἐν τῷ νῷ; the truths which are of most moment in the opinion of a
good and wise man are written on the "fleshly tables of the heart", not on tablets
of wax or sheets of parchment. He bears them about with him and does not need
to store them in a library.

[2] εἰς ἀναρμοστίαν καὶ ἀπρέπειαν ἐκβάλλειν. If Dionysius had really any understanding of philosophic truth, he would have avoided casting it before swine.
He would not have exposed it, by circulating his σύγγραμμα, to the disordered
and lewd minds of his court circle.

if he was greedy of the reputation of having participated.

"Now if Dionysius was affected thus by our only interview (perhaps it might be so, though *how* it happened 'Goodness only knows', to use the Theban phrase, for I went over the subject in the way I have described, and that once only, and on no second occasion[1]), he who would learn how the effect fell out as it did, must ask himself why we did not go over matters a second and third time, and yet oftener. Does Dionysius after a single hearing fancy that he has knowledge, and has he really sufficient knowledge, whether from discoveries of

[1] In this difficult sentence I would punctuate thus : εἰ μὲν οὖν ἐκ τῆς μίας συνουσίας Διονυσίῳ τοῦτο γέγονεν,—τάχ᾽ ἂν εἴη, γέγονεν δ᾽ οὖν ὅπως "ἴττω Ζεύς", φησὶν ὁ Θηβαῖος· διεξῆλθον μὲν γὰρ ὡς εἶπόν τε ἐγὼ καὶ ἅπαξ μόνον, ὕστερον δὲ οὐπώποτε ἔτι—ἐννοεῖν δὴ δεῖ , . . τίνι ποτ᾽ αἰτίᾳ τὸ δεύτερον καὶ τὸ τρίτον πλεονάκις τε οὐ διεξῆμεν· That is I take, εἰ μὲν οὖν . . . γέγονεν as a protasis to which ἐννοεῖν δὴ δεῖ κτλ. forms the apodosis. The general meaning is "I only spoke with him once; hence the question arises why we did not go over the ground again and again". The three possible explanations of Dionysius's conduct in not asking for a second interview, viz. that he thought himself after the first conversation competent to carry on his studies by himself, that he thought what he had heard disappointing, that he felt unequal to the demands of philosophy on his intellect and character, correspond to the three possible results of the πεῖρα suitable to a prince enumerated on p. 340.

As for points of detail, I assume with some hesitation that γέγονεν δ᾽ οὖν ὅπως ἴττω Ζεύς stands for ἴττω Ζεύς ὅπως γέγονεν, " we may leave it to Zeus to know *how* it happened", *i.e.* "only God can say how it came about". Hence I have removed Burnet's comma after ὅπως. In the apodosis I would also remove the comma after τὸ τρίτον, since Plato is insisting that there was only *one* interview, and the οὐ must therefore negative the whole clause τὸ δεύτερον καὶ τὸ τρίτον πλεονάκις τε. The only point now left obscure is the meaning of the τοῦτο of 345 *a* 1. *What* is it that might be supposed to have happened, God knows best how, to Dionysius after his interview with Plato? Apparently the τοῦτο means the "compassing of the truth" referred to in the previous sentence (ἐὰν ἅπαξ τῇ ψυχῇ περιλάβῃ), so that the whole sense is, "if Dionysius really understood that part of the subject which I put before him at our only interview, —perhaps he did, though God knows how he could,—why did he not seek further instruction?" Two explanations, viz. that what, on the supposition, he already knew was enough to qualify him to philosophise for himself in future, or that he was disappointed in what Plato had to say, are then examined and dismissed, and the implied, though unexpressed conclusion is that the only remaining alternative, viz. that he felt his unfitness for the vocation of a philosopher, must be the true one. (I should say that I owe this explanation of the reference of τοῦτο to a suggestion of Prof. Burnet.)

his own or from previous instruction by others? Or does he think my exposition worthless (φαῦλα τὰ λεχθέντα)? Or, for this is the third possibility, does he think the subject beyond him and admit that he has not the ability to live in the practice of wisdom and virtue? If he thinks the exposition worthless, he will find himself in disagreement with numerous witnesses whose judgement in such matters is of much greater weight than that of a Dionysius. If he holds that he has discovered the truth or been instructed in it, and that it is at any rate worthy of a liberally educated mind, how could he ever have been so ready to affront one who had been his master and guide in these studies, unless he is a very singular fellow? The nature of the affront I can explain from personal experience."

The concluding paragraphs of our passage from 344 *a* 1 on do not seem to me to require any particular explanation or elucidation. They merely restate for us the view which had long before been expressed in the *Phaedrus* of the one reasonable ground on which *written* works on φιλοσοφία may be defended, viz. that they serve to refresh a man's fading memories of the actual converse in which two minds have followed up the trail of truth, and urge that that ground is not pleadable on behalf of the work ascribed to Dionysius. Either his character or his judgement is proved to be bad by his seeking no second interview with Plato, and his boasts of his own proficiency,—and Plato inclines strongly to the view that the defect is not merely one of judgement. I have therefore to confess that if my interpretation of the two pages against which Mr. Richards' strictures are specially directed is substantially accurate, I see nothing either in the matter or in the manner of the whole digression which interferes with the ascription of the letter as we have it to Plato.

And I think I have already shown that (*a*) the whole passage as I have rendered it is too much of a unity for one-half of it to be excised without the excision of the remainder, and (*b*) that if the whole is excised the result is immediately a sensible gap in the continuity of the letter. Whence I conclude that for those of us who lack the face to condemn the whole letter on the flimsy grounds which have been urged against it, apart from the objection to this particular section, the only alternative is to recognise the whole as from the hand of Plato. We may feel that Plato's hand has lost something of its cunning; there are unnecessary repetitions in the narrative, and the grammatical construction is sometimes loose, though both charges may be made with equal truth against, *e.g.*, *Laws* vii.-ix. But these are no remarkable faults in a man well over seventy, and most of us, even in our prime, do not carry out in correspondence, and should not employ even in a published pamphlet to which we had purposely given the form of a personal letter, the same strict rules of composition as in a formal treatise or essay.

I will add only one further remark, which seems to me of some weight. The seventh epistle, whether by Plato or not, bears every mark of being a genuine document of the date at which it purports to have been written. The *Epinomis*, indeed, has been quoted as a like example of imitation, but the argument is worthless until some better evidence than that of a φασιν in Diogenes Laertius has been produced against the Platonic authorship of the *Epinomis*. Moreover, even those who think the *Epinomis* an imitation at least account for its exact correspondence with the style of Plato by assigning it to an immediate intimate and personal companion of the master. If we are to ascribe the seventh letter to another than Plato, I do not see how

we can avoid a similar view of its origin. It will have
to be regarded as a manifesto in the name of the
Academy, produced at the latest within a very short
time after Plato's death. Indeed, I think, we may go
further. Such a manifesto could hardly have been
written after the direction of Sicilian affairs had been
put into the hands of Timoleon, and it is scarcely more
likely to have been later than the horrible catastrophe
which ended the tyranny of Dionysius in Locri (346).
Thus we are driven to date the supposedly spurious
letter before Plato's death, and to assume that, even if
he did not actually write it, it was composed in his name
and with his approval. It follows that if the philosophical digression which we have been examining is
"rubbish", it was rubbish which imposed on Plato and
was taken by him for an expression of his own theories.
I, for one, cannot believe in such a theory. The only
rational view of the matter, to my mind, is that a letter
which purports to have been written by Plato shortly
after the death of Dion in 353, cannot have been
written later than 346, and is indistinguishable in style
from Plato's latest work, really was written by Plato,
and that its philosophical part is therefore very unlikely
to be "rubbish" and very likely to be excellent sense.

[1912]

VI

ST. THOMAS AQUINAS AS A PHILOSOPHER

IF an educated Englishman had been asked a hundred
years ago who are the great original philosophic
thinkers of the modern world, what answer would he
have been likely to give? His list of names would, no
doubt, have depended partly upon his personal pre-
ferences, but there are some philosophers whom he
would have been sure to mention. He would certainly
have named Descartes, Locke, and Hume, and almost
certainly Francis Bacon, then all the more admired
because the real character of his theories in logic was so
little understood. A widely read man would probably
have given the names of Leibniz and Spinoza, and the
few who had any knowledge of German literature
would no doubt have added that of Kant. It is almost
certain that no mention would have been made of St.
Thomas or any of the great schoolmen of the thirteenth
century. The current estimate of them is indicated by
the remark made in 1828 by Macaulay that "we extol
Bacon and sneer at Aquinas". If the same question
were put to-day, there would still be individual variations in the answers, but there are some names which
would be contained in them all, and I think it safe to
say that among these would be that of St. Thomas. We
are not to-day all of one mind in philosophy any more
than our great-grandfathers were, and I do not know
that it is desirable that we should be. But if we are not

all of us professed Thomists, we are all, I believe, agreed to recognise in St. Thomas one of the great master-philosophers of human history whose thought is part of the permanent inheritance of civilised Europeans and whose influence is still living and salutary. It is worth while to ask ourselves what is the real ground for the great difference between our own estimate of the worth of the Thomist philosophy and that of our great-grandfathers. Their depreciation of the Angelical Doctor, however unjust, presumably had some sort of reasons for its existence, and if we can discover them, we may learn a lesson which will be profitable in serving to keep us from repeating the same kind of mistake on our own account.

To indicate some of these reasons and to point out their inadequacy will be the modest purpose of the remarks I now proceed to make.

There are two qualities which we may fairly demand from the work of any man whom we are to recognise as a really great philosopher with a permanent importance in the history of human thought. In the first place the work must be original, and in the second it must be critical. When I say that the work must be original, I do not mean that it need be startling or revolutionary, but that it must be the achievement of genuine personal intellectual effort. The great philosopher must be one who has thought for himself and has thought hard. No mere skilful borrower or adapter, no mere eloquent exponent of the ideas of other men can permanently retain his place on the roll of honour of the world's great thinkers. And by saying that the work must be critical, I do not mean that it must necessarily be chiefly devoted to criticism of other men's thoughts, I mean that it must be something more than the construction of a brilliant but undisciplined speculative imagination. The great

philosopher cannot, indeed, have too daring an imagination provided only that its exercise is controlled by a
profound sobriety of judgement, a massive common
sense. Commonly we find the two gifts in an unequal
combination. The daringly imaginative mind is apt to
be deficient in sobriety of judgement, the emphatically
sensible mind to be wanting in imaginative power. And
perhaps, when this is the case, since the object of philosophy is the attainment of truth, the thinker of really
massive common sense, even if his imagination is
slower in its flights, really does more for philosophy
than the dazzling but erratic and unsystematic specu-
lator. The greatness of St. Thomas as a philosopher
seems to me to lie in this, that his work combines high
originality with an unsurpassed sobriety of judgement
and sense for reality. To our great-grandfathers this
statement would have seemed a paradox, and it is precisely because it would have struck them as a paradox
that they could permit themselves, in Macaulay's
phrase, to "sneer at Aquinas". May I attempt to state
briefly what I take to have been their case?

Thomas, I think they would have said, is not one of
the world's great philosophers for the double reason
that he is not original and that he is not critical. He is
not original because his so-called philosophy is all borrowed and all borrowed from one man, Aristotle. And
what he has taken from Aristotle is simply a framework of barren and verbal formal logic. He is content
to treat every philosophical question as a mere matter
of bringing the issue at question under the caption of
some Aristotelian antithesis, like that of matter and
form or potentiality and act. No doubt in effecting the
reduction, he shows great skill in the construction of
formal syllogisms and the multiplication of subtle verbal
distinctions. But the syllogisms and distinctions do not

bring us one step nearer the real understanding of concrete fact, and that is why, as was assumed, the sciences
made no real advance from the thirteenth century to the
seventeenth. The scholastic philosopher might devote
himself as much as he pleased to the elaboration of
further and further deductions from arbitrarily assumed
major premises, but so long as the premises were not
tested by confrontation with empirical fact, all this *a-
priorist* ingenuity was worse than wasted. In the early
nineteenth century view, at least, what science needs is
not formal logic but guaranteed empirical fact, first,
last, and all the time.

And again, St. Thomas and his contemporaries are
uncritical, and that in more ways than one. They are
uncritical, it was held, in the first place in the selection
of their great authority, Aristotle. It is an arbitrary
thing to pick out this one man from among all the
thinkers of the past and reject all the valuable lessons
which might have been learned from other sources. It is
uncritical, again, when the authority has been selected,
to follow it with a blind trust in its infallibility on every
subject on which it has delivered itself. And finally, it
is uncritical in the highest degree to submit the conclusions of philosophical thinking to the constant over-
ruling control of theological authority, as it was commonly assumed that St. Thomas and the other great
schoolmen had done. This, I believe, is the substance
of what would have been stated as the anti-scholastic
case, and it must be allowed that if it could be sustained
it would be enough to justify the men of a hundred
years ago in their refusal to reckon seriously with the
scholastic philosophies.

But the anti-scholastic case cannot really be sustained. In all that is most weighty in the indictment it
rests upon complete misconception of the real situation

of thought in the thirteenth century and the work which was done by St. Thomas and his teacher Albert the Great. I will deal first with the charge of want of originality and then make some remarks about the other charge of want of critical judgement. I have not, indeed, anything novel to say, but on an occasion like this, when we are assembled expressly to "praise famous men", it is worth while to remind ourselves of the facts which abundantly prove the real originality of Thomas.

If we are to put ourselves at the right point of view for appreciating that originality, we must begin by understanding quite clearly that the thirteenth century, like the seventeenth and the nineteenth, in their various ways, was not one of traditionalism, acquiescence in a heritage from the past, but one of restless and audacious innovation, and that to the eyes of contemporaries "Brother Thomas" was one of the most audacious of the innovators. To speak accurately Thomism, to those who were living at the time of its birth, was not the defence of a tradition but doubly a revolt against established tradition. It is, in the first place, of course, not true that the discovery of Aristotelian logic was the work of the thirteenth century. No doubt scholasticism in its latest days did degenerate into something like the substitution of the mere reduction of a problem to the technical terminology of Aristotle for the real examination of the facts. But if we are to make this a ground of attack against the first introducers of formal logic into the modern Western world, the scapegoats ought to be looked for in the twelfth and not in the thirteenth century. It was not the latter which wasted the best of its energies in unfruitful quarrelling about the old problem of Universals, nor were Thomas and Albert primarily formal logicians at all. Their Aristotle,

as I need hardly remind you, was very different from
the Aristotle known to Peter Abelard. The interest of
the thirteenth century was not in Aristotle's logical doctrines but in the teaching of his *Metaphysics, Physics,
De Caelo, De Generatione, De Anima,* and the rest of
the treatises which were recovered for the Western world
early in the century from the hands of Jews, Persians,
and Moors, and the fascination of this literature lay
precisely not in its logical form but in its matter. As
M. Gilson has said, the recovery of the cosmological,
physiological, and psychological work of Aristotle
meant to the Western world the rediscovery of Nature
herself as an object of investigation in her own right
and by the "natural light of reason". We must recollect
that the world into which Aristotle's metaphysics and
science, as distinct from his formal logic, were reintro-
duced in the early years of the thirteenth century was
one which for centuries had known only one work of
real value on what we nowadays call science — Chal-
cidius' fragmentary version of the *Timaeus,* and that
the *Timaeus,* with all its profound insight into the character of scientific problems and scientific method, does
not even aim at being a repertory of scientifically
ascertained conclusions of fact. In the Aristotelian
works rediscovered in the thirteenth century, Western
Christendom was, for the first time since the closing of
the ancient Hellenic schools by Justinian, being confronted with an encyclopaedia of the Natural Sciences
as a *fait accompli* and put in a position to realise that
the external world is something more than a useful key
to the hieroglyphics of the Scriptures. There was, indeed, to be a period, some centuries later, when a re-
kindled interest in the remains of the pre-Aristotelian
Greek thinkers would serve the same purpose of recalling men from fancy to fact, but we misread the facts of

history if we do not realise that the enthusiasm of the
thirteenth century for Aristotle was prompted by the
very same spirit as the protests of Galileo against the
Aristotelian traditionalism of the universities of Northern Italy in the seventeenth century. Hence M. Gilson
seems absolutely right in his contention that the return of Aristotle from his Oriental captivity opened
for scientific thought an era not of subjection but of
liberation.

This, however, is not all that has to be said about the
attitude of Thomas toward the great Greek thinkers,
nor the half of it. The next point I would raise is one on
which I have already said a passing word—the point
that, whatever Thomism in some later phases may have
temporarily sunk into being, St. Thomas himself was
no traditionalist but a vigorously independent thinker
who impressed his older contemporaries as a daring
innovator. In fact, as I said, he was doubly in revolt
against tradition. The main tradition in Christian philosophical thinking, as you all know, had right down to
the days of Albert and Thomas been the Platonic as
derived through Augustine and Boethius; the substitution of Aristotelianism for Platonism as the basis of a
specifically Christian philosophy was a revolution and
a rather paradoxical revolution. The greatest admirer
of Aristotle among you would probably be ready to
allow at least that, on the face of it, Platonism impresses
us as a deeply religious view of existence with the closest
affinities to Christianity in its doctrines of Providence,
moral judgement and retribution; on the face of it,
again, Aristotle's thought, at first at any rate, certainly
looks to be what it has been called in recent years by
one who has a right to speak on such matters, the least
religious of the great philosophies. The task of finding
a basis for a Christian philosophy precisely in the "First

Philosophy" of Aristotle was thus a singularly bold one from which any thinker without the highest intellectual independence must have flinched.

And if Thomas was thus a bold innovator on the Platonic tradition of earlier Christian thinkers, we must remember that he was equally an innovator in the interpretation he put on Aristotelianism itself. Here again there was a definite tradition confronting him, a tradition built up by men to whom, as his repeated references show, he felt that grave respect was due, Alexander of Aphrodisias, Avicenna, Averroes, and the tradition was decidedly in favour of a pantheistic and naturalistic interpretation of Aristotle which would have been fatal to the very cause Thomas had at heart, the creation of a system of thought which was to be at once reasoned closely out at every step and wholly true to the religious demands of Christianity. The complete victory won by Thomas over the Averroists and their naturalism must not blind us to the simple fact that philosophically it was Siger of Brabant and not Thomas who was following the lines of traditional Aristotelianism. In fact, the Aristotelianism of St. Thomas triumphed over that of the Averroists not because they were *philosophically* heretics and schismatics (they, in fact, stood for the main tradition of centuries), nor because it is demonstrably the more faithful interpretation of Aristotle's own thought—a position on which one might argue for ever without reaching a definite conclusion—but by its sheer merits. One may convince oneself on that point very readily by a simple study of that exquisite masterpiece of philosophical polemic, the *de Unitate Intellectus contra Averroistas*. There is no pretence here that the issue at stake is decided in any way by mere exegesis of an authoritative text. The question is not what Aristotle personally meant to say, but what is true. Even if the Averroists are right in their exegesis of Aristotle, it still has to be considered whether the doctrine presented, perhaps rightly, perhaps wrongly, as Aristotle's is true or false. It is not concealed that the doctrine the writer of the essay believes to be true and holds to be compatible with the not very explicit utterances of Aristotle is in conflict not only with the teaching of Averroes but with the whole tradition of Aristotelian exegetes. There is no pretence that we have simply to discover what Aristotle meant, and that his opinion, once ascertained, must be taken as true because it is his.

The writer's position is the very different one that it would not be at all surprising that Aristotle or any other philosopher should have fallen into an error. Our business is to satisfy ourselves by independent hard thinking, if we can, about the truth of the matter; if we subsequently find that Aristotle's deliverances admit of being understood in a sense compatible with the truth, so much the better for him, but if they cannot be so interpreted, we have simply to say that, like every-body else, Aristotle was not infallible and has made a mistake. On the merits of the controversy it seems to me unmistakable that the Averroists receive, what is a rare thing in metaphysical controversy, a direct and crushing defeat which makes the reading of the essay a delight to anyone who can appreciate the art of "mental warfare". That Thomas felt this, too, I should infer from the departure at the end of the essay from his usual calm impersonality of tone. I think I detect in the sentence in which the Averroists are invited if they really have anything worth calling an argument, to produce it and see what will happen to it, an innocent chuckle, so to say, over the completeness of a triumph which the Saint evidently recognises as due not to

superior acquaintance with Aristotelian texts but to
honest personal clear-headed thinking.

The plain fact, indeed—though I am here anticipating for a moment—is that the Aristotelianism of
Thomas, if we are to call it so, is not borrowed from
anyone, except in the sense in which the most original
of human minds may be said to "borrow" the suggestions it needs as the pabulum for its own thinking.
It is a genuinely new systematic doctrine, indebted to
Aristotle of course, and to many others besides, but
owing its specific form and its systematic coherency
to its deviser; the right name for it is not Aristotelianism
but Thomism.

How completely the new philosophical doctrine
revolutionised accepted tradition in the Christian West
may perhaps be seen from two little facts doubtless
familiar to all of you.

One is the fate of the famous *a priori* argument of
Anselm for the existence of God, named by Kant the
"ontological proof". From the careful study of Father
P. A. Daniels it appears that out of fifteen leading
schoolmen of the thirteenth century who reproduce the
argument, three, of whom Albert the Great is one,
express no opinion on its validity, ten accept it, only
two reject it, St. Thomas and Richard of Middleton. I
think we may infer that the discredit into which the
argument fell with philosophers and theologians, to
whom one would have expected it to be specially wel-
come from its simplicity and apparent finality, is wholly
due to the vigour and originality of the famous criticism
to which it was subjected by Thomas. It is highly significant that the moment Descartes attempted to revive
the same line of thought in the seventeenth century, the
critics of his *Meditations* raised the objection that his
employment of it would render his philosophy suspect

in the eyes of theologians—the very class, as I say, whose natural bias one would expect to be in its favour. It is not for me, here, of course, to express any opinion of my own on the soundness of the famous argument; I want simply to make two observations about the rejection of it by St. Thomas. The first is that there could be no better proof of the independence of mind of a thinker whose principal task in life was the philosophical defence of religion than that he should have insisted on rigorously criticising and rejecting the very line of argument which promised to be the shortest of routes to Theism, and that in the face of the general consensus of the *docti* in its favour. The other is that it is a point of the highest interest that there are just two great philosophers who have independently, and on different grounds, rejected the ontological argument, Thomas and Kant, and that whenever you meet a philosophic thinker to-day who rejects it, you regularly find, when you come to scrutinise his ground, that he is moved directly by the considerations long ago urged by one or both of these great men. Kant and St. Thomas have often been, and still are, pitted against one another by their respective followers as natural antagonists; this makes it all the more significant that they are in complete agreement on this fundamental point, rather to the scandal of many of the so-called "idealists" of our own day, who would like to regard Kant as their legitimate ancestor. The secret explanation of the agreement I believe is to be found in the fact that both philosophers are really, in the best sense of the phrase, "critical realists" with all the realist's distrust of brilliant speculation which has no solid root in a firm grasp of empirical fact.

The other example is equally significant, and to you it will be equally familiar. Thomas seems first to have attracted attention as a thinker with an individuality of his own by his declaration that the philosophical arguments in vogue for an absolute beginning of the world's history will not stand scrutiny and that, apart from a supernatural revelation, it must remain an open question whether the created world has not existed *ab aeterno*, a position in which he agrees with Rabbi Moses. In our own day the bias of metaphysicians seems to be preponderantly in favour of the Aristotelian tenet of the eternity of the world, and the fact stands in the way of our appreciating the originality of this declaration at its full merits. We have to remember that the philosophical bias of the contemporaries of St. Thomas was, quite naturally, in the other direction. Since no one who was an orthodox Christian thought of doubting that the world had had a beginning at no very remote date, the tendency was naturally to attempt philosophical demonstration of what was unquestionably accepted as a known truth, and living thinkers, including St. Thomas' own teacher Albert, had professed to be able to supply the required proof. There is abundance of evidence that Thomas' early declared and persistent denial of the worth of all these demonstrations was felt as something like a veritable scandal. It would naturally wear that appearance all the more that the rising philosopher would inevitably seem to be playing straight into the hands of the "naturalists" of the time, the Averroists. To appreciate the disturbance created, we have only to remember the alarm caused to well-meaning and pious men by the appearance of Darwin's *Origin of Species*. We know the kind of thing which would have been said in the middle of the nineteenth century if a rising divine or Professor of Theology or Moral Philosophy had publicly declared that all the arguments by which opponents of Darwin were trying to refute the doctrine of the origination of new species by natural selection are invalid and will not stand examination. But to the contemporaries of St. Thomas the assertion that there are no sound philosophical arguments against the creation of the world "from eternity" involved at least as great a revolution in traditional thinking as the doctrine of the origin of species by natural selection demanded of our grandfathers. It could have come from no one but a thinker of the most marked originality and determined courage, the last kind of man in the least likely to allow his judgement as a philosopher to be determined for him by extra-philosophical considerations or bias in favour of a venerable tradition.

These remarks lead me naturally to the part of my subject which happens, from the character of my own studies, to be most interesting to myself—the attitude of Thomas to the philosophical thought of the world's past. The persons for whom Macaulay is speaking in the words I quoted at the beginning of this lecture supposed this attitude to be sufficiently described by saying that St. Thomas subjected human thought to the despotism of Aristotle. But the judgement is only intelligible when we remember that the accusation dates from a time when the serious revival of Aristotelian study in Europe had barely begun. The Aristotle of the "advanced thinkers" of the eighteenth and early nineteenth centuries was not the Aristotle of history as we have since learned to understand him, nor even Aristotle as seen through the eyes of St. Thomas himself, but Aristotle as falsely conceived by the *epigoni* of scholasticism in its feeblest and least original period. From our point of view such an estimate ought to be at once and for all impossible. It would be truer to say that what Thomas effected for the first time in history since the expiry of neo-Platonic learning in the sixth century was a magnificent and original synthesis of past philosophical thought. He took his materials freely from the whole record of the classic past, so far as it lay open to him, and what he constructed out of them was no chaotic eclecticism but a coherent system welded into a unity by the presence throughout its details of a few great ruling principles, won by permanent hard thinking and held with the clearest consciousness of their implications. It is not true that he changed the existing philosophical tradition by dethroning one un-critically accepted authority and enthroning another. It would be much truer to say that he retained and built upon the thought which had been accessible to his predecessors, enriching and integrating it with the wealth of new matter made accessible to his own age by the recovery of Aristotle. Indeed, I do not know that it would be going beyond the mark to say that, for the first time in the life of the modern world he at-tempted something like a critical and thoroughly his-torical appreciation of past philosophy in its entirety. I cannot develop this thought so fully as I should like to do, but there are certain aspects of it upon which I should like to make a few remarks.

To a student of Greek philosophy it is of great interest to note how frequent are the references in that great philosophical masterpiece, the *Summa contra Gentiles*, to the very thinkers about whom the men of the thirteenth century could have the least trustworthy information, the pre-Platonic men of science. It is curious how often the author goes out of his way to comment on the theories of men like Anaxagoras and Empedocles, and what earnest efforts he makes to understand them and to call attention to the truths they may be supposed to have been struggling to convey.

To be sure, many of his guesses at their meaning are such as we can now see to be unhistorical, but we have to remember the paucity of his information. In the main his knowledge about the earliest Greek thought is necessarily based on scattered notices in the text of Aristotle. He has thus to reconstruct under the double disadvantage that his knowledge is full of *lacunae* and that Aristotle's statements about his predecessors are often both obscure and vitiated by the defect, shared by Aristotle with Hegel, of inability to appreciate the ideas of others except with reference to his own system. This, however, is a difficulty common to him with all writers about the beginnings of Greek science down to a very recent date. We have to remember that the work of collating the various sources of information, correcting the often grave errors in the traditional texts and establishing the historical affiliation of the sources, an indispensable preliminary to satisfactory interpretation, can hardly have been said to have begun before the publication of Diels' *Doxographi Graeci* and the great Berlin edition of the commentators on Aristotle, well within our own lifetime, and is not even yet fully completed. Bear all this in mind, and then, comparing Thomas' treatment of those of the early thinkers about whom the literature available to him contains a reasonable amount of information with Hegel's treatment of the same subject in his lectures on the *History of Philosophy*, ask yourselves which of the two men, when proper allowance is made for superiority of the material available to Hegel, has used his material in the more objective and scientific way. I honestly do not think the advantage will be found to be on the side of the German.

A more important question is that of the relation of Thomas to Plato and to Aristotle himself. Here I am afraid I shall be bound to be a little more prolix. There is a misleading but common impression that down to the middle of the thirteenth century the foundations of the philosophy of the Christian ages had been Platonic, but that at that date Thomas and Albert effected a sudden revolution by rejecting Plato for Aristotle. There is, of course, a certain truth at the bottom of this statement, but, like all summary statements, it is dangerously misleading unless it is very carefully qualified. In the first place it suggests the thoroughly unhistorical view that the philosophies of Plato and Aristotle are in principle opposed to one another, whereas the truth, as all careful students of both philosophers know, is that the differences between the two thinkers, important as some of them are, are comparatively few and are mostly on points which are quite secondary by comparison with the fundamental principles in which the two great philosophies agree. That Aristotle himself was clearly alive to this is manifest all through his work. The undisguised object of the standing polemic which he urges against the contemporary Academy is to suggest that, in spite of all differences in formulas, in spirit it is himself, not Speusippus or Xenocrates, who is the legitimate heir to the intellectual achievements of Plato. Nor do I think Plato himself would have resented this attitude. No doubt, if he could have returned to earth, he would have protested that much of the Aristotelian criticism rests on misconception of his meaning, the kind of misconception inevitable when a biologist attempts to follow the thought of a mathematician. But the philosopher who deliberately refused to compose a treatise on his own philosophy on the ground that philosophy is not a body of formulae or doctrines, but the living spirit of personal devotion to the pursuit of truth, would have been the last man to disown a successor on the strength of a difference in expression or opinion.

The popular conception again completely misrepresents the facts about the actual achievement of Thomas. It is true that on a first perusal of him we are struck by the uniformity with which the familiar Aristotelian technical formulae recur in his treatment of all questions. His logical equipment, in particular, comes direct from the *Topics* and the *Analytics*. This is, in any case, what we should expect. There was, in fact, no other body of articulated logical doctrine with which to work. But when we penetrate to the matter which is presented to us in this vesture of Aristotelian logic, the case is altered. The Augustinian exemplarism, itself a direct derivation of the Platonic doctrine of Forms, is, as we know, an important and integral part of the Thomist philosophy. Intimately connected with it is the equally fundamental conception of causality as a process in which the effect imperfectly "mirrors" the cause, and this, with the great notion of the ladder of being, or scale of perfection, is wholly a legacy, through Augustine, from the neo-Platonists. It is, I think, safe to say that none of these conceptions could have been derived from the text of Aristotle unless Aristotle had first been read by the light of Platonism and neo-Platonism as mediated through Augustine.

Indeed, I should like to go rather further than this. It seems to me at least an ambiguous statement to say that Thomas directly opposes Platonism in metaphysics at all. He certainly opposes particular doctrines of the *Platonici*, but it is another question whether he can be said to oppose the doctrines of Plato. (I am speaking, of course, of the Platonic metaphysic; I do not refer to psychology and the theory of knowledge, where we all know that Thomism is definitely Aristotelian.) Before we can say that Thomas opposes the Platonism of Plato, we need to be quite sure what Plato's own ripest thought was, and to be sure on that point is a very difficult matter. The trouble is that Plato has himself been at some pains to warn us that his deepest thoughts are not to be found in his writings; he reserved them, in fact, for oral exposition to the students of the Academy. Our knowledge of them has to be gathered in the first instance from the allusions of Aristotle, who notoriously treats as the distinctive doctrines of Plato propositions which are not to be found in the Platonic dialogues at all. Unfortunately Aristotle is most commonly content to make enigmatic statements without explaining what they mean, a task which would be superfluous while the original hearers of Plato were alive and active, and even when he gives an explanation we cannot be sure that it is one which Plato himself would have accepted as accurate. The dramatist's gift of entering with ready sympathy into the inmost thought of another mind appears, indeed, to have been one with which Aristotle, with all his other gifts, was not richly endowed. The indispensable preliminary to real comprehension of Plato's personal thought would seem to be a careful collection of all the notices of his oral teaching to be found in Aristotle and a confrontation of them with all the similar records of such notices by Xenocrates and other Academics as still survive in the commentaries of Simplicius and other men of learning in later antiquity. This preliminary work has only been systematically undertaken within the present century by the industry of M. Robin,[1] and the task of interpreting the material he has collected for us cannot be said to have advanced beyond its bare inception. It will be time to raise the question whether Thomism and Platonism are really in fundamental antagonism when we have rediscovered,

---

[1] L. Robin, *La Théorie platonicienne des Idées et des Nombres d'après Aristote.* Paris, 1908.

if we ever do rediscover it, the real tradition of the first generation of the Academy. Meanwhile, I may perhaps be allowed to utter a word or two by way of caution.

If, as seems perhaps probable, Plato really meant to make the world of Forms which is the object of science something existing apart from God, independent of Him and above Him in the scale of perfection, it need not be said that Thomas completely rejects that part of his teaching, though the rejection is not a conscious repudiation of Plato, since no one in the thirteenth century understood Plato in this sense. So far as I have observed in my own reading, what polemic there is against the *Platonici* in the principal works of St. Thomas is principally connected with two points, (1) that Plato regards "natural species" as substances and (2) that the *Platonici* have said that the soul is in the body as the sailor is in his ship. The first of these statements about Plato is certainly borne out by well-known polemical passages in Aristotle, though it is interesting to remember that the precise meaning and the justification of these Aristotelian criticisms is still hotly controverted among special students of Greek philosophy. The second statement seems to an outsider like myself a little of a puzzle. The phrase about the sailor and the vessel does not actually occur anywhere in Plato and is not really well-chosen to illustrate the view about the relation between the soul and the body suggested even in the *Phaedo*. St. Thomas presumably took the phrase from the passage in the *De Anima*[1] where Aristotle says that the problem is one which will have to be considered. The curious thing is that the ancient commentators were all completely in the dark about the bearings of the observation; they are quite uncertain whose theory is alluded to, and even uncertain whether Aristotle

[1] 413 *a* 9.

meant to express approval or disapproval. The one thing they do not suggest is that the reference is to Plato. Possibly, then, St. Thomas was mistaken in seeing any reference to Plato in the words. In any case the real attitude of Thomas to the great thinker who had inspired the philosophical thought of Augustinianism cannot be properly determined by reference to this rather special and limited polemic. It is much more significant, though it is too often forgotten, that Thomism incorporates in itself the whole of the Augustinian exemplarism. This really brings Thomas much nearer to Plato than Aristotle himself is, at least in his controversial moods. Aristotle often allows himself to speak as though the whole Platonic doctrine of Forms or Ideas had been "moonshine", "empty words"; Thomas never says anything of the kind. In his theory the archetypal Forms have an important part to play; it is only that Plato was mistaken in supposing that they are directly accessible to *our* imprisoned intelligence.

And what of the relation of Thomas to Aristotle himself? Is not this equally misrepresented when he is spoken of as an "Aristotelian" or a "follower of Aristotle" without further explanation? Clearly I think in using such unqualified expressions there is the danger of creating a thoroughly false impression. There is one sense in which Thomas is no follower of Aristotle nor of any other man. He never accepts a doctrine because it has been taught by a man with a famous name and an established reputation; what he accepts he accepts because he believes it to be true, or if not absolutely and certainly true, the nearest approximation that can be made to the exact truth. If then he, in many parts of his philosophising, follows Aristotle so closely, it is because he is convinced by the independent exercise of his personal thinking powers that Aristotle is on the right lines. You will remember how explicitly this point is made in the annihilating critique of the Averroist doctrine about the "unity of the intellect". We are told there, as plainly as we could be told, that our real concern is not with what Aristotle taught but with what is true. If the Averroists could succeed in showing that their own exegesis of Aristotle is correct, that would be so much the worse for Aristotle, but none the better for Averroes. The sanction of Aristotle is never an adequate refuge for error. One remembers, too, how in the commentary on the *De Caelo*[1] we are explicitly warned against the very mistake made by the traditionalists of the time of Galileo. We may be content, we are told, to accept the scheme of the Aristotelian (or rather Eudoxian) astronomy, because "it saves the appearances", but we must not insist that the machinery it assumes of the rotating spheres is real, "because it is quite possible that the appearances may equally well be saved by some other theory yet to be put forward." That is, in modern language, we may use the current astronomy as a convenient descriptive theory on the strength of which eclipses and other astronomical events may be correctly calculated, but we have no right to treat the description as if it were an explanation. It is plain, I think, that if Thomas, who was, of course, well acquainted with the fact that a heliocentric astronomy had been taught in antiquity by Aristarchus and Seleucus, could have been confronted with the revival of the theory by Copernicus, he at least would have been ready to consider with an absolutely open mind the question whether the heliocentric theory does not "save the appearances" better than the geocentric.

In general, as to this matter of the degree of de-

---

[1] ii. 17, forte secundum aliquem alium modum, nondum ab hominibus comprehensum, apparentia circa stellas salvantur.

pendence of St. Thomas on Aristotle, there are, it seems to me, one or two things well worth saying even in a brief paper like this. (1) I suppose no one has ever made an extensive and repeated study of the *Corpus Aristotelicum* without feeling strongly that there were, so to say, two Aristotles. There was the Aristotle whose tendencies are to "naturalism" in philosophy and to detailed and specific research in the sciences, and there was the Aristotle who was "carried off his feet", as Professor Burnet has said, in the Academy by the Platonic passion for the divine and eternal. The consequence of this manifest clash in the philosopher's own soul between the "naturalistic" bent, presumably acquired in early education, and the "other-world" tendency due to Platonism is a curious "fault" which runs through all the chief Aristotelian treatises. Thus, just by way of indicating the presence of the "fault", let me suggest the questions: (*a*) What is, according to Aristotle, the proper specific object of "first philosophy"? Is it "being as such," or is it the eternal and absolute being, the "unmoved first mover"? (*b*) Is it really possible to fit on the few broken and enigmatic remarks of the *De Anima* about the imperishable "active intellect" to the general straightforward naturalistic account of the process of knowing and its presuppositions? Does not one feel of all the exegeses alike, "this may be, in point of fact, what Aristotle ought to have said, but I cannot convince myself that it is what he actually meant to say"? (*c*) Or again, does any of us believe that Aristotle has really succeeded in his *Ethics* in harmonising the view that the good for man is the special object of the science of "Politics", and thus belongs altogether to the "active life", with the other view which he springs on us at the end of his argument that our truest good can only be found in "contemplation"?

On the face of things, Aristotle's philosophy as Aristotle himself left it, is an imperfectly achieved attempt to hold together a secular or "one-world" and a religious or "two-world" view of things. The ordinary "naturalist" is content to see only the one world of the sensible and present; the "Platonist" is so interested in the "other" world of the unseen and eternal that his tendency is to come as near as he dares to treating "this" present world as a shadow or a bad dream. For a thoroughly critical philosophy the problem is precisely how to combine aright the two complementary attitudes of frank acceptance of the "secular present" and the noble "detachment" which refuses to accept it for more than it is worth. In Aristotle's own philosophy, as it seems to me, both attitudes find their recognition, but they are not harmonised; they simply alternate. The general rule is that in any considerable work of Aristotle you start with what seems to be a thorough-going "empirical" "secular" or "this-world" attitude to the world and an avowed opposition to everything that is "transcendental". But by the time you reach the end of the treatise, you find yourself landed in the full-blown "transcendental"—"the unmoved mover", the "imperishable active intellect", "the contemplative life", without any clear indication of the way in which the transition has been effected. Here, as it seems to me, the so-called Aristotelianism of Thomas is much more thoroughly thought out and coherent than what I may call the Aristotelianism of Aristotle. The "this-worldly" and the "other-worldly" are not juxtaposed; the one is subordinated to the other in virtue of definite guiding principles clearly laid down and the relations of the superior to the subordinate are made logically transparent. To my own mind the clarity which is thus brought into the treatment of this supreme problem of the relation of the eternal and the secular is the best proof of all of the genuine originality of the Thomistic thought and of its perennial significance for all generations of men. I may give as an instance of the quality I have in mind the treatment of the relation of the temporal and eternal good of man in the third book of the *Summa contra Gentiles*, as compared with the treatment of the relation between the life of practice and the life of speculation in the *Nicomachean Ethics*. I do not think there can be much doubt here which of the two philosophers show the coherency, lucidity, and assurance which mark the utterance of one who is really master of his theme.

For my immediate purpose, which is to urge that the Thomist philosophy is no mere Aristotelianism revised but a masterly synthesis of both Plato and Aristotle with one another and with Augustine, effected by original insight of the first order, it is particularly important to make two remarks.

As I have said, in the thought of Aristotle himself, when one tries to study it in a strictly historical spirit without preconceptions, there appear to be two conflicting strains, the naturalistic or positivist and the Platonist. Hitherto students have been content to note the fact without attempting to discuss the question of the historical development of Aristotle's own mind. From the rise of the succession of expert Aristotelian exegetes in the first century of our era down to the dawn of our own twentieth century, the encyclopaedic "work" of the great thinker has only too successfully hidden his personality from us. The first serious systematic attempt known to me to reconstitute the features of the son of Nicomachus as a living personality with a history of growth behind it, has only just been made by Werner Jaeger in his fascinating *Aristoteles*, published only last year.[1] Many of Jaeger's special results must, no doubt, be considered tentative, and I have elsewhere tried to show that in some cases he has fallen into definite errors. But in the main I believe he has made out his principal thesis, and that we can distinguish in all the principal works of Aristotle well-marked earlier and later sections, the general formula being that Aristotle starts on his personal career as a convinced and enthusiastic Platonist, passes through a phase in which he attempts to show that all that is most fundamental in the "other-worldly" Platonic metaphysic and ethics can still be retained when the doctrine of "Separate Forms" has been eliminated, and ends by approximating more and more closely to the cultivation of an almost purely empirical and positivist cultivation of the details of the special sciences. If this is so, I think we may safely say that it is Aristotle the Platonist rather than Aristotle the positivist who influences the thought of Thomas.

To illustrate by one or two examples. Jaeger has, I think, made it clear that there is a shift in the *Metaphysics* as it stands from the conception of "first philosophy" as the study of "being supreme and eternal" to the thought of it simply as the study of "being as such", and the only reasonable explanation of the shift is that the parts of the work where the conception of "theology" as the crown of science is dominant come from manuscripts of the transition period, in which Aristotle is still concerned with the exposition of a real though remodelled Platonism, those in which "first philosophy" is equated with the science of "being as such" from those of the later and more positivist period. So with special reference to the famous book of the *Metaphysics* which expounds the conception of God as the "unmoved first mover", I cannot resist the arguments used

[1] Jaeger, *Aristoteles*. Berlin, 1923.

by Jaeger to prove that in the main we are dealing with Aristotle in his earlier vein, while the chapter which introduces the fifty odd "unmoved movers" of the planetary spheres is a later addition in the interests of positive science, but wholly out of keeping with the tone of its context. As Jaeger says, from the point of view of this addition, God sinks from the position of being the one supreme and abiding source of all temporality to the position of something like a mere unknown cause of the diurnal revolution of the heavens, an astronomical hypothesis much on the same level as gravitational attraction in the *Principia* of Newton, or, if you prefer it, of the as yet undiscovered cause of gravitation of which Newton speaks in the concluding *Scholium Generale*.

Now there cannot be the slightest doubt that it is Aristotle in what seems to be his earlier vein, the Platonist Aristotle, who means so much to Thomas. One may doubt whether if the *Metaphysics* had been completely worked over from the point of view of the chapter on the planetary movers, so that God appeared throughout simply as the first member of a whole series of unknown causes of movements of rotation, the book would have had much fascination for him. Or I may make the same point in another way. I have sometimes asked myself what are, when all is said, the two or three leading conceptions drawn from Aristotle which are all-pervasive in the system of Thomas. I believe, though I am of course offering only my own personal impression, that we may reduce the list, if we confine ourselves to matters of absolutely first-rate importance, to two. One is the great conception of "potentiality" and the significance for every branch of science of the distinction between potentiality and act. I know that in modern times there has been a violent revolt against this

R

distinction and that many philosophies have made determined attempts to get rid of the notion of potentiality
once and for all and to recognise nothing but actuality.
The revolt was primarily intelligible and in many respects salutary. I take it, it would be generally admitted
that there is some foundation for Francis Bacon's complaint that Aristotle and his followers had corrupted
natural science by this *frigida distinctio*. The schoolmen of the decadence really did tend to forget that the
distinction never affords a sufficient description, not to
say an explanation, of the specific detail of any process
in nature, and for my own part I think to some extent
they could plead the unfortunate example of Aristotle
himself for their error. Since no philosopher is infallible,
I should not be much surprised if Thomas himself can
be proved to be sometimes a sinner in this way. But the
history of biology or psychology, or any science which
deals with objects which live and grow on characteristic lines, is enough to prove that in philosophy to
ignore potentiality and treat the not yet actual as simply
"what is not" leads to nothing but confusion and dis-
aster. Insistence on the conception of the "potential"
seems to me to be one of the most valuable features of
the intellectual inheritance which we have to thank the
great men of the thirteenth century for preserving for
us. The other great fundamental principle which strikes
me as all-important is the famous doctrine of the equi-
vocity of "being" (or, if you like to put the point
differently, of the irreducibility of the categories to any
one supreme category), which is perhaps even more
important for Thomism than for Aristotle himself, since
it is the foundation of the whole theory of analogical
knowledge as the means of escape from sheer ignorance
of the supra-temporal in philosophy. It happened that
some time ago I was reading simultaneously Eriugena's

famous *De divisione naturae* and the *Summa contra Gentiles*, and naturally found myself led to make some comparisons. On one point, to be frank, I had to confess that Eriugena seemed to me to have an advantage; whatever one might think of his conclusions, one could not but be impressed by the extraordinary vigour of a speculative imagination to which one seemed to find no later parallel until one came down to Giordano Bruno in the full tide of the anti-scholastic reaction. Yet, on the other hand, quite apart from any consideration of theological consequences, one could not help feeling that, regarded simply as philosophical speculations, the speculations of Eriugena, like those of Bruno after him, were undisciplined and fanciful; one was dealing with the work of an imagination hardly controlled by sober judgement. The question this reflection suggested to me, as I thought by contrast of the magnificent sobriety of Thomas, was this. Was there any fundamental philosophical principle, unknown to John the Scot, which served to keep the thirteenth-century thinkers secure from the excesses of an unregulated imagination? If there was, was it a principle which they derived from their study of Aristotle and could not equally well have learned from Plato and the Platonists, who were as well known to a learned man in the ninth century as to the learned in the thirteenth? My own answer was that, so far as I could see, the principle wanted, a principle which could not well have been thoroughly learned except from Aristotle, was precisely that "being is predicated equivocally" or, in other words, that the categories form an irreducible plurality. This, as it seems to me, is the ultimate principle on which all the wild and dangerous philosophical Monisms must be shipwrecked, the safeguard of sane and sober critical thinking, the one indispensable form of "pluralism" which must reappear in any philosophy with pretensions to be true.

Now both these principles belong as much to the earlier Aristotle as to the later. The distinction between potentiality and act, though best known to us from the prominence given to it in Aristotelianism, appears to have originated in the Platonic Academy and to have been the common property of the school. The immediate proof of this is that we find the distinction already employed without explanation, as something familiar, in a fragment of Aristotle's lost *Protrepticus* which must have been written before the death of Plato, and can be seen from the remains preserved from it by later writers to have been an eloquent exposition of Platonism. Indeed we may fairly go a step further back. In the famous passage of the *Theaetetus* where Plato is making the distinction between knowledge in actual use and knowledge which we have acquired and can revive on occasion but are not actually using (*Theaet.* 197 c) we have the very phrase that "in a sense we have none of these pieces of knowledge, when we are not using them", what we have is the "power" of putting our hand on them. It is, I think, not unlikely that this observation is the starting point of the whole doctrine of potentiality and act, though, if it is, this of course in no way lessens our debt to Aristotle for his recognition of the fundamental importance of the distinction and its significance for the whole study of nature and of man.

The other great principle of the irreducibility of the categories is nowhere, so far as I know, expounded in Plato, and I do not feel sure that the later world would have arrived at it without great difficulty if it had not been able to learn the lesson from Aristotle. At the same time, it is fully in accord with the principles of Plato. Even of Xenocrates, against whom in particular,

the majority of Aristotle's attacks on the Academy appear to have been aimed, we happen to know that he
contented himself with the reduction of the categories
to two, Substance and Relation. We may say then, I
believe, that if the Thomistic metaphysics may be
called Aristotelian in the sense that it is to Aristotle
they are directly indebted for their most fundamental
formulae, it is a misapprehension to regard them as
Aristotelian in the sense that they are in principle anti-
Platonic. They represent rather a rich and full synthesis
and co-ordination into a systematic whole of the results
won by the thousand years' long travail of Greek philosophical thought, a synthesis only possible to a mind
of the first order. It has been said that Kant, by far the
most epoch-making of modern philosophers, aims at a
synthesis of Hume and Leibniz, as imperfectly apprehended through Wolff. The remark was not, of course,
meant as a disparagement of Kant's originality; the
suggestion is that the very achievement of such a synthesis is itself only possible to a thinker of the most absolute originality. But, by comparison with the Thomist
synthesis of Plato, Aristotle, and Augustine, how comparatively incoherent and loose is Kant's synthesis of
Hume and Leibniz. The one has the unity of a great
work of art, the other is by comparison an ill-con-
structed amalgam which visibly falls to pieces under
the reader's eyes.

In epistemology and psychology the case stands
rather differently. Here the foundations of the Thomist
edifice may really be called Aristotelian in the more
special sense which I have just deprecated for the
Thomistic metaphysics. And I confess that it is just
here that my own difficulties about what seems to be
St. Thomas' teaching begin. I find it for example—
perhaps the fault lies simply with my own failure to

understand—hard to reconcile the character of our
knowledge in pure mathematics with the restriction of
the functions of the intellect in man to the work of
abstraction from what is given in sense, and again to
satisfy myself that the theory of the part played by the
"sensible species" in perception is quite consistent with
itself, and with the surely sound conviction that the perceived qualities of things are real qualities of real things
and not "psychical additions" to the reality. And yet,
for all my difficulties, here again I feel convinced that
if we would make progress to a sound theory, we cannot
do better than go to school to St. Thomas. It is a
striking sign of the times that contemporary philosophy
is coming more and more to busy itself with precisely
the problems which confront us in the Thomist epistemology and psychology of knowledge. The tendency is
certainly spontaneous, since most of those who exhibit
it in a very marked degree are pretty obviously quite
unacquainted with all mediaeval philosophy. Yet it is
undeniable that something like a return to the mental
outlook of the thirteenth century is being forced upon
us to-day in at least two ways. We have witnessed a
widespread and vigorous revolt against the type of
epistemological theory — ultimately derivable from
Kant—which attempts to safeguard scientific knowledge against sceptical criticism by pronouncing the
scientific characters of that knowledge, its universality
and necessity, to be a "psychic addition" put into
things by the human mind *de suo*. If we choose to define
the very ambiguous word "Idealism" arbitrarily as
meaning the doctrine that universality and necessity
are "put into nature by the knowing mind", we may
fairly say that there are no "idealists", in this sense,
left to-day. The epistemologist of to-day, as compared
with his predecessors of forty years or more since,

usually has the advantage of superior knowledge of some specific branch of science, and the influence of science, both natural and mathematical, is shown in this widespread conviction that a true theory of knowledge must treat knowing of all kinds from the outset not as a process of "creating" but as an adventure of discovery. We do not put "the categories" into Nature; we find them there. This view of the relation between the knowing mind and the Nature it knows, of itself, takes us back to the "critical Realism" characteristic of the philosophy of an age earlier than the unfortunate subjectivisation of the philosophical problem by Descartes.

It is significant also that, as the current literature shows, the reaction towards what I may call an epistemological realism has once more made actual a whole class of problems prominent in Thomistic philosophy but until recently too lightly dismissed by most later thinkers. When we have convinced ourselves that the apprehension of Nature is not, as Descartes too long led us to believe, indirect, through the mediation of "ideas", but direct and first-hand, so that we immediately perceive the genuine qualities of real things, we are confronted, of course, with the difficult task of correctly explaining the facts which have been the stronghold of the theory of indirect or representative perception (facts about double vision, hallucinations, dreams, etc.), and of devising a really sound scientific account of the function of the processes which *in the organism*, though not in the mind's apprehension, intervene between stimulation of the sense-organ and awareness of the apprehended quality. In a word we have back on our hands precisely the same questions which in the philosophy of Thomas are answered by the theory of the sensible and the intelligible "species". As I have confessed, I have never been able to feel sure that I quite grasp St. Thomas' thought on this subject, though I do seem to discern that it is much subtler than the rather crude psychology apparently intended by Aristotle himself. But this at least is clear, that a theory of perception and perceptual knowledge which is to meet the acquirements of modern science will have to be something in its general character very much like that of Thomas. It will have to combine, as he at any rate meant to combine, the two complementary positions that our knowledge of the world around our bodies is mediated in fact by highly complicated processes of a very special kind, and that *as knowledge* it is *direct, unmediated* apprehension not of "ideas" or "images" but of actual physical reality. No one, so far as I know, among the great modern philosophers has ever seen more clearly than Thomas that the problem is precisely not to sacrifice one of these true positions to the other. Hence we may fairly say that the great task awaiting the epistemologist at this moment is no other than the task of providing us with an equivalent, expressed in terms of all that we know about the physiology of the brain and sense-organs, for the Thomistic doctrine of the part played in perception and perceptual knowledge by the sensible and intelligible "species". For all I know, it is possible that the theory as it stands only needs to be translated into the language of modern physiological psychology, without further modification, to prove the very truth of which the epistemology of the present moment is so anxiously in search. Even if it should not be so, and modification as well as translation is called for, I am at least sure that the careful study of the Thomist doctrine on the subject is the best preparation for fruitful meditation of one's own, and that the bad habit of beginning the study of so-called "modern" philosophy with Descartes, in whom the epistemological problem is falsified from the first by "representationist" assumptions, is responsible for generations of mere fumbling in the dark which might have been escaped if the gentlemen of the eighteenth and nineteenth centuries had been willing to do less "sneering at Aquinas" and more study of him.

[1924]

VII

FRANCIS BACON

It is now three hundred years and a few odd months since the Easter Sunday[1] on which Francis Bacon, Viscount St. Alban, ex-Chancellor of England, and author of the *Great Instauration*, passed from this temporal scene a disgraced and broken man. In his Will, executed some four months earlier, stand the words familiar to us, "for my name and memory, I leave it to men's charitable speeches, and to foreign nations, and the next ages". The appeal for charitable construction has been deprived by lapse of time alike of its force and its justification. Educated countrymen of Gardiner and Acton are no longer in danger of corrupting the story of our past into a deceitful legend for the greater glory, or shame, of a sect in politics or divinity. Time has also, and that none too soon, brought the opportunity for a sane and sober judgement on the services of Bacon to the cause which lay closest to his heart, the advancement of the sciences. The future to whose censure he submitted himself, as we may fairly think, has arrived. That the verdict of the "foreign nations" may not be wanting, the last year has brought us what I may perhaps call the most thorough, elaborate, and impartial study of the Baconian philosophy hitherto produced, the acute and learned monograph of Dr. Adolfo Levi,

---

[1] April 9 (O.S.), 1626.

258

Il Pensiero di Francesco Bacone.[1] We should now be in
a position to judge of Bacon's services or disservices to
scientific and philosophical thought in the only way
befitting the historian of ideas, with severe and serene
disregard of all questions affecting his character as a
friend, a statesman, or a judge. These are matters for a
different, it may be a higher, court: in this place and on
this occasion, Bacon comes under our consideration as a
thinker, not as a man, and it would be an impertinence
to forget the distinction. With the rights and wrongs of
his treatment of Essex or Peacham or Aubrey we have
as little to do as the student of Shakespeare's tragic art
with the morality of the sorry intrigue half disclosed in
the *Sonnets.*

We may doubt whether it would have been easy to
pronounce a thoroughly impartial judgement even on
this question of Bacon's real merits as a natural philosopher before the opening of the present century.
Science and philosophy, no less than politics, have their
sectaries and partisans. Among ourselves, all through
the first fifty or sixty years of the nineteenth century,
the period which saw the two great editions of Bacon's
Collected Works—those of Basil Montagu and of Ellis,
Spedding, and Heath—as well as Macaulay's only too
famous article in the *Edinburgh*—the dominant mood
was one of uncritical and unhistorical magnification.
What Pindar said of Hiero[2] Englishmen of that age
said in their hearts of their "national" philosopher;
whatever fell from his lips was presumed to be great
because it came from him. It was a point of honour,
even with zealous Whigs like Macaulay, whose political bias led them to put the harshest construction on

---

[1] *Il Pensiero di Francesco Bacone considerato in relazione con le filosofie della
natura del Rinascimento e col razionalismo cartesiano.* Turin, 1925, Paravia &
Co.

[2] *Pyth.* i. 87 εἴ τι καὶ φλαῦρον παραιθύσσει, μέγα τοι φέρεται | πὰρ σέθεν.

all the acts of the Chancellor, to insist that the thinker
had revealed once for all the one "true way" in science
and philosophy, and that nothing was left for after
ages but to tread meekly in his steps, *in* Verulami
ponere ficta pedum pressis vestigia signis. Then, as
might have been expected, followed the natural re-
bound from this idolatry, marked, for example, by De
Morgan's vigorous and mirthful criticism of Bacon and
his *fervent*, Macaulay[1] and Jevons' piquant contrast
between the false scientific method of Bacon and the
true method of Newton,[2] and culminating in the open
contempt avowed by philosophers whose own conception of science had been chiefly inspired by Kant, a
contempt expressed pithily in the complaint of Lewis
Nettleship that Bacon, though Nettleship owns to "finding a good deal in him", is "typical of the inferior English characteristics, a sort of swagger and ignorant independence".[3] A generation for which both the wave
of adulation and the counter-wave of detraction are
spent forces should be able to judge more historically
and with more certain discernment.

It is not difficult, in the light of history, to understand
the source of the perturbing influences which vitiate
both the estimates to which I have referred. The supreme outstanding feat of the eighteenth century, so far
as natural philosophy is concerned, had been the definite conquest of the mind of Europe by the Newtonian
mechanics of the heavens. As developed and translated
into the language of analysis by Lagrange and Laplace, the Newtonian gravitational astronomy appeared
to be not only the last word of astronomical science
itself, but the flawless model of explanatory theory to

---

[1] *Formal Logic*[1], 216-24;   *Budget of Paradoxes*[2] (ed. 1915), i. 76-90.
[2] *Principles of Science*, 581-6.
[3] *Works*, i. 69 (from a letter of January 1880).

which all genuine natural science ought to conform.[1] The key to all nature's mysteries, it was thought, must be found in the conception of "attractive forces" acting at a distance,[2] and the work of the new century was expected to be the reduction of molecular physics and of chemistry to the Newtonian pattern. It is true that it would have been hard to prove that Bacon had exercised any special direct influence on Newton, but it is not surprising that no one should have been troubled by scruples on such a point in the first flush of the great triumph of the Newtonian ideas. What was undeniable and patent was that physical science, after remaining, to all appearance, stationary for so many centuries, had, in the hundred and odd years since the publication of the *Principia*, come triumphantly into its own, and seemed likely to extend its domain indefinitely by the mere process of applying the concepts of the Newtonian mechanics systematically in one field of fact after another. And it was not difficult to see where the Newtonian methods in science differed most obviously from those of the preceding ages of sterility. It was well understood that, as Dr. Whitehead has reminded us,[3] science had won its resounding victories by a revolt against *rationalism*—the metaphysician's characteristic demand for principles which completely justify themselves to the reflective intelligence—and a stubborn loyalty to "brute" fact for which no reason can be produced except that "we see it happens so". The great outstanding triumph of brute fact over "rationality" was, indeed, just the peculiarly Newtonian element in

[1] J. T. Merz, *History of European Thought in the Nineteenth Century*, vol. i. chaps. iv., vi.

[2] We may recall the way in which the conception is made central for natural science in the *Metaphysische Anfangsgründe der Naturwissenschaft* of the convinced Newtonian, Kant.

[3] *Science and the Modern World*, chap. i.

the Newtonian mathematical physics, the gravitation-formula. There is nothing self-luminous about the "law of the inverse square", no superior rationality inherent in a system pervaded by that law rather than by another which might be a possible mathematical alternative:[1] there is an apparent *irrationality* about the scheme which would have been resented by the typically rationalist intellect of the great thirteenth-century schoolmen and was actually resented by the equally rationalistic intellect of Leibniz, the most universal genius of the Newtonian age. To a thoroughly rationalist mind it was a rock of offence that the Newtonian celestial mechanics require as a first principle a formula which has no logical connection with the general Newtonian laws of motion and can only be supported by an appeal to brute fact. For the same reasons it is to-day an advantage of the "general theory of relativity", in the eyes of a rationalist, that its laws of motion are so stated as to include the facts of gravitation and dispense with the need for a special gravitation-formula.[2]

Thus Newton's famous *hypotheses non fingo* was naturally understood, all the more for its explicit allusion to the arch-rationalist Descartes, as the formal repudiation of rationalism, *i.e.* of the demand that natural science shall admit none but transparently self-evident premises.[3] As everyone knew, two full generations before Newton, Bacon had been foremost in complaining of the scientific sterility of the mediaeval rationalism,

---

[1] This explains why Leibniz complained that Newton, by appealing to gravity as an unexplained property of "matter", was, in effect, reviving the belief in "occult qualities": cf. *Nouveaux Essais*, Avant-Propos, p. 203 (Erdmann).

[2] É. Meyerson, *La Déduction relativiste*, 284-6; M. Schlick, *Space and Time* (E. Tr.), 44.

[3] The premises of geometry are, indeed, not self-evident. But it is clear that Descartes, from long familiarity with them, supposed them to be so. We may be sure that Euclid's parallel-postulate was taken by him to be "evident by the natural light".

and preaching the doctrine that the one hope of progress lies in a true induction from observed and given fact. It was thus not without reason that the men of a hundred years ago saw in the *Novum Organum* the first plain enunciation of the programme of the return from rationalism and ontology to reverence for the given in all its inexplicability and apparent lack of justifying reasons.

This view was, no doubt, one-sided. The direct and immediate inspiration of Newton's work came from a different quarter. It is Kepler and Galileo whom Newton has really to thank for the services without which there could have been no Newtonian mechanics of the heavens, and Kepler and Galileo, while fully sharing Bacon's reverence for the factual and directly given, had understood, as Bacon never did, that mere acceptance of the given will never of itself give birth to science, but needs to be quickened by the fertilising influence of mathematics, the very type of strictly rationalistic thought. We have to allow here for the pardonable consequences of a failing most incident to man in all ages, national pride. The conqueror who had taken European thought captive was an Englishman; the more rationalistic philosopher whom he had dethroned in the universities and academies, a Frenchman. If it could be plausibly asserted that the precursor who had heralded the advent of the conqueror had also been one of our own countrymen, the story of the revival of science in the modern world would become a tale of the victories of the English intellect. How completely patriotic pride could obscure the facts for our grandfathers we may see from the confident air with which Macaulay lays it down that all great discoveries, in science, as in politics, are "ours"; France, the only rival whom the essayist deigns to mention, is relegated to the humble position of interpreter of the English genius to an inferior world.[1] The complacent pronouncement forgets Copernicus, Galileo, and Kepler, Torricelli and Pascal and Lavoisier, Maupertuis and Lagrange, and a host of other hardly less illustrious names, but the omission is characteristic of the writer's time. The critics of the next generation naturally recoil from this fond exaggeration. A mathematician like De Morgan, really familiar alike with logic, with the text of Newton, and with the history of science—all subjects in which Macaulay was not truly at home—has no difficulty in showing that Macaulay misstates his facts, that the theorems of the *Principia* were not, and could not have been, reached by the induction described in the *Novum Organum*, and that Macaulay's own conception of Bacon's methods is so loose that, when he proceeds to give an example of their value, he gives us one in which they are misapplied to bring out an unwarranted conclusion. Later critics with their own minds full of the *Critique of Pure Reason* find it still easier to observe that Bacon leaves the fundamental questions of the metaphysician and the "epistemologist" untouched; we can understand why they go on to draw the conclusion that a writer with so little to say on the issues most interesting to themselves can only be called a "philosopher" by a stretch of courtesy. But it is for us to beware that in anxiety to avoid undue glorification we do not fall into undeserved detraction. Metaphysics and the theory of knowledge are not the only fields in which there is work for philosophy to do, and it is well for philosophical students in this country, after fifty years of preoccupation with the problems raised by Kant and

---

[1] *Essay on Horace Walpole*: "the great discoveries in physics, in metaphysics, in political science, are ours. But scarcely any foreign nation except France has received them from us by direct communication."

his continuators, to rediscover the external physical
order itself as a fitting object of philosophical examination. Our professed philosophers have long enough
been engrossed with the contemplation of mind; they
may profitably go to school once more to the men of
the seventeenth century whose most direct concern was
with the world of natural objects, and it may well be
that Bacon, in particular, has a valuable lesson to
teach.

In my own judgement he has, and if we are blinded
to his real performance we are blinded by the very
largeness and spaciousness of the design. Like others
among the first-rate men of his marvellous century,
Bacon has still before him the philosophical ideal—a
legacy from the magnificent audacity of the great scholastics—of a single unified science embracing, in a single
survey, and by a single method, the whole field of the
knowable. We have been accustomed for more than a
century to think of him chiefly in terms of that part of
his vast project most fully represented by accomplished
work, as the author of a treatise on scientific method,
or, more narrowly still, as the author of a theory of the
process of inductive generalisation. But it is necessary
to remember that, from his own point of view, the
elaboration of a new scientific method was only one
part of the gigantic task of the revivification of science.
Equally important were to be the survey of the domain
of science and estimate of its derelict territories (only
represented in Bacon's actual output by the *De Augmentis Scientiarum*, an expanded Latin version of the
Two Books of the Advancement of Learning, which had
been originally designed independently of the main
work on the Interpretation of Nature) and the improved *Natural History*, the great repertory of carefully ascertained and documented facts, for the actual

execution of which Bacon never succeeded in accomplishing anything of moment. If he could appear to plead his own claims on our grateful remembrance, he would certainly ask to be judged as the author, not of the *Novum Organum*, but of the *Great Instauration*, in which the theory of induction is but one part among others, not as the mere logician, but as the man who had "taken all knowledge for his province".

When we judge Bacon from this point of view, many of the condemnations which the critics of the last half-century have passed on the defects of his theory of scientific generalisation will be seen to be of only secondary importance. The truth of the strictures has, indeed, often to be granted. We cannot deny, and Bacon himself often confesses, that his statements about the actual facts of nature are often gravely vitiated by a large admixture of falsehood due to acceptance from tradition of alleged facts for which there is no adequate testimony from known and competent observers—reliance on *experientia vaga* in the absence of a proper *experientia literata*. The reasonable attitude in such cases is not that of the detractors who condemn the men of the seventeenth century because they were not in a position to reject peremptorily the reports of an Aristotle, a Pliny, or an Albert the Great. It is more reasonable, as well as kinder, to recognise the open-mindedness which made Bacon and his fellows slow to dismiss as mere fable reports of strange things found in the best repertories of facts to which they had access, and to give them the fullest credit for their insistence that care must be taken for the future that all alleged observations shall be documented with a rigour unknown to earlier ages. Had Bacon and his contemporaries simply disregarded all accounts of strange things to be found in earlier authorities on the score of insufficient documentation, some ancient delusions would have died less hard; so far there would have been gain to science. But, I take it, the gain would have been more than offset by loss, if all records of facts puzzling to the seventeenth-century English or French or Italian student had been summarily rejected on such grounds. (History would suffer in the same fashion from the summary rejection of everything for which there is not fully convincing contemporary documentary or inscriptional evidence.) The true scientific method is rather that professed by Bacon, provisional acceptance of what appears to have a body of respectable testimony behind it, even though the testimony has never been subjected to the severe controls of the laboratory, coupled with the determination that these severe tests shall be regularly applied for the future. We may fairly hope that, by this method, the *experientia literata* of the present may be made gradually to correct the *experientia vaga* of the past without any incurring of the very real risks attendant on sweeping scepticism. The errors which will be retained will only be retained for a time ; radical scepticism about all observation not made under "laboratory" conditions would entail error of a much more widespread and durable kind.

So again, we have to admit the truth of the main unfavourable criticisms of De Morgan and Jevons on Bacon's "induction". It is manifest that Bacon was not—as so busy a man could hardly be—abreast of the greatest discoveries of his own age, and that he had no inkling of the truth stated by Galileo when he said that the script in which the book of nature is written is that of geometrical symbolism; that geometry is, so to say, the accidence of nature. There is no gainsaying De Morgan's pithy contrast between Bacon's and Newton's views on the place of observation in natural science.

The great use of observations is to test theories, not to furnish them.

De Morgan is in the right of it when he criticises Bacon's picture of the rapid progress of science in his imagined Atlantis (where one body of specialists are occupied for life in making endless random observations and experiments, which are then handed over to an entirely different group, who are to elicit theories from this mass of miscellaneous observations), by remarking on the fewness of the actual experiments and observations which play any important part in establishing the results of the *Principia*. But defects like these, though they might be serious if we had to estimate Bacon solely by his contribution to the theory of scientific generalisation, become less considerable when we take the whole scheme of the *Instauration* into account and avoid the easily committed mistake of judging the projected whole by the part its author happens to have brought nearest completion. This is a mistake committed, as it seems to me, equally often by the eulogists and the critics of Bacon. The eulogists select for magnification just those features of Bacon's doctrine which are most open to objection—his curious faith in the fertility of random uncontrolled experimentation, his rejection of the "anticipation of nature" by the method of hypothesis, his apparent conviction that mere empiricism, uncontrolled by "regulative ideas", can be the foundation of assured and continuous scientific advance. The critics, alive to the vulnerability of all these positions, assume that to dispose of them is to dispose of Bacon's claim to be remembered as a thinker of permanent significance.

Both parties might have been saved from misunderstandings if they had not apparently both begun and finished their study of Bacon with the *Novum Organum*.

It is not the least among the many excellences of the monograph of Mr. Levi that he follows a different and more promising path. The first three-quarters of his book are given to a full and careful study of Bacon's conceptions about the scope of science, the classification of the sciences, and the general character of the "scientific view of the world"; it is only in the last quarter of the book that the author proceeds to examine the *Novum Organum* and its theory of generalisation. This is the philosophically right way by which to approach Bacon and his doctrine; when we adopt it, we discover that the real significance of Bacon for the development of European thought is independent of the merits and defects of his particular views on induction. We also win the right point of view from which to appreciate the special Baconian theory of induction itself, since we approach the method, as a reader who begins his Baconian studies with the *Novum Organum* cannot do, possessed of a real understanding of the question to which Bacon expected induction to provide the answer. Hitherto, as Mr. Levi says, the verdicts of both admirers and hostile critics of the "Baconian method" have nearly always been vitiated by the simple fact that the problem Bacon expected science to solve is different in character from the problems it has historically been the glory of modern natural science to have solved. He has received high praise on the ground that, as has been alleged, his method enables us to answer a question which he was not raising, and has been depreciated on the ground that the true method for dealing with this question is not that which he recommends. Until we are quite clear on the nature of the fundamental scientific problem as Bacon conceived it, both laudation and depreciation are premature.

Before we can either praise or depreciate Bacon as a

thinker with understanding, we need to put to ourselves
the question which Mr. Levi has, with true philosophical insight, made primary for his discussion of the
Instauration. On which side of the great dividing line
drawn in science by the seventeenth century does Bacon
fall? Is his right place with the latest of the men of genius
who draw their inspiration from the mainly humanistic
ferment of the Italian Renaissance? Or should he rather
be counted among the earliest of the creators of the
"modern scientific" conception of nature; the way of
looking at the world about us which is at bottom common to Hobbes, Descartes, Spinoza, Newton, seemed a
century ago to have been definitely established by Lagrange and Laplace, and is only now beginning to be
severely criticised from within by the physicists themselves? On the right answer to this question, whether
Bacon is the last and most eloquent of the men of the
Renaissance or the earliest of the moderns, will depend
our view of the character of the supreme scientific
problem as Bacon understood it, and consequently,
also, our view of the worth of his famous inductive
method.

Naturally, I cannot undertake to reproduce here the
substance of the elaborate argument by which Mr. Levi
reaches his answer to this question; I can only express
my conviction that the answer he reaches is the right
one. Bacon is definitely among the first of the "moderns", not among the last of the mediaevalists. The main
proof of this is to be found in his insistence on the discovery of what he calls "forms" of "simple natures" as
the last and highest problem for a true science. The
natural world, as he sees it, appears to be a complex of
bodies, each exhibiting a plurality of distinct sensible
qualities, a colour, a smell, a taste, a specific hardness,
a specific density, and the like. Each of these qualities

is what Bacon calls a "nature", and his conviction is that the number of independent simple "natures" is strictly limited; they are perhaps not more numerous than the letters of an alphabet.[1] What we call "things", in their apparently infinite variety, are but the words of a language of nature, all reducible to arrangements of this small number of primary vocables. The problem of discovering the "form" of a simple "nature", assigned by Bacon to that highest exercise of the scientific intellect for which he appropriates the name "metaphysic", is then declared to be the problem of finding a "nature which is convertible with the given nature, present wherever the given nature is present, absent wherever it is absent, and is, at the same time, a specification of a more generic nature".[2] Thus to discover, for example, the "form" of whiteness is to discover a character which is always found where white colour is found, never found where white colour is absent,[3] and is, moreover, a specific determination of some character more generic than itself. A further light is thrown on the real meaning of this conception of a "form" by Bacon's famous and characteristic doctrine of the strict correspondence of knowledge and power. The "form" must be of such a kind that to know what it is is also to know how to produce the corresponding "nature" without limitation, wherever its production is physically possible. To know the "form" of white is, in Bacon's view, equivalent to knowing how to produce a white colour in anything capable of exhibiting colour, that is, wherever there is a surface which can have any colour at all.[4] The vast range of the transformations which knowledge of the "forms of simple natures"

[1] *De Augmentis*, iii. 4 (*Works*, Ellis and Spedding, i. 566).
[2] *N. O.* ii. 4.
[3] *Ibid.* ; *De Aug.* iii. 4 (E. and S. i. 566).
[4] *N. O.* ii. 5 ; *De Aug.* iii. 4 (E. and S. i. 568).

would render feasible explains why Bacon chose for the practical art of the successive production of such transformation the name *magic*. It explains also why he held that knowledge of the comparatively few ultimate "forms" of such "natures" would enable its possessor to change the whole complex of the sensible qualities of a body, by superinducing one fresh "nature" after another, so that the transmutation of metals dreamed of by the alchemists would be among the everyday operations of a properly informed and equipped "applied science".[1]

If we remember that Bacon has also laid it down that all human skill can really effect in nature is to displace bodies, to move them to and from one another,[2] we see at once—as, in fact, was already suggested by the conception of a "form" as a specification of a character more "generic" than itself—that the ideal Bacon has before his mind, though he has not realised the supreme position to which that ideal elevates mathematics as the key to science, is the correlating of all qualities in nature with configurations, or kinematical patterns. Clearly, if all the events of nature are to be expressible as syllables of one and the same language, the letters which compose the syllables cannot be colours or sounds or odours; the common measure of all natural events must be sought in characters which are themselves *common* to all events. This means that the common measure must be looked for in properties directly arising from the fact that all events fill a certain volume and duration and are bounded, spatially and temporally, in various ways by other events. When events have been, so to say, translated from the vernacular of the eye, the ear, the nostrils, the palate, the skin, into

[1] *N. O.* i. 85 ; ii. 4,
[2] *N. O.* i. 4,

nature's "Latin", they must all appear as space-time patterns. This is the thought which underlies the development from Galileo, through Descartes, Newton, Lagrange, and many another, to the full-blown "mechanical theory of nature" of our own days, though it is only of late that we have possessed a philosophical terminology which allows us to formulate the thought with precision. Accurately stated, it is the doctrine named by Dr. Whitehead[1] that of "simple location". Mr. Levi's careful study makes it abundantly clear that Bacon held this doctrine no less than Galileo, though the lack of mathematical training, for which not Bacon but the Cambridge of his youth was to blame, prevented him from giving the thought the same lapidary expression. It is no accident that the one example Bacon has given us of the process of search for a "form" ends by the divination that the "form" of heat is a particular kinematical pattern, a specific type of motion in what we should call the molecules of a body,[2] or that he should have more than once hinted that all the wealth of colours, sounds, fragrances, and other sensible characters of the world of daily life are a mental addition of our own to the bald reality,[3] which consists of "indivisible bodies exhibiting motions conformable to a law", and again, that the "forms" of the various "natures" are no more than the several clauses or sections of this law.[4] Patterns of rhythmic movement across space and time the sole reality, everything else a mass of "psychic additions" embroidered on this monotonous ground by the human senses and imagination: these are the fundamental positions characteristic of the "mechanical" interpretation of nature

[1] *Science and the Modern World*, 71-3, 84, 98.
[2] *N. O.* ii. 20.
[3] *Valerius Terminus*, ii. (E. and S. iii. 235) ; *N.O*. i. 41.
[4] *N. O.* i. 51, ii. 2.

wherever it makes its appearance in man's thought, whether in Democritus, in Lucretius, in Galileo, in Newton, or in our modern positivists of science. Bacon's acceptance of these positions clearly stamps him as belonging to the beginnings of modern "naturalism", not to the last stage of the confused "vitalism" characteristic of the men of the Renaissance, who were trying to move back from the elaborate qualitative physics of Aristotle and the Aristotelians to the cruder picture-thinking of the old pre-Socratic fathers of science.

The "mechanical" view of nature has yet several steps to take before its full implications will become clear. Before we can advance from Bacon's position to Newton's, Galileo and Descartes will first have to enunciate the programme of the geometrising of nature explicitly. Even the one vestige of an extra-geometrical reality which persists in Newton, the conception of "gravitational mass " as an ultimate property of his particles, with its consequence, the appearance of gravitation as an independent outstanding fact irreducible to the general laws of motion, will have to disappear, as it does in the kinematics of the "general theory of relativity", before the complete reduction of physical science to geometry is accomplished. But Bacon has already taken the first step on the path to this goal; the taking of the rest is a mere matter of logical consequence. And yet, when we come to think of it, with all his lack of insight into the full consequences of his own assumptions, Bacon has kept true to the reality of things in a way which makes him, rather than the great physicists who were to succeed him, the most instructive guide for ourselves at the present moment. Beautiful and consistent as the "classical" kinematical interpretation of natural processes may be, needed as it was for the development of physics and chemistry, it has just one defect, but one which is fatal to it as a philosophical account of the real. As Dr. Whitehead says,[1] it is simply unbelievable; the more faithfully we keep to it, the farther away shall we get from anything we can regard as the final truth about the world. How unbelievable it is we shall see, if we will make two reflections.

(1) The kinematical view, taken seriously as a full statement of the truth, absolutely demands as an immediate consequence the doctrine, only hinted at by Bacon, but expressly avowed by Galileo[2] and Descartes, that the sensible qualities of bodies, all, that is, which gives nature her apparent inexhaustible wealth and variety, all that is of primary importance for the life of animal organisms, must be simply unreal, fabricated by the mind as an unauthorised comment on nature's text. Fully thought out, this must mean that the colour of the sapphire, the scent of the rose, and the like, belong, not to the sapphire or the rose, but to the mind of the sentient perceiver. It is the notorious fact that, throughout the animal creation, it is these characters, colours, sounds, smells, and the like, which count in the life of the organism. By their means creatures are attracted to their mates, directed to their prey, warned of the approach of their enemies; yet, on the theory, the characters which play this all-important part in the life of animated nature are purely illusory. The behaviour of the animal organism to its environment is based on awareness of something which is *not* there. In the nineteenth century it was fashionable to disguise the paradox by misstatement. The eye, it was said, apprehends vibrations "as" colours, the ear apprehends them "as" sounds, and so forth. The equivoca-

---

[1] *Science and the Modern World*, 80.
[2] Galileo, *Saggiatore* (*Opere*, iv. 332); Descartes, *Meditatio* vi., *Principia*, i. 70.

tion should be too patent to need exposure. It should be clear that the eye apprehends no vibrations at all; it sees only colours: the ear hears not vibrations, but tones. If then, all that is real in the object apprehended is vibratory motion, it follows by consequence that sense-awareness is throughout awareness of things as they are not, and this should be incredible. For, in the last resort, it is from the very senses the argument would disable that we have learned of what it declares to be the only realities, shape, volume, situation, movement. An argument which is to discredit the senses as revelatory of the characters of real objects should make the characters treated by the "mechanical" theories as the key to the truth about nature as much of an illusion as all the rest. We only escape the admission by adroit juggling with words.

(2) For much the same reasons, the theory is doomed to fail us when we advance from the sciences of the inorganic to the sciences which study the manifestations of life itself. If the clue to the whole interpretation of nature is the reduction of all processes to changes of configurations of systems of given units which do not themselves change—whether we call the units "hard impenetrable corpuscles" or "point-events" makes no real difference—then, since sentient organisms and rational human persons are themselves components of the "kingdom of nature", it is necessary that the explanation should work for organisms and persons, no less than for everything else. We are thus committed to all the difficulties which attend the attempt to work out a consistently "mechanistic" scheme in biology. These difficulties are sometimes met by the biologist with a retort which ignores the real problem. The defender of "mechanism" will point triumphantly to recent successes in the "synthetic" production of com-

pounds once believed to be obtainable only by the
agency of living organisms, as proof of the needless-
ness of "vitalistic" hypotheses. As a defence of "mechanism" the retort misses its mark. On the face of it,
the successful production of urea, for example, in a
laboratory affords no adequate ground for expecting
that the world will ever see a laboratory-made man, or
even a laboratory-made rabbit. But the real reply goes
deeper than this. The very plausibility of the general
"mechanical view" of nature rests all along on the tacit
presupposition that there remains something outside
and independent of the nature which has been identified
with kinematical configurations, viz. the sentient creatures which apprehend the configurations, and in appre-
hending them perform the miracle of translating them
into colours, sounds, smells, savours. Without the sentient as an independent term the sensible world, in which
we all move and have our being, could not even be an
illusion, for there would be no one and nothing to be
illuded. Either there is something real, not included
in the nature which has been reduced to patterns of
movement (viz. the sentient aware of the patterns),
and then the reduction to kinematics is not applicable
to nature as a whole; or else the sentient is, like everything else, a kinematical pattern and nothing more,
and the sensible world cannot be so much as a misapprehension.

Since we cannot well deny the fact that there is sentience and a sensible world, we are thrown back on the
former of these alternatives. The whole of nature, the
whole of what there is for our observation, cannot be
reduced to an intricate kinematical pattern. The living
and sentient, at least, refuses to submit to the treatment, and the more we learn of the impossibility of
drawing a hard and fast line between the sentient and

the merely animate, or again, between the animated and the inanimate, the more irresistibly we are driven to the conclusion that the patterns of a mathematical physics cannot be a final and complete account of the reality of any natural process, that it is the sciences of the organic to which we must go for our very interpretation of the patterns of the inorganic domain itself. This explains why a philosopher like Dr. Whitehead finds himself attracted by the comparative fluidity of Bacon's thought and, in particular, why he has singled out a striking passage of the *Silva Silvarum*, where Bacon is anticipating the fundamental conceptions of a greater man still, Leibniz, as significant for our own age, on which the task of purging natural science from bad "materialistic" metaphysics is so urgently laid. "It is certain", Bacon says, "that all bodies whatsoever, though they have no sense, yet they have perception: for when one body is applied to another, there is a kind of election to embrace that which is agreeable, and to exclude or expel that which is ingrate: and whether the body be alterant or altered, evermore a perception precedeth operation; for else all bodies would be alike one to another. And sometimes this perception, in some kind of bodies, is far more subtile than the sense; so that the sense is but a dull thing in comparison of it: we see a weather-glass will find the least difference of the weather in heat or cold, when men find it not. . . . It is therefore a subject of a very noble inquiry, to inquire of the more subtile perceptions; for it is another key to open nature, as well as the sense; and sometimes better."[1]

Bacon is here preluding to Leibniz's well-known doctrine of the reflection in the state of each "monad" at any moment of the simultaneous states of all other

[1] *Silva Silvarum*, cent. ix *ad init.* (E. and S. ii. 602).

"monads" and to Lotze's contention that the inter-action of two things implies that either "takes note of" the state of the other. From the rigidly "mechanical" point of view, all such language, implying as it does that the *selective* activity of the organism, so funda-mental in biology, is only a special case of a character common to all natural agents, would have to be dis-missed as a mere "anthropomorphic" metaphor. Yet we know very well that selection is something much more than a metaphor in the organic realm, and our inability to find a real lower boundary of that realm ought to make us careful of declaring the word to be a mere metaphor anywhere. It seems plain that we can-not escape Bacon's shrewd conclusion that if selection were, in any domain of reality, only a metaphor, within that realm all bodies would be "alike" one to another. Historically, the remark may be accounted for by the consideration that the animation of nature at large was a common conviction of the Renaissance age, and that Bacon has not clearly seen how inconsistent the con-viction is with the "mechanical" conceptions clearly foreshadowed by his own utterances. But precisely be-cause he has not wholly committed himself to that radically erroneous *identification* of reality with a kine-matical pattern which was to dominate the unconscious metaphysics of post-Newtonian men of science, his thought has a living significance which that of the reck-less post-Newtonians has not. He is happily in the right where they were unhappily in the wrong; he sees, as we are learning to see, that a true philosophy of nature must be sought by trying to follow the cate-gories of the organic sciences downward into the realm of the inorganic, not by treating categories which only suffice for the formulation of laws of the inorganic as a sole and sufficient clue to the structure of a unity which embraces organic and inorganic alike in a supreme and all-inclusive pattern of patterns.

We might state the flaw in the "mechanical" theory once more in a more precise form: to do so will afford a natural transition to the brief consideration of Bacon's characteristic doctrine of logical method with which I shall bring these remarks to an end. When the "minute philosopher" denies that selection is a universal feature of natural process, he is in effect maintaining that, in the domain studied by physics, the internal state or structure of anything which is a genuine unit is independent of its transactions with other units. Modification of the internal characters of A and B in virtue of the transactions between them is relegated to the organic realm, where, as we all know, or think we know, the transactions between organism and environment are correlated with profound modifications of the internal character of both. In the inorganic domain the component units of any system are, on the theory, to run through the whole series of their transactions with one another without any internal change, remaining all through simply self-same. What exhibits internal modification is to reveal itself by the very fact as not a real unit. The conception naturally took time to develop. Even Newton could speculate about what he called "old, worn" particles. But in the full-blown "mechanical" theory all such conceptions have disappeared; there are no "old, worn" atoms in the nineteenth-century kinetic theory of gases, and it is interesting to note that Sir John Herschel[1] actually came very near accepting what Bacon means to treat as the impossible paradox of the complete "likeness" of bodies. He makes it an argument for Theism that one atom of a given chemical element is so exact a replica of any other that

[1] Quoted in Ward, *Naturalism and Agnosticism*, i. 100.

atoms must be regarded as turned out from a divine factory. Such conclusions are direct consequences of the assumption that the "classical" mechanics is the universal clue to the structure of nature, since in mechanics motions, the only processes taken into account, are regarded as persisting unaltered and merely compounded with one another. This was the real reason why Leibniz rejected atomism as the last word about the constitution of nature. If it were the last word, he argued, sufficient knowledge of the present motion of a single atom should enable us to reconstitute the whole history of the physical world, whereas, in fact, there are always a countless plurality of alternative routes through space and time by which the atom might have reached its present state.[1] That is, the kinematical states of the unit constituents of nature, as conceived by the "mechanical" theorist, are too wholly external to the constituents to admit of our thinking of the unity of nature as a whole as more than a mere resultant of transactions between the members of the aggregate of atoms. But such a unity of nature as a whole as is implied by a sound philosophy of the sciences must be something less superficial; it must be a real pervasive character, not an *Aggregatzustand*.

Leibniz thus reproduces Bacon's thought when he requires us to substitute for the atom, as the genuine unit in things, the monad, which has an internal principle of development and is, at every moment, charged with its whole past and pregnant with its whole future. Unfortunately, Leibniz felt bound to make the development of the individual monad wholly self-contained, so that it is only *its own* past and future with which each is charged. Each behaves as though it were a universe to itself. Genuine interaction is thus replaced by the creative

---

[1] *Opuscules et fragments inédits*, ed. Couturat, 522.

T

activity of God, who has fashioned the monads in such a way that their various developments keep one tune and time. How, on this theory, Leibniz could so much as have come to suspect that there is anything in the universe beyond himself is a difficulty he never quite succeeded in explaining. Bacon's thought is much more truly reproduced by Dr. Whitehead when he conceives of each of the monads of his own philosophy as weighted by the past and big with the future not only of itself, but of each and all the rest. The unity of pattern in nature thus gets adequate recognition as dominant of all partial sub-patterns. As Dr. Whitehead puts it,[1] it is true that the living body may be regarded as a highly complex pattern of electrons and that electrons of the same kind are to be found in the lifeless bodies surrounding it; but the behaviour of an electron which enters into the pattern of a living body is differentiated by the fundamental fact that it belongs to that pattern and not to any other. In this way the nightmare of "epiphenomenalism", which was threatening fifty years ago to make the selective action of the living organism superfluous, disappears, as the relation of organism to environment is made the clue for understanding the relation of the monad, the particle, or the electron, to its surroundings. Dr. Whitehead has worked out the thought with a power which is his own, but the germ of it is to be found, as he himself insists, in the passage already cited from Bacon. For the immediate future of scientific thought it was of the first importance that physics and chemistry should be developed as sciences of number, weight, and measure; relatively, therefore, the "materialistic" concepts which served as admirable instruments for the immediate purposes of physicist and chemist were entitled to their temporary

[1] *Science and the Modern World*, 215.

domination over the scientific mind. The developments
of the biological and historical sciences since the middle
of the nineteenth century make it necessary that our
own age should revise its fundamental scientific conceptions by removing from them limitations imposed
in the special interest of the extreme abstractions of
chemistry and physics, and we may well pay our
tribute of gratitude to the far-reaching vision of the
man who so long ago gave the clearest hints of the line
that revision will need to take.

Bacon's peculiar logical theory, like his philosophy
as a whole, has been both unintelligently belauded and
unintelligently decried. In the days of laudation,
Macaulay could persuade himself not only that Bacon,
alone among logicians, had made a correct analysis of
the process of induction, but that he had given a universal rule for sound reasoning, that Baconian induction is the one and only method of human thinking.
The statement might have surprised Bacon, who is
never tired of reiterating the complaint that the true
method of science is something as yet unknown and
undreamed of, and that his account of it is likely to
be discredited precisely by its novelty. In the reaction from uncritical laudation, naturally enough, the
Baconian rules were depreciated almost to the point of
denying them all worth.

It had been foolishly asserted that the results of
Newton's *Principia* are illustrations of the power of the
method. Men like De Morgan and Jevons, who knew
what the methods of the *Principia* are, were naturally
quick to point out that however Newton reached his
conclusions, he did not reach them by any process like
the construction of tables of presence, absence, and
degree, and the routine performance of eliminations
described in the second book of the *Novum Organum*,

and they were not slow to infer that, since Bacon's method would not have served Newton's purpose, it serves no purpose of any particular value. The true state of the case is different. As Mr. Levi has said, the tragedy of Bacon's method is that it does provide solutions for a certain kind of question, but unfortunately not for the kind of question Bacon was most anxious to solve. We should therefore be judging too favourably of the Baconian induction by elimination if we were content to remark that it is in principle the method afterwards called by Mill the "Joint Method of Agreement and Difference", and that we all know the usefulness of that method in biological and sociological inquiry. For Mill's conception of the scientific problem itself was radically different from Bacon's. Mill thought it the typical business of science to establish laws of uniform sequence between observed events, on which we may rely with sufficient confidence for practice. From Bacon's point of view this is a task which science can execute, but it is not the main task. The supreme problem is to discover the "forms" of "simple natures". Mill is satisfied with knowing the order of sequence between events; Bacon is asking after the formal structure of the events themselves. Unhappily his method of induction by elimination, though it will often give a reasonably adequate answer to Mill's question, is quite unsuitable for the solution of his own.

We can illustrate this from any of the familiar examples used in text-books to exhibit the working of the method. Thus, let the question under investigation be concerned with the outbreak of a local epidemic. If we find that the houses which have been visited by the disorder, though they present no other discoverable feature in common, all get their milk supply from a particular dairy, while other houses which have not suffered seem to have nothing much in common but the fact that they do not get their milk from this dairy, we shall be reasonably safe in suspecting that the milk of the dairy in question is the carrier of the disease. But even if the investigation should enable us to lay our hand on the actual offending cow, we should be no nearer knowing what Bacon would call the "form" of the disorder, the specific derangement of physiological function which is to blame for the symptoms. The "form" could only be identified properly on the strength of a correct theory of the infra-molecular physics of the human organism, and it is idle to imagine that such a theory can be elicited by comparison and elimination directly from facts taken over unanalysed from inspection through the senses, even if the senses have been fortified by the most elaborate instruments of precision. No procedure of mere generalisation from observed data could conduct us to the knowledge of the intimate structure of the patterns of nature called by Bacon knowledge of "forms", and the advantage claimed by Bacon for his "induction", that it functions mechanically and quasi-infallibly, thus making the interpretation of nature a matter for mere plodding industry, is therefore imaginary. So long as we are content, as on the whole Mill was, with mere detection of regularities of sequence among events directly accessible to observation, it is perhaps possible to approximate to this substitution of mere industry for insight. If a sufficient number of painstaking observers were employed in the construction of "tables" of presence, absence, and degree, it is likely that the tables would be reasonably full; mere accuracy in the recording of observations is a virtue which can be inculcated on the dull and laborious.

The confrontation of the "tables" with a view to affecting eliminations, again, need not call for much more than industry. So it is not surprising that the mere formulation of laws of sequence is, in actual fact, often accomplished by very commonplace persons. If the work of science went no farther than the detection of such regularities, it would have been no extravagant anticipation to hope, with Bacon, that all men, once provided with instruments of observation and taught rules for the elimination of the irrelevant factors from a problem, might be equipped fairly equally for the work of the scientific man. If science were the simple business it is made to look in those chapters of Mill's *Logic* which present it as a mere matter of conforming to the four "inductive methods"—themselves merely slightly differing forms of Bacon's *exclusiva*—there would be no good reason why all of us, except the "feeble-minded", should not make ourselves a name in science. The trouble is that authentic science is so much more than this. If you have the true scientific spirit, you will not fancy you have penetrated very far into nature when you have merely qualified yourself to say, "As a general rule and where there are no interfering factors, A will be followed by B". You will not be content until you see definitely why the "regular sequence" should be $A - B$ and not $A - C$ or $A - D$. To know so much, you need to have discerned the pattern of the event A, that of B, and that of the more complex event $(A - B)$, and to see how the patterns of A and B demand, while those of A and C or A and D refuse, integration into a larger pattern.

Again, you will not even be content with a general scheme of this type. In actual fact the patterns A and B never occur in their typical abstract generality; we are confronted with a specific a and β which fall under the types of A and B, but have their own irreducible concreteness. And similarly a and β are not integrated into the mere complex typical $(A - B)$, but into an $(a - \beta)$ with its specific concreteness, and you want to account for just those concretions. Since it seems to be involved in the thoroughgoing unity of the world-process miscalled the "uniformity of nature" that the special concretion of the actual event is what it is because its total setting in the rest of "nature at the moment" is what it is, we readily understand why Dr. Whitehead should comment on Bacon's method with the remarks that "induction has proved to be a some-what more complex process than Bacon anticipated. He had in his mind the belief that with a sufficient care in the collection of instances the general law would stand out of itself. We know now, and probably Harvey knew then, that this is a very inadequate account. . . . I do not hold induction to be in its essence the deriva-tion of general laws. It is the divination of a particular future from the known characteristics of a particular past. . . . Inductive reasoning proceeds from the par-ticular occasion to the particular community of occa-sions, and from the particular community to relations between particular occasions within that community."[1] In other words, it is not generalisation, but the inter-pretation of the individual in terms of concepts trans-parent to the intellect, that is the never completely realised goal of a science awake to its task.

This is a just criticism of Bacon's method of elimina-tion, but it equally hits the weak point in the positiv-istic conception of science championed by Avenarius, Mach, and Pearson, as a mere labour-saving trick of summing up the "routine of our perceptions" in com-pact formulae. What we really ask of science is not to abbreviate the "routine" but to make it intelligible. For that reason, I should not myself regard Bacon's

---

[1] *Science and the Modern World*, 63.

inadequate appreciation of the importance of precise *quantitative* determinations in science as the *fundamental* defect of his doctrine. It is true, to quote Dr. Whitehead once more, that it is just this which is the most readily recognisable difference in "tonality" of mind between Bacon and Galileo or Newton,[1] and the characteristic he most conspicuously shares with the Aristotelianism he was anxious to dethrone. But we think inadequately of the mathematical method which has proved to be the true key to physical science if we make quantitative precision its primary recommendation. Mathematics, as Descartes long ago said, and as the modern creation of rigorously pure mathematics has abundantly proved, has not necessarily to do with quantity. What is distinctive of the mathematical sciences is not that they are concerned with quantity, but that they are in a special degree transparent to the intellect. In mathematical thought we deal, more truly than anywhere else, with "ideas" which—to use Hume's terminology—are not merely "conjoined", but "connected". It is this substitution of connection for bare conjunction without "rhyme or reason" that a mathematical foundation brings into our study of the course of natural events. We can, indeed, never hope to see conjunction completely transformed into connection; the element of bare given fact never quite disappears from a science of nature, for the simple reason that the nature we are trying to understand is primarily given to our minds, not created by them. But it is the supreme task of science, as it advances, to reduce the element of mere "conjunction" in our apprehension of nature, "without limit". The grave fault of Bacon's proposed inductive method, as of all merely inductive methods, considered as an instrument of

[1] *Op. cit.* 66.

science, is that it could do nothing to effect this reduction. However often and successfully we might employ
it, it would leave us everywhere with conjunction not
converted into connection on our hands. It might do
much to make our forecasts of events more probable,
and so to serve our practical utilitarian ends, but it
would not advance our understanding of the world.
That is, it would be useless for the discovery of
"forms".

Had Bacon been the mere vulgar utilitarian he has
sometimes been taken to be, the perception of this
defect, supposing it had been possible to him, need
have caused him no concern. From the merely utilitarian point of view, we should praise Bacon, if we
praised him at all, for the very limitations of his
method, and regret that he retained so much of the
old metaphysical leaven as even to raise the problem
about the discovery of "forms". But in truth it is in
this other strain in his thought, the recognition of the
discovery of "forms" as the true problem of the
sciences and the identification of "forms", so far as the
physical sciences are concerned, with space-time patterns, that his real significance for living thought must
be found. If the labours of Dr. Whitehead and other
eminent thinkers who are engaged on the work of re-
stating the first principles of natural knowledge in a
form free from "materialistic" metaphysical assumptions should be crowned with success, it is not hard to
name the great men of the past to whom the natural
philosophers of 1950 will be found looking back as
their intellectual ancestors. Foremost on the list of the
forerunners of a philosophy of nature at once organic
and mathematical should stand the names of the two
great mathematical metaphysicians of the ancient and
the modern world, Plato and Leibniz. Between them

as a connecting link, for all his personal want of mathematical equipment, might well stand Bacon, who
found in Plato an anticipator of himself,[1] as he was in
turn recognised with generous appreciation by Leibniz.[2] To be remembered as one, even were it the least,
of such a triad would have been, I believe, glory
enough to satisfy Bacon. Whatever were the failings of
his character, and it is my business neither to exag-
gerate nor to extenuate them, excessive self-conceit
does not seem to have been among them. Of himself
we may well believe he would have wished us to say
what he has said of the great men of an earlier time:
"So let great authors have their due, as that Time,
which is the author of authors, be not deprived of his
due, which is, further and further to discover truth".[3]

[1] *N. O.* i. 105; *De Aug.* iii. 4 (E. and S. i. 565); *Advancement*, ii. (E. and S. iii.
355), *Cogitata et Visa* (E. and S. iii. 662).

[2] *Confessio Naturae contra Atheistas*, Erdmann, p. 45, "divini ingeni vir
Franciscus Baconus"; *De Stilo Nizolii*, ib. 61, "incomparabilis Verulamius"; *In
specimina Pacidii introductio*, ib. 91, "feliciter accidit ut consilia magni viri
Francisci Baconi, Angliae Cancellarii, de augmentis scientiarum ad manus
adolescentis pervenirent".

[3] *Advancement of Learning I.* (E. and S. iii. 290).

[1926]

VIII

SOME FEATURES OF BUTLER'S ETHICS

WE are told on the best of all authorities that the last place where a prophet must look to be honoured is his own land. Whether the fame of Butler may be considered as illustrating this adage is a difficult question. From our great-grandfathers and grandfathers he certainly received admiration enough, but it is not so clear that their descendants of to-day rate him at anything like his real worth. To my own mind, at least, there is something niggling about a great deal of the criticism it has long been fashionable to bestow on the "philosopher of Anglicanism". The explanation is presumably to be found in the domination of so much of the best philosophical work of the last generation by influences from Germany. When the ardent youth of our Universities were being taught, with abundance of persuasive eloquence, that in philosophy Kant and Hegel had made all things new, men were not likely to see much merit in the thought of the "home-keeping" wits of the eighteenth century, even if they condescended to study it at all, except in so far as, as in the case of Hume, some knowledge of it was necessary for the understanding of Kant. When the full history of the Germanic influence on our nineteenth-century literature comes to be written in a thoroughly critical spirit, a great deal will have to be done over the whole field in the way of rehabilitating reputations which have been unduly depreciated from this cause; it will then, I believe, be acknowledged that one of the more unfortunate effects of the intellectual conquest of Britain by Germany has been the curious neglect of the very rich and valuable ethical literature which begins with Cumberland and Cudworth (or perhaps, taking dates of publication into account, one should say Samuel Clarke) and culminates in Richard Price.

We might, indeed, have expected that men like Green and Bradley would have found a kindred spirit in the author of the *Sermons on Human Nature*, but in fact Bradley, so far as I can recollect, shows no knowledge of the British rationalistic moralists, and in the *Prolegomena to Ethics* Butler receives only the barest incidental mention. It is too much, perhaps, to say that the attitude of the younger men who would probably have agreed to recognise Green as their spiritual father has usually been unappreciative where Butler is concerned; it is, at any rate, no more than the truth to say that their sympathy has been as imperfect as Charles Lamb's with Scotsmen. The late Dr. Rashdall was in many ways more independent in his thinking and much more interested in our native traditions in ethics than most of the "men about Green", as was even more manifest in the admirable lectures he used to deliver in Oxford some thirty-five years ago than in his writings; and from him I should have expected a higher measure of appreciation. Yet I know from our long-continued private correspondence that the unqualified admiration he accorded to Price was hedged about with all sorts of qualifications and reserves as soon as one ventured to claim it equally for Butler.

On the Continent Butler seems not yet to have received serious attention. Possibly the explanation may be that he has too much of the traditional English

Augustinianism to be altogether acceptable to the more religious thinkers of countries where the Thomist theology is dominant, while to the less theological the mere fact that he was a prelate and an apologist would be sufficient reason for not taking him seriously. Whatever the reason may be, in the one German manual of the history of philosophy where I remember to have seen his name, he was curtly dismissed as a divine who regarded "funk of hell-fire" as the principal reason for a virtuous life, while in France and Italy even his name seems to be hardly known. It was quite recently that a very eminent French philosopher wrote to me of Butler as an author whose name he had only just learned, and of whom he knew nothing beyond the fact that he appeared to have been a Bishop. For those of us who are persuaded that Butler is in fact a thinker of singular depth, as well as nobility, it is plainly a duty to show, if we can, that the comparative neglect into which his memory seems to have fallen is undeserved. It is particularly opportune to undertake such an *Ehrenrettung*, so far as the *Sermons* and their ethical teaching are concerned, at the present moment, since the present year is the bicentenary of their publication. The *Analogy* I may leave on one side, all the more that Dr. Broad has written of it so recently and so well.

I believe that most of the disparagement to which Butler's ethical teaching has been subjected, so far as it rests on anything more than carping at words, arises simply from a lack of historical perspective. His utterances are judged, as no man's utterances should be, without taking into account the circumstances of his life. Readers, especially young readers, are too apt to think meanly of the Bishop because he gave the world neither a completed system of metaphysical philosophy nor even a system of morals. They rightly feel that he has said nothing on many of the issues which would have to be considered in a systematic treatment either of metaphysics or of morals, and they proceed to the wholly unjustified conclusion that since he has left so much unsaid, the permanent worth of what he has said must be slight. This is the line taken in most of the familiar unfavourable criticism of the *Sermons* in particular. Butler, we are told, has no systematic psychology of moral action. He "hedges" on the issue between reason and feeling as the source of our awareness of moral distinctions; he has no worked-out psychology of "conscience"; he does not face the problem created by the disagreements in the deliverances of the "consciences" of individuals and social groups; he ignores the fact that "conscience" develops; he does not discuss the question whether, even for myself, my own "private conscience" is an infallible guide; according to the fashionable interpretation of his language, he even leaves it in the end an open question whether "conscience" would not lose its authoritativeness if it could be shown to be in opposition to "self-love". On all these grounds, his contribution to a definitive moral theory cannot be anything of much moment.

Now much of this criticism may be at once disqualified by one very simple reflection. Before we venture to say that any man ought to have done certain things which he admittedly has not done, and proceed to depreciate his performance because he has not done them, we need to know whether the circumstances in which his work was undertaken made it feasible for him to do these things, and if so, whether doing them would have been relevant to the purposes determined for him by his situation. It is no reproach to any man not to have done what his situation would not permit of doing, still less not to have done what his situation would have made irrelevant to his purpose. In Butler's case it must not be forgotten that his situation and his purposes were those neither of an academic Professor nor of a leisurely man of letters leading the "speculative life", but those of an active and busy Anglican clergyman. As a preacher at the Rolls Chapel, and subsequently as the parson of a North Country parish, his work was primarily that of a practical "preacher of righteousness" and a Christian priest; as a prelate his time must have been taken up pretty completely by administrative cares and duties. At no time in his not very lengthy life had Butler the leisure to work out in detail a speculative system, and it is absurd to depreciate him on the ground that he never executed a task which he could not have executed without being false to the vocation he had chosen. Had Butler's situation been like that of Locke before him or Gibbon after him, the case would be altered. But the performance would probably have been different too. For my own part I think it not impossible that in a situation of life which would have made devotion to pure speculation a moral duty or even morally permissible, Butler might have approved himself the greatest metaphysical intellect of his century. But that is, no doubt, a mere matter of personal opinion.

With reference to Butler's ethical doctrine in particular, we must never forget that, except for the *Preface to the Sermons* and *Dissertation* appended to the *Analogy*, it is conveyed to us through sermons actually delivered in a London pulpit, and that the sermon is a literary *genre* determined by its special object. The preacher aims at producing a very specific result and at producing it by a spoken appeal to an audience with a specific psychology. Butler's object, as appears abundantly from the text of his *Sermons*, was not to construct

elaborate and subtle psychological analyses, but to impress on a London audience the necessity of conducting
their lives virtuously. Elaborate psychological refinements would have been badly out of place in sermons
intended to dispose of the sophistries by which a
fashionable audience tries to excuse itself for its neglect
of what it really knows all the time to be its duties. For
the immediate purpose what is wanted is what Butler
undertakes to give, a convincing indication of the claim
of the known moral law to absolute direction of our
conduct. To a man of leisure sitting in his study, it is
an interesting and a proper subject for discussion
whether we apprehend that law by a "perception of the
heart", or by a "sentiment of the understanding", or by
both at once; the issue is irrelevant to the preacher
dealing with a congregation whose excuse for misconduct is either that they do not apprehend the law at
all or that, if they do, they do not see any obligation to
regard it when they would prefer to ignore it.

So it is no fault of the *Sermons* that they disregard
the apparent or real variations in the deliverances of
"conscience". We must remember that these *Sermons*
are what they profess to be, actual discourses addressed
to audiences of educated citizens of London in the last
years of George I., a body with perfectly definite
educational and social traditions. For the purpose in
hand, it is irrelevant to dwell on minor differences
between the moral convictions of individual members
of the audience. It is quite certain that in all essentials
Butler's hearers would be agreed (as educated citizens
of the same age, the same class, the same language, and
the same historical traditions must necessarily be agreed),
on the question what sort of conduct is right and what
is wrong. The question Butler rightly reckons with as
the one which will be raised is not what it is that "con-

science" tells us to do, but why we should do it if we are minded otherwise.[1]

All through the argument it is assumed that there are two points on which there is no dispute. We know what "virtue" is, and we are agreed that the reasonable and right course of life is to live "conformably to our nature". The only point disputed between Butler and the opponents whom he wishes to convince is whether the way of living which is admitted to be "virtue" is or is not that which is conformable to our "nature". Butler does not consider the possibility of conflicting moral codes and the grounds on which a choice could be made between them; and rightly not, because he knows that his audience will not justify their misdeeds, after the fashion of Shelley's coterie in a later generation, by arguing that they are "virtuous" when judged by the standard of the "higher morality". The early Georgian man of the world was too full-blooded a sinner to take that line of defence. To have foisted into an argument addressed to him reflections on the fact that the moral code of an Englishman of 1725 was not that of a Spaniard of the days of Philip II., nor of a contemporary of the First Crusade, nor of a Hottentot at the Cape, would have been the merest irrelevance. (Not that there would be any great difficulty in dealing with the suggested problem from Butler's point of view.)

In principle these elementary reflections appear to dispose of all the usual criticisms made on Butler with

---

[1] *Sermon III.* "Let any plain honest man, before he engages in any course of action, ask himself, Is this I am going about right or is it wrong? Is it good or is it evil? I do not in the least doubt but that this question would be answered agreeably to truth and virtue, by almost any fair man in almost any circumstance. Neither do there appear any cases which look like exceptions to this; but those of superstition and of partiality to ourselves. Superstition may perhaps be somewhat of an exception; but partiality to ourselves is not; this being itself dishonesty."

Dissertation. "Nor is it at all doubtful to the general, what course of action this faculty, or practical discerning power within us approves, and what it disapproves."

the single important exception of the allegation that in the remarks of the *Preface* on the "ambiguous case" in the ethical doctrine of Shaftesbury, and again in the well-known passage in the *Sermons* on the *Love of our neighbour*, he compromises the authority of "conscience" by admitting that it could not be maintained if there were ever any reason to think "conscience" and "self-interest" opposed. But I should like to make some more special remarks on the principal features of his moral teaching with a view to the clearing-up of what seem to me persistent misunderstandings about its real character.

(1) What is Butler's real position on the questions which must be answered differently by a "rationalist" and by a "sentimentalist" in ethics? In the *Sermons* themselves he avoids taking up any definite position, and, as I have said, I think him justified on the ground that, for his immediate purpose, which is simply to insist on the authority of the moral law, a discussion of the precise way in which that law is apprehended would be irrelevant and disturbing. It does not follow that Butler had not a definite view, and the *Preface* to the *Sermons*, taken along with the explicit statements of the *Dissertation*, should make it fairly clear what that view is. It is true that even in the last-named work Butler does not expressly identify the "reflective faculty" by which we approve and disapprove our own conduct either with "reason" or with "feeling", either with the "sentiment of the understanding" or with the "perception of the heart", but seems to hold, as is the fact, that moral approbation and disapproval imply both factors.[1] But the real issue at stake in the con-

---

[1] *Dissertation.* "It is manifest great part of common language, and of common behaviour over the world, is formed upon supposition of such a moral faculty; whether called conscience, moral reason, moral sense, or Divine reason; whether considered as a sentiment of the understanding, or as a perception of the heart; or, which seems the truth, as including both."

troversy between rationalist and sentimentalist can be stated in a way which involves no special psychological refinements, and when it is so stated, it becomes pretty clear what Butler's attitude towards it is. I take it that no "rationalist" ever meant, by saying that moral distinctions are apprehended by reasoning or understanding, to affirm that moral approval and disapproval are purely unemotional intellectual states.[1] In any man who asserted such a proposition it would be self-stultifying to appeal to our widespread human detestation of cruelty or ingratitude, or our sympathy with and admiration of the contrary virtues, as evidence for his theory. Yet such appeals are constantly made by "rationalists" no less than by "sentimentalists". The real question at issue is not so much that of the "origin" of our approbations and disapprobations as that of their content.

The typical contention of all the writers who have been called "rationalists" is that, whatever may be the way in which we come by our moral convictions, what we approve or disapprove is always an objective character of our voluntary reactions to our situation, which can be identified by the intellect *après coup*. Or, in other words, the rationalists' point is that the intellect can apprehend principles which are implied in and justify our approbations and disapprobations. The essence of the rival view, expressed most forcibly by Hume, is precisely that we cannot do this. Hume, for example, holds that we know what we approve and what we disapprove, but we can discover no rational principle at

---

[1] Butler's at first sight singular phrases "sentiment of the understanding", "perception of the heart" are perhaps chosen deliberately to make this point. It is hard to believe in Whewell's "emendation "of them to "perception of the understanding", "sentiment of the heart". Whewell should have remembered Pascal's *Le cœur a ses raisons*. [And I believe there is truth in the contention that the more explicit recognition of "sentiment" in the *Dissertation* is due to study of Hutcheson.]

the bottom of our verdicts of approval and disapproval. The issue, at bottom, is as unpsychological as the very similar issue in speculative philosophy about the presence or absence of *a priori* principles of interconnection in our scientific knowledge. To be a rationalist in your epistemology does not mean that you deny the difference between thinking and sensation, or that you hold that science draws no premises from sense-perception. It means simply that you regard the world as in principle through and through intelligible, as a system of "facts" or "events" interconnected by principles which justify themselves to the intellect on scrutiny. To be a rationalist in morals means in the same way to hold that the body of moral approvals and disapprovals which make up the content of morality is permeated by recognisable principles luminous to the understanding. This, and nothing else, is what, in fact, "rationalists" like Cudworth, whose ethical work has never been completely published and was wholly unpublished when Butler was preaching his *Sermons*, and Clarke, of whose work he had been a close student, had set themselves to show. And at this point I trust I may be pardoned if I make a brief digression from my immediate subject.

In the interests of clear thinking, I should like to enter a protest against attaching any undue significance to the common distinction between Intuitionism and Rationalism in ethics, or, what I suppose comes to the same thing, the distinction between Particular and Universal Intuitionism. I cannot believe that there ever has been a sane thinker who held either that all our moral approvals are "universal" or that they are all "barely particular". In point of fact, in actual life we pass moral verdicts of both kinds. We approve or disapprove certain general ways of behaving, *e.g.* generosity, gratitude, cruelty, revenge; we also approve a particular act as the proper act to be done in a certain concrete situation for which no accepted code of duties provides any rule at all. I cannot believe that writers like Clarke, who devote most of their space to the consideration of the broad general lines of right action, meant to imply, what none of them ever says, though they are sometimes criticised as though they had said it,—that our verdicts of right and wrong have been from the first couched in this "universal" form. I can see no reason to suppose that Clarke would have felt called on to dispute the sensible observation of Adam Smith, that our approvals and disapprovals are *called out* by individual acts, but express themselves in a form which "universalises" the character of the act evoking the verdict, as for instance, to take Smith's own example, when we are revolted by a strikingly cruel act and say to ourselves, "I must never do that kind of thing". On the other hand, I cannot believe that any sane "particular Intuitionist" ever supposed that when he approved or disapproved an act, his verdict was so "barely particular" that he could not indicate the character in the act at which it was aimed. And, of course, in singling out for attention any character of the concrete and individual, you are already "universalising". Thus, as it seems to me, the attempt to make a distinction in principle between Rationalism or Universal Intuitionism and Particular Intuitionism is doubly objectionable. The distinction is not really applicable to the doctrines it is intended to classify, and it further rests on the importation into ethics of irrelevant and misleading psychological considerations.

Now, if the real ethical issue as between Rationalist and Sentimentalist has been rightly stated in what I have said, there can be no doubt where Butler stands.

He is definitely on the side of the Rationalists. This is, to begin with, indicated by the simple fact that he rests his case against his opponents on the question what kind of conduct is rightly to be called "natural", when we have regard to the consideration that "nature", in our ethical discussions, means "human nature", and that human nature is a "system" of "principles of action". The question here is not one of "psychological origin", it is one of justification, and justification at the bar of the intellect. That is the bar at which you would have, if required, to justify the assumption that the "natural" rule of life is the rule it is good to follow; it is again the bar at which the further question what way of living *is* the "natural" life for men in particular must be argued. It is for intelligence to pronounce what is the natural life for man, as it is for intelligence to decide what is his "natural diet". The reason in both cases is the same, that it is intelligence which supplies us with our standard, by revealing what is, as Butler likes to put it, in point of fact *our* "nature". Butler, to be sure, gives a special name to intelligence as declaratory of the line of conduct conformable to our nature; he calls it "conscience".[1] But he is careful to define conscience simply as "the reflex principle of approbation and dis-approbation", the principle by which we *judge* approvingly or disapprovingly of our own conduct, and this ought to place his meaning beyond doubt.

---

[1] *Preface*, "reflexion or conscience or approbation of some principles, or actions, and disapprobation of others". "Conscience, or reflexion, in the nature of man plainly bears upon it marks of authority over all the rest"; "that natural authority of reflexion"; *Sermon II*. "that particular kind of reflexion which you (*i.e.* Butler) call conscience"; "a superior principle of reflexion or conscience in every man . . . which passes judgment upon himself". *Dissertation*, "a capacity of reflecting upon actions and characters, and making them an object to our thought"; "our perception of vice and ill-desert arises from, and is the result of, a comparison of actions with the nature and capacities of the agent".

Passages like this show that "conscience", "reflexion", "thought directed on the quality of our own acts and characters" are, for Butler, strictly synonyms.

If we could feel any uncertainty on the point after reading the *Sermons* themselves, our doubts ought to be dissipated by the study of their *Preface* and of the *Dissertation*. It is significant that in the *Preface* Butler is careful to explain that he is fully in accord with the teaching of Clarke and has no strictures to make on his attempt to vindicate morality by reasoning from the "nature of things" in general.[1] By his own avowal, the thoroughgoing rationalism of Clarke is formally the most satisfactory way of treating moral philosophy; his own more specific and restricted appeal to the nature of the human agent in particular has only been adopted because it has, for the purposes of the preacher, the advantage of being more readily apprehended by and making a more immediate impression on, the average congregation.[2] So the rationalism of the *Dissertation* comes out unmistakably in one of its most important passages, that in which dissatisfaction with our situation is contrasted with censure of the conduct which has led to the situation.[3] Butler is not arguing that, viewed as so much emotion, there is some special unique character in the uneasy feeling of the man who judges that he has, *e.g.*, ruined his prospects by misconduct, which distinguishes it from the disagreeable feeling of the man who finds that he has been ruined

[1] When Butler speaks in the *Preface* to the *Sermons* of a way of treating the subject of morals which "begins from inquiring into the abstract relations of things" and concludes that "vice is contrary to the nature and reason of things", the language shows that he is thinking in the first instance of Clarke, though he may also mean to include Wollaston, to whom he refers later on as a "late author of great and deserved reputation". Cudworth's *Eternal and Immutable Morality* was published too late to be referred to in Butler's volume.

[2] *Preface*. "The first seems the most direct and formal proof, and in some respects the least liable to cavil and dispute."

[3] "This approbation and disapprobation (*sc.* of a "due concern about our own or others' happiness" and of the neglect of it) are altogether different from mere desire of our own or of their happiness, and from sorrow upon missing it. . . . In one case, what our thoughts fix upon is our condition . . . in the other our conduct."

by accidents for which he is not accountable. (Suppose, the failure of his banker or the miscarriage of his ship.) He finds the relevant difference entirely in the intellectual judgement that my position has been caused by my own wrong-doing. And similarly, both in the *Sermons* and in the *Preface* to them, the reason why man, unlike the brutes, would be living an unnatural, and therefore an *ex hypothesi* wrong life, if he simply acted on the prompting of the "strongest impulse" is found in the fact that man has a power, which the brutes have not, of *judging* his own actions as good and bad. He is alive to a real character of his acts which has no meaning for a brute, and therefore it is unnatural that he should act as though he were not alive to it.

To criticise this straightforward Rationalism on the ground that Butler gives to understanding, in its practical function as the discernment of good and evil in our own conduct, the special name of "conscience" is surely to fall into the fault of mere carping at words. Aristotle, too, has his own special name for thought exercised upon questions of choice between acts and inspired by an "end" to be realised; he calls it definitely *phronesis*, by way of antithesis to the *sophia* which is the pursuit of purely speculative truth. Yet no one accuses Aristotle, as some men are not ashamed to accuse Butler, of the crime of accepting a "faculty psychology". No one doubts that Aristotle's meaning is that it is one and the same intelligence, whole and entire, which displays itself differently in the creation of science and in the creation of a system of morality. What reason is there to suppose Butler to mean anything else? In general, the accusation of belief in a "faculty psychology" is one of those criticisms which are too facile to be really enlightening. If the proof of the charge is taken to be found in the mere fact that an author gives different names to the functions of thinking, understanding, and judging, according as they are employed upon a different matter, it will be hard for any philosophical writer who finds it necessary to achieve lucidity and brevity by the use of a technical terminology to avoid a conviction. If we further require, as we should, evidence that the accused has really committed the error of substituting a plurality of "faculties" for the single intelligent thinker as the agents in the mental life, most of the writers whom it is fashionable to condemn summarily as guilty of the fallacy of the faculty psychology will probably be entitled to an honourable acquittal. The *word* "faculty", taken by itself, may be *démodé*, but is as innocent as the word "capacity", or any other of the equivalents which the most determined enemy of Associationism finds himself quite unable to expunge from his vocabulary. As for Butler, his own language leaves it beyond dispute that when he speaks of "conscience", he means to describe the fact that we are capable of judging, and habitually do judge, our own acts and characters as right and wrong, good and bad, and that such a judgement carries with it the conviction, which it is his object to justify, that we "ought" to give it effect in our actual "choices and avoidances". It is a convenient thing to have a simple name for this capacity of judging our own conduct and character, and the name "conscience" is readily supplied by current popular language. To say, as I have had it said to myself by one distinguished moralist, "I should have had no quarrel with Butler if he had only used the word *reason*", is to agree with him about the facts, but to make one's self the pedant of a particular vocable.

(2) To return to the series of more specific accusa-

tions which have been levelled at Butler's account of conscience, they may be reduced roughly to the following heads. (*a*) Butler does not deal with the problem of the historical growth of conscience; (*b*) he seems to leave us with no more certain and authoritative guide in action than the "private conscience" of the individual; (*c*) he does not explain in any systematic way what it is that conscience enjoins. Why Butler does not deal with these questions at length has, I think, been sufficiently explained. The reason is that he does not think that the great practical deficiency of his hearers is want of acquaintance with their duties; it is an insufficient sense of the obligation to take duty seriously. If we read the three *Sermons on Human Nature* in particular with careful attention, we shall find that they form an argument addressed to two classes of persons. The first class are those who, under the influence of a false theory of human nature, hold that egoistic self-seeking is the only possible motive of all human acts. "Virtue", being *ex hypothesi* not self-seeking, is unnatural, in the sense that it is impossible. Anyone who bids us cultivate it is either a dupe or a designing impostor, a theory which it is not hard to identify with that of Mandeville; if indeed Mandeville was seriously intending to expound any theory at all, and not merely to amuse himself by cynical contemplation of the "seamy side" of human affairs. These opponents are met in principle by the argument for the disinterestedness of all the "particular passions".

The virtuous man is as much, and no more, of an exception to their theory as the gambler who wastes a noble estate to gratify the passion for excitement, the rake who ruins splendid bodily and mental gifts in the service of Bacchus and Venus, or the vindictive man who throws away his life to gratify his grudge.

And it is undeniable that the gambler, the profligate, and the revengeful man are only too real types of humanity.

The second class of persons with whom Butler has to reckon have a theory of human conduct which is not that of Mandeville, but is common enough for all that. They are the type who admit the reality of the promptings of virtuous impulse, but see no reason why we should be virtuous when we do not happen to be strongly under the influence of these impulses. Their view, unlike the former, does not involve the confusion between "self-love" and the "passions". They hold that the natural and proper course of life is to have no settled rule of action whatever, to let every impulse, good or evil, "take its turn as it happens to be uppermost". If such irresponsible creatures were capable of enunciating a principle, the principle they would own to is that of "living in the moment and for the moment". As the distinction between "self-love" and the "passions" is meant to supply the refutation of the first class of immoralists, so the subsequent argument for the supreme authoritativeness of "conscience" is intended specially for the benefit of the second. We see that this is so from the simple consideration that throughout this argument it is the "passions" in opposition to which the authority of conscience is asserted. There is no corresponding demonstration that conscience has "manifest authority" over the promptings of cool and reasoned regard for our own "interest". We have to discover Butler's view on this point by collation and comparison of passages which occur in several different contexts. No doubt this absence of a direct assertion of the supremacy of "conscience" over "self-love" can partly be explained by Butler's avowed conviction that in the main "interest" and "duty" coincide; to disregard the second also means disregarding the first.[1] (Hence his emphatic statement that most men do not care too much, perhaps do not care enough, about their own interests; it is not considered pursuit of self-interest which is the worst enemy of practical morality.) But it remains a curious fact that Butler does not think it necessary to deal with a third possible view of the conduct "natural" in a human being, the view that it is neither abandonment to the passion of the moment, nor yet strict obedience to "conscience", but the calculating pursuit of my own "greatest happiness on the whole", the "rational egoism" of Henry Sidgwick. I do not see how the omission can be fully accounted for except by the consideration that Butler's purposes are strictly practical and that he did not contemplate "rational egoists" as forming an appreciable part of his audience.

We can, however, perhaps collect the answer he would have given to the "rational egoist" from certain striking passages of the *Dissertation*. In the second *Sermon*, where the case of a man who rushes open-eyed on his own destruction is contrasted with that of a beast which does the same thing, for the purpose of proving that in man "self-love" (which has no existence in the beasts) is a "superior" principle by comparison with the "passions", it is clear enough that Butler holds wanton indifference to our own "happiness" to be unnatural and therefore wrong. But the treatment given in the *Dissertation* to the question whether we are "more at liberty" to make ourselves miserable than to make others miserable, suggests that if he had been asked

---

[1] The most unqualified statement is that of *Sermon III. ad fin.* "Conscience and self-love, if we understand our true happiness, always lead us the same way. Duty and interest are perfectly coincident." But here Butler is speaking from the pulpit and is free to assume the teachings of the Christian faith about God and immortality. In the *Preface*, where he is considering things as they appear without the light of faith, he has, of course, to speak without this confidence.

why it is wrong to neglect your own happiness, his considered reply would not have been "because neglect is contrary to self-love", but "because conscience forbids neglect".[1] His final view seems to have been that "self-love" is never, to use Kantian language, a source of *imperatives*. It is concerned with the formation of probable judgements of fact. Its utterances are all of the form "this will probably add to (or will probably detract from) my happiness". The *imperative* "I ought to do what will make me happy and ought not to do what will make me miserable" is clearly assigned to "conscience". It is in keeping with this that in the *Sermons* themselves conscience is always spoken of as *the* reflective principle, or *the* principle of reflex approbation and disapprobation.

"Self-love" is, of course, reflective, in the modern sense of the word; it is intelligent and "calculates", as the "passions" do not. But Butler clearly means to use the word "reflective" or "reflex" in the strict sense. Conscience is said to be reflective, not simply because it is intelligent, but because its judgements are judgements about our *own* conduct; the agent is also the judge who turns his scrutiny upon his own act. Hence one of the most serious allegations against Butler (which shall be examined shortly), has, in my opinion, always been wrongly expressed. It is not true that Butler ever "co-ordinates" self-love and conscience as principles of action; he never considers self-love as having a right to prescribe acts which conscience condemns. The real way to make the complaint intended by his critics

---

[1] *Dissertation.* "It should seem that a due concern about our own interest or happiness and a reasonable endeavour to secure and promote it, which is, I think, very much the meaning of the word *prudence* in our language; it should seem that this is virtue, and the contrary behaviour faulty and blameworthy; since, in the calmest way of reflection, we approve of the first, and condemn the other, conduct, both in ourselves and in others."

would be to ask whether Butler had not sometimes talked as though conscience might contradict *itself* by commanding regard for our own "interest" and yet also commanding some act which would be in conflict with that interest. The question is not whether there are two "authorities" who may disagree, but whether the one authority may possibly be inconsistent in its injunctions. All the "imperatives" are imperatives of conscience, but there may be a doubt whether any of them except the command to aim at my own happiness is wholly categorical.

I do not see that any serious ground to take exception to Butler's principles is furnished by the evidence about the gradual growth of conscience or the differences between the conscientious convictions of individuals. It is important to note two points. Butler never speaks of "private conscience", and what he ascribes to conscience is authority, not infallibility. Of divergences of moral judgement between members of his audience he speaks as trivial and secondary,[1] and as I have argued, he was fairly entitled to take this view. It is a fact that persons of the same age and social tradition will "in the main" agree on the broad general question what kind of conduct is morally good. Those who talk of "conscience" as though it were a set of whims and fads confined to the individual are attaching far too much importance to the "conscientious objector". Even his conscience is not active simply in "objecting". He may have his personal fad, a belief that vaccination is sinful

---

[1] *Sermon II*. "The appearance there is of some small diversity amongst mankind with respect to this faculty, with respect to their natural sense of moral good and evil; and the attention necessary to survey with any exactness what passes within, have occasioned that it is not so much agreed what is the standard of the internal nature of man, as of his external form. Neither is this last exactly settled. Yet we understand one another when we speak of the shape of a human body. So likewise we do when we speak of the heart and inward principles, how far soever the standard is from being exact or precisely fixed."

or the like, but ninety-nine-hundredths of the things his
conscience commands or forbids are precisely the things
commanded or forbidden by the consciences of his
fellows. And even in the hundredth case his disagreement with them is usually on a question of *fact*, not on
a question of *right*. The anti-vaccinationist does not
dispute his duty to protect his children from smallpox;
he merely denies that vaccination is protective. His disagreement with the rest of us is on a point of medical,
not of moral, theory. The vegetarian, for all his language
about "wanton cruelty" to the animals, is always careful
to insist that a vegetarian diet is more wholesome than
a flesh diet. If he could be convinced that flesh-eating
is desirable on dietetic grounds, he would apparently
lose most, or all, of his moral scruples. Even the
"objector" who refuses his services to his country in
war-time commonly justifies himself not so much by
denying the ethical principle that a society righteously
defending itself may require those services, as by
alleging that the facts about the special circumstances
in which his country has entered on hostilities make the
case one of unrighteous war. On the question what *kind*
of war is righteous, he is often in complete agreement
with everyone else.

There are ultimate moral disagreements, but they
only cover a minority of the cases, and even they are,
in the main, disagreements about *axiomata media*, not
about principles. For example, there are those Englishmen who regard fox-hunting as inexcusable cruelty to
animals, and those who do not. But both parties would
probably agree in the propositions that some infliction
of suffering on the lower animals is morally permissible,
and that some is not. The point in dispute is only
whether the amount of pain inflicted on the fox, when
weighed against the enjoyment of the hunter, comes

under the head of the permissible. Butler thus appears to me right in treating genuine variations of moral judgement among members of the same group, with the same traditions, as a secondary matter. But, incidentally, we may note that by taking this line he makes it clear that he supposes the deliverances of conscience to be universal principles, *e.g.* the commands to practise generosity, gratitude, justice, and the other great typical virtues. He cannot have supposed that there would be anything like the consensus he assumes, if the question were whether a particular act, in a given complex situation, is the generous or just act to do. So his recognition of veracity as one of the things enjoined by conscience cannot be interpreted as committing him to the view that there are no circumstances in which "verbal misleading" can be right. This inference as to his meaning is strictly in keeping with the approving tone in which his *Preface* speaks of the moral theory of Clarke.

Again, I do not see why Butler need have been disturbed by the fact that the "conscience" of Englishmen of his own time differed widely from that of the heroes of the First Crusade, and both from the conscience of a Hottentot. As far as "historical development" goes, conscience would be in no worse case than any other form of knowledge. There is really no reason why we should defer more to the judgement of the Crusader or the Hottentot on a question of morals than on a question of science. If the Crusader regarded it as unquestioned truth that it is good to kill an "infidel" for being an infidel, he also, if he thought about the matter at all, presumably held that there is no land between the West of Europe and the East of China, and that the infidels whom he slaughtered worshipped Mahound. We do not regard ourselves as bound to doubt the competence of the human intelligence because men have made these errors in geography and historical knowledge; why are we not equally free to admit that they have also judged wrongly in questions of morals? It cannot be fairly demanded of the believer in the authority of conscience that he should regard every opinion about right and wrong which has ever been entertained by any man as equally authoritative with every other. There are, however, two further remarks which ought to be made in this connection, as necessary to a reasonable interpretation of Butler.

The first is that there is a real danger of exaggerating the amount of disagreement between the "consciences" of society in different ages. Much which would be commonly put down loosely to "variations" in "conscience" does not really come under this head. Thus we disapprove strongly of the man who prosecutes the blood-feud, or, in other ways, attempts to right himself and his friends with the strong hand. In earlier ages and ruder societies the prosecution of the blood-feud had been regarded as a positive duty and a very sacred one. Yet it does not follow that the virtuous man of to-day who regards private revenge as absolutely prohibited really differs on the principles of right conduct from a man of the past who thought it a sacred duty to avenge the innocent blood with his own hands. The difference is, at bottom, a difference in the situation of the two men. In the one case there is an organised society which will make the punishment of the homicide its business, and will execute it with a certainty and an impartiality impossible where the repression of crime of this kind must be undertaken by private enterprise; in the other, unless a kinsman of a murdered man has the public spirit to devote himself to the prosecution of the feud, murder will often be committed with impunity by the violent. The man who makes it a duty to pursue the slayer, and the man who, in happier times, makes it a duty to "leave the offender to the law", may be entirely agreed on the question what justice is and both may have the same respect for justice. The difference between them may simply be that the methods for securing the execution of justice are much more developed in the society of the second than in that of the first, and this does not amount to a difference in the deliverances of "conscience". Similarly, the great scholastics explained the polygamy of the patriarchs by saying that though the principles of the moral law which regulates human marriage are the same in all ages, there was a need in the world's youth which there is not now for numerous offspring, in order that the earth might be brought effectively under the dominion of man. What would in us be only explicable as "licentious" disregard of the sanctity of conjugal ties was in the patriarchs respect for the moral law which enjoins the subjugation of nature by man. And it might not be hard to find other illustrations of the point.

If, as I have already argued, what Butler understood "conscience" to reveal was the great principles of moral conduct rather than the precise way in which they are to be applied to particular cases, considerations of this kind will make it clearer that he might have extended to many of the so-called variations of conscience from one age to another his remark about individual disagreements within the same community, that they are, after all, secondary.

However, it is, of course, clear that we cannot treat all the relevant facts in this way. We cannot, when all legitimate deductions have been made, deny that as intelligence develops there is real advance in delicacy of moral discrimination; men do become alive to obligations of which they had formerly been ignorant. But here comes in the second of the considerations I wish to urge. Butler never says or suggests that conscience, in his own or any other age, is *infallible*. What he says is that it is *authoritative*. Now authority does not necessarily imply infallibility in moral matters any more than in others. A guide who is far from infallible may be the best guide I can get, though the distinction is so constantly forgotten in the controversies about the place of authority in theology. In matters of science, history, and the like we all understand the point well enough. A man who is not himself competent to form a personal opinion on a question of history or archaeology or textual criticism is expected to regard the general *consensus* of the acknowledged "experts" as authoritative; even a man who is qualified to form a personal judgement is rightly expected to allow great weight to such a *consensus* and not to reject it without being prepared to give convincing reasons for his dissent. This does not, of course, mean that the "experts", when agreed, are infallible, or that anyone thinks them to be so. We all know that they may agree in a mistake and sometimes do so. But it means that in the main we are likely to be most often right, and right on the most important matters, if we follow their guidance. Of course, there are exceptions. For instance, a man who accepted the authority of the leading "experts" in Greek scholarship some seventy years ago would have had to reject a good many of the ripest of the Platonic dialogues as spurious and to declare the Homeric poems badly constructed pieces of patch-work. We know to-day that the "experts" of the fifties of the nineteenth century were wrong on the first point, and the conviction among Greek scholars themselves is happily spreading that they were wrong on the other point too. And yet, on the whole, the man with little or no Greek scholarship would have done better to read the history of Greek literature by their aid than to venture on it without that help. His "authorities" would have been very fallible indeed, but they would still have been the best *he* could get.

In principle the case seems to me to stand no otherwise with the authority of "conscience". As I have tried to urge, Butler does not mean by "conscience" something peculiar and private to the individual man. He seems rather to have meant the body of moral convictions which is common to the "best" men of a society—a "public" rather than a "private" conscience. That he never, even by implication, claims infallibility for this body of convictions yields at least a presumption that he did not suppose it to be infallible. His teaching never requires us to hold that even the "best" morality of one age may not be improved on by a later. But, for all its possible deficiencies, it may still well be the case that the conscience of the best men in my society is the best guide I have and ought to be followed as such. If I find myself in sharp opposition to it on some question of conduct, I may be right, but, if I am a modest man, I shall be well aware that I am very likely to be wrong. And I shall think it a duty to discover what the best men I know think of my proposed line of action, and, if they condemn it, to make very sure indeed of myself before I venture to decide that, on the particular point in question, the "best" moral opinion of the age happens to be that which is incarnate in just one personality, and that personality my own. I can see nothing in any of Butler's statements about the authority of conscience which would warrant the view that I am doing right in always acting simply on my own personal impressions, or that it is not my positive duty to attach the greatest weight to the judgement of good men generally. Indeed, I believe it would be quite consistent with all he has to say, that a given man should recognise some other man as a better judge than himself on a specific class of moral questions (*e.g.* on matters involving a delicate sense of sexual purity), and consequently resolve in those matters to follow the other's spiritual direction closely. Though, we must note, even in such subjection to spiritual direction, a man does not divest himself of ultimate responsibility for himself. The selection of the adviser is his own act and it is his business to select wisely.

I believe one might, without abandoning any claim made by Butler for "conscience", go a step further. Probability, we must remember, is, according to Butler himself, the guide of life. Hence the recognition that, when all care has been taken to listen for the voice of the inward monitor, and to eliminate the possibilities of misjudgement due to unconscious bias, or to unfamiliarity with the kind of situation in which I am called upon to act, by humbly seeking the judgement of men better and wiser, or more experienced in the kind of affairs with which I find myself called upon to deal, I *may* honestly fall into moral error. The question will thus arise, not in connection with the broad principles of morality, but in connection with their application to the special situation, can I ever be absolutely certain, beyond all possibility of error, that the act the "reflective principle" pronounces right is exactly and perfectly right? It seems to me that absolute certainty is not attainable and that Butler's moral theory does not require that it should be. We can be certain that some ways of acting in the given situation would be wrong because they would involve, *e.g.*, injustice or ingratitude. But we cannot, in many cases, be sure exactly what act would, *e.g.*, be most fully in accord with the demands of justice or again of moral prudence.

Suppose, for example, that I am left as guardian and executor to the child of a friend or relative, with a very considerable latitude of action, neither the utmost scrupulosity nor the most careful consultation of the more experienced can ensure that I shall make no mistake in selecting an investment or a school for my ward. And the situation is only typical of those which are arising every day for every man whose notion of right action is anything more than mere abstention from the ways of behaviour which good social opinion has definitely classed as "not respectable". The problem recurs for a magistrate every time he has to decide for himself what penalty to inflict for an offence, for a citizen every time he is called on to exercise the franchise.

It does not seem to me that in cases of this kind we can ever expect to be absolutely certain of the "path of duty". We have always to make the reservation which Prince Florizel makes in Stevenson's tale when he decides to throw the Rajah's diamond into the river, "God forgive me if I am doing wrong, but its empire ends to-night". I doubt if any of us who has ever had to take a momentous decision in the course of his life has been able, in the act of taking it, to avoid uttering the prayer "God forgive me if I am deciding wrong". But, at the same time, I cannot see that this possibility in any way diminishes the authority claimed for conscience, when we have honestly done our best to make sure that the decision taken has been dictated by conscience. To demand more certainty than this would be to require that "conscience", when due pains have been taken to enlighten it, shall have not only authority but infallibility, and this is a claim which Butler never advances.

Indeed, it is just in not advancing this claim that Butler appears to me to show a decided advantage in sobriety over that other great moralist of duty, Kant. Kant does more than once make the extravagant assertion that no honest man can ever be in doubt about the path of duty, because he can always discover that a proposed course of action is wrong by simply applying the test of universalising its "maxim". But manifestly this test is hopelessly unsatisfactory. Not to dwell on the point that there seems to be a great deal of very bad morality which would stand the Kantian test quite successfully, it is obvious that at the best the test will only secure you against "flagrant sin". It would, for instance, have been of no use whatever to any British citizen anxious to know how he ought to use his vote at the last General Election. Before voting for the Labour candidate or the Conservative candidate a man certainly ought to ask himself whether he would be doing right by voting for either, or again by abstaining from using his vote, but no "universalising" of any maxim would decide that very pertinent question. All you can say is that I ought to use my vote, having regard to the general issues at stake, the particular choice between candidates in my own constituency, the probable consequences of the return of each of the contending parties to power, in such a way as to do the most good and the least harm. It is certain that, however I vote, I shall be voting for a party which, supposing it to be victorious, will do some good and also some evil, and I have in the first place to judge which party is, on the whole, likely to do most good and least evil. And the problem is usually still more complicated. I may be satisfied that on the whole it is desirable that one of the parties should

come into power, and equally satisfied that it is desirable
that it should be sobered and balanced by not having
too large a majority over its rivals, and in some cases
this, I take it, would be a valid reason for thinking
it my duty to vote against "my own party". And there
is still a third complication created by the fact that I
may be convinced that one of the candidates between
whom I in particular have to choose is a man of such
outstanding character and ability that his services
ought not to be lost to the Legislature, irrespective of
the question what his party is.

To make the illustration more precise, let us suppose
I am satisfied that on the whole the Labour party stand
for the best interests of the inhabitants of the country
as a whole, and therefore desire to see that party returned. I have to set against this desire the consideration that it is very undesirable that they or any other

party should be able, from the weakness of the Opposition, to do pretty much what they like for four or five
years. Such complete domination of the situation is very
likely to mean that they will effect that very part of
their programme which I regard as bad and unwise, as
well as that on the strength of which they have my
approval. Or, alternatively, it may mean that the
discipline and vigilance of the party will suffer; they
will be free to develop internal differences and to
quarrel among themselves, and the very measures on
the strength of which the party has my general approval
will be less effectively carried out. And finally, I have
to ask myself whether, supposing one of the rival candidates to be a man of exceptional character and ability,
it would not be better that the majority of "my party"
should be diminished by a defeat in this constituency,
where their candidate is a man of no special qualifications, than that the exceptionally valuable man should

be lost to the counsels of the nation. I am not using my vote conscientiously unless I balance all these considerations against one another, and it is not an easy thing to decide what relative weight should be given to each of them. Any moral theory which professes to provide a short cut to the right decision in such a case stands self-condemned by its own pretensions. It thus seems to me proof of the judiciousness of Butler's mind that, with all his insistence on the authoritativeness of the "reflex principle", he never advances for it the claim to infallibility. To use the valuable distinction of Hutcheson, at best one can secure "formal rightness" in one's conduct by obedience to conscience; there can be no guarantee of "material rightness".

(3) I have left to the end the most serious imputation which has been brought against Butler as a moralist; I mean the charge that in the end he runs away from his own professed position by admitting that the obligation to obey conscience depends on the coincidence of the path of duty with the path of self-interest. So far as I can discover, the case for his critics rests on two passages, one paragraph from the first Sermon on the *Love of our Neighbour*, and the section in the *Preface* to the *Sermons* which discusses Shaftesbury's problem of the "sceptic not convinced of the happy tendency of virtue". There could, of course, be no ethical objection to what is clearly Butler's view, that in point of fact a man does always promote his own truest interest by the strict practice of virtue. It is possible to hold that the fact is far from certain; but to believe it to be certain is no derogation from the claims of virtue, so long as you also hold that, though virtue does always make for our personal happiness, it is to be pursued, not for that reason, but because it is virtue. In Aristotelian language one may perfectly well hold that virtue and interest

"are the same", in the sense that they are inseparably conjoined in fact (the virtuous act is always also the act which is "to my interest"), but that their εἶναι or *esse formale* is not the same, just as according to Aristotle the truly virtuous life and the truly pleasant life are the same, though virtue is not pleasure. Thus the mere fact that Butler, like all Christians, holds that virtue in the end always coincides with interest has no relevance to the charge we are considering. We may therefore confine our attention to the two specific passages to which I have referred.

Now if we had only the one sentence from the Sermon to go upon, we might, I think, have to admit that Butler has perhaps fallen into inconsistency.[1] He certainly does appear there to be saying in so many words that we could not regard "benevolence" or any other conduct as morally obligatory unless we were convinced that it is also to our interest, and if he means this to be an expression of his own opinion, he is unsaying what

---

[1] *Sermon XI.* "It may be allowed, without any prejudice to the cause of virtue and religion, that our ideas of happiness and misery are of all our ideas the nearest and most important to us; that they will, nay, if you please, that they ought to prevail over those of order, and beauty, and harmony, and proportion, if there ever should be, as it is impossible there ever should be, any inconsistence between them; though these last two, as expressing the fitness of actions, are real as truth itself. Let it be allowed, though virtue or moral rectitude does indeed consist in affection to and pursuit of what is right and good, as such; yet, that when we sit down in a cool hour, we can neither justify to ourselves this or any other pursuit, till we are convinced that it will be for our happiness, or at least not contrary to it."

The phraseology here, "it may be allowed", "if you please", "if there ever should be, as it is impossible there ever should be", "let it be allowed", makes it, to my mind, almost certain that the position is meant to be one which Butler himself does not accept, but is content to assume for the purpose of reasoning with an audience who regard "self-love" as the one rational rule of conduct. He had said at the beginning of the discourse, "there shall be all possible concessions made to the favourite passion, which hath so much allowed to it, and whose cause is so universally pleaded; it shall be treated with the utmost tenderness, and concern for its interests". We must therefore expect a touch of "irony" in the sermon. It is monstrous to discuss the incriminated passage without taking into account Butler's sarcastic words about the indulgence he proposes to show the "favourite passion" of his auditors.

he himself had said about the "manifest authority" of conscience; the famous phrase "had it power as it has manifest authority, it would absolutely govern the world" becomes meaningless, if it is true that we need to satisfy ourselves that an act will be for our interest before we can pronounce it obligatory. Even so, it would be fair to urge that no one is ever absolutely consistent with himself in his every utterance, and that an author's convictions ought to be judged by the tenour of his work as a whole and not by a single phrase which contradicts his own emphatic and repeated declarations. The reasonable thing would be to discount the isolated sentence as not really faithful to the writer's convictions.

But this is not all that may be said. It is almost certain that the words complained of are not intended to convey Butler's own opinion at all. They are a sarcastic concession to the audience he wishes to carry with him. Many of them, we can hardly doubt, would hold that, when all is said, there is force in the point of view put brutally by a character in *Pickwick*, "damn hurting yourself for anyone else", and Butler may mean no more than that, even if you grant this principle, "benevolence" is not "hurting yourself". Even if a man agrees with Lowten, you want him in practice to perform kind acts, and you may fairly urge that, after all, even on his own principles there is every reason for doing so, because he will not be hurting himself but very much benefiting himself. And there is one consideration in particular which, as I think, goes a long way to show that Butler's language in this particular passage is meant to be no more than a dialectical concession to the audience. We may reasonably suppose that if he has taken special care anywhere to adapt his language closely to his thought, it will be in the *Preface*,

in which he is at pains to explain the precise drift of
the discourses which follow. Unlike the *Sermons* themselves, the *Preface* is not a spoken address from the
pulpit aiming at making an immediate impression; it is
a literary production addressed to readers, composed at
leisure to be studied at leisure. And the very passage
critical of Shaftesbury, which is made part of the count
against Butler, contains an express statement flatly inconsistent with the sentence we are now considering.
There Butler claims to be proving that the "utmost
scepticism" about the coincidence of virtue and happiness of which we can conceive leaves the obligation to
the strictest practice of virtue unaffected. Now he cannot have meant both to affirm this and also to affirm
that no obligation is binding unless we are satisfied that
it is to our interest to recognise it. If one of these utterances represents his convictions, the other cannot. And
there can be no doubt which of the two passages may
be most reasonably taken to represent the author's
deliberate view. The criticism of the "ambiguous case"
in Shaftesbury's system is the one elaborate and express
discussion of the problem which Butler has given us;
the remark in the discourse on *Love of our Neighbour* is
made at the end of a discussion proceeding on different
lines, and has much more the character of an incidental
obiter dictum. We must therefore conclude either that
Butler has by a mere oversight allowed himself to make
an incidental remark which is not really consistent with
his considered position and forgotten to correct it, or,
more probably, that the remark was not intended as
more than a temporary concession to the prejudices of
an audience.

There remains the actual discussion of the case put
by Shaftesbury, the case of the "moral sceptic".
Butler's determination of the case has, I believe, been

sometimes misunderstood from neglect of the dramatic form in which it is given. If we examine it carefully we shall see that the argument has two stages which must be carefully discriminated. The misconception comes in when it is supposed that Butler discloses his own hand in the first stage of the answer. The following analysis will make the point clear.

Butler begins by asserting that it is Shaftesbury's neglect of the notion of obligation which led him to the view that the case of the "sceptic" is "without remedy", *i.e.* that you cannot expect a man to see any reason for acting virtuously if he doubts whether it will be to his interest to do so. He then supposes the defenders of this position to retort that it makes no difference to the situation to "take in the authority" of conscience, since, they urge, even if you admit it and grant that there is an obligation on the side of virtue, still there is also a counter obligation to pursue my own interest. The immediate answer is that, even if this is granted, the conclusion they wish to draw would not follow. It would only follow that, in this statement of the case, there are two contrary obligations which cancel one another, not a "formal obligation to be vicious".[1] That is, if you leave the authority of conscience out of account, it might be fairly argued that a man who thinks he would promote his happiness by a vicious act is absolutely justified in being vicious. If you admit the authority of conscience, then, even on your own theory that there is *another* independent obligation to pursue my own happiness, there is at least as much justification for preferring virtue to interest as for preferring interest to

---

[1] *Preface*. "But does it much mend the matter, to take in the natural authority of reflexion? there would indeed be an obligation to virtue, but would not the obligation from supposed interest on the side of vice remain? If it should, yet to be under two contrary obligations, *i.e.* under none at all, would not be exactly the same, as to be under a formal obligation to be vicious."

virtue. (It is true that Shaftesbury had never expressly said that the sceptic would be formally "bound" to be vicious in the supposed case, but it is part of Butler's fairness that he wishes to state the case against virtue, which he has to meet, as powerfully as he can, and is therefore at pains to point out that, on the principles of a "morality without obligation", a man would not merely be *free* to be vicious, if he thought vice to his interest, but would be acting in a way such a morality must pronounce wrong if he were anything but vicious.)

The all-important thing to be observed here is that the conclusion that the sceptic would "be under no obligation at all" is not Butler's. The conclusion rests on premises which he rejects. "Granting this to be so" means no more than "allowing this to be so, for purposes of argument, though I deny it is so", *dato ma non concesso*. Hence Butler continues by denying the relevant premise; "the obligation on the side of interest does not remain". His own solution of the problem is exclusively contained in the sentences which follow on this denial.[1]

---

[1] *Loc. cit.* "But the obligation on the side of vice does not remain. For the natural authority of the principle of reflexion, is an obligation the most near and intimate, the most certain and known; whereas the contrary obligation can at the utmost appear no more than probable; . . . and thus the certain obligation would entirely supersede and destroy the uncertain one, which would yet have been of real force without the former." (The important words here are "utterly supersede and destroy", which show that Butler is not thinking of anything in the nature of a "gamble in futures".)

"Take in then that authority and obligation, which is a constituent part of this reflex approbation, and it will undeniably follow that though a man should doubt of everything else, yet that he would still remain under the nearest and most certain obligation to the practice of virtue." "Though men should be ignorant of or disbelieve any authority in the universe to permit the violation of this law; yet, if there should be such authority, they would be as really liable to punishment, as though they had been before-hand convinced, that such punishment would follow."

Thus "hell" does not come into the argument, since Butler holds that the reasoning would be equally valid if no one had ever heard of "hell", if "through stupidity" mankind were "universally ignorant" on the subject.

It may, however, be said that, even so, his own appeal is to interest. For does not his argument that "no one can be certain that vice is his interest" amount merely to the suggestion that perhaps vice does not pay? This is, I think, a complete misconception, as may be seen from the absence of any reference to what would be the central point if the argument were an appeal to interest, the *magnitude* of the disagreeable consequences which may, for all we know, attend on vice. The argument sometimes supposed to be Butler's *must* take this point into consideration. Fully stated it would run thus. Even if there is only a very trifling probability that "all tales are true" about hell, still, *if* they should be true, the pains of hell are so terrific that a wise man will not run even a distant risk of suffering them. But Butler is wholly silent about this question of the "value of the expectation" of future suffering. The contrast he makes is simply the contrast between the *uncertainty* that vice will be to our interest and the absolute *certainty* that the moral law carries its authority with it. The point is simply that this authority is "certain and known". It is because of its certainty that Butler goes on to say that the authority of "conscience" absolutely destroys all the weight of the appeal on the other side to considerations of interest, which "would have been of real force" but for the known certainty of moral obligation. Had Butler held the position ascribed to him by some of his critics, he would have had no right to express himself thus. His argument should have been that even if the probability that vice will lead to misery appears slight, yet the magnitude of the misery to which, according to the theory of future rewards and punishments, it does lead is so overwhelming that it must be imprudent to take the risk that the theory may prove true. The probability

of "damnation" may be low, but the "expectation",
which is what a wise man would be guided by in
deciding whether to run the hazard, is another matter.
As it would be reasonable to risk a penny on the tiniest
of chances of winning a "million", so it would be
reasonable not to incur the faintest risk of the penalties
of damnation.

But when the argument is stated in this way, it becomes a variant of "Pascal's Wager"; it is differentiated
from Butler's reasoning in two ways. The magnitude
of the penalties which the sinner may expect if there is
a moral government of the world becomes the pivot on
which the argument turns, and the consideration which
is crucial with Butler, the intrinsic authority of the
moral law, ceases to be relevant. In an argument intended simply to prove that the faintest probability
that there may be a hell makes it imprudent to run the
risk of going to hell, if a hell there be, it is superfluous
and irrelevant to raise the question whether the moral
law has an intrinsic authoritativeness or not, just as it
would be irrelevant if one were captured by brigands
and threatened with torture, to ask for a sight of the
warrant empowering the infliction of the tortures. It
should be noted, as further proof that Butler's argument is not in principle that of the Wager, that he goes
on to lay stress on the point that what renders a man
justly liable to punishment is not fore-knowledge of the
penalty but the transgression of a known law. Obviously this is no more than the truth. It would be no
relevant defence on the part of an alien in this country
standing his trial for murder to plead, what might be
the truth, that he had not known that the penalty for
murder by our law is death. He knows, at least, that
murder is prohibited, and, consequently, by violating
the prohibition he renders himself justly liable to what-

ever penalty, known or unknown to him, the law assigns to the crime of murder. Similarly it would be no defence to a charge of any kind to urge, even with truth, that hitherto the administrators of the law have winked at the offence in question, and that it has been committed by others with complete impunity. This might (or might not) have some force as a plea after conviction for mitigation of sentence; as a defence it would be worthless. But the fact that Butler calls attention to this analogy of itself shows that the magnitude of the transgressor's "expectation" of misery, the central consideration in every form of the prudential argument for virtue, is not intended to come into account at all in his own theory. His point is simply that we know with certainty that we have specific moral obligations, and that uncertainty whether neglect of them will affect our "interest" does nothing to destroy this certainty of their reality. Their reality would, in fact, remain, even if I could be certain, as I cannot be, that vice will do nothing to diminish my happiness, or even that a vicious act will augment it. If you grant the intrinsic "authoritativeness" of the moral law, even certainty that I should gain by violating it would not in any way affect the other certainty that I ought not to violate it, any more than certainty that I shall be rewarded by the Government for committing a convenient crime would make the commission of the crime a lawful act.

[1926]

Y

DAVID HUME AND THE MIRACULOUS

WHEN the University of Cambridge did me the high honour of inviting me to deliver this lecture, I could not but feel that the invitation, in some sort, determined for me the subject of my discourse. The character of the field of letters in which Sir Leslie Stephen achieved such well-deserved renown made it plain that my theme must be the life or doctrine of a British philosopher, by preference a philosopher of that eighteenth century which Sir Leslie Stephen himself had done so much to illustrate by his writings. To the occupant of a Chair of Moral Philosophy in the University of Edinburgh the philosopher could not well be anyone but David Hume, the most famous, even if not the greatest, of all Scottish metaphysical thinkers and, with the single exception of Walter Scott, the most distinguished man of letters whose life has been closely connected with the city of Edinburgh. The philosophical thought of Hume, as a whole, is no topic for the discourse of an hour, but that space of time may be profitably, and I trust not un-entertainingly, spent on a consideration of the side-issue raised by the once notorious tenth section of the *Enquiry Concerning Human Understanding* which deals with *Miracles*. Historically, this essay is interesting by reason of the scandal it created, and was perhaps intended by its author to create. To it, and not to the *Dialogues Concerning Natural Religion*, which were

not published during Hume's life, our philosopher
owed the ill-repute he enjoyed alike with the orthodox
Presbyterians of Aberdeen and the High Anglican
Churchmen of Oxford, the set of Johnson and Wesley;
to it, in the main, he owes the admiration of modern
"anti-clericals", who have regarded him as a hero of
militant "free-thought".

The entertaining feature of the situation, to the reflective mind, is that this reputation, for good or ill,
is quite undeserved. It is as certain as anything in
biography can be that Hume was, in point of fact, no
anti-clerical zealot, but an amiable and easy-going
man of the world whose chosen social circle consisted
largely of the "moderates" among the Edinburgh
Presbyterians. The members of that circle, to be sure,
were not men of the faith which removes mountains
and conquers the world. But they valued established
beliefs as a bulwark of comfort, peace, and social order,
and would have been the last persons to sanction a
violent and wanton attack on any set of doctrines which
serve to keep the "vulgar" in their place and to guarantee the "thinking" minority against disturbers of their
ease and leisure. They may fairly be presumed to have
understood that Hume's assault on the "bigotry,
ignorance, cunning and roguery" of that considerable
"part of mankind" who profess belief in the miraculous
meant very much less than it looked, on the face of it,
to mean. They would be confirmed in the suspicion, if
they entertained it, by observing that, for the purposes
of the *Enquiry*, the whole section is superfluous, while
the known character of Hume makes it impossible to
account for its presence as the irrelevancy of the fanatic
who has got, for the time being, upon his dangerous
topic. The irrelevance is, indeed, so manifest that it
seems best explained by the suggestion of Hume's

learned editor, Mr. Selby-Bigge, who supposes that the philosopher's motive in the assault was a simple craving for notoriety at any cost. The "learned world", as we know, "said nothing to the paradoxes" of Hume's *Treatise*; he was determined that it should say something to them in their amended version, and none too scrupulous about the methods by which publicity was to be ensured. Hence the combined violence and irrelevance of a section which was at least certain to get the *Enquiry* talked about, as it very effectually did.

A similar explanation can, as I hope to show, be given of the apparently strange logic of Hume's argument. On the face of it, there would seem to be something amiss with reasoning which proceeds from the principle that "a wise man proportions his belief to the evidence" to the conclusion that in a vast, if none too well defined, field, the "wise man" will simply refuse to consider "the evidence" at all. We cannot be surprised that Hume's admirer, Huxley, should have been much more perturbed by reasoning of this kind than his unfriendly critic Green, whose objection to the argument, indeed, does not go further than to urge that it does not come with the best of grace from the mouth of our professed sceptic. If we look more closely, I believe we shall see that the reasoning, interpreted in the light of Hume's professed general doctrine, certainly proves something, but something very different from what Hume had suggested by his boast of having discovered an argument which "will, with the wise and learned, be an everlasting check to all kinds of superstitious delusion". What has really been proved, as Hume himself says at the end of the whole discussion, would certainly not destroy the faith of the average Presbyterian of the eighteenth century, though it should leave a thinking Presbyterian dissatisfied; as Hume does not say, it

should also leave the serious believer in science at least
equally concerned. The "academic" or "sceptical"
philosopher of Hume's own type is, in fact, left in the
position of an amused spectator of the conflict between
two irrationalities. We miss half of Hume's irony unless
we understand that it is meant to hit not only "dangerous
friends or disguised enemies to the Christian religion",
but also "dangerous friends or disguised enemies" to
Newtonian science. I trust I need not say that I do not
myself regard amused detached contemplation of either
Christianity or natural science as a right attitude in a
rational man. But it is an attitude very characteristic of
the century of so-called "good sense", and none the less
likely to be the secret attitude of David Hume, that it
is hard to say which would have been more enraged by
it, if he had understood it, John Wesley or T. H. Huxley.

It is desirable, before we go any further, to set out
the steps of the argument we are to consider as briefly
and baldly as we can. If we try to do so, it will be found,
I think, to fall into eleven successive propositions, which
I will state in order, with a minimum of exegetical
comment. We begin (1) with the proposition, taken
from Archbishop Tillotson, that the evidential value
of the testimony of others, so long as it is considered as
the testimony of others and nothing more, is always
inferior to that of our own senses, a thesis I should not
be too ready to concede myself without a great deal of
qualification, since in many cases I should put vastly
more confidence in the report of a trained observer than
I should in my own eyes. (2) We are next told that this
general principle is now to be applied to "accounts of
miracles and prodigies found in all history, sacred and
profane". "Miracle" is here apparently equated with
"prodigy", and neither word receives any definition.
In the course of the argument, we shall find two other

incidental definitions of "miracle" introduced. Unfortunately, the definitions are not coincident, and to adopt either seriously obscures the nature of the reasoning. For the present, so far as can be seen from the context, "miracle" and "prodigy" both mean any very unusual and unexpected event, anything which, to use a definition I once heard given by a divine, makes one say "O!" (3) We now take it into account that some events are found in experience to be "constantly conjoined"; other conjunctions are more variable. Here we must, of course, remember that it is part of Hume's general metaphysical doctrine that there is no "necessary connection" between events. All events are separate, and there is nothing in the character of any event which demands that it should be continued in one way rather than in another. All our information is that certain types of event have been found, we do not and cannot know why, to be continued in certain ways and not in others. (4) A wise man, then, will always "proportion" his belief in any statement about a succession of events related to have taken place "to the evidence". This is interpreted to mean that he will *count* the number of "instances" in which a conjunction of the kind in question has occurred, and the number of instances in which one member of the conjoined pair of events has occurred without being continued by the other. It is on this counting that the wise man will base his judgement of the *probability* of the alleged narrative.

(5) Further, all inference is founded solely on "our experience of the constant and regular conjunction" of events and on nothing else. Among the events covered by this principle are the true and false statements made to us by others. Hence the principle applies, among other things, to our inferences about the trustworthiness or untrustworthiness of human testimony. (6) Hence,

when we are offered testimony to alleged facts which "partake of the extraordinary and the marvellous", there is a "conflict of opposite experiences". We have, in fact, to balance our knowledge that the unusual and unexpected sometimes happens against our knowledge that informants sometimes, from various causes, speak falsely, whether intentionally or not. This is why it was reasonable in "the Indian prince" to be incredulous when he was first told of the freezing of water in our northern winter, though it would have been unreasonable to persist in his incredulity if he had had numerous independent reports to the same effect from informants with no motive for deception. The general result, so far, then, is that the strangeness of an alleged sequence of events diminishes the probability of its reality, except when the testimony for the sequence is so strong that it would be still stranger that all the witnesses should be mistaken or untruthful. (7) There is one case in which the value of testimony is not merely diminished by the "conflict of experiences", but actually reduced to zero. This is the case when the event testified to is a "miracle", that is to say, a *violation* of the "laws of nature", or, what comes to the same thing, of "the common course of nature". This would be the case with testimony to the resuscitation of a dead man, since such a conjunction between death and subsequent resuscitation has "never been observed". There is "uniform experience against it".

Here we observe that the reasoning is affected by the introduction of a disturbing element, a new definition of "miracle". We have been concerned with the general question of the worth of testimony to the unusual and unexpected *in genere*, and it has been assumed that we know nothing of "laws" or "patterns" in nature which prescribe one continuation of a course of events rather

than any other. The only difference permissible according to our fifth proposition is that between a familiar and
an unfamiliar continuation, and the only conclusion to
which we are really entitled is that it is *natural* to be
incredulous when we are told of the unfamiliar, as the
Indian prince was mistakenly incredulous about the
freezing of water. The shift from the unfamiliar to the
"contrary to uniform experience" is confusing and unjustified, but indispensable to the further development
of the argument, and directly causes the inconsequence
on which Hume's critics have remarked. It is quietly
forgotten that, on the premises, there cannot be said
to be "uniform experience" against the resuscitation of
the dead man or any other sequence of events. At best
I have only a uniformity within the range of *my own*
experience to urge; a narrator who professes to have
seen the resuscitation is actually appealing to *his own*
experience as the foundation of his story. Thus, unless
I am to assume that my own personal experiences are
the standard of the credible—and if I do assume this,
there is an end of all correction of expectations—it is a
petitio principii to say that there is "uniform experience"
against any event to which any man claims to be able
to testify, and there is no basis for any distinction
between the "miraculous" and that which is merely unfamiliar, and therefore startling, to a particular person.

The paradox that the principle that "belief should
always be proportioned to evidence" justifies, in a certain class of cases, rejection of testimony without
examination, is only established by the illegitimate
device of changing a fundamental definition in the
course of the argument. A footnote which introduces a
further *distinguo* seems to show that Hume is a little
uneasy about this procedure. It admits that the testimony may, after all, really justify belief in a fact which

seems "miraculous", *i.e.* a fact to which my experience affords no analogy, though it does not justify belief in the "miraculous" character of the fact. This leads to a fresh definition of a "miracle" as "a transgression of the laws of nature *by a particular volition of the Deity or by the interposition of an invisible agent*". Apparently, then, in spite of what has been said, Hume would admit that there may be adequate testimony to the resuscitation of a dead man. There might be evidence which would require us to admit the fact, though none which would establish the point that the fact was due to a "particular volition of the Deity". (The reference to other "invisible agents" appears to be a needless rhetorical amplification.)

This new definition of "miracle", sprung on us in a footnote, seems to be the most unfortunate feature of the argument. It obviously disposes at once of all which had apparently been secured by the appeal to the inviolability of "laws of nature", since it permits us to accept as facts the sequences of events which that appeal was intended to rule out, provided only that we do not profess to have proved by testimony that the facts have "a particular volition of the Deity" as their cause. In this version of the matter, there is no story of legend or folk-lore which a sufficient number of testimonies might not require us to accept as a genuine account of facts, provided only that we eliminate all reference to "the Deity" or "invisible agents". It is not clear how a principle compatible with this position is to be of any use to "the wise and learned" as an "everlasting check to all kinds of superstitious delusion"; yet it is clear that this, and not the much more radical procedure of dismissing a whole class of alleged events without scrutiny of the testimony for them, is the only consequence really compatible with the principles on which Hume's polemic professedly rests. The upshot, after all, is no more than the statement, which might be made about all testimony to anything, that no testimony can establish a fact unless the falsity of the testimony would be more unlikely than the unreality of the alleged fact. This is virtually admitted when Hume proceeds to formulate his eighth proposition.

(8) In no actual case of a reported "miracle" do we find the testimony to be of this strength. This is, of course, itself an allegation about a fact, and we observe that before we are entitled to make it we must tacitly surrender what appeared to have been secured by the appeal to "inviolable laws". If the weakness of the testimony is to be a relevant consideration in determining the credibility of the supposed event, we must examine the testimony before we can pronounce it to be weak. The proposed dismissal of testimony without examination has thus led us to nothing, and ought to be eliminated from the reasoning as a superfluous complication. How completely the ambiguity of the word "miracle" has vitiated the argument is shown when Hume goes on, in this connection, to urge it as a grave objection to stories of alleged marvels in the career of Mohammed that Plutarch, Livy, and Tacitus record marvels as occurring in an earlier age at Rome. This is meant to suggest the objection that the marvels, if they occur, must be regarded as "evidences" in favour of a religion, but evidences in favour of incompatible religions may be considered as destructive of one another. Plainly, this consideration, whatever it may be worth, has no bearing on the value of the historical testimony, considered simply as testimony to the actual occurrence of an unusual fact. It concerns not the fact, but the "theological" interpretation of the fact. Thus it appears

to be an authenticated fact that the first volley of the firing party told off to execute the Bāb severed the cord by which the victim was secured without doing him any injury. Hume's reasoning would require us to discount the excellent testimony to the fact, on the plea that similar stories related in the *Acts* of Christian martyrs may be regarded as so many *testimonies* against the occurrence of the fact in the case of the Bāb.

(9) We now reach what is meant to be the conclusion from all the considerations so far put before us. No testimony to a "miracle" has ever amounted to a probability, much less to a proof, and even if the testimony, in any case, did amount to proof, it would be opposed by another proof derived from the "very nature of the fact which it would endeavour to establish". Here, as it seems to me, confusion of thought reaches a maximum. To know that it is a fact that no such testimony *has* ever amounted to a probability, we must, of course, have examined the amount and character of the testimony, and thus have made it a duty to do the very thing Hume originally proposed to show superfluous. It is at least difficult to understand the suggestion that there could be a *proof* of any proposition if there were also a *proof* of a second and incompatible proposition, unless the remark is meant as a mere rhetorical amplification of the statement that proof of the "miraculous" is not forthcoming. The final appeal to "the very nature of the fact", which proof of the "miraculous" would "endeavour to establish", takes us back again to the position which has just been incidentally abandoned, that there is a whole class of cases in which testimony may properly be dismissed *without* examination, and this, if justified, makes the weakness of the testimony, the very point on which Hume is specially insisting, irrelevant.

(10) We next have a curiously qualified retractation of this attempted return to the abandoned position. The occurrence of "violations of the usual course of nature" may actually be *proved* by testimony, but they cannot be so proved as to make them "the foundation of a system of religion". Since we have never been told exactly what is meant by a "religion", this admission is not very enlightening, but it is illustrated by a singular example. There might be testimony which would not merely make it probable, but actually prove, that the whole earth was covered by a mysterious darkness for the first week of January 1600. If the testimony were abundant and of good quality, we should have to accept this as a fact, and look for an explanation, though our present knowledge of science suggests none. But no testimony whatever could give us any ground to believe that Queen Elizabeth died on January 1st of that year, was buried, reappeared again and resumed the government in the following month. And "if this miracle should be ascribed to any new system of religion", we might dismiss the testimony without examination. I confess I cannot see on what ground Hume makes any distinction between the two cases he has, with notable bad taste, been pleased to imagine. If it is true that experience is our only criterion, the two imagined sequences seem exactly alike in being wholly startling and unfamiliar, and I should have thought that the same kind and amount of testimony might serve indifferently to accredit either. There is as much or as little precedent for one as for the other. And, again, it is hard to understand why testimony to either, seeing that on Hume's own theory it would have some initial value, however slight, should lose all that value merely because the belief in the event had led *ex post facto* to the appearance of a "new system of religion".

Presumably, the thought in Hume's mind is that the partisans of a "system of religion" already in existence, especially of one fighting its way to victory over its rivals, are likely to be unduly disposed to believe in, or even to invent, stories of marvels which recommend it, and that this diminishes the evidential value of their testimony. This, no doubt, is a truth, though not a specially novel one. But he appears to be using this obvious reflection in a surely illegitimate way to destroy the whole value of testimony, even outside testimony, to marvellous events which have preceded and caused the "new system of religion". Where the "system" has actually been called into being by antecedent belief in the occurrence of a "miracle", manifestly the fact that the belief has had this historical effect cannot in any way diminish the antecedent probability of the truth of the belief, except in so far as we might have reason to suspect the adherents of the "new system" of successful suppression of evidence which would tell against the truth of their story. This would be a relevant consideration, but one which could only be taken into account on the assumption that we scrutinise testimonies and do not dismiss them unexamined.

(11) We come at last to the surprising and famous *volte-face* with which Hume ends his essay. There is nothing in what we have heard, in spite of obvious allusions in the worst of taste, which plays into the hands of opponents of "our most holy religion". For that is founded altogether on faith, not on reason. The Scripture history is full of incidents which are infinitely improbable. The testimony for them, judged by the principles which have been laid down for our guidance, amounts to nothing at all, and we might therefore suppose that the benefit promised at the beginning of the essay to the "wise" would prove to be the abolition of

Christianity. But Hume reminds himself at the close that since, on his own showing, "the Christian religion . . . cannot be believed by any reasonable person" without a miracle, anyone who does believe "is conscious of a continued miracle in his own person, which subverts all the principles of his understanding", and the arguments against "miracles" must obviously fail when addressed to a person who has the actual present experience of one in himself. The lameness of the conclusion, when it is compared with the vaunting of Hume's *exordium*, has naturally given rise to the current view that it is a mere piece of mockery—a transparent substitute for the true ending, like the *finale* of a Euripidean tragedy on Dr. Verrall's interpretation of the poet. That there is mockery in the language is undeniable. The question I propose to raise is whether, after all, the conclusion, satisfactory or not, is not that which follows from the reasoning on Hume's principles, and the violent contrast between *exordium* and peroration itself a part of the mockery.

If we are to find any coherence in Hume's argument, we must, in the first place, eliminate an ambiguity which can hardly be accounted for except by the writer's determination to make a sensation, the ambiguity of the term "miracle" itself. A "miracle" may mean either of two very different things; it may mean simply an unusual and arresting event, an event "out of the common course", or it may mean an event, not necessarily particularly unusual, which is held to disclose, as most events do not, the *direct* activity of God as author and controller of events; a miracle may be either a mere "wonder" or it may be a "sign", and, as everyone knows, in the language of theology no event is called a "miracle" unless it combines both characters. But the second is, from the theologian's point of view, the more important. St. Thomas,[1] for example, reckons among minor "miracles" such events as the relief of a "fever" by the offering of a prayer, a process which he must have believed to be illustrated by daily occurrences, and Dante is following the same doctrine when he appeals to the story of the opportune cackling of the Capitoline geese as evidence that "miracles" prove the divine selection of the Roman people for universal empire.[2] Manifestly it is clear that there are two quite distinct, though connected, questions which need to be carefully distinguished: (1) What sort and amount of evidence is needed to justify belief in the reality of an unusual occurrence? (2) Whether such occurrences, if there is evidence for them, can rightly be employed as proof of the control of events by a divine purpose? It is one question whether there can be adequate evidence of the occurrence of events "out of the common course", another what the evidential worth of such events as testimony to the doctrines of a "religion" may be. The first question belongs to inductive logic, the second to theology, and nothing but confusion can come of the attempt to treat the two questions as one.

It is also clear on the face of it that Hume's essay begins as a discussion of the first question, and that the introduction of the second is a piece of irrelevance. The conclusion which was to deliver the "wise" from "superstition" once and for all should have been that events sufficiently out of the daily routine are so inherently improbable that any counter-probability suggested by the amount of testimony in their favour may be dismissed as infinitesimal. This, if it could be established, would make the raising of the theological issue superfluous. Or, at most, all that it would be relevant to urge would be the subsidiary consideration that the theological convictions of

---

[1] *S. c. G.* iii. 101.   [2] *Monarchia*, ii. 4.

witnesses of the alleged events are likely to be a source of antecedent bias. Even this reflection should, in strict logic, be dispensed with, if it can be independently established that *no* amount of testimony, biased or not, has any weight, if only the event testified to is sufficiently strange. Now if Hume had confined himself to this contention, his argument would have gained in force and coherence: there would have been none of the perplexities introduced by the repeated change of the initial definition of a "miracle", nor would the whole reasoning have been imperilled, as it is, by the damaging concession that a departure from "uniform law" may after all be accepted as a fact, if the testimony is abundant and good enough, or by the arbitrary decision that testimony might be sufficient to prove the occurrence of a world-wide darkness of a week's duration and yet not deserve any examination if it were offered in favour of a "resurrection". We do less than justice to Hume's acuteness if we imagine that he was not alive to the havoc made in his argument by this confusion of the issues, and it is only reasonable to suppose that the irrelevance is due to a purpose. Without the sensational attack on the theologians, the main argument would probably have attracted no particular attention from anyone; the *Enquiry* would have been as little talked about as the *Treatise*, and Hume was, above everything, determined that he would be talked about.

What remains to be considered, then, is the question what Hume's main argument amounts to when all the irrelevance has been removed, and it is taken simply as an argument about the value of testimony to the strange and unprecedented. Even when taken in this way, at first sight the argument is bound to seem curiously wrong-headed. We are apparently told that assent should always be based on a careful weighing of the direct and indirect evidence on both sides of a question, and this is, then, strangely enough made the ground for asserting that, if only an alleged occurrence is unusual enough, we need not weigh the evidence produced for it. We may confidently dismiss our witnesses unheard. If this were really Hume's meaning, it is clear that his conclusion and his premises would be oddly at variance, and it is not surprising that a disciple like Huxley, who was anxious to maintain the conclusion, but to maintain it with some appearance of logic, should have restated the case in a way which abandons Hume's main contention. With Huxley, the main weight of the conclusion is made to rest on the assertion that in actual fact the testimony which has been produced to the occurrence of "miracles" has always been dubious or inadequate. Whether this is the fact or not, it is at least an appeal to what is itself ascertainable fact, and can only be made after that very scrutiny of the testimony in the particular case from which Hume promises to deliver "the wise". If we are careful, however, to remember certain fundamental positions of Hume's general philosophy, we shall see that, before we can get at the real meaning of his argument, we have to translate its terms into the language of Humian scepticism, and that when we do so, the reasoning proceeds to a conclusion which is valid enough, though quite unsensational.

We have to bear in mind, to begin with, Hume's peculiar doctrine about the nature of assent or belief, a doctrine proclaimed loudly enough both in the *Treatise* and in the *Enquiry*. A belief, we must remember, is explicitly asserted to be simply "a lively idea" associated with a "present impression"; it is only in respect of its superior "liveliness" that a belief differs from a fancy, or assenting to a proposition from merely framing it. "I believe this", we are told in so many words, means only "I feel at this moment a strong propension to consider things in this light", and it is because belief means no more than this, that Hume professes to believe his own metaphysic, though, as he ingenuously says, he forgets about it and virtually denies it whenever he mixes in the social life of his fellows. While he is meditating alone in his study, though at no other time, he feels a strong propension to consider things in the fashion of the *Treatise*, and this, of itself, *is* believing, for the time, in the *Treatise* and its doctrines. It is another of Hume's convictions that, though beliefs have causes, they never have sufficient justifying reasons, and that in the sequence of events, there are "customary conjunctions", but never discernible "connections". There is no pattern in the course of events in virtue of which any event should require one continuation into the future rather than another. Each event has its own special character and all events are loose and separated. There is no discoverable reason why any one event should not be "conjoined" with any other whatsoever as its sequel. What events are followed by what we discover only by experience, and experience is a purely passive awareness of sequence. It follows that, when we hear from Hume of "uniform experience" and of "laws of nature", uniform experience can mean no more than a type of sequence which has been regular so far as our own recollection and that of the other persons with whom we are in communication, goes. (Indeed, it is plain that it is only by the courtesy of an opponent that Hume is entitled to bring in the reference to the experience of any one but himself. A second person who makes a statement to me about *his* experience may always be mistaken or untruthful, and, in the end, it will be my own personal acquaintance with the sequence of events by which I have to judge whether or not he is a credible witness.) Similarly, an "inviolable law of nature", when we translate the words into their equivalent in Humian metaphysics, means no more than a type of sequence which, so far as my own recollections, eked out by those of any other persons in whom I rightly or wrongly put credence, go, has been uniform.

Next we have to remember that the same considerations must be applied in interpreting the statement that our knowledge of the sequences in nature depends on "customary experience". This does not mean, and in the *Treatise* Hume is at pains to make the point clear, that there is any discoverable reason why there should be a fixed routine in the course of events, and a routine which each of us can discover from the small fragment of the sequence open to his personal observation. There is no logical ground for expecting that the sequence of events will conform to any rule; any one event might perfectly well be succeeded by any other. All that is meant is that it is an inexplicable, non-rational tendency of the human mind to *expect* that the usual will happen and that the unusual will not. Repetition gives rise to a subjective "association of ideas" and therefore to expectation; in fact, the probability of an event, as is explained in the *Treatise*, means neither more nor less than the degree of "vivacity" with which some one imagines, and therefore anticipates, it. "Customary sequence" is thus only a cause, not a justifying ground, for our anticipations. To put the point quite simply, all our judgements are judgements, true or false, about actual fact; there are no judgements of value, neither a logical *ought* nor a moral *ought*. Just as "this is right" means only "the disinterested spectator, as a fact, contemplates this with pleasure", so "this is probable", "this is certain", means only that "actual observers expect this with a less or greater degree of confidence". This universal reduction of all propositions to statements about actual occurrences is the most characteristic and important peculiarity of Hume's whole philosophy. The ideal before his mind is the same which inspires the chief work of Avenarius, the elimination from all assertions of every element which is not "pure experience", simple record of the event without interpretation or valuation. The problem he has not faced is that directly suggested by the *Critique of Pure Experience*, the question whether intelligence, as distinguished from mere insignificant reaction to stimulus, would not vanish completely from a community in which the ideal had been realised.

Let us, then, re-state Hume's main argument in the terms of his own philosophy. It will be seen, I think, that it amounts to this. It is a fact, and a fact of which no explanation can be given, that repetition gives rise to "associations of ideas", and that the strength of these associations depends on the frequency of the repetition. The more often I have seen *A* followed by *B*, and the less often I have seen *A* occur without being followed by *B*, the harder I find it to believe that *A* will occur, or has ever occurred, without being followed by *B*. Similarly, if I have never seen *A* followed by *C*, I shall not imagine *C*, and consequently shall not expect *C* to occur, as a continuation of *A*. This is the ultimate causal explanation of habits of thought and expectation. They are, in fact, prejudices without logical value, as the *Treatise* declares in deliberately provocative language, but the strength of the prejudice may be, as a fact of my mental make-up, invincible. This, and no more, is all that Hume is entitled, on his own principles, to mean when he talks of the inconceivability of the violation of a uniform law of nature. Properly speaking, there are no laws of nature to be violated, but there are habits of expectation which any one of us, as a fact, finds himself unable to break through. Since, again, we discover, also as a fact for which we can give no reason, that it is "customary repetition" which appears to be the foundation of these habits, it is also the fact that we expect a certain sequence with the greater confidence the more familiar its type is to us, and that, if an alleged sequence of events is sufficiently startling and contrary to our expectations, we feel a stronger propensity to consider the statements of witnesses as mistakes or lies—things of which we have some experience—than to accept them as true. We find it easier to imagine vividly that our witness is deceived, or is deceiving us, than to imagine the events he describes. The conclusion to which we are led is thus, like the premises from which we started, a simple proposition of fact. Men find the unusual hard to imagine in proportion to its unusualness, and there is a point, for any one of us, when the difficulty amounts to a psychological impossibility. When this point is reached, the unimaginable event is a "miracle". Thus the conclusion to which the argument is leading us is really the assertion of fact that a "miracle" *is* not believed in by anyone, being *ex vi termini* simply an event so unexpected that we find it easier to imagine the falsity of the testimony than to imagine the occurrence of the event.

Now, if Hume had ended his essay at this point, it could have brought him no notoriety, and it would not have proved anything which could well be disputed. The pious and the impious, the orthodox and unorthodox alike, might well have agreed that there are some things which any man does find incredible. The trouble is that men differ so much from one another in the matter of what, in particular, each finds incredible. What we want to know, if we are to write or read history, is not what a given man finds credible or incredible, but what we *ought* as rational beings to pronounce credible or incredible, and the philosopher of "pure experience" can give us no guidance here. Hume, for example, indicates that in his opinion a resurrection from the dead is flatly incredible, no matter what the apparent testimony for it may be, whereas a week of world-wide darkness is credible, if there is enough testimony for it, though both events seem equally to baffle our powers of rational explanation. Any one of us who does not feel the special "propensions" of Hume on this point, may obviously ask him to justify his position, if he can, by showing that there is some difference in principle between the two cases. What is more, any man who finds any event whatever not wholly unimaginable may pertinently ask Hume why that particular event should be placed in the category of those which may be disposed of as unreal without examination of testimony. It is this obvious reflection which both justifies and demands the apparently inconsistent concession to the Christian believer with which Hume has seen fit to end his essay. The tone of persiflage is manifest throughout the paragraphs, but the whole is not persiflage; there is a real concession which is absolutely demanded by Hume's own radical "positivism".

The main result really reached had been that, in point of fact, men find it hard to believe the marvellous, and if the marvel is sufficiently astounding, they refuse to believe. In plain language, this ought to mean that no one ever does believe in the reality of a sequence of events quite unlike the routine of his customary experience. But this conclusion would be manifestly false in fact. For Hume could not deny that, to take the most familiar example, there were many sincere orthodox Christians in his own society and that they did, as a fact, believe in the reality of certain events to which their customary experience afforded no analogy. It might be argued, though not very reasonably by an avowed irrationalist, that the orthodox have no right to hold their convictions; but the fact that they did hold them, and hold them with assurance, was beyond dispute, and it has to be shown that this fact is itself consistent with Hume's own principles. Otherwise the principles would themselves be completely discredited as leading, by logical necessity, to a conclusion false in fact. This explains the serious motive for the apparently paradoxical concessions which Hume proceeds to make. There would be a real paradox, if it were part of Hume's case that "customary experience", and it only, provides a rational justification for our beliefs about the course of events. But his position is that none of these beliefs have any rational justification; belief, as the *Treatise* says, is more of the nature of sensation than of the nature of reason. The only problem that can be raised about our beliefs is that of their cause, and Hume has insisted strongly on the point that all we can say about the cause of belief is that, as a fact, it is commonly produced by "customary experience". We could not say that it cannot be produced in any other way, for to say so would be to go beyond the limits of the factual. And the existence of a single genuine believer in the unusual is empirical proof that, as a matter of fact, "customary experience", though the commonest, is not the only cause of belief.

Now Hume has been careful to protest against any assumption that there is a rational connection of any kind between customary repetition and belief. That the repetition of a certain sequence of events should make us expect its recurrence with the greater confidence, the oftener the repetition has been noted, is, according to him, a fact of human nature which we can observe, but for which we can allege no justifying reason. (It is on a par with the gambler's belief in the continuation of a run of luck, a belief neither more nor less rational than the opposing belief, also found among gamblers, that the "luck must change".) It is thus only what might be expected —if in a world where there are only "conjunctions" we can talk of what may be expected—that "custom" should be only the customary, not the invariable, cause of belief. And, since there is no discoverable connection between repetition and belief, you cannot tell the man who confidently believes in the reality of the unparalleled that his belief is unreasonable. He finds in himself, as Hume takes care to put it, "a determination to believe what is contrary to custom and experience". But, on Hume's own showing, to believe what is contrary to custom is neither more nor less reasonable than to believe what is conformable to custom. It is less usual, and we have no right to say anything more. This is, in fact, what Hume does say, in more provocative language, when he speaks of the Christian believer as having a standing "miracle" within himself, which makes him proof against all reasoning against the miraculous. The strict meaning of the statement is simply that in this case the believer's "propension to see things in a certain light" has causes which are not those of other men's belief, nor of his own beliefs about the majority of things. Stated thus baldly, Hume's conclusion would be at once proper to a consistently "sceptical" philosophy and quite acceptable to the vast majority of the orthodox. In fact, what would be shocking to any man who was deeply religious as well as orthodox would be the suggestion that the motives of credibility in matters of religion are of the same order as those involved in believing or disbelieving a newspaper report of travel or exploration. Why the statement that this is not so should have been couched in language which was certain to create scandal can hardly be explained, except by Hume's resolution to attract notice at all costs.

There is another side to the matter which demands a word or two. From the position of his own sceptical philosophy, Hume is not entitled to regard the belief of the man who "has the miracle in himself" as inherently more or less unreasonable than his own. But there can be no doubt in what light Hume was himself "strongly inclined" to view all such matters, and we can quite understand that he would contemplate the orthodox, whose "propensions" are so unlike his own, with a detached amusement. To his eminently secular mind they would be no better than entertaining oddities. But there is another party whom Hume must have found equally entertaining for precisely the same reason, the militant rationalist who assails orthodoxy in the name of science. Rational science goes outside the limits of a philosophy of pure experience in much the same way as dogmatic theology. The greater part of Hume's *Treatise* had been devoted to an attempt to demolish the foundation-stones of a rational science of nature. Necessary connection, the permanence of substance, the extramental reality of the physical world, are all dismissed as superstitions. To use more modern language, no "constants" are left in nature, unless we can give the name of a "natural constant" to our own inexplicable and unjustified prejudice in favour of the usual and familiar. From this point of view, the man of science, who builds on the "uniformity of nature", and the divine, who appeals to the immutable attributes of his God, are alike constructing dogmatic theories on a basis of "extra-belief". Spinoza, the typical assertor of natural necessity, and the theologians may both be beaten equally effectually with the same stick, since both go beyond the limits of fact in precisely the same fashion, by "feigning" that there is real "connection" where they should have been content to record mere "conjunction". It follows that "our most holy religion" does not stand alone in being founded on a "faith" which has no foundation in reason. The same faith is also the foundation of our most admirable science. The only difference which could be pleaded as giving an advantage to science is that the predictions of the scientific man, up to the present, have largely been found to be verified by the course of events; the predictions of the theologian, which concern an unseen order, are naturally incapable of this verification. On closer scrutiny the apparent advantage is found to vanish. For we have no means of knowing that the theologian's predictions, too, *may* not get their verification; the predictions of science are never verified more than approximately, and we do not know that the course of events may not change its character at any moment in a way which would deprive them of even approximate verification. That they have proved trustworthy up to the present is no more than a curious and inexplicable "happy coincidence".

Hume's light-hearted irony has, then, a double edge. As he says, in effect, the Christian believer is staking his all on a mere promise which, for all we can prove, may remain eternally unfulfilled. As he does not say in the context, but in effect urges all through his polemic against rationalist dogmatism, the convinced believer in science is equally staking everything on a promise of the same kind to which the course of events may give the lie at any moment. The believer in God and the believer in an order of nature both have the same consciousness of a "miracle" within their own breasts. That either should excommunicate the other for their common guilt of "extra-belief" is the feature of the situation which the "academical" philosopher finds entertaining. The "naturalist" who derides his neighbour's "groundless" anticipations of the joys of Paradise forgets that, on Hume's showing, his own anticipation that the sun will rise to-morrow is equally groundless. If only one half of this condemnation of all anticipations of the course of things as alike unintelligent is actually expressed in the essay, the reason must be that notoriety was to be got by an attack on the Church; an attack on the Royal Society would pass unregarded.

As a contribution to logic, Hume's essay is thus an attack not so much on the credibility of "miracles" as on the validity of induction. His point, if one works it out, is that all inference from the present occasion to anything beyond itself presupposes some metaphysical theory of the structure of the world as a whole, whereas the world revealed to us by "experience" has *no* structure; it is a mere series of loose and separate incidents. Now this is half the truth. Even if it were the case, as Dr. Broad has so brilliantly shown that it is not, that scientific induction can be reduced, as Hume tries to reduce it, to a mere application of the theory of Probability, the difficulty would still remain. For—to appeal again to a principle which has been made specially clear by the work of Cambridge philosophers—there is no such thing as *the* probability of a given event, there are only probabilities relative to a given set of premises, and such a set of premises inevitably includes some metaphysical assumption about the structure of the world as a whole. Hume himself makes one such wholly undemonstrable assumption of the utmost importance when he rests his whole philosophical edifice on the proposition, admitted by himself to be incompatible with other equally indispensable postulates, that "all our perceptions are distinct existences, and the mind never perceives any connection between its ideas", in other words, that all events are loose and separate. This assumption, once made, ought to dispose not merely of all dogmatism, theological or scientific, as Hume intended it should, but of every attempt to regard any one event as more or less probable than any other. In principle it excludes all inference from the particular occasion to anything beyond itself, and therefore leads direct to the denial of the very possibility of science, even when the pretensions of science have been reduced to the most modest proportions. If the doctrine is to be carried out regardless of consequence, even the most abstract pure logic and mathematics cannot escape condemnation. For if there is really no means of transcending the particularity of the particular occasion, even my statement that two and three make five can be no more than a record of the event that I have, on this occasion, counted with this result; I can have no guarantee that the result will be the same the next time I perform the counting. All I am entitled to say is that at present I feel a "propension" to consider the matter in that light.

It would be of no avail to introduce a distinction between particular data of sense and "universals" which pervade the data, in the hope of preserving, at any rate, scientific knowledge of the inter-relations of "universals", for, if all events are loose and separate, there can be no warrant for assertions about "pervasive" elements in them. The attempt at analysis itself already implicitly transcends the supposed disconnection of events. Dr. Whitehead thus seems to me wholly in the right of it when he insists on the point that the "induction" indispensable to science is not to be regarded as a process of generalisation but as one in which we "divine" some characteristics of a particular future from the known characteristics of a particular past, except for the slight oversight by which he has spoken of the conclusion inferred to as though it must be "future". No one, I take it, knows better than Dr. Whitehead that the inference may equally well be from one particular past occasion to another equally past. But, of course, the very admission that it is a legitimate procedure to divine any of the characteristics of one occasion from what we know of another occasion demands the surrender of the assumption that "occasions" are simply loose and separate, or in other words, that "experience" is mere awareness of a series of disconnected "events" which are only externally "conjoined". I cannot dwell long on the point, but I would only urge that in principle this must mean that a scientific view of nature must be much more like that of Leibniz than like that of Hume. So far from being merely "conjoined" as earlier and later, events must have a pattern in virtue of which each brings with it traces of all that has gone before and is big with all that is to come. And to admit so much is to admit that, in the end, the course of events as a whole has a supreme pattern which appears, with the needful modifications, as the dominant factor in determining the patterns of its parts. What the dominant pattern is, in its detail, we naturally cannot say, since we never see more than fragments of it. But we can, on the supposition that such a pattern is really there, make "divinations" which are more or less true to the main scheme, and these divinations, without which inference could not advance a single step, are the (commonly unconscious) meta-physical presuppositions which guide us in our judge-ments of probabilities. They furnish premises without which we should have no logical justification for pro-nouncing any one anticipation of experience more or less probable than any other. Were it true that "con-nection" is, as Hume supposed, not "divined" but simply "feigned", induction would not even be what Earl Russell once called it, a method of making "plausible" guesses. It would be guessing without any method, and there would be no sense in calling one guess any more plausible than any other.

The very existence of a dispute between the divine and the man of secular science about the reality of "miracles" is only possible because, unlike Hume, the parties are both, at bottom, rationalists in their con-scious or unconscious metaphysics. In a purely non-rational world, any one occurrence is just as much or as little of a "wonder" as any other. You may say, with Hume, that it is only from customary experience that we can derive the expectation that an event will have a given continuation, or, with the most supranaturalistic of Mohammedans, that the only reason why anything happens is that "Allah almighty disposes it so"; the formulae are different, but their sense is identical. The distinction between the "ordinary" or "normal" and the "astounding" or "miraculous" (in the etymological sense) can only be made on the basis of a metaphysic which recognises a real connection of events by a co-herent and all-pervasive pattern. Only where this is a common metaphysical dogma does it become justifiable to raise the question whether better testimony is re-quired to establish the unusual and surprising.

If by a miracle we mean simply an unusual occur-

rence, it may then become a mere problem in the estima-
tion of opposing probabilities to determine whether the
reality of such an occurrence is credible. From this
point of view there could be no question of dismissing
testimony unexamined as intrinsically worthless, but it
would be possible to accept the general principle that
the antecedent unlikeliness of the facts testified to make
it reasonable to demand exceptionally abundant and
weighty testimony. The one criticism one would feel
inclined to pass upon Hume's version of this principle
would be that he forgets that the probabilities with
which we have to reckon in matters of history are
mostly not of the kind which admit of exact mathematical expression. A wise man is regularly determined
in his decision to credit human testimony by "im-
ponderables" to which no calculus can assign prob-
ability-coefficients.

The real issue, in the case of "miracles" appealed to
as of significance for religion, is not the bare antecedent probability of unusual events. The unusual
event gets its significance as a "miracle", in the religious
sense of the word, from the conviction that it is an event
in which the character of a divine purpose underlying
the whole course of events becomes exceptionally transparent; it is a "sign" of the mercy, the justice, the power
of God. It follows at once that our whole attitude towards the credibility of miracles is profoundly affected
by our ultimate metaphysical position. The problem
cannot even be discussed with any profit between two
parties of whom one is a theist and the other an atheist
or a pure agnostic. For they will differ profoundly about
the nature of the pattern which binds nature into a connected system. On any rationalistic hypothesis, startling and singular events must be reasonably expected
to occur from time to time, and there can, so far as I

can see, be no means of saying in advance how startling the surprises which the course of events contains may prove to be to us, who are familiar, after all, with so small a fragment of the whole. But, in an atheistic or neutral metaphysical scheme, there would be no reason to expect the surprises to wear any special character, or to be distributed in any special way over space and time. We should expect them to make their appearances as simple "freaks". If our philosophical world-scheme is definitely theistic, the case is altered completely. For we shall then conceive of the pattern of events as a whole not merely as providing a connection between them, but as providing a connection which is intelligent in the sense that, like the structure of a symphony, or a well-lived life, it exhibits the realisation of an end of absolute value. We should, thus, antecedently look for the "singularities" in nature and history to exhibit a special kind of concentration, exactly as the surprises in the construction of a great piece of music or the conduct of a life of wise originality exhibit the same concentration. The intelligence of the great musician or the great statesman shows itself neither in unbroken adherence to an iron routine nor in wild eccentricity. It reveals itself in the way in which conformity to routine, where there is nothing to be gained by departure, is combined with bold and original departure from routine because the situation makes the demand for it. A theist, conceiving of the pattern of events in the light of such analogies, will thus reasonably regard it as to be expected that surprises of a certain kind and in certain historic connections, surprises which contribute, so to say, to a plan, "worthy of God", should occur in history and that others should not, exactly as one would expect some kinds of musical surprises in a newly discovered symphony professing to be by Beethoven, but would emphatically not expect others. Thus the difference in ultimate metaphysical outlook between a theist and a non-theistic philosopher would make a difference between the two sets of initial premises relatively to which each estimates the probability of certain events. It is not in the least unreasonable, for example, in a convinced theist to be satisfied with evidence for the resurrection of Jesus Christ which would not satisfy him of the resurrection of his next-door neighbour, since he may well ascribe to the resurrection of Christ a unique spiritual value for the whole history of the human race which he could not ascribe to the resurrection of his neighbour. We should be misconceiving the whole issue if we did not bear in mind that what is affirmed by the Christian creed is not simply the resurrection of *some* man, but the resurrection of just this one man and no other.

This is what I meant when I said, a little while back, that the motives of credibility to which the religious man, who is also a thinking man, appeals are of a kind quite other than those which Hume takes into consideration. The determining factor in leading him to believe in certain "miracles", assuming for the moment that he professes a religion which includes this belief, is his underlying conviction that the plan of the world is dominated by certain absolute values, and that these events are the most striking and transparent examples of the dominance of just these values. They are like the comparatively few critical moments in which we find a revelation of the inmost character of a friend and from which we then proceed to interpret the whole of his more ordinary behaviour. It follows, of course, that the whole question of the reality of "miracles", in any but the bare etymological sense of the word, is secondary to the much graver question of the legitimacy of a

2 A

theistic interpretation of life. The alleged occurrence of miracles cannot itself be rationally made a premise for the argument for Theism. Two theists of different creeds, provided they agree in attributing a certain character to God, may discuss the question whether the "miracles" of one of the different creeds are or are not worthy of the character of God. It would be idle to ask any man to accept Theism in any form on the evidence of any kind of "miracle", since, unless he already admits what you are seeking to prove, the most irrefragable evidence that the facts to which you appeal are genuine facts would establish no more than the hardly disputable conclusion that strange things do sometimes happen. It is thus not surprising if, as Francis Bacon remarks, miracles have been wrought to convince idolaters, but none to convince atheists.

The point I want to make, then, is this. The problem of Hume's essay, as Hume himself states it, is vitiated by illegitimate simplification. When we are dealing with testimony to a startling event which claims also to have the value of a "sign" from the unseen, we have two questions, not one only, on our hands. There is, of course, the preliminary question, which arises whenever we have to decide for or against accepting testimony, the question of the quality of the testimony, the intelligence and *bona fides* of the witnesses, the nature of the agreements and disagreements between their reports, the presumption that these reports are independent, and the like. When we have satisfied ourselves, if we succeed in doing so, that our evidence is unexceptional in all these respects, there still remains two real questions, not to be disposed of by these antecedent considerations: (1) Is it more likely that the most unexceptional witnesses should fail us in this case or that the event to which they testify is a fact, and (2) if it is a fact, is it merely a puzzling fact, or has it the value of a "sign"? Our answer to *both* questions, I hold, is legitimately influenced by our metaphysic. If our metaphysic is definitely theistic, it will be rational to regard such "signs" as likely to mark the course of history; if it is anti-theistic or neutral, the same expectations will not be, for us, rational. Whether it is rational to be prepared to acknowledge "miracle" as a feature of the historical process is thus a question which depends on a prior question: Is it irrational to be theists in our metaphysics?

As I have said, it would involve an obvious circle in our reasoning if we alleged the occurrence of miraculous events as the ground for adopting a theistic metaphysic. If a theistic interpretation of the course of events is to be justified, the justification must be based on the *cursus ordinarius* of nature. Our metaphysic, if it is to be more than an idle play of fancy, must be a response of thought to the full concrete reality of the world in which our life is set. And I think it follows that we cannot expect to arrive at a metaphysic of any great worth so long as we confine our contemplation to the domain of formal logic, or epistemology, or even of experimental science. We and our fellows are ourselves a part of the world to be interpreted, and we have no right to assume at the outset that we may not even be its most significant part. The material for interpretation is supplied not only by the natural sciences of the laboratory, the observatory and the field, but by the whole history of man with his ideals, his achievements, his failures, his self-condemnations, his hopes and his fears. For the tissue of life is inextricably woven of all these strands, though we are tempted, in an age of un-avoidable specialism, to forget the fact when we retire to our studies or our laboratories and concentrate our

attention on the artificial and poverty-stricken extract
from the wealth of the real world which we call our
special "subject". Like the Ephesians of the time of
Heraclitus, we retire each into a poor little private
world of our own, and forget the "common", and this,
as that great man said, is to live like men half-asleep.
Indeed, it is so to be logicians, or chemists, or historians
or ethnologists that we forget to be men. The fault is
not wholly our own, and it cannot well be escaped by
our generation, though we may be permitted to imagine
with innocent envy the possible happier lot of our successors, if some great social and economic change
should simplify this intellectual problem by leading to
the destruction of the masses of accumulated misapplied
"erudition" which are our nightmare. But it is our fault
if we make no attempt to escape complete subdual to
that in which—for our sins—we have to work. The
final verdict on the question whether Theism is not a
legitimate, or, it may be, a necessary feature of a metaphysic which can "give account" of the real world in all
its real fullness could be expected neither from an age
of specialists like our own, nor from an age of gentle-
manly loiterers, like the literary coteries of the eighteenth century. For a voice which might speak with
compelling authority we have to look to a society which
has an intensely rich and full life of its own and yet is
not mastered by it but masters it, "sees it steadily and
sees it whole". For my own part, I think I know what
the verdict of such a society would be. I cannot, of
course, expect that all my hearers should be of my
mind. What kind of response one makes to life will, no
doubt, for better or worse, depend on the sort of man
one is for good or bad. One will respond with a different
metaphysic according as one thinks that "we are such
stuff, As dreams are made on", or μέγας ὁ ἀγών, οὐχ ὅσος

δοκεῖ. But we can all make it our purpose that our philosophy, if we have one, shall be no mere affair of surface opinions, but the genuine expression of a whole personality. Because I can never feel that Hume's own philosophy was that, I have to own to a haunting uncertainty whether Hume was really a great philosopher, or only a "very clever man".

[1927]

X

KNOWING AND BELIEVING

WE are all accustomed in everyday life to draw a distinction between some things which we know and other things which we only believe, but do not know. But what is the precise difference we mean, or ought to mean, to mark by this distinction? Is there a real difference in kind between the act, or attitude, of knowing and that of believing? If there is, is this difference one which the psychologist could detect by an examination of the two acts as such, independently of any consideration of the intrinsic characters of their objects, the *scitum*, that which is known, and the *creditum*, that which is believed, or is it only by explicit references to the natures of *scibile* and *credibile* that the correlated acts of knowing and believing can be discriminated? The question is not, of course, whether that which is known to one mind may not be merely believed by another; it is manifest that there is much which he or you may know, but I can only believe without knowing. It is whether there are certain things which, from the nature of the case, are capable of being known, whether a given mind knows them or only believes them, and others which, again from the nature of the case, can be believed but cannot be known by any mind —or at any rate any human mind. Plato, as I presume we all know, teaches emphatically that to know (ἐπίστασθαι) and to believe (δοξάζειν) are radically distinct intellectual attitudes, each with its own class of appropriate objects, so that there are two distinct domains, in either of which truth is attainable; the domain of that which is, in its own nature, adapted to be known, the *eternal*, and the domain of that which is, not from any incidental disqualification on our part, but inherently, incapable of being known, and can only be believed, the *temporal*. Only the immutable and eternal can be known in the proper sense of the word; of the temporal we have, at best, only "true belief or opinion", though it is not denied that belief or opinion can be true. This is why, in the symbolic language of the *Timaeus*, "*true* discourse" about matters of sense-perception is called "opinion" and "belief" (πίστις, δόξα), and assigned to the "circle of the Other", but true discourse about the non-sensible is named "understanding" and "knowledge" (νοῦς, ἐπιστήμη), and given to the "circle of the Same" (*Tim.* 37, *b*, *c*). Aristotle also—though he never, I believe, expressly denies that the temporal can be known—appears in principle to agree with this Platonic view, since he does deny that "sense" can yield knowledge, and demands that the name shall be restricted to conclusions which can be demonstrated with formal logical necessity from premises which are themselves materially necessary, and by insisting that such premises must be strictly reciprocal as well as universal, in effect, makes knowledge and demonstration impossible outside mathematics.

On this view, then, objects which properly belong to the domain of the *scibile*, may accidentally be objects of mere belief to a particular mind, like the propositions of Euclid to the mind of the distinguished Oxford man of the story who "could not say that he had precisely proved them, but flattered himself that he had made them appear highly probable".

But objects which properly belong to the domain of belief can never become matter of knowledge for any mind. This consideration seems to me to make a difference between the position of Plato or Aristotle and that of the mediaeval philosophers and theologians who depend so closely on Aristotle for their general logical and metaphysical doctrine. At first sight, indeed, the great schoolmen, with their insistence on the indispensability of a faith which is not knowledge, might seem to be retaining the principle of the Platonic distinction and merely reversing Plato's estimate of the relative worth of belief and knowledge. But the actual facts are hardly as simple as this. The theory was, indeed, that to us in our present condition on earth the most momentous of all verities, the specifically Christian affirmations about God, are matter of a belief which is not knowledge, but, in the phrase of St. Thomas, "in a sense midway between knowledge and opinion". But this was regarded as incidental to our present earthly state; in our "fatherland" in glory, it was taught, we shall know what are at present to us the "mysteries of faith" with the same direct apprehension of their truth that we now have of the truth of the principle of Contradiction; thus it was not thought to be an inherent consequence of the character of these *credenda* that they are not now objects of knowledge. Though it is admittedly true that no one can simultaneously know and believe the same truth, yet, it was said, there is no more difficulty in understanding how the triune nature of Deity can be at once known to the beatified and believed by us on earth, than in understanding how a geometrical theorem can be at once known by the mathematician and believed by the layman. On the other side also, it was held to be a consequence of divine omniscience that God knows, in the

full sense of the word, all those "contingent" truths
about matters of fact which fall outside the limits of
demonstration and remain matter of belief for the
created mind. "Future contingents", in particular, being
contingent, cannot be demonstrated, and being future
cannot be known through experience. Hence no created
intelligence, not even that of a seraph, can *know* what
I shall be doing five minutes hence, but this has been
eternally known by God.

Thus, the position, I suppose, comes to this: whatever is in its own nature an object of knowledge
may be also, *per accidens*, to some mind the object
of a belief which is not knowledge. There are some
truths which can never be matters of more than belief
to any created mind, if only for the reason that no
such mind knows all "contingents". Since, however,
they are all said to be known to God, their admitted
unknowability to us does not quite constitute them into
a domain distinct from that of the inherently knowable,
any more than "truths of fact" are made unknowable
for Leibniz by his theory that the knowledge of them
would demand an infinite analysis which no mind but
that of God can complete. It will only be, to use a
scholastic distinction, *quoad creaturas*, not *simpliciter*,
that there is a realm of *credibilia* which are not *scibilia*,
though it might possibly be said that this account requires to be modified in the light of the principle that
the identity of knowledge in God and in the creatures
is only one of analogy. However that may be, it is
interesting to observe that it is precisely the great
Greek thinkers—whom it is fashionable in some quarters
to depreciate for their "intellectualism"—who most
explicitly refuse to make the domain of the knowable
coextensive with that of the actually true.

The modern world has not taken kindly to this

Platonic doctrine of the two radically distinct domains; its tendency is rather to assume that whatever is true is inherently knowable though circumstances may prevent us for a time, or even permanently, from knowing it. But if we reject the distinction of domains, the question is obviously at least suggested whether we can still retain a radical distinction between the acts or attitudes. If whatever can be an object of either may also, with suitable conditions, be an object of the other, we may fairly ask why we should be at the trouble to assume two mental attitudes or activities, when one would possibly serve our turn equally well. We have a reasonable motive for considering whether one of the two terms may not be the genus of which the other is a further specification. May it not prove either that knowing is a specific way of believing, or believing a peculiar way of knowing?

Clearly it would not be promising to treat knowing as the generic term and believing as a subvariety of knowing, for the obvious reason that many, if not most, of men's actual beliefs appear to be false, and it seems preposterous to admit that anything which is false can be known. But it is tempting to regard believing as a genus, and to define knowing as believing a proposition which is, in fact, true. From this point of view there will be no difference between the mental attitudes or acts of believing and of knowing. To know will be to believe a proposition which happens to have the peculiarity of being true; the act, or activity, of believing such a proposition, considered as an act or activity of the believing mind, will be in no respect different from that of believing what is false, since the difference between the true and the false will be a difference of some kind in what is apprehended, not the manner of its apprehension. It should follow that a psychologist who keeps strictly to his subject has not to concern himself with knowledge. He is within his province in treating of belief as a distinctive mental attitude and discussing the various ways in which it is generated or destroyed; but he strays over the borders of that province if he ventures to discriminate between beliefs which are true, and others which are false, since true and false are "extrinsic denominations", just as he would be violating the same frontiers if he undertook to deal with the distinction between virtuous habits and vicious. The sharp discrimination thus effected between logic or epistemology and psychology is a real attraction to many minds. It is true that we get into difficulties when we go on to ask whether such a view really allows us to believe in the possibility of "epistemology" as a *tertium quid* which is neither quite the same thing as logic nor quite the same thing as psychology. But we may ignore this consideration for the moment, as the possibility of "epistemology" seems problematic on any theory of the relation of knowing to believing. What I wish to ask is whether this undeniably attractive view will really work within its own limits.

Obviously, if we are to identify knowing with believing that which is in fact true, we shall need to be careful to distinguish believing itself from some attitudes of mind with which it is often confused in careless speech. None of us would say that a man knows a proposition which he merely holds to be either more likely to be true than to be false, or even much more likely to be true than to be false, though we sometimes talk of "believing" in these cases. Thus I myself think it more likely that Plato wrote the *Epinomis*, and overwhelmingly more likely that he wrote the seventh Epistle, than that he did not, but I hope I should never say that I *know* either of these things. If I were betrayed in the

heat of argument into making such assertions, I should
expect to be properly checked for the careless temerity
of my language. Again, I think there are good grounds
for holding that Plato did not write the *First Alcibiades*,
and should in ordinary conversation, say without hesitation that I "believe" it to be unauthentic. But suppose
it were discovered to-morrow that the real name of the
author had been preserved in some newly discovered
scrap of papyrus, then I should all along have been
holding an opinion which was true, but on any theory
about knowing, it would be an abuse of language to
say that I had "known" all along that the dialogue is
spurious. If we are to do reasonable justice to a doctrine
which identifies knowing with believing what is true,
we must at least add that it is not every degree of assent
to a proposition that amounts to belief. We shall have
to say of belief in general what St. Thomas says of
belief in the articles of religious faith, that it is not mere
cogitatio cum assensu, but *cogitatio cum fixo assensu*,
thinking of the proposition accepted with *firm* assent,
as distinguished from the imperfect and wavering
assent which amounts to simple *opinion*. And this consideration at once leads to an important question. St.
Thomas, whose purpose in making the distinction is to
determine the precise character of the assent to the
Christian creeds required for salvation, does not tell us
how firm assent must be, to remove it from the level of
mere opinion to that of belief, but other utterances
make it clear that he does not regard a man who merely
thinks the statements of the creeds more likely to be
true than not, or even considerably more likely to be
true than not, but still subject to a real possibility of
falsity, a "believer". The inferiority he admits in belief,
as contrasted with the vision anticipated in a future life,
lies not in any uncertainty of conviction but in the

absence of clear and distinct apprehension. The difference between the states of probation and of glory, as he
conceives it, is not that the same verities are held in
the one problematically, in the other with assurance,
but that in the first they are perplexing and mysterious,
in the second they will be obvious and self-evident; in
both they are taken to be certain. I take it, however,
that in a more mundane connection he might have been
willing to regard convictions which, though firm, fall
short of such absolute assurance, as fairly entitled to be
called beliefs, and whether St. Thomas would have
admitted this or not, I feel sure that it ought to be
admitted.

What, for example, is the status of my conviction
that William Shakespeare, the player from Strat-
ford, was the author of *Hamlet* and *Othello*? It is not
quite that of the unshakeable assent to articles of
faith, not to be disturbed by any accumulation of
appearances to the contrary, demanded by St. Thomas
of the Christian believer. I can *conceive* evidence which
would be destructive of the conviction. And yet it would
misrepresent the facts to say that I only entertain the
proposition "William Shakespeare wrote *Hamlet*" in
the same fashion in which I entertain the proposition
"William Shakespeare did not write any part of the
Two Noble Kinsmen". That is a personal opinion, of
which I am ready to admit that it may quite well be
mistaken; that I myself wrote the sentence I have just
read is, to me, matter of knowledge. That William
Shakespeare wrote *Hamlet*, I should say, is neither
merely the one nor quite the other, and I can only distinguish it from both by saying that whereas I think, or
opine, that Shakespeare did not write any part of the
Two Kinsmen, and know that I am writing this address,
I neither opine nor know, but *believe* that Shakespeare

wrote *Hamlet*. There is thus, as it seems to me, a state of mind which is neither wavering and uncertain opinion, nor yet knowledge (even on the view we are now examining that absolutely assured conviction is knowledge, when that of which I feel the assurance is true), and for this state of mind I can find no other name in our language but belief. On the theory under consideration the only *intrinsic* character which discriminates opinion, belief, and knowledge must be the degree of assurance and confidence with which assent is given to a proposition. But if it is admitted that any distinction can be made in this respect between a belief which does not amount to knowledge and a mere opinion, there is the difficulty that it is quite impossible to say what degree of assurance is required to convert opinion into belief. We clearly must not say, unless we mean to deny manifest facts, that any opinion becomes a belief when it is held with any degree of assent whatever going beyond the mere admission that it may possibly be true. It would be monstrous to say that I believe in the guilt of the accused in a sensational trial for murder the moment I concede that the very imperfect and fragmentary "evidence" obtainable tells rather for conviction than for acquittal. On the other hand, it is equally impossible to deny the name of belief to all convictions which are held subject to the possibility of doubt and correction, for this would be to reduce the practical convictions by which we govern our daily lives to the status of mere opinions. But the conviction shown, for example, by a life assurance company, when it accepts me as a "first class life", clearly has a status very different from the opinion of one of the directors about the authorship of *Junius* or the authenticity of the Zinoviev letter which played a part in the General Election of 1924, or the probable

issue of the coming General Election of 1929. And there
is a further special difficulty about such a position if it
is combined with the definition of knowledge as a belief
which is, in fact, true. For from the combination of the
premises that all opinions, and only they, which are
held without any qualification of the recognition that
they may be mistaken are beliefs, and that a belief
which is true is knowledge, it would follow that I know
any proposition whatever which I happen to hold very
confidently, whenever that opinion happens to be a
true one. If, for example, I very stubbornly hold that
Philip Francis wrote *Junius*, for no better reason than
that Macaulay said so, then, if to-morrow documentary
proof of that fact should be discovered, I should have
known to-day who was the author of *Junius*; and this
seems quite unreasonable. However hard it may be to
say precisely what the distinction to be made is, a sound
theory will need to distinguish not two terms only,
belief and knowledge, but three, opinion, belief, knowledge, where the theory in question only enables us to
discriminate two.

The impossibility of identifying knowledge with confident belief of what is true in particular, is well illustrated by the example Plato has selected in the
Theaetetus, the effect of advocacy on a jury. Skilful
advocacy will frequently lead a jury to pronounce with
complete confidence on a question of fact where the
evidence is patently incomplete. Indeed, we may
imagine a case—and I do not think it would be hard
to produce actual instances of such cases—in which such
evidence as there is all points in one direction, and yet
the jury are induced to return an unhesitating verdict
in the opposite sense by clever and eloquent but wholly
irrelevant appeals to sentiment and prejudice. And in
a case of this kind it may well happen that such a

finding is in accord with fact; the available evidence may have pointed unmistakably in one direction and yet have been misleading. I might myself, for example, be brought to trial for an alleged offence in some country where Englishmen happen to be very unpopular, and there might be evidence tending to establish my innocence, but none of my guilt which could stand examination. I might then be convicted on the strength of a moving appeal by the prosecution to the local dislike of the English, and it might be the case that I had actually committed the offence laid to my charge, though the evidence of my guilt was worthless. Or I might be an innocent man with a formidable mass of incriminating evidence against me which could not be shaken in cross-examination and no evidence in my favour, and might owe my acquittal to a pathetic but irrelevant insistence by my advocate on the distress of my invalid wife and helpless babes. In such a case it would be an abuse of language to say that the jury who found the correct verdict *knew* me to be guilty or innocent, though they were undeniably led to believe with complete conviction something which, in fact, was the truth. And, as against the view that the *differentia* of belief may be found in the peculiarity of being attended by some doubt or uncertainty, some admission that the thing believed may, after all, be false, I would add that if the appeal to sentiment or prejudice were sufficiently adroit and eloquent, every member of the jury might leave the box without a shadow of hesitation in his mind, and yet it would be monstrous to call this unqualified conviction knowledge.

It seems to me, in fact, that what those who make it a *differentia* of belief to be entertained with a conscious residual uncertainty really have in mind is *opinion* rather than belief proper, and even so, they are not, I think, distinguishing opinion and belief quite accurately. Thus, to take an example, *A. B.* is accused of the murder of *C. D.* and acquitted because the evidence for the Crown proves to be wholly inadequate. I may know that the evidence is inadequate, and yet may hold either that it is overwhelmingly probable that *A. B.* did not wrongfully cause the death of *C. D.*, or that there is no more than an "off-chance" that he did not. In the first case I should say *I believe* in *A. B.*'s entire innocence; in the second that I do not. I believe the Crown has not made out its case, and I may, in addition, *opine* that *A. B.* was wholly blameless, or I may not. The difference is one which any one of us would recognise in practice, and it seems to me an important difference The difference between opining and believing is thus a psychological one. It need not necessarily have a logical ground. I may, for instance, know that all available evidence supports one conclusion, and yet be absolutely firm in my belief that, in spite of the evidence, a different conclusion is the true one. Whether this is an admissible frame of mind or not, it is one with which we are all familiar. We can believe, and believe intensely, in the direct face of evidence, and it is generally held that there are cases where it is a duty to do so, *e.g.* that Othello ought to have believed in the loyalty of Desdemona against any evidence that could have been amassed. But we cannot believe in this fashion against demonstration or against *self*-evidence. The difference between opinion and belief thus seems to me to be properly psychological. A conviction, false or true, held with a certain degree of confidence which we cannot exactly define, is a *belief*. But the difference between belief and knowledge is of another kind. When we know, we are indeed absolutely certain; but we may be, and often are, absolutely certain where we do not know, but merely believe. The difference between believing and knowing is thus not primarily psychological, not to be detected by any mere examination of the act or process of knowing or believing; and, again, if what we have said so far is sound, it does not lie in the mere fact that what is known is true, since we often believe what is true without knowing it. Yet it seems clear that there is a difference. What then is it?

It is natural enough to attempt to answer the question in the way in which it is at once answered by one of the interlocutors in the *Theaetetus*, by saying that what makes the difference between believing and knowing is that when one knows a proposition one can "give an account of it", or, more precisely, one can produce demonstration of it. Where one cannot do this one merely believes, but does not know. One half of this statement, that knowledge and demonstration are co-extensive, if knowledge is taken in the fullest and strictest sense, is, of course, exactly the teaching of Aristotle, and would, I suppose, be generally admitted so far as this, that we cannot be said to know any truth which can be demonstrated, unless we are acquainted with, and could, if called upon, produce the demonstration. If, for example, I cannot demonstrate that the series of prime numbers has no last term, I can hardly be said, without justification, to know the proposition. I may have known it once, at school or college, but at present, until I have recovered the lost demonstration, I can hardly be said, except by courtesy, to know the proposition. The case is still clearer if the proposition asserted is one of which I admittedly have never had any demonstration. Thus suppose I were now to assert the proposition "there is a consistent geometry in which the total number of points is less than twenty"; if the

only justification I could produce for the statement
turned out to be that I had once heard my distinguished
colleague, the Professor of Mathematics in the University of Edinburgh, assert it, I might fairly be told that
I do not know the proposition I am affirming; I only
believe it, though, in view of my colleague's eminence,
I do well to believe it. What I really *know* is not that
there is such a geometry, but that I once heard my colleague say that there is such a geometry. If Russell
spoke truly when he said that in the time of Kant no
proposition of geometry had ever been correctly demonstrated, we may fairly say that no geometrical truth
whatsoever was known by Kant and his contemporaries,
though this leaves it possible that they believed a great
many such truths. It is another question whether the
negative half of our statement (in which it diverges altogether from the doctrine of Aristotle), "where we cannot
demonstrate, we merely believe" can be sustained. As
both Plato and Aristotle saw, the identification of
knowledge proper with awareness of demonstrations
at once raises the question about the status of the
"first principles" of demonstration, the ultimate major
premises of knowledge. Do we know these premises or
do we not? Obviously if we know them, it cannot be by
demonstration. If we said that no one knows the conclusion of a demonstration unless he has first demonstrated its premises and the premises which have been
used in demonstrating them, we should be making all
knowledge depend on an infinite analysis, and thus, in
effect, denying that a "creature" can know anything.
If we say that the ultimate premises are not known but
only believed, we should have to admit that this defect
in our cognition of the premises affects the whole super-
structure which is built on them, and so, once more,
there would be no genuine knowledge.

We do not really escape this difficulty by pointing out, what is true enough, that in mathematics, the type of strictly demonstrative knowledge, it is not the ultimate postulates, but only the implication of further consequences by the postulates, that is formally asserted. The difference, we are sometimes told, between the modern philosophical mathematician and his less cautious predecessors is that the predecessors asserted both a conclusion, such as the Pythagorean theorem, and the various more ultimate postulates from which the demonstration of the theorem is drawn; their more philosophical successor is content to assert only that the theorem is a consequence of the postulates without committing himself to any further assumption about the truth of either postulates or theorem. This is true, so far as it goes. As a mere device for securing a necessary subdivision of intellectual labour it is an excellent arrangement that the mathematician should be set free to develop the implications of a set of premises without being called on to concern himself with asking from what quarter his premises have come, or how they can be justified. In acting so, the modern philosophical mathematician is, after all, only carrying further a procedure begun by Euclid himself when he substituted the colourless names of "common notions" and "initial demands" (κοιναὶ ἔννοιαι and αἰτήματα) for the older designation of unproved premises as "axioms", obviously with the intention of excluding controversy about the source and justification of these initial premises. But no device of this kind can obscure the central fact that there are undemonstrated principles which the most cautious of mathematicians cannot avoid asserting, at least tacitly. He must, at least tacitly, assert all the principles, whatever they may be, of a logic of implication itself. However true it may be that one asserts

neither the Pythagorean theorem nor the postulates
which virtually define an "Euclidean space", but only
the consequence of the first on the second, still, in
asserting as much as this, one is assuming as *known* the
structural principles of the logic of implication. If these
are not known, I cannot know that one specific conclusion rather than another "follows from" a given set
of premises. If they are merely believed, then I cannot
know, but can at best believe, that any given consequence "follows from" the premises from which I assert
it to "follow". Indeed, the profession even of a complete
scepticism about the possibility of attaining knowledge,
if it claims to be a reasonable scepticism and not a
personal "fad", involves the claim to know that "nothing can be inferred with certainty", and he who says as
much as this is plainly claiming by implication to *know*
what conditions would be required to make inferences
valid.

The point is luminously illustrated by the notorious *crux* in which Mill involved himself in his *Logic*.
Nominally Mill's account of inference is intended as an
analysis and justification of the procedure of the experimental sciences. But in view of his belief that "induction" is a method, and in the end the sole method, of
demonstration, his book becomes a theory of demonstration, with the peculiar characteristic that it is committed to justifying demonstration from the point of
view of pure experience, that is, without presupposing
any ultimate principles of demonstration. It is no incidental and removable oversight, but a result dictated
by the nature of Mill's undertaking that, in the end, all
knowledge is made to repose on "induction by simple
enumeration", a procedure for which Mill has really
no justification to offer except the old one of Hume that
it is quasi-instinctive and has some remarkable and

quite unaccountable successes to its credit. (And even this allegation is only made on the strength of the very curious assumption that the results of such men as Galileo and Newton have, in fact, been reached by reliance on "enumeration".)

I hope I need not say that I have not the slightest quarrel with the doctrine that the *prima axiomata* are disclosed to us by "induction", if only the nature of the induction is rightly understood. The all-important point is not that this induction is not proof of any kind. We do not "prove" such an "axiom" by an enumeration of particular instances; we *see* it, or as Aristotle says, "recognise" it in the particular instance, and this recognition is direct and immediate. (This is the explanation of the fact, found so mysterious by Mill, that one "observation" is sometimes sufficient, whereas, in other cases, thousands may be inconclusive. The collection of the thousand is not the "induction", it is preliminary to it.) It is the clear perception of this point which gives Aristotle's brief statement about "induction" at the end of the *Posterior Analytics* its immense superiority over the accounts of our modern "inductive" logicians, who have been seduced by Bacon into mistaking "induction" for a method of demonstration. In intention, I suppose, I do not differ much from the position which writers like Bosanquet really mean to adopt, but I feel that they have not quite shaken themselves free from the notion that "induction" is proof, and are thus involved in the insoluble difficulty about "circular" proof.

It seems to me, then, that it is quite impossible, unless we take refuge in a personal scepticism which does not even profess to be able to offer any rational justification for itself, to get away from the familiar Aristotelian doctrines that we possess knowledge, and knowledge which is direct and immediate, not mediated through inference, and that knowledge is something really different from belief though the difference is one which cannot be detected by the psychologist. Neither knowledge nor belief can be treated as a special sub-variety of the other with a *differentia* of the kind an observational or experimental psychologist can identify. (I may remark in passing that I know, of course, that so far as terminology goes, Aristotle restricts the *name* knowledge (ἐπιστήμη) to awareness of the conclusion of demonstration as guaranteed by its premises, and speaks of the immediate apprehension of premises and principles which cannot be demonstrated by another name, νοῦς, or as the schoolmen said *intellectus*. But the point which is important for my purposes is that νοῦς or *intellectus*, like knowledge, is sharply discriminated from opinion and belief (δόξα and ὑπόληψις), and held to have a still higher "epistemological" status than demonstration, knowledge of proved conclusions as guaranteeed by their premises.) It is this recognition of an immediate knowledge as genuine knowledge, and indeed as the type of complete and perfect knowledge, which I am concerned to defend.

For a full defence, no doubt, it would be necessary to examine the position of a logician like Bosanquet who believes himself able to admit the reality of knowledge which is something more than a belief in that which happens to be true, and yet to deny that there are "unproved premises of proof". I cannot undertake such an examination because, no doubt by my own fault, I have never been able to understand what Bosanquet's position really comes to. I suspect that he may partly have been influenced by the consideration that the formal principles of deduction (for example, the principle of the syllogism in Barbara) do not themselves appear as the actual premises of deductions of which they are the principles. At most, however, this would only go to prove that the unproved and unprovable implications of a deduction should not in strictness be called its premises, not that there are no such principles. And it has also to be remembered that the general principles of the logic of implication are not the only unproved truths presupposed by the demonstrations of the sciences. Each of them has also, as Aristotle insisted, its own special postulates (οἰκεῖαι ἀρχαί), and these may and do figure as actual "premises" in its deductions. In a system of Euclidean geometry, for example, the "fifth postulate" will occur as an actual premise, though the principle that "if equals be added to unequals, the wholes are unequal" will perhaps not. As far as I understand Bosanquet's view on the general question, he seems to hold—and this is why I suspect that I must be misunderstanding him—that all knowledge involves a circle. Our conclusions are guaranteed by the consideration that they follow from certain ultimate presuppositions, and these presuppositions, in turn, are guaranteed by the fact that they lead to these conclusions. If this is really what is meant, it should seem that at any rate the principles of a logic of implication are themselves exempt from the asserted dependence on conclusions; if they are not, how can I know that an alleged conclusion does or does not "follow" from the premises from which it is alleged to follow?

If, as is perhaps more likely, all that is really meant is that what we commonly call our "existing scientific knowledge" consists, outside the domain of pure mathematics, of propositions which have never been and never will be demonstrated, and do *de facto* acquire a higher probability from their "consilience" with fresh records of the independently observed, this seems irrelevant as an objection to the Aristotelian account of the "undemonstrated principles of demonstration". It is, of course, to be remembered that the recognition of a real difference between knowing and believing does not carry with it the consequence that I am never mistaken when I think I know. That I sometimes suppose myself to know when I do not really know is a fact having the same sort of signification as the equally familiar facts that I sometimes suppose a demonstration which really involves a fallacy to be cogent, that I sometimes suffer from hallucinations of the senses, and that my memory is sometimes at fault. What the fact really shows is merely that there is no psychological criterion by which we can infallibly discriminate knowledge from belief, any more than there is such a criterion for the discrimination of sense or memory from imagination.

What I am concerned to suggest, then, is this. If it is really impossible to get away from the positions that knowing and believing are different in kind and that some knowing is immediate, there must be something wrong with certain conceptions of complete or perfect knowledge which have been popular in our own lifetime. Neither inference nor judgement can be the type of the most profound and thorough knowledge. For the inferentially known is always mediately known, known as Aristotle says, "on the basis of a previously existing knowledge", and it is in the right of this knowledge previously existing that the inferentially known can claim to be known. Even judgement, though it is an abuse of language to identify it with inference, or inference with it, not only tends, as Bosanquet used to say, to "expand into inference", but tends always to provoke the demand that it shall be justified by exhibiting it as the conclusion of a process of inference, though in the case of the "unproved principles", the demand can only be met by refusing to meet it. It is never transparently absurd to ask about any judgement offered for our acceptance, "What are the grounds for it?" even though the answer may have to be that no other judgement or judgements can be produced as grounds for that I have made. This is notoriously not the case with perception. When I have justified an assertion about present matter of fact by saying that, for example, I actually *see* the mercury rising in the thermometer-tube, it would be strictly meaningless to ask *why* I can see this. The characteristic peculiarity of the Aristotelian account of knowledge which, I suggest, is necessitated by the impossibility of making the "unproved principles" mere matters of belief, is that it frankly recognises the same directness which marks our apprehension of sensible fact, at one end of the scale, in the apprehension of ultimate principles at the other end; both are strictly *vision*. As in the case of vision with the bodily eye, there are a bewildering multitude of links intermediate in the causal order between the occurrence of the event which is the stimulus and the event which is the sensation, but nothing whatever intermediate in the order of apprehension between percipient and *perceptum*, so also in the case of what we see with the mind's eye when we apprehend an undemonstrable principle, there is nothing intermediate in the order of apprehension between the knowing mind and the principle it knows. And it is this kind of direct and immediate apprehension of truth which we should regard as the type of true knowing. All that we commonly call our scientific knowledge is an endeavour, never fully successful, to recapture for our mental vision of facts this immediacy and obviousness from which we begin by passing away, the moment judgement supervenes on sense-perception.

Judgement has sometimes been spoken of as the

characteristic form of the apprehension of truth. It seems to me that the very fact that most of what we know about the world has to be couched in the form of judgement is the characteristic mark of the inevitable imperfection of our apprehension. This was well understood by the philosophers of the Middle Ages, and it is because they understood it so well that there is a curious point, not often remarked upon, in which their language about God differs from that of philosophers of a later time. When a modern philosopher allows himself to talk of God, he makes no scruple to speak of God as "thinking", or even "cogitating". Locke, for example, in his attempted demonstration of the being of God proceeds at once, after establishing the point that "something has existed from eternity" to argue that this something must necessarily be a "cogitative" being. So in Green's *Prolegomena to Ethics* the cardinal point for which it is contended against the naturalist is that both the existence of nature and our knowledge of it are dependent upon the reality of a "self-distinguishing principle" which *thinks*. St. Thomas, on the other hand, expressly denies that *cogitatio* is found in God. God *knows* all truths, but God does not "think", just as God wills the whole creation but does not "deliberate", or "make up His mind". It is just because judgement is the characteristic form of *thinking* that, to the mind of St. Thomas, it is an unjustifiable anthropomorphism to say that God thinks. God does not *think*; He knows with a knowledge which is vision.

The thought is that in a knowledge which is always completely "in act" there is a complete and intimate interpenetration and possession by the knower of the object known which is absent from judging. Judging is not "being in possession of" or "being possessed by" the object; it is a preliminary step on the way to such

possession, inevitable in us who begin without knowledge, and have to obtain it in successive fragments
and parcels; we make our way in the direction of knowledge by thinking "about it and about". But if we
could completely achieve the ideal of knowledge which
guides us all through the process, the perfect *adaequatio
intellectus cum re*, as we cannot, our knowledge would
no longer be thinking, or wear the form of judging; it
would have recovered the directness characteristic of
the perception from which it began by setting out. It is
this conception of complete knowledge as a direct vision,
to which the form of judgement is inadequate, which,
as it seems to me, is already implied in the admission
of a real distinction between knowledge and true belief.

I hope I shall not be understood as suggesting either
that to know anything completely I must *be* that which
I know, or that in so far as we know objects it is not
properly we who know, but the objects which "know
themselves through us". What I mean is not this. I
mean rather that the type of perfect knowledge is an
apprehension which is at once direct and, as I may say,
"self-luminous" or "transparent". The absence of
either directness or transparency—what I might call
the colour of "of-courseness"—is an indication that our
apprehension is not all that complete knowledge should
be. In this respect, sense-perception, though it gives us
our most familiar illustration of one of the characteristics of complete knowledge, the directness, falls short
in respect of the other, because it is apprehension of
"brute" fact, about which there is no "of course", but
which, for all we can see, might perfectly well be quite
otherwise. At the other end of the scale, in the "highest
universals" which are indemonstrable, we approximate
again to a knowledge which may fairly be called
"vision", and is called insight. These principles are no

mere tautologies; they are all, in that sense, "synthetic", and yet there is no "because" behind them; they carry their own evidence with them, they are so "of course". The trouble is that this "of-courseness" cannot be communicated to the whole system of what we know. It is communicated to the conclusions which follow by demonstration from the principles, but these conclusions remain incurably abstract; there is always a gulf between them and full concrete actual fact.

And yet it is undeniable that there is a kernel of something which is not merely believed but known in our apprehension of actual fact. Perception, I mean, is knowledge, and perceiving is knowing, and yet perception is not judgement, and nothing but confusion comes of the attempt to talk of it, as some modern logicians have done, as though it were judgement. There is a difference difficult to express clearly by any form of words, and yet unmistakably real, between seeing a green leaf and judging "that the leaf is green". I cannot attempt to communicate the content of a perception to anyone without converting perception into judgement, and hence the possibility of confusing knowledge with mere belief comes in at once, since there is always the possibility of error in the description, or analysis, of the perceived which is involved in the simplest of judgements. The ideal type of knowledge would only be realised if we could substitute for our crude piecemeal perceptions an apprehension of the actual in which we should see it articulated by the ultimate principles, as a system of geometry is articulated by its postulates, and see the articulation not progressively but in one complete act of insight, carried through to the whole of the actual detail, not stopping short, as our scientific insight always does, at the "proximate" universals. This would be nothing other than the *scientia visionis* ascribed by the mediaeval thinkers in its completeness to God and only to God. We, of course, never reach its completeness just because of the curious position of the mind which is the standing crux at once of naturalism and of a really "absolute" idealism, as at once standing outside and above the complex "event which is nature" and also implicated in it τρόπον τινὰ δύσφραστον καὶ θαυμαστόν. In actual perception, in a very real sense, we may say that the whole of the actual is given to us at every moment, but it is given in a form which is opaque and non-communicable; in our most exact scientific knowledge, when we know, as Aristotle would have us know, our conclusions through, and as guaranteed by their ultimate οἰκεῖαι ἀρχαί, our insight is direct and there is transparency and the "of course" quality, but the whole transparent structure still stops short with "separated" universals, and, if we are to speak strictly, we must say that our application of the system to the actual "passage of nature" is, as Plato maintained, at best "true belief" rather than knowledge.

The point I am anxious to make is that just because "vision" is the ideal type of knowledge and vision in its completeness is impossible for us, who enter ourselves, in virtue of our temporality, into the "passage of nature", it is quite impossible for us to construct on a single principle a flawlessly coherent scheme of the *omne scibile*, after the fashion of philosophers like Hobbes, who take demonstration falsely as the ideal of knowledge and deny the name to all that cannot be demonstrated. It is inevitable that, for us, there should be a rift in the scheme of the *scibile*, the rift which separates the sciences of demonstration from our knowledge of the historical and individual. And there is one characteristic of this historical knowledge on which I think it may not be superfluous to offer a remark; I

mean its inarticulateness, or, as I might say, incom-
municability, a quality it shares with actual perception.
I suppose it is impossible for any man to immerse himself long and thoroughly in the study of the life and
work of a great personality or a great age without feeling that he in the end comes by a direct insight into
purpose and meaning which he can call by no name
but knowledge, though it is quite impossible to demonstrate the correctness of his insight to anyone or even
to communicate it. The point has been admirably put
by my lamented friend, Prof. John Burnet, with special
reference to his own life-long study of Plato and his
circle, and I cannot do better than quote his words. "A
man who tries to spend his life in sympathy with the
ancient philosophers will sometimes find a direct conviction forcing itself upon him, the grounds of which
can only be represented very imperfectly by a number
of references in a footnote. Unless the enumeration of
passages is complete—and it can never be complete—
and unless each passage tells exactly in the same way,
which depends on its being read in the light of in-
numerable other passages not consciously present to
memory, the so-called proofs will not produce the same
effect in any two minds. That is the sense in which
philological inquiry, like every other inquiry, requires
an act of faith. In the long run the positive construction
must be left to the individual student, and no two
students will see quite alike."[1]

Much the same experience, as I cannot doubt, would
be confessed by every historian of a man or an age.
And yet, in spite of the impossibility of demonstration
and the disagreements of individual students about
this or the other point of detail, it seems undeniable
that we do, in favourable cases, succeed in getting an

[1] *Greek Philosophy*, Part I. 2-3.

"understanding" of a great historical personage which is no mere affair of the more or less likely, and can be recovered by successive students for themselves, though none of them can directly impart it to another. We can, if we will, succeed in knowing, not merely opining or thinking, what the "historical" Plato, or Cromwell or Shelley was, no matter what uncertainty may hang over many of the alleged incidents of their lives. Where we understand, we may fairly say we know; in fact, in our relations with the members of our circle of personal intimates, it is precisely what we thus understand of their inmost purposes and characters that we may claim with the best right to know; it is details of events in their lives, not related to character and purpose, in connection with which it is most rash to profess more than opinion or belief.

The one great outstanding defect in the Platonic-Aristotelian account of knowledge, inspired as it is, naturally enough, by reflection on the character of the one body of knowledge which had already acquired a high degree of organisation by the opening of the fourth century B.C., the mathematical, is that, by insisting too exclusively on one side of the ideal of a completed knowledge, its thoroughgoing articulation, it really leaves no room for the recognition of historical insight into the individual as genuine knowledge, a one-sidedness which has left its traces on all subsequent philosophical methodology. Against Aristotle's οὐδὲ δι' αἰσθήσεως ἔστιν ἐπίστασθαι, I should like to set as a true and important *aperçu* Locke's recognition of the reality of "sensitive" knowledge itself, only with the already given caution that in the very attempt to communicate the content of "sensitive" knowledge we are passing away from perception itself to the "perceptive judgement", as Bosanquet, I think, calls it, and substituting for immediate apprehension the mediated, with the possibility that it may be the incorrectly mediated. And the possibility becomes an overwhelming probability when we consider that, in the case of any "perceptive judgement", the implied premises are immensely numerous, and far the greater number of them, possibly the most important of them, are commonly held only implicitly. The premises which would justify our affirmation have to be sought partly in a vast mass of un-analysed and imperfectly analysed perceptions, partly in an intellectual scheme or pattern embodied in a linguistic structure which we have received as an in-heritance, and with a very imperfect comprehension of the complexities of its articulation. It is only when our thought is moving in the realm of "abstractions" which constitutes the domain of the "exact sciences" that we can be confident that the first of these two sources of unrecognised "tacit premises of mediation" is pre-cluded; even there we are at the mercy of the second, as is shown clearly enough by the actual history of the critical search for a complete and accurate list of the postulates of mathematical science.

We readily understand, then, why in the past the tendency among great philosophers should have been to make "exact" science into the one type of all genuine knowledge, and to minimise the importance, or even to deny the existence of "sensitive", or, as I should prefer to say, "historical" knowledge. The fact, as I take it, is that in the rationalisation of the given we are always moving between two extremes, one which we have left behind us when we take the initial step towards science, that of merely immediated "given-ness", not as yet even "recognised", the other, one which we never reach, that in which we should possess and be possessed by vision of the *whole* system of the true, apprehended in all its articulation and apprehended all together. Here the antithesis between immediate and mediated would once more be done away with, and we should at last have an actual knowledge fully adequate to our ideal of knowledge which is through and through, in all its detail, knowledge and nothing but knowledge. But, in fact, we never achieve the completion of the process. Our human thought is always, as the phrase is, "discursive", advances from point to point, or, as the schoolmen said, proceeds by composition and division, that is judgements, affirmative and negative *about*, or *upon*, a material not itself apprehended by judgement. We leave perception for judgement the moment we begin to recognise, to reflect and to communicate the results of recognition and reflection; not being able to complete an "infinite analysis", we never return, at the other end of the process, to the kind of apprehension we are seeking, a vision which has the directness of perception without its inarticulateness. And, as I take it, the ultimate reason why this must be so is the simple one that time and movement are as radically characteristic of our thinking as they are of the processes of our physical life. Thinking and judging are what, so far as I can see, complete knowledge cannot be, temporal processes. Our attempt to say what knowledge is leads us back to a conviction which we may equally reach along very different lines, the conviction that time is at the bottom of our profoundest and most perplexing metaphysical problems.

There is a great passage in Augustine's *Confessions* (xii. 18) which puts the point I am very inadequately labouring with admirable clarity. "Will you say", exclaims Augustine to a supposed opponent of his exegesis of the opening words of *Genesis*, "that what truth rounds so loudly in my inner ear concerning the true eternity of the Creator is false? That it is false that His substance is invariable by succession of times, and that His will does not fall without His substance? Whence He does not now will this and again that, but wills once, all together and always, all that He wills; He wills not subsequently what before He willed not, unwills not what formerly He willed. Such will is mutable, and nothing mutable is eternal, but our God is an eternal God. Again, is that false which truth rounds me in the inner ear, that anticipation of things to come becomes vision when they have come, and vision, again, becomes memory when they have passed; that all activity of mind (*intentio*) which is thus variable is mutable and nothing immutable eternal, but our God is an eternal God? I combine these positions together and discover that my God, the eternal God, created the world by a will that was not novel and that His knowledge admits of no transitions".

What is here said with special reference to the knowledge of the Creator seems to be simply true of all knowledge which realises the ideal implicitly aimed at in every attempt to know; an apprehension which is not such vision, whatever its excellence, does not wholly amount to what we really mean by knowledge, and it is just for this reason that, without the slightest desire to depreciate science, or to suggest any doubt about the imperative duty of its prosecution, I feel bound to say that such "science" as is possible to beings as temporal as men—I mean, of course, in the conditions familiar to us from our experience as those of man in the life we see—is never quite identical with "knowledge". Even in our exactest of exact science (in the most philosophical of philosophical arithmetics, for example) there is always, I take it, the possibility that we have overlooked some premise really required by the system, or formulated it without due circumspection, and so there is always the possibility that we are claiming to know where we should be content to say that we believe. What is more, we can, in such a case, make no absolutely clear and sharp cut between the propositions which we know and those which, it may be, we should only be said to believe, any more than I can make such an absolute distinction between what I actually perceive and what I remember. The nature of the distinction between knowing and believing, like that of the distinction between seeing and remembering, may be clear and intelligible enough, but it furnishes no infallible criterion for application to the specific instance, just as, in the realm of moral practice, the doctrine of the Categorical Imperative, accepted without reserve, would furnish no infallible criterion of the rightness of the individual act.

Let me, in conclusion, try to put together, in a set of theses, the results of these rather desultory reflections:

(1) Knowing and believing are two quite distinct attitudes of a mind to that which it apprehends. Knowing is not a special way of believing, nor believing a special way of knowing.

(2) The difference between the two attitudes is not one which can be discerned in an individual case by observational scrutiny, and is, in this sense, not psychological, and cannot be justified by an empirical science of psychology.

(3) Nor does it lie in the fact that what is known is *true*, since this may equally be the case with what is believed, but not known.

(4) The reality of "sensitive" or "historical" knowledge shows that the difference cannot be simply that the object of knowledge is non-temporal.

(5) Yet the difference must lie somehow in the respective characters of that which is believed and that which is known.

(6) What the difference is seems to be indicated by the consideration that *perception* affords knowledge, though a knowledge which is inarticulate and incommunicable. Belief is a sub-species of *judgement* and judgement is mediate, in the sense that it presupposes reference to grounds for judging which fall outside the judgement itself. This is not the case with knowledge.

(7) The ideal of knowledge is that it should be at once immediate and articulated. In actual life, the immediacy is most manifest in perceptional knowledge, where articulation is at a minimum. The articulation is clearly manifest in scientific knowledge, as conceived by Aristotle, where conclusions are known along with and through premises which are, in the last resort, themselves immediately apprehended. But, even in the case where such scientific knowledge is best exemplified, that of pure mathematics, the whole of the premises relevant to the conclusion are not consciously envisaged in the act of "knowing the conclusion through its premises". Hence the ideal of knowledge is not actually attained even here, since the apprehension is not full and complete "vision".

(8) It follows that while Aristotle was justified in his demand for "intuitive apprehension of unproved premises of demonstration", his account of knowledge is defective at the other end by not explicitly recognising the reality of the inarticulate and incommunicable knowledge belonging to sense-perception as such.

(9) The impossibility of limiting knowledge to awareness of the universal, thus implicitly denying that historical fact can be *known*, arises directly from the fundamentally temporal and successive character of

human mental activities, not from the nature of knowledge itself.

I would add two corollaries to these theses:

(1) It is unfortunate that some eminent recent philosophers should have spoken habitually of logic as concerned with judgements rather than with propositions. This language inevitably tends to obliterate the very real distinction between knowing and believing by the misleading suggestion that knowing is a kind of "cogitation".

(2) Since knowledge, so far as it really is knowledge, is immediate, there can be no "theory of knowledge" in the sense of a theory of the way in which knowing is done. The whole of what can properly be called "theory of knowledge" is contained in an answer to the question "How does knowing differ from opining and believing?" And the true answer to this question can be given in three words, "By being vision".

[1928]

XI

IS GOODNESS A QUALITY?

THE observations I am about to make are likely to be both confused and irrelevant, since I am not sure that I know either what *goodness* and *quality* mean in this connection, or what the framers of our programme intended us to be discussing. But I will try to indicate what is in my own mind, so far as I know my own mind, in some prefatory remarks about the extent to which I suppose myself to be agreeing or disagreeing with the distinguished speakers who have preceded me.

I do not find the passage in Aristotle's *Ethics*, from which the discussion presumably starts, as obscure as Mr. Moore seems to do. The point, I take it (and I presume I am here in accord with Mr. Joseph), is that the word *good* has a variety of senses, and yet is not merely *equivocal*. As in the case of the word *surgical*, the different senses are interconnected by analogy. I say (1) *Hannibal was a good strategist*, (2) *Gladstone was a good Chancellor of the Exchequer*, (3) *a good epitaph must be brief*, (4) *Easter Monday is a good day for a public demonstration*. In no two of these cases do I mean precisely the same thing, yet it is no mere accident of language that I use the same word in all four cases. The range of values of *x* for which the statement *x is good* is significant forms a *series* with an order of before and after between its terms. As Aristotle himself puts it, "good is predicated in all the categories", and categories are an ordered series. (There is a metaphysical order of dependence between the primary category of all, *substance*, and the rest, and the relation of dependence is a different one in each case.) The point might, indeed, be made without going outside the bounds of a single category. A lead-pencil and the penknife with which I point it may both be good, but a good pencil must have a soft lead, and a good knife must have a hard blade. Good drinking-water must be odourless; good wine, I presume, must have an aroma. It would be possible that all the characters on the strength of which I call A good should be the same as those on the strength of which I pronounce B bad. This of itself seems to show that when I truthfully call different things *good*, it is not, at any rate, one and the same "simple indefinable quality" that I intend to denote in all cases, though, so far, it might still be true that what is denoted in each case is *some* simple indefinable quality, and further, that there is some sort of connection between all these simple indefinables. But I cannot myself believe even this statement to be true. I do not think that any such simple quality is denoted when I truly speak of a given poem or novel as a good poem or novel, and I think it a pity to equate simplicity, where it exists, with indefinability. I do not see why the simple need be indefinable, or why in *Principia Ethica* Mr. Moore should have identified definition with the analysis of a complex whole into its constituents. Given an indefinable A and a second term B, however unanalysable B may be, it seems to me that I can define B if I can point out some relation which B and only B has to A, and has not to any term but A, and this, I should have said, is the procedure regularly adopted in the most precise of our definitions, those of numbers and numerical functions.

But I agree with Mr. Moore when he urges against
Mr. Joseph that the goodness of a poet or a poem is not
identical with the poet or poem, and again when he
adds that the goodness of either is not identical with
the "complex of characters" on the strength of which
we call poet or poem good of its kind. I do not even
understand the first thesis, the one Mr. Joseph appears
to defend. If the goodness of the poem *is* the poem, it
must also be true that the poem *is* its own goodness.
What, then, about the badness of the same poem?—and
the best poem can be bad in some ways, and sometimes
surprisingly bad. *Paradise Lost* is an astonishingly
good poem, but it is amazingly bad too, in respect of its
total lack of humour; it would not be the poem it is if
it were not perversely unhumorous as well as sublime
or rhythmically beautiful. Its badness does not fall outside the character which belongs to *Paradise Lost* as
Paradise Lost; the badness is as peculiarly "Miltonic"
as the goodness. The vulgarity of mind in Dickens is
quite as inseparably Dickensian as the humour and
imagination. In fact, to anticipate for the moment, the
schoolmen, I should say, were entirely right in holding
that it is only of God that it can be said that He *is* His
own goodness.

Even the more mitigated second thesis seems to me,
as to Mr. Moore, untenable. I think it plain that the
goodness of a poem is not the same thing as the complex of characters on the strength of which it is judged
to be good. If a poem has this complex of characters,
and if they really are a sufficient ground for calling it
good, the poem always is good. When I go on from
saying "the poem has these characters" to say "the
poem is good", I am not, indeed, in any way crediting
the poem with an additional character, and far less con-
ferring such an additional character upon it; I am

recognising that it is good, and good because it has the characters already indicated, and the goodness would none the less be there if I did not recognise it. In this sense we may say of the goodness of the poem and its possession of the characters in question that, to use a familiar Aristotelian *cliché*, ἔστι τὸ αὐτό; but with Aristotle we have to add τὸ μέντοι εἶναι οὐ τὸ αὐτό. The added statement, "and, since it has these characters, it is good", has brought in something which was not present in the mere statement that the poem has these characters. What is added is a valuation by reference to a teleological standard, a recognition that the poem is what it *ought* to be. I shall presently attempt to elucidate some of the implications of this *ought*; for the moment I would merely note the fact of its presence when we speak of the poem as a good one.

I do not mean, of course, that the standard is an externally imposed one, an *extrinsic denomination*. When I say "this is a good tragedy" I am not intending a comparison with some imaginary tragedy other than the one before me. What is implied is that in being a tragedy at all, the composition aims at exhibiting a certain typical structure, in the phrase of Plato, it βούλεται εἶναι, "means to be", something which it may conceivably not succeed in being. So far as it does succeed, it is a *good* tragedy. In fact, the thought I want to defend is the old one that what makes the difference between all created things and their Creator is that this *nisus* to self-transcendence is present in all of them. They all "mean to be" something which they never quite succeed in being, and this is why none of them is identical with its own goodness.

This, I think, is the real point of the account of the ἰδέα τἀγαθοῦ in Plato's *Republic*, to which Mr. Joseph alludes in a passage of his recent book referred to by

Mr. Moore. According to the *Republic*, the source of the goodness of everything other than the Form of good lies outside the thing; it lies in the Form of good. The goodness of other things, in the last resort, is not their own; it is a reflection, and an imperfect reflection, of the goodness of the Form, just as their being itself is a similar reflection of the being of the Form. Hence they are neither their own being nor their own goodness. Their "becoming" is a never-completed process of self-transcendence, and at the same time a *nisus* towards a goodness which is never fully actualised in them. So far as Mr. Joseph's language indicates such a view, I am in accord with it. But I should diverge from him if he meant, as I do not think he does, that the meaning of the doctrine which he accepts—viz., that God, and presumably God only, is His own goodness, is completely conveyed by saying that God cannot get or lose His goodness. For this would be equally true if goodness were thought of as an "inseparable accident" of God, but the point of the thinkers who invented the famous formula was precisely that in God the distinction between what is *essential* and what is *accidental* has no meaning: there are no *accidentia* of God, and there is no *essentia* of God, or "nature of deity", primordial or otherwise, distinguishable from God Himself. Plato is human, but Plato is not humanity, and even the phoenix, the "*sole* Arabian bird", if it existed, would not be "phoenicity", but God *is* Deity. The reason why God was said to be His own goodness is not, as Mr. Joseph seems to suggest in one passage of his book, no doubt by an inadvertence, that God is *substance*, but that the whole scheme of the categories is inapplicable to God. In the scholastic sense of the word *substance*— and it is the scholastic, not the Cartesian sense which is relevant to the scheme of categories—Plato is a substance, and a good one, but no schoolman could have said of Plato as Mr. Joseph is prepared to say of a good poem, that Plato is identical with his own goodness. Their point was that the *composition* characteristic of created things (whether thought of as composition of form with matter, or of *essentia* with existence), is not found in God. God is absolutely *simple*, so that, so to say, in every one of His acts His whole being receives complete expression. It is not with Him as it is with us. A man may be at once powerful, just, merciful. But some of his acts will exhibit one of these characters at the expense of, or in the absence of others. The justice may get in the way of the mercy, or there will at least be occasions when the man's act discloses his justice but discloses nothing one way or the other as to his mercifulness. But every act of God, just because God is *actus purus*, exhibits the whole of God.

There is one other point on which I should like to express entire agreement with Mr. Joseph. I hold, as he does, that moral rightness must not be confused with "tendency to *produce* good", and that a right act is itself good, not merely productive of something else which is good. I cannot deny that wrong acts may be productive of good, and even of *moral* good, and right acts of evil, and even of *moral* evil. An atrocious crime produces good, and moral good, when it brings home to many minds the neglected duty for giving proper public protection to the defenceless; the just punishment of a criminal—*e.g.* a political assassin—is productive of moral evil when it gives rise to sentimental sympathy with the murderer and condonation of his offence.

I turn now to exposition of the view I want to put before you. For the moment I propose to put reference to God on one side, and to start with elementary reflections about the use of the word *good* as a predicate of

the things and persons of everyday life. I confine myself to these because though we often speak of the characters or attributes of persons and things as good, I
think what we mean in such cases is that it is the person
or thing which is good, and that the character or attribute is specified as the *ground* for the judgement of
goodness. We say "truthfulness is good", "cruelty is
bad". But we mean, I think, that a truthful man is
good in virtue of being truthful, a cruel man bad, in
virtue of being cruel. Now it seems to me misleading to
say that what such a predicate means is that its subject
possesses a certain *quality*. The only alternative way of
expressing all that I mean when I call a thing good, I
believe, is to say that the thing in question is what it
ought to be, and it is the presence of this implication
of an *ought* which makes it improper to treat the pre-
position *x is good* as being of the same type as *x is white*
or *x is sweet*.

I do not mean by this that the thing I call good is
what I like it to be, what I now want it to be, or am
resolved that it shall be. I may call *A*'s music good, and
B's novel bad, though I know at the moment of speaking that I neither like *A*'s music nor want to hear it,
and that I do like *B*'s novel, or am bursting to read it.
I may, for my own purposes, want to make another
person do, and take pains to induce him to do, what I
myself judge to be very bad acts, or may be anxious to
keep him from doing a very good act. Still less need I
mean that the good thing is productive of, or instrumental to, something else. I judge great poetry good,
though I do not know that it is instrumental to anything, and though honesty or classical scholarship may
be instrumental to various valuable results, I am not
thinking of these results, or not primarily of them, when
I say that honesty or scholarship is good. Also, in using

the word *ought* in this way, I am employing it in a wider than the specifically ethical sense. I mean the word to cover such cases as those in which we say that this epigram, or this finish to a game at chess, is what it ought to be.

Mr. Moore would perhaps say that I am here committing a "circle in definition", since if I were asked what I mean by saying that the epigram is what it ought to be, I should be brought back to the original statement that it has the character *x*, and that *x* is such that the proposition *if an epigram has the character* x *it is good*, is true. But I think the alleged circle is not real. The change of expression from *this is good* to *this is what it ought to be* brings out in high relief a genuine fact, the teleological reference implied in the use of the predicate *good*, and it further indicates that when the word *good* is used in its proper sense, and not as a loose equivalent of useful, the teleology is internal, inherent in the very nature of the thing which is pronounced good. The "nature" of the person or thing in question is not merely to *have* certain characters, but to *tend to* a certain completion or fulfilment. In this sense what I may call a *forward-looking* reference is embedded in the very structure of the subject of the predication. The persons or things of which we are speaking in the class of judgements now under consideration are all persons or things which come to be what they are by a process of development. Their characters are not a mere bundle or complex, nor, again, are they interconnected by relations of mere logical implication: they belong together in virtue of an extra-logical structural plan, which controls the development and expresses itself through it. It is in this sense that they all presuppose a τέλος, a culminating stage in which the structural plan embodied in the whole process finds full completion without either excess or defect. If, or when, this finality of expression is reached, the person or thing actually is just what it was all along tending to be, it is perfect in its kind. So far as it has, as it stands, embodied the plan in its attained development, it is good, though not perfect; so far as it fails to do so, and thus falls short of the exigence of its own "nature", it is defective, and if it falls short of what its own nature demands at *this* stage of the development, it is *bad* of its kind. Where, if anywhere, we come across anything in the natural world, like the atom as conceived by the popular science of the last century, which has no internal structural law of development, and so neither grows into, nor is fashioned into anything, but is merely inertly there without any fulfilment of tendency, the predicates *good* and *bad* seem to be strictly inapplicable.

This is why, when Spinoza is indulging his more anti-teleological mood, he quite consistently treats good and evil as mere illusions. The difficulty about the doctrine is not merely that on his premises, since he denies that there is any "nature of man" distinguishable from the "nature of *this* man", he has no right to call Nero a bad *man*, or bad specimen of man, though this is a serious difficulty enough for a philosopher who sets out to write on ethics: he has not even the right to believe that there is a "nature of Nero", since to admit so much is to allow that Nero βούλεται εἶναι, tends to be, something which Nero actually is not, and so there will be a possible other than the actual. If Spinoza's professed metaphysic is sound, whenever we speak of the unactualised potentialities of Nero's nature, or of any man's nature, we are saying what has no real significance. Hence Blyenbergh was perfectly right in telling him that he had cut himself off from the possibility of having an ethic, as a philosopher who treats potentiality as mere not-being is bound to do. To identify the goodness of a thing simply with its "possession of a quality of some kind" seems to involve this fatal attempt to eliminate process, γένεσις εἰς οὐσίαν, from the world.

When we consider any concrete thing which forms part of the actual world of historical fact, we find it always at once a *Werdendes* or γιγνόμενον, and a *Gewordenes* or γεγενημένον. Its history is the record of the passing into actual fact, or the failure to pass into fact, of a nature which belongs from the first to the thing and yet is not, in the first instance, actual in it. The passage may be the growth of an organism or a mind, or it may be the conscious and largely deliberate shaping of a work of art by the craftsman or artist. It is, I would urge, in the realisation of such internal plan or structure as no longer mere possibility, but actual fact, that the goodness of the thing lies. Nor do I think it any real objection to retort that we may say of the bad person or thing, as we do of the good, that it has a history of fulfilment of the "law of its nature", so that I am apparently committing myself to the view that the artistic or moral monster is at once monstrous and also beautiful or virtuous. After all, the old Greek view seems to be sound, that definite form is a principle of goodness in its embodiments, and that evil as such is formlessness. The process by which the bad man, or play, or picture, becomes what it is is not really one of advance to relevant and adequate embodiment of coherent form, but rather one of failure to embody form, or of positive resistance to it. The effect, in these cases, really is an "effect defective". The bad work of art is anarchical; either it exhibits no recognisable controlling form to speak of, or it exhibits one which fits the content no better than a bed of Procrustes, and in either case, it is anarchic. Anarchy again, as Plato reminds us in his

picture of the "tyrannical man", is distinctive of the
"moral monster". A real Nero is a man distracted; a real
Iago is a stunted man.

It is fundamental to the view I am trying to present
that there should be no division of the knowable into
two disjunct realms, one of the merely real or actual, and
another of ideals, or values, or goods, and it is to exclude
this separation that I am anxious to insist upon the distinction between the persons and things which are the
true subjects of predication of goodness, and the characters in virtue of which goodness is predicated of them.
That which is good is, properly speaking, a person or
thing: it is Paris, not some character of Paris, that is
handsome, Hector, not some character of Hector, who
is brave. A character, divorced from its embodiment in
a thing or person, is just a concept, and I can see no
sense in saying that concepts are good, or bad, or that
one is better or worse than another. So again with
things and persons which are purely imaginary, like the
characters of a play or novel. I do not think anything
more can be meant by saying that Wycherley's Manly
is a scoundrel than that if there were a real man who
acted as Manly is made to do in the play, that man
would be a scoundrel. So if a man were to say that the
imaginary society of Plato's *Republic* is better (or
worse) than London society to-day, I could only understand him by taking this for an abbreviated way of
saying that if there really were such a society as Plato
depicts, it would be better (or worse) than that of contemporary London. A thing, to have anything significantly predicated of it, must at least *be*, and so far
as I can see, there is no such mode of being as the "being
merely for thought" of which philosophers have sometimes spoken. Would there be any real meaning in the
statement that the imaginary *Iphigenia* of which

Aristotle has sketched the plot in his *Poetics* is a better or worse play than the *Iphigenia* of Euripides or of Goethe, if the meaning is not simply that if a poet actually constructed a play on the lines laid down by Aristotle the play, in respect of its plot, would be better, or be worse, than the actual play with which the statement compares it?

I am not, of course, denying the reality or importance of the distinction between existence and essence; on the contrary, it is vital to me to insist that the distinction is both real and important. But it is a distinction within what is real, not a distinction between what is real and an unreal something else. That can hardly have been the true meaning of Plato, or of any other supreme philosopher.

In a word, I want to maintain that we shall never understand either judgements about good and bad, or historical judgements unless we are clear on the point that the subjects of such judgements are genuinely individual, that an individual—or at least a finite individual—is a complex of existence or actuality, and *essentia*, real possibility, and that the *essentia* is a factor, and ought to be the controlling factor, in its own actualisation; it is at once an efficient cause, as the Americans say an "urge", towards actualisation along certain lines, a formal cause, or law of the process, and a final cause; the whole process of the development is directed upon it, its actualisation "tends" towards it, and will bring it about, if not thwarted or prevented. This is familiar Platonic and Aristotelian doctrine, and calls less for explanation than for vigorous reaffirmation. For the purposes of ethical and aesthetic, as well as of historical studies, it is vital to understand that tendency, or real possibility, is neither unreal, nor is it the same thing as actualisation in fact. The range of real possibility is not

indefinite; *non omnia possumus omnes* is true to the
letter; on the other hand, it is wider than that of actual
fact. A possibility which is never converted into
actuality may none the less be a real possibility. If
Shakespeare had been carried off by one of the visita-
tions of plague in the 1590's, it would still be true that
Shakespeare had the possibility of writing *Hamlet* in
him, and that Francis Bacon had not, or that I have not.
Even those philosophers who try to believe that an
unactualised possibility is nothing at all have not been
able to deny that a sentence like that I have just written
is at least a popular way of saying something which may
be true and be known to be true. But on their theory of
the matter, I do not see what the statement "I have not
'got it in me' to write a play like *Hamlet*" means, unless
it is a mere guess about the future, "I shall never write
a play like *Hamlet*, and if I went on living for ever, I
never should". But if unactualised possibility is nothing, how do I know that I never shall write such a play,
to say nothing of knowing that, with an unending life
before me to do it in, I never should? Am I entitled to
say more than that I have not yet written a *Hamlet*?
Or to leave self-judgement which is proverbially un-
trustworthy, out of the question, consider a case of a
kind with which we are all familiar. There is a literary
work of which we are certain that it must have been
produced by one or other of several persons, *A*, *B*, *C*,
others being excluded by external evidence of some
kind. Is a judgement of the type "This work must have
been written by *A*, because it transcends the powers of
B and *C*, and we may therefore eliminate them" ever
more than an arbitrary guess which it is impossible
either to make probable or improbable by reasons?
Swinburne, for example, ascribed the anonymous play
Arden of Faversham to Shakespeare on grounds of this

kind; I confess that to myself—if my opinion had any right to count—the ascription seems not only baseless, but preposterous. But will anyone say that a judgement on the point either way can in the nature of the case have *no* genuine grounds at all?

I hold, then, that the character in a thing in virtue of which we denominate it good is precisely this domination of the process of its "becoming" by an immanent form which is also an end, and that consequently the thing which we can call good, or "the nature" of the thing, is regularly a factor in its own production; in a real sense a good thing is *causa sui*. Of course, it may be retorted that a work of art, a picture or a poem, does not paint or write itself, it is painted or written by someone. But I do not believe that the objection has any real weight. Even in ordinary language we speak more often of the work of art as "growing" in the artist's mind, or under the strokes of his chisel or pencil, than we do of its being "made" by him, and we should intend to cast doubts on the artistic quality of the work if we spoke of it as a "manufactured product". Whatever we may think of some of Mr. Alexander's views about artistic creation—and I own that some of them seem to me strange—he is surely right in saying that the artist has always mixed his mind with his materials, and that the embodied product itself contains the factor of "mind" as well as the factor of "material". The great portrait, for example the Strafford in the National Gallery, is something more than an arrangement of pigments which have been transferred from the tubes that once held them to a certain canvas by the efficient causality of Van Dyck's mind; it is that, no doubt, but it is also an exterioration or embodiment of Van Dyck's mind through the medium of pigment on canvas, and this is why we speak of the painter not as manufacturing it but as creating it. If it were only a manufactured thing, we might perhaps call it *useful*, we should have no reason to call it *good*. When we judge of the work of art as a work of art, we are thinking of it not merely as having been produced by mind, but as *embodying* mind; the dominant constituent in it has actually been also the agency in the production.

It follows that for this very reason that the thing which can be called good in such judgements is at once a product and the controlling factor in its own production, the *essentia* of the thing and its existence tend to fall apart. The thing is not its own goodness, because it is not identical with its own *essentia*. Hence we can *attribute* the goodness to it, but we cannot identify the two. The *essentia*, as I have said, is a real possibility actualising itself. At any stage in this process of self-actualisation there is still possibility not yet actualised, a *beyond* yet to be attained, and in this sense the goodness of the thing lies outside its own existence. Also we have to remember that a thing in the historical world with which we are concerned is not the only finite factor in its own production; it does not, like a Leibnizian monad, simply unfold its own possibilities from within, subject to the *concursus* of God. The natures of other things—I should myself say with Mr. Whitehead the natures of *all* other finite things—are negatively or positively factors in the development. Thus, to express the point in scholastic terminology, the composition characteristic of the good or bad things with which we have actual acquaintance may be characterised more precisely than by calling it composition of *essentia* with existence; it has the specific character of composition of *form* with *matter*. It is an interesting speculation, which I do not wish simply to dismiss, that there may be finite creatures, like the angels of Thomistic philosophy, in whom there is the composition of *essentia* and existence, but not the more specific composition of form and matter. But I have no actual acquaintance with angels; if I believe in them, it is not on any empirical evidence, and even actual converse with an angel would not of itself be proof that the Thomist theory of the angelic nature is sound. So far as my actual experience of things goes, it seems to be a consequence of the *commercium* in virtue of which all are factors in the development of each, that in the *existentia* of each there are elements which are recalcitrant to domination by the form or *essentia*, and that the completest domination of the first by the second which is ever actually attained is imperfect and impermanent. And thus the same *nisus* towards complete and relevant embodiment of form in virtue of which a thing has goodness attributed to it appears to be also regularly a *nisus* towards self-transcendence. In this way, too, the goodness of a thing seems to be outside itself.

We see this, of course, most notably in the life-history of organisms and species of organisms. The goal of the *nisus* towards complete embodiment of significant form in the history of the individual organism seems to be its own state of adult maturity, its ἀκμή, and yet, so far as the goal is reached, it is only reached to be lost again, as the organism becomes middle-aged, senile, and finally dies. It is an old story, that while the good to which the organism is unconsciously aspiring is its own ἀθανασία, "the complete adjustment" of *its own* "inner relations" to "outer relations", the good it achieves is something else—the perpetuation of its species in the next generation. And, of course, it is only on a short-sighted view that even this can be said to be really attained; species are not, as the Greek philosophers once fancied, coeval with time; they do not, so far as

we can see, even enjoy the privilege of "Dionysiac recurrence"; when they disappear, they disappear once
and for all. Hegel spoke once of the "cunning of the
Absolute", which dangles an unattainable good before
the individual, like the donkey's bunch of carrots, which
is always at the same irreducible distance from the
animal's nose. No doubt, the thought in his mind was
that the "race" no more ever gets the carrot than its
individual members do. We have, in fact, as Aristotle
remarks, in talking about the good, or end, or οὗ ἕνεκα
of a process, commonly to distinguish between the οὗ—
the actualisation of the possibility—and the ᾧ—the individual in which it is effected, the beneficiary. Thus, in
the case of the physician, the οὗ is the establishment of
the organic balance which is health, but the ᾧ is the
patient who is restored to health, and it is only exceptionally and accidentally, when a man takes his own
prescriptions, that the physician's patient is himself.

If a process of historical development really is, as I
have assumed it to be, what Plato calls a γένεσις εἰς
οὐσίαν, a process controlled and sustained by and culminating in the embodiment of significant form, where,
in the case of the development of the living organism,
does the process really reach its goal? Where is possibility finally translated without remainder into actuality? Not within the individual organism, nor yet in the
species, or the "kingdom" to which the species itself
belongs, nor in any yet wider whole that we can think
of. For they all carry within themselves at their fullest
attainment the possibilities which will, sooner or later,
lead to the breaking down of the embodiment and the
"withdrawal" of the form. The goodness of these
various wholes, like that of the individual organism, is
still not identical with themselves, but beyond them,
and so may be said to be adjectival to them, though, for

the reasons I have already given, it would not be an adequate statement to call it a "quality" of them.

How far is the case altered if we turn from the growth of the plant or animal to the shaping of a work of art, or the building up of moral character? We have here, of course, to reckon with a new and important factor in the process, intelligent awareness of the self-constitutive *nisus* and of the general character, at least, of the embodiment to which it is moving. A work of art, no doubt, is born, as we say, in the throes of inspiration; it is not put together in cold blood. And, similarly, a moral character worth having could hardly be acquired by a methodical skill in acquiring one specific "virtuous habit" after another. So far it is true of the artist and the moral hero, *nascitur, non fit*. But, on the other hand, we may be sure that no real work of art was ever made in the fashion described untruthfully by Aaron, when he said that he threw the people's offerings into the melting-pot, and "there came out" the golden calf. And I am probably not alone in suspecting that Mr. Alexander's vision of the statue somehow emerging from the block as Praxiteles struck it at random with his chisel does less than justice to the brooding intelligence which presumably controlled the blows of the implement. Moral character, again, grows, but it does not grow to any purpose apart from an intelligent self-discipline which involves prevision. Whether it be a work of art or his own soul a man is making, to make with any result he must have some prevision, though, no doubt, his foresight only becomes clear and articulate slowly and gradually enough. As Mark Tapley rightly hinted, public buildings do not "grow spontaneous" in the most fertile of soils, and fine moral character, even with the most favourable of social "environments", does not really come up like a flower;

it must be worked for and thought taken for it. In virtue of this presence of conscious controlling prevision, the making of a work of art, the building up of a character, are less at the mercy of "haphazard" than the growth of an organism. The *essentia* of the work of art or the character *in fieri* can dominate the external factors in the process more thoroughly than the "form" can control the growth of the individual animal or plant; less allowance has to be made for the presence within the "matter" of the development of elements intractable to "form". I suppose that we may add that it is in the case of the formation of character that this tractability is at a maximum, since here the "material" itself is peculiarly intimate to the "nature of the individual".

In this respect the work of art, or the personal character, has its good within itself in a sense in which this would not be true of the animal organism. It is at least possible to understand the view that the animal organism fulfils its function completely in making its contribution to the continuance of its species; we could imagine Nature saying, without palpable absurdity, to the creature whose share in this work has been done: "You have no longer any significance for me, and may go to my scrap-heap: you were made for the whole, not the whole for you". But even were it the fact, as it is not, that the example and influence of every work of art and every fine human character are regularly productive of a series of equally good works of art or personal characters, we could not without absurdity, take such a view in these cases. It is no part of the goodness of the *Iliad* that it should contribute to inspire Virgil to produce the *Aeneid*, or of the *Aeneid* that it should be a chief factor in the making of *Paradise Lost*. It is only the other side of the same fact that the work of

art or the human character is not intrinsically subject
to old age, as organisms appear to be. The work of art
does not decline from its ἀκμή with the passage of time;
the worst that happens to it is that it may grow out of
fashion. We may lose our appreciation of its beauty,
but the beauty remains there *herrlich wie am ersten
Tag*; it is *always* young, always at its ἀκμή. And when
we come to consider personal character, it becomes
positively preposterous to conceive of the process of its
formation as culminating in an ἀκμή to be followed by
a curve of descent. In the nature of the process itself,
there is no reason why it should not go on for ever, as
Kant held that it does, or why, if it does culminate in
an attained perfection, this perfection itself should not
simply persist. When both these alternatives are rejected, as they are by so many among our contemporaries, they are rejected, not on the ground of their inherent absurdity, but on the strength of a conviction
that the permanence of personality is causally dependent upon the preservation of a physical organism.
I am not here to enter on the question whether this is
or is not a true conviction; I am only concerned with
the point that impermanence is no part of the intrinsic
character of the individual moral person, as it seems
perhaps to be of the intrinsic character of the individual
organism. The *nisus* of a moral person towards his own
"personal good" does not necessarily burst the mould
of his own personality. This does appear to be what
happens to the natural organism, which has to take
leave of its own existence in attaining what Whitehead
calls its "objective immortality"; and so has its good
"outside itself" in a way in which we may hope that a
person has not.

Yet, when all this has been said, however nobly we
may "think of the soul", and however generous the

hopes we allow ourselves to entertain of its destiny, it
remains true that the good man's personal goodness is
not identical with him; it is something which is his, but
is not himself, and so must be said to be adjectival to
him. In the first place, as Mr. Joseph's language reminds us, it is something he does not possess without
having to win it first, and it is also something he conceivably may lose, without *ipso facto* ceasing to be
himself. At least, this must be so if man is really an
historical being, if *process* is the very stuff of his being.
And if each of us is really a strictly eternal being, a god
mistaking himself for something else, like the persons
who compose the Absolute in the philosophy of
McTaggart, I confess I do not understand how the
"misperception" which infects our experience of ourselves and of one another gets its first hold of us. Indeed, in spite of all the acuteness McTaggart shows in
repelling the objector—an acuteness which I can only
admire and envy—I think he leaves the really fundamental objection to his construction untouched. The
one apparent reality of our human situation, into which
no element of illusion due to misperception enters, is, as
I understand McTaggart, the love of each person for
his personal friends, and McTaggart, at least, seems to
be fully aware that the reality of the love demands that
the various persons who feel it are constitutive of the
being of one another. But how can they be thus related
if process itself is the illusion which he pronounces it
to be? If he is to be consistent with his treatment of
becoming as illusory, must he not convert his persons
into self-contained Leibnizian monads, none of whom
ought, in strictness, to have any suspicion that there *is*
anything except itself? My standing difficulty with a
metaphysic like McTaggart's, is that it seems to me to
demand at once that each of us shall be such a monad,

and that he shall not be. If he is to love his friends, he cannot be such a monad; if he is to have the character McTaggart describes as a "fundamental differentiation of the Absolute", he can be nothing else.

Let us look again for a moment at the reasons for denying that I am my own goodness. If we do so, shall we not see that though I am certainly the possessor of my own goodness, the subject to which it is truly attributed, I am, so to say, not a possessor in my own solitary and exclusive right? My goodness, such as it is, is the actualisation of *my* real possibilities, and I have myself been a causative factor, and the determining causative factor, in the process of actualisation; it has been brought about by my use or neglect of my opportunities, and neither the use nor the neglect has been forced upon me. But my "real possibilities" themselves are rooted in my various relations with the living and the dead, the animate and the inanimate, in the whole world-wide scheme of beings of whom I am only one. Positively or negatively, all of them have gone to constitute the whole system of the possibilities. My *essentia* is, indeed, mine and not yours, or that of any other being, but it could have no subsistence if it stood alone, just as the *essentia* of the circle defined by Euclid is other than that of any other of the figures he defines, but that there should be such an *essentia* at all implies that there should be a region of space as defined by Euclid's scheme of postulates, and thus implies the *essentia* of all the other figures of Euclid's geometry. So far, then, is my goodness from being me, that while I can say that I have it, and in a real sense that I have made it, I cannot say that I have *created* it. When I say that I have it, I am to remember also that you can retort on me with equal truth, "What has thou that thou hast not received?" And the same question may be asked with the same force of any being into whose actuality any element of historical becoming enters, even of a being with as little unrealised potentiality about itself as one of the angels of the Thomist philosophy. None of them all can be identical with its own goodness, because all are characterised by the composition of *essentia* and existence, potentiality and "act".

Whether there can be any good thing which is its own goodness, then, depends on the answer we give to a question of ultimate metaphysic—is it true, or is it not, that "real possibility" presupposes a ground—a principle of distinction between the possible and the impossible—which is itself an actuality? We are all familiar with this position from the prominence given to it in the metaphysic of Lotze, and before him by Kant in the "pre-critical days" when he made it the foundation of a repeatedly urged "demonstration of the being of God" which, so far as I can see, is left untouched by the furious assaults of the *Kritik* upon the "cosmological argument". It is also, of course, the foundation of the Aristotelian theism, and so of the famous "five ways" of St. Thomas. And I need not remind you of the part it has played in our own day in the *Naturphilosophie* of Dr. Whitehead. It would take us too far afield from our immediate subject to enter on a discussion of the truth of the principle, and therefore I will only say here that I see no way to escape from it. If it is a sound principle, then there must stand at the source of all historical development a being which is strictly eternal and superhistorical, because it, and it alone, is *actus parus*, complete actuality without any element of the merely "possible", and it would not be hard to show that such a being, and only such a being, possesses the full character of God. Such a being could have no "nature" distinguishable from, and making itself through, the phases of its actual existence. Here, and only here, the distinction between *essentia* and existence could have no meaning, and consequently the distinction between an attribute and that which is the subject of the attribute would be meaningless too. Such a being would be good and perfectly good, and that in an "eminent" sense. It would be more than even the complete actualisation of all potentialities, since it would be the eternally actual source of them all. Hence, unlike anything which has a history, it would eternally be its own goodness. To say that it is good would be to say that it is that which it is, whereas to say of anything else "this is good" is only to say "this is becoming, or this has become, what it ought to be". Thus here, at last, we should have found something which has what it has not "received", indeed has *received* nothing, but is what it is, and is good, strictly in its own right. If there is such a being, as I believe there is, we can say of it that it *is* its own goodness. Its goodness is not adjectival to it because, as I say, in it it is all one to be and to be good. But though this may be true of God, it is not true of me, or of anything which is not God. What I have I have "received" and received from many quarters, and however true it may be that I make my own goodness out of what I have thus received by "free" volitions of my own, I can only exercise free volition "under God"; my own volition is itself part and parcel of the historical process which is only possible in virtue of the actual existence of the strictly eternal and actual source of all possibility. Hence my goodness—even in "heaven", if I ever reach "heaven" —is *communicated* and dependent, not inherent and *original*.

[1932]

Printed in Great Britain by R. & R. CLARK, LIMITED, *Edinburgh.*